Access 2003 Programming
Weekend Crash Course®

Access 2003 Programming
Weekend Crash Course®

Cary N. Prague
Jennifer Reardon
Lawrence S. Kasevich
Diana Reid
P.V. Phan

WILEY

Wiley Publishing, Inc.

Access 2003 Programming Weekend Crash Course®

Published by
Wiley Publishing, Inc.
10475 Crosspoint Boulevard
Indianapolis, IN 46256
www.wiley.com

Copyright © 2003 by Wiley Publishing, Inc., Indianapolis, Indiana

Published simultaneously in Canada

Library of Congress Card Number: 2003101926

ISBN: 0-7645-3975-2

Manufactured in the United States of America

10 9 8 7 6 5 4 3 2 1

1B/SV/QZ/QT/IN

About the Authors

Cary N. Prague is an internationally known best-selling author and lecturer in the database industry. He owns Database Creations, Inc., the world's largest Microsoft Access add-on company. Its products include a line of financial software: Business! for Microsoft Office, a mid-range accounting system; POSitively Business! point-of-sale software; the Inventory Bar code manager for mobile data collection; Check Writer; and General Ledger. Database Creations also produces a line of developer tools including the appBuilder, an application generator for Microsoft Access; the EZ Access Developer Tools for building great user interfaces; appWatcher for maintaining code bases among several developers; and Surgical Strike, the only Patch Manager for Microsoft Access.

Local and national clients for Database Consulting, LLC, consist of many Fortune 100 companies, including Microsoft, United Technologies, ABB, Smith & Wesson Firearms, Pratt and Whitney Aircraft, ProHealth, OfficeMax, and Continental Airlines.

Cary is one of the best-selling authors in the computer database management market, having written more than 40 books that have sold over one million copies. His software topics include Microsoft Access, Borland (Ashton-Tate) dBASE, Paradox, R:Base, Framework, and graphics. Cary's books include various editions of the *Access Bible, Access 97 Secrets, Access Crash Course, dBASE for Windows Handbook, dBASE IV Programming* (winner of the Computer Press Association's Book of the Year award for Best Software-Specific Book), and *Everyman's Database Primer Featuring dBASE IV.*

Cary is certified in Access as a Microsoft Certified Professional and has passed the MOUS test in Access and Word. He is a frequent speaker at seminars and conferences around the country. He is on the exclusive Microsoft Access Insider Advisory Board and makes frequent trips to Microsoft headquarters in Redmond, Washington.

Cary holds an M.A. in computer science from Rensselaer Polytechnic Institute, and an M.B.A and Bachelor of Accounting from the University of Connecticut. He is also a Certified Data Processor.

Jennifer Reardon is a leading developer of custom database applications. She has over 10 years experience developing client/server and PC-based applications. She has accumulated much of her application-development experience working as lead developer for Database Creations. She has partnered with Cary Prague in developing applications for a number of Fortune 500 companies.

Jennifer's most significant projects include a spare parts inventory-control system for Pratt & Whitney's F22 program, an engineering specifications system for ABB-Combustion Engineering, and an emergency event-tracking system for the State of Connecticut. She was also the lead developer of many of the Database Creations add-on software products including Business; Yes! I Can Run My Business; Check Writer; and the User Interface Construction Kit.

Jennifer has coauthored the *Access 2003 Bible, Access 2002 Bible,* and the *Access 2000 Programming Weekend Crash Course.* She has also written chapters in other books on subjects including Data Access Pages, the Microsoft Database Engine, the VBA programming environment, creating help systems, and using Microsoft Office 2000 Developer. In addition, she has authored chapters for *Microsoft Access 97 Bible* and *Access 97 Secrets.*

Ms. Reardon owns her own consulting firm, Advanced Software Concepts, which provides custom applications to both the public and private sectors. She specializes in developing client information systems for state-managed and privately held healthcare organizations. She has also developed a job costing and project management system for an international construction company. Her corporate experience includes seven years with The Travelers, where she was an Associate Software Engineer serving on numerous mission-critical client/server software development projects using Easel, C, SQL Server, and DB2.

Jennifer holds a B.S. degree from the University of Massachusetts.

Lawrence S. Kasevich has over 30 years of experience in engineering, information technology, and management. As the vice-president of development for Database Creations, he has developed several Microsoft Access-based products that have sold worldwide. He also supervises the consulting division and manages the project efforts for clients and new product development. His writings have encompassed computer technology, business solutions, and many other topics .He has written six books and numerous articles. He has shared his experience by making presentations at developer conferences and professional organizations nationwide. He was a member of the adjunct faculty at Rennselear at Hartford where he taught information systems courses for 10 years. He earned a B.S. degree in Electrical Engineering from the University of Connecticut in 1974. In 1986, he received an M.S. in Management from Rennselear at Hartford.

Diana Reid is responsible for the design and development of the company's corporate and client Web sites, as well as managing the company's accounting product line. Diana is a contributing editor for several books on Microsoft Access and has been a technical editor for several editions of the *Access Bible* books. She is a speaker at Microsoft-sponsored developer conferences, speaking on FrontPage, HTML, and other Web technologies. Diana received a B.S. in Finance from Central Connecticut State University in 1991.

P. V. Phan currently serves as Director of Information/Technical Services for Database Creations, Inc. In this capacity, he heads a support team for both in-house and customer technical support for end users and developers. He is a member of the development and consulting team for the full line of Database Creations, Inc. products, as well as serving as a consultant on numerous projects for many companies, including some Fortune 500 corporations. He has over 8 years of Access training and programming experience and over 14 years of computer experience in business and academic settings. He holds degrees from the University of Connecticut in psychology and biology.

Credits

This book is dedicated to my son, David Prague. David, who will be a freshman at Roger Williams University in the fall of 2003, proved what rewards hard work, dedication, and a commitment to excellence can bring. Despite my constant involvement, tough love sessions, and his own personal challenges, he rose to overcome the obstacles of our times, become employed, win scholarships, and become a fine young man. As he embarks on the next major opportunity of his life, I dedicate this book to him to let him know how much he is loved and respected. —Cary N. Prague

This book is dedicated to my friend Sara Schilling in honor of her 21st birthday. Thanks for being such a good friend and a devoted stable companion. You are always there when we need you. Thanks for your input and encouragement for my equestrian pursuits, which keep me focused and grounded (although broke). —Jennifer Reardon

This book is dedicated to my wonderful wife, Debbie, who gives me incredible love and support in all I do. I love her dearly. It is also dedicated to our children and their families: Cheryl, Tom, and Victoria—a truly beautiful family; Alissa and Nathaniel—a special and loving couple; and Ashley—a smart and talented young lady. I am so thankful for and proud of them all! — Lawrence S. Kasevich

To my father, Robert Smith, who has struggled bravely with his fight against cancer for the last four years and taught me to achieve in order to be the best. Also to my mother, Joan, for always being there. And finally, to my husband, Matt, and to our two wonderful children, Elizabeth and Aiden, who make my life complete. —Diana Reid

This is dedicated to my mother, Nhu Mai Nguyen, for her boundless love for all of her children. —P. V. Phan

Preface

Microsoft Access is an outstanding environment for application development on any level. It is one of easiest database managers to use, and one of the most powerful. People with all levels of skill and experience have found that Microsoft Access can help them create applications to meet nearly any need. New users can quickly master using simple tables, queries, forms, and reports. They can even learn and use macros quite easily. However, when users need modules and VBA code, they sometimes run into a virtual brick wall and cannot proceed.

This book teaches you how to program in Microsoft Access and VBA, whether you are a complete beginner or an experienced information system professional who wants to add another language to your box of tools. Organized according to the Weekend Crash Course approach, this book consists of 30 short chapters. Each chapter teaches you a different part of Access VBA development. The first few chapters start with programming basics, teaching you system design, an understanding of logical constructs, and an introduction to the VBA editor environment and testing and debugging. After the initial chapters, you learn hard-core VBA and ADO programming with a variety of topics including client/server, working with data, and even programming external data imports and exports.

Using one cohesive example—a common check writer, register, and reconciliation form, along with a banking interface—you learn visual programming using Microsoft Access. Each chapter features easy-to-follow text and lots of screen shots to keep you on track. The Check Writer sample application is written completely in ADO for Microsoft Access 2003. You also see an .ADP version linked to an MSDE (SQL Server 2000) back-end database.

Structure of the Book

Each part of this book is organized into four to six sessions. Each session is designed so that you can complete it in about half an hour. At the end of each session are review questions that let you quiz yourself immediately on what you just read. At the end of each of the six parts, you'll find 20 additional questions to test what you learned throughout that part.

Friday Evening

In the first four sessions, we teach you the basics of programming. You learn how to make the transition from macros to modules and then learn about the Visual Basic Editor and how to debug programs with the built-in tools like syntax checking, auto quick info, and auto list members. You learn the basics of system design and learn the concentric-circle method of development that Microsoft follows. You learn how to trigger code from various types of events and how to declare the various types of variables.

Saturday Morning

On Saturday morning, you move beyond the basics. You first learn the logical constructs that every programmer uses, including decision-making and looping. You learn the difference between functions and procedures, and you write your first program in Visual Basic, the language of Microsoft Access. Access architecture is then covered and you are exposed to the Access Object Model. ADO is next, as you learn how to access and manipulate data in tables. You also learn not only how to retrieve data from tables, but how to add, update, and delete data.

Saturday Afternoon

You begin Saturday afternoon by learning how to create switchboards and menus and how to handle keypress events programmatically. You learn about unbound forms, which are used in client-server systems. The rest of Part III teaches you how to work with the various controls on a form or report through programs. You first learn how to program combo and list boxes and how to work with option groups through programming. Next, you learn how to manipulate subforms through code and how to use tabbed controls in ways you never thought possible. A session on advanced message boxes and error handling wraps up this part.

Saturday Evening

By Saturday evening, you are learning how to import and export data programmatically from other databases, spreadsheets, and text type files including delimited and fixed-width file types. You learn the secrets of improving processing speed and keeping your programs compiled. Finally, in this session you learn how to create animated splash screens, about boxes, and other forms that appear when a program starts. Part IV ends with a session on adding help systems to Microsoft Access programs.

Sunday Morning

On Sunday morning, you are ready to learn how to handle more advanced types of Access requirements. It starts with dialog boxes for printing and then covers finding data using dialog boxes for searching any field in a table. The next session covers topics after your development is complete, including packaging your application and Access runtime and Setup utilities. You also learn how to create wizards for starting or shepherding the user through complex tasks. Finally, you learn about building Add-In libraries and using references.

Sunday Afternoon

The final part of the book covers a group of advanced programming topics. It begins with programmatically checking file attachments and programming an interface to link to files.

You learn how to program Access security and create true client-server applications using ADPs and the Microsoft Database Engine (MSDE) or SQL Server 2000.

Appendix

The appendix provides the answers to the test questions located at the end of each of the six parts of the book.

The Companion Web Site

The companion Web site for this book, located at `www.wiley.com/compbooks/prague`, contains all the sample files created or referred to in the book, as well as a self-assessment exam that lets you test what you've learned.

The Web site also includes links to sample products and demos that you can download and try. These sample and demo products, developed by the authors and third-party companies, provide you with useful tools for developing Microsoft Access applications.

Layout and Features

No one should try to simply power through this material without a break. We've arranged things so the sessions in this book each last about half an hour, and they're grouped into parts of two or three hours. After each session, and at the end of each part, you'll find some questions to check your knowledge and give you a little practice at exercising your newfound skills. Take a break, grab a snack, refill that coffee mug, and plunge into the next one!

Along the way, you'll find some features to help you keep track of how far along you are, and point out interesting bits of info you shouldn't miss. First, as you're going through each session, check for this in the margin:

20 Min. To Go

This icon and others like it let you know how much progress you've made through each session as you go. There are also several icons to point out special tidbits of info for you:

This is a flag to clue you in to an important piece of information that you should file away in your head for later.

This symbol denotes helpful advice on the best ways to do things, or a neat little technique that can make your work easier.

Don't do this! 'Nuff said.

This symbol tells you where to find more information on the current subject elsewhere in the book.

 This symbol refers you to this book's companion Web site for more information.

SYNTAX ▶ Watch for places where we've flagged a passage where essential syntax is modeled for you. The bar to the left shows you the extent of the passage. Usually, it'll be something like this:

To check something and make a decision based on it, you use the If...Then statement. The If...Then statement works like this:

```
If this is true Then do this
```

Here's an example:

```
If Check1.Value = 1 Then Form1.Text1.FontBold = True
```

The part after the If is a condition; if the condition is true, the computer will do whatever comes after Then.

Conventions Used in this Book

Aside from the icons you've just seen, such as *Tip*, there are only three conventions in this book:

- To indicate a menu choice, we use the ⇨ symbol, as in:

  Choose File ⇨ Save Project to save your work.

- To indicate programming code within the body text, we use a special font, as in Form2Hide.

  Notice that line at the end: Form2.Hide. When the user clicks the OK button, you want Form2 to disappear. The Hide command does just that.

- To indicate a programming example that's not in the body text, we use this typeface:

```
Private Sub Command2_Click()
Form2.Hide
End Sub
```

Ready, Set . . .

One little weekend—such a small amount of time to invest for so much knowledge. *Go* get it!

Acknowledgments

We wish to thank the following people who greatly contributed to the success of our book. First, and foremost, we want to thank the staff of Database Creations, Inc. and Database Creations Consulting LLC for supporting our band of writers as we completed the book. To Julie Frattaroli, Kim Manzone, Karen Prague, and Debbie Schindler. Your work keeping the lights on and customers happy is most appreciated.

One of our motivations was the desire to create a book that could be used to teach Access programming. We needed a test bed and found it at the high school in South Windsor, Connecticut. When we approached the Board of Education with the idea, we thought we had no chance of actually convincing them to let our developers teach a course that didn't even exist. To our amazement, they agreed.

To Allan Mothersele, a true educator, who lives more hours than not at South Windsor High School. He lets us practice our ideas on students as we muddle through our Access database and programming course. His love for children, robots, things mechanical, and the entrepreneurial spirit truly lives within his teaching.

To our agents, Matt Wagner and Bill Gladstone, and our financial guru, Maureen, at Waterside Productions. They are the best agents and people in the business! Thanks for making our trips through contract-land easy and profitable.

Thanks to our friends at Wiley. First, to our acquisitions editor, Sharon Cox—we thank you for being a fair negotiator. To our project editor, Jodi Jensen, who read, changed, rewrote, replaced, removed, condensed, expanded, and generally turned our characters on the page into English but never complained whined, insisted, or ranted at our obviously poor writing skills. It turned out to be our best book yet, and we appreciate it. We also promise to learn your version of English as our first language some day—as well as our second and third.

Thanks to our other friends at Wiley, including Richard Swadley, Joe Wikert, Andy Cummings, Greg Croy, and Mary Bednarek.

Finally, to all our families, loved ones, horses, cats, dogs, and friends whom we ignore for months at a time when we write our books.

Contents at a Glance

Contents

Access 2003 Programming
Weekend Crash Course®

☑ **Friday**

☐ Saturday

☐ Sunday

Part I — Friday Evening

Session 1
Introduction to Microsoft Access and Programming

Session 2
From Macros to Modules

Session 3
System and Process Design, Testing, and Debugging

Session 4
Events — A Place to Run Your Code

PART

I

Friday
Evening

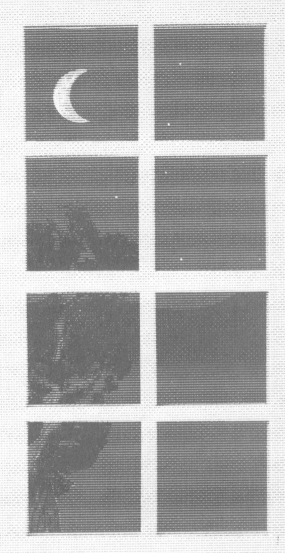

Introduction to Microsoft Access and Programming

Session Checklist

✔ Understanding what programming is

✔ Using the Visual Basic language

✔ Programming for the contemporary developer

✔ Examining database programming

✔ Using the Check Writer example database

✔ Reviewing the basic Access program structure: modules, functions, and subprocedures

**30 Min.
To Go**

Microsoft Access is an outstanding environment for both database users and professional developers. In this session, you learn the difference between programming with the Visual Basic language and using Microsoft Access tables, queries, forms, and reports. You also learn how professional developers use Microsoft Access to create applications, and you are introduced to the Check Writer application example used throughout this book.

In order to get the most from this book, you should be familiar with most of the Microsoft Access objects — including tables, queries, forms, and reports. You should also know the basic concepts of building tables and creating relationships. If you have never created a Microsoft Access form, this book is probably not for you. All the examples start from forms that have been created and explain how to add functions and procedures using Visual Basic, the internal language of Access.

If you have created simple or complex macros, you already understand the basics of events and programming. This book does not teach macros because professional developers use macros only on rare occasions. For example, macros are used for creating certain types of menus or for avoiding .mda library-referencing problems, which cause compile errors when the libraries are not connected. This book does explain how to convert your macros to modules and thoroughly covers event-driven programming, which is used in Microsoft Access applications.

What Is Programming?

Programming is the name given to the process of creating instructions to accomplish a task. This is just one of the many phases of development. Microsoft Access contains a set of tools, one of which is called a *language*. Just as you build words, sentences, and thoughts when you speak or write using human language, you use the programming language to create the program. The language consists of a series of commands that tells the computer how to accomplish the task at hand. Computer programming languages have rules and grammar just like spoken languages.

 Computer grammar is called *syntax*.

Programming can be defined in many ways, but usually words such as *logic*, *structure*, *commands*, *sequence*, and *order* are part of the definition. Professional programmers today generally prefer to be called *developers*. A developer is a person who creates computer applications. Traditional programming is not a necessary element. Creating a form using Microsoft Access can be considered development. When an error message or process is added to the form with a macro or language element, that is also programming. Programming is only one element of development. Analysis, design, testing, and debugging are other key elements of application development.

Microsoft Access contains a variety of tools that enable you to build applications without using the built-in language. These include queries, forms, and reports. Microsoft Access is known as a *database management package* because it gives you the ability to create tables that hold data. If you have created macros using Microsoft Access, you have already programmed, whether you know it or not.

Visual Basic is the language that is used internally with Microsoft Access. It is also called VBA or Visual Basic for Applications, Visual Basic — Applications Edition, and the Visual Basic language. It was called Access Basic in the first versions of Microsoft Access. Whatever you call it, the Visual Basic language is an integral part of Microsoft Access. For the purposes of this book, the Microsoft Access programming language is referred to simply as Visual Basic.

Why Use the Visual Basic Language?

Although Microsoft Access allows you to create process-oriented programs using macros, it is the language that gives you unlimited flexibility. Many Microsoft Access programmers started with macros and eventually realized their limitations. Eventually, you will find that to meet all your needs in Access, you need to program using the Visual Basic language.

There are many things that macros cannot do. Macros cannot

- Create error trapping routines and run a process based on the error
- Use repetitive looping or incrementing of variables

- Perform complex decision making
- Replace runtime parameters to change form display

Don't confuse the Visual Basic language within Microsoft Access with the product Microsoft sells called Visual Basic or Visual Basic .NET. Although Visual Basic (the product) and Microsoft Access share the common Visual Basic language, the products themselves are very different. All Microsoft Office products contain roughly the same Visual Basic programming language. These products include Access, Excel, Word, PowerPoint, Outlook, and even MapPoint.

Programming for the Contemporary Developer

If you are fairly new to Microsoft Access and have been a programmer for several decades, you may be wondering, "Why program at all?" You may have already discovered the incredible power of tables, queries, forms, and reports. You may have created fairly complex forms including combo boxes, option groups, ActiveX Objects, and the like, which provide more power than many programs you used just 10 years ago. You also may be very comfortable using macros.

If you have already been programming in languages such as COBOL or dBASE, you may be looking for the window that lets you type in commands so that you can start programming. Although there is such a screen in Microsoft Access, you don't use the Visual Basic Editor window to write a program (as you might have back in the '80s). In the early days of personal computers, you started with a blank screen and an editor similar to a simple word processor. You wrote line after line of computer language code to do such mundane things as

Draw a rectangle	`@12.15 To 25.40`
Display a text label	`@13.17 SAY "Customer Name:"`
Allow the user to enter data	`@13.31 GET CUSTNAME`

In those days, you had to worry about where the cursor was and where it was going. Today's visual tools, such as the Form Design window, make it easy to build forms without ever entering a line of computer code. In fact, using Microsoft Access, you can build fairly sophisticated applications without ever writing a single line of Visual Basic code. You could easily spend a day creating the program for a simple form in dBASE II. In Microsoft Access, you can create the same form with a wizard in a couple of minutes or from the Form Design screen in half an hour.

Microsoft Access uses an event-driven visual programming environment. This means that, generally, you create a form to display something and then, in the Design view of the form, you use the events of the form — the form's controls, mouse movements, or keyboard keypresses — to add programmed instructions that go beyond just simple form display and data editing. It is a visual environment because you see the user interface at all times. Additionally, as you will learn in the next session, you can view the results of your work nearly instantaneously with only a few mouse clicks. If you are used to the mainframe world, you know the pain of compiling and linking.

An *event* is just that — an event. Examples include a form being opened, a user placing the cursor in a field on a form, a data value being changed, your mouse moving to a specific control, or more than 50 other distinct occurrences for which you can write Visual Basic code. You can also write Visual Basic code for many other things that happen to forms and reports: printing reports, trapping for potential errors, and even checking the passage of time and performing some task after a certain number of seconds. Each of these events serves as a trigger for code to be run (or *executed*, as it is also called in programming vernacular). Figure 1-1 shows some of the events that are behind a form and a Visual Basic window where a simple program has been created to check the value of text box entry and to display an error message if it is null.

Figure 1-1   *Sample events behind a form and the Visual Basic window showing a simple program.*

**20 Min.
To Go**

Database Programming Is Incredibly Flexible

A number of popular software products today include or are built primarily around programming languages. Some of these are .NET, C++, Java, Visual FoxPro, Delphi, Visual Basic, Microsoft Access, and Microsoft Excel. Many more products from small companies with smaller followings are also available, but Microsoft Access is one of the most flexible because it is built around a database management system. Database management systems include the capability to build tables and relationships and to store data.

Microsoft Access is a multidimensional product because it also includes an easy-to-use but powerful set of form and report tools. Its Visual Basic language capability allows the automation or addition of extensions to your simple forms and reports, making them incredibly powerful.

Microsoft Access comes with a *back-end* database management system, which means it has two different data engines to manage data. The first engine is known as *Jet*. You may not be aware of this engine because Jet is built into Microsoft Access. Each time you create a new database, design a table, or write a query, you are using the Jet database engine. The second engine is a smaller version of SQL Server 2000 called the Microsoft Database Engine.

The Microsoft Database Engine is also known as MSDE and has to be installed separately. You can find it in a separate directory on your Office 2003 installation CD.

If you create professional Microsoft Access applications using the Jet engine, you should always create two separate .mdb database files. One database file contains just your tables, whereas the other contains links to those tables, along with your queries, forms, reports, and module code. This technique is known as *file/server computing* because you have a program file and a data file. You may have heard it referred to as *client/server computing,* but the Jet database engine is not a true client/server database engine. Instead, it is a file/server database engine.

Real client-server database engines such as SQL Server or Oracle actually do all their processing on the database server hardware and minimize data sent across the network. Although Microsoft Access uses Jet as a database manager, all processing is done on the client workstation each time the entire data table is sent across the network. The optimum solution for large database applications is to use Microsoft Access as the front-end and to use SQL Server or Oracle as the back end.

Although SQL Server and Oracle are also very powerful database managers, they do not include a set of integrated tools and have no specific programming language. In fact, SQL Server uses Visual Basic to handle its own internal event model known as *triggers and stored procedures*. *Triggers* are events that respond to a change in a data value. This change triggers (or starts) a block of code known as a *stored procedure* (so named because it is also stored in the data table).

Microsoft Access 2003 contains a client-server database model called *projects* and uses the file extension .adp. This built-in client/server model uses the personal desktop version of SQL Server known as the Microsoft Database Engine (MSDE). You can create applications that work with MSDE instead of Jet and then use the more powerful SQL Server when you are ready.

Using the Check Writer Example Database

Included on the companion Web site for this book are sample files that we refer to in various sessions throughout the book. Many more free software samples and demo versions of business systems and third-party tools are available from leading Microsoft Access add-on vendors.

The example used in this book is a fairly simple application that is representative of the types of applications you can develop with Microsoft Access. The example is a working check writer, which is an electronic version of the checkbook you probably use all the time. The example is written in Microsoft Access and programmed with the latest version of Access 2003, Visual Basic, and the internal data access language ADO.

You will use these two files:

CheckWriter.mdb   The program file, including Queries, Forms, Reports, and Modules

CheckWriterData.mdb   The data file, containing only the tables used in the example

If you have never worked with linked databases, this is a great time to start.

 Professional Microsoft Access application developers always keep the program and data in two separate database files. That way, if the programs or design objects (forms, reports, and so on) require changes, the developer can replace the customer's program file without disturbing the data files.

The sessions in this book use various parts of the Check Writer example to show you how to build any professional application. The application is constructed specifically to demonstrate what you must know to be successful in application development, including Visual Basic programming, data design, and forms and report creation.

Using the Check Writer main menu

When you first open the Check Writer application, you see the main menu shown in Figure 1-2. The main menu consists of a few simple buttons and some graphics. When you click a button, that function runs.

Figure 1-2   *The Check Writer example main menu.*

You can choose from the following functions on the main menu:

Check Writer/Register   A tabbed dialog where you can add, edit, delete, or display checks, deposits, adjustments, and a visual check register.

Bank Accounts	A data entry form to enter bank account information for your accounts.
Check Reconciliation	A complete electronic check reconciliation screen to help you balance your checkbook.
New Bank Account Wizard	A wizard form to create a new bank account and set up the starting balance.
Import	A utility form to demonstrate data import and integration.
Export	A utility form to demonstrate exporting data.
Recurring Payments	A form to demonstrate creating a payment that occurs more than once, including saving or retrieving the data.
Setup	A simple form to enter your company name and address.
Exit	A function that closes the Check Writer application and exits Microsoft Access.

Using the Check Writer tabbed data entry form

The main Check Writer/Register application consists of four tabs. Each tab contains a separate subform that displays one or more records. The tabs filter the data to show only checks, deposits, or adjustments in the first three tabs. The fourth tab shows a check register containing all types of transactions. Figure 1-3 shows the first tab, displaying the check form itself. The check form lets you enter the check number, enter the check date, select or enter a new payee, and enter the amount of the check.

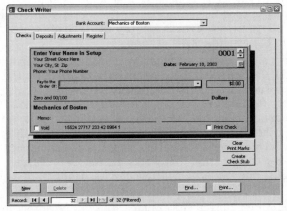

Figure 1-3   *The Check Writer/Register example tabbed data entry form.*

As you learn throughout this book, this form requires a great deal of programming. A function behind the Amount field is used to automatically convert the amount to words. A pair of spin buttons in the upper-right corner of the check let you automatically increase or decrease the check number. When a new payee is added, a program makes sure that you want to add the new value and adds a record to the separate payee database.

Several check boxes appear at the bottom of the form. One check box voids the check and displays a large VOID stamp across it; the other check box prints the check. You can fill in the stub below the check using a button to retrieve values from the check and format them into a single string.

The area in the footer of the form also contains buttons that display great examples of a search-and-print dialog as well as New and Delete buttons that use professional error-trapped subprocedures for handling New and Delete tasks.

Understanding the Check Writer data model

The data model used in the Check Writer example is shown in Figure 1-4. Most of the transaction data is stored in the tbl_CheckWriter table. This table is used to store checks, deposits, and adjustments.

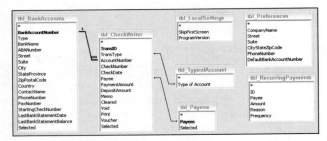

Figure 1-4   *The Check Writer example data model.*

Whereas all the data fields necessary to enter check, deposit, and adjustment data are contained in this table, some fields are also used for reconciliation (balancing your checkbook), printing, and voiding. The TransType field is used to identify the type of transaction and to filter the records for each tab in the frm_CheckWriter form.

The tbl_BankAccounts table contains all necessary information for adding bank accounts and relating this information to the tbl_CheckWriter table. The primary key field for the tbl_BankAccounts table is BankAccountNumber, whereas the primary key in the tbl_CheckWriter table is an AutoNumber field named TransID. The foreign key field to the tbl_BankAccounts table is the AccountNumber field in the tbl_CheckWriter table. An AutoNumber field is used because the other more distinctive keys don't make sense in a check writer. Although checks usually have sequential numbers, deposits and adjustments do not. Therefore, there is no foreign key combination that works. BankAccountNumber, Date, and TransType cannot work because you can have multiple checks, deposits, or adjustments on the same day.

There are two additional tables used for lookups in the example. The tbl_TypeofAccount table contains a list of transaction types including check, deposit, and adjustments such as Error Correction, Interest, Wire Transfer, ATM, and so on. The tbl_Payees table contains a list of unique payees used by the checks. Each time you enter a new payee into the frm_CheckWriter form payee line, you have the option to add any new payees into the table.

Using the Check Register

The Check Register is found in the last tab of the frm_CheckWriter form, as shown in Figure 1-5. There is not a lot of code behind this form, but the subform is a great example of a continuous form with a complex calculation to display the continuous balance.

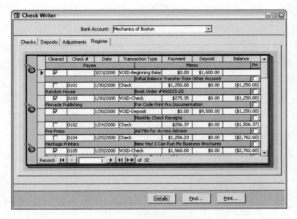

Figure 1-5　*The Check Register form.*

The Check Register subform is made up of multiple lines. In later sessions of this book, you learn how to use multiple-line subforms that include a surrounding OLE object and an editable data source. You also learn how to change the record source of the subform programmatically (using code) when the form is initially opened and how to change a control's calculated control source programmatically.

Viewing the Print Checks dialog

The Print Checks dialog shown in Figure 1-6 is displayed when you click the Print button at the bottom of the Check Writer form. This example is used in several sessions to illustrate the interaction between Visual Basic and dialog boxes. Based on the choices the user selects in the dialog box, various blocks of Visual Basic code are run to select different reports, change query dynasets (the results of a query) that are passed to different reports, and even determine fields that are printed or hidden on reports.

Managing the Check Reconciliation process

The frm_CheckReconciliation form is shown in Figure 1-7. This screen contains a set of tools that allows the user to visually reconcile a checkbook. The user first enters the bank balance to view the difference between the checkbook balance and bank balance, and then the user clicks the Cleared button and watches the difference shrink. Using the combo box on the form, the user employs Visual Basic code to switch between bank accounts. The EDIT button in the continuous subform also allows the user to display the selected transaction by opening the Check Writer form, changing the tab, and finding the record programmatically. This provides a good lesson for navigation within multiple forms.

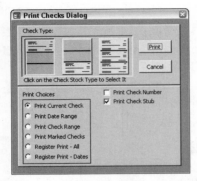

Figure 1-6   *The Print Checks dialog box.*

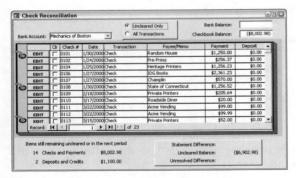

Figure 1-7   *The Check Reconciliation form.*

**10 Min.
To Go**

A Typical Visual Basic Screen

In the next session, you learn how to create Visual Basic programs, and you should begin to understand the process of working with Visual Basic. Figure 1-8 shows the Visual Basic Editor window that, in Microsoft Access, is a separate program in a separate window.

Because the Visual Basic Editor is a separate program in Microsoft Access, you can see both Microsoft Access and the Visual Basic Editor in your task bar at the bottom of your Windows screen. Although this is a huge difference internally for Access, it simply means that you can view both windows simultaneously and the editor does not use memory that could otherwise be used by Access. With more memory available to Access, programmer productivity may be increased and Windows itself is more stable, which causes less stress on machines running Access programs.

The more clean and free memory you give Microsoft Access, the faster your programs will run and the more stable they will be. You should reboot your machine at least once a day, and if you have been moving between design screens and running your Access forms programs frequently, you should close Access once in a while (every hour perhaps) and restart it. Each time you move from a design screen to a datasheet or forms view, Access leaves behind a little dirt known as a *memory leak*. Eventually, your system will report "out of memory," or Access will report errors where there are none. Closing Access and restarting it or rebooting your system will clean up the internal memory. These problems are well known to professional Access developers.

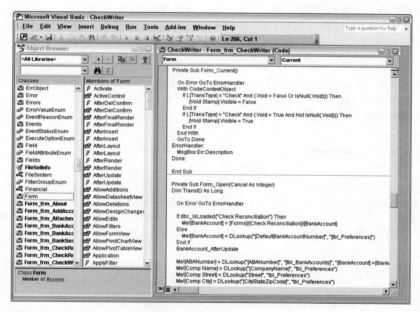

Figure 1-8   *The Visual Basic Editor window.*

Modules, Subprocedures, and Functions

You should understand a few more terms before moving on to the next session. When programmers think of programming in Microsoft Access, they think of Visual Basic modules. You already know that there is a Module tab in the database window. The Modules tab in the database window displays the module libraries created by you. You can have up to 1024 module libraries in a database. Each module library can contain many procedures, just as a bookcase can contain many books.

There are two types of procedures: functions and subprocedures. Functions and subprocedures are the building blocks of modules. Each module contains one or more function or subprocedure, and each function or subprocedure contains one or more Visual Basic statement.

You will often see the term *procedure* used interchangeably with the Microsoft Access term *subprocedure* and sometimes with *function*.

Procedures hold the Visual Basic program statements that make up modules. Just as a library has both hard-cover and soft-cover books, a module library has two different types of procedures. Both work exactly the same: they allow passed parameters to affect the way they process Visual Basic statements, they can contain error checking, and they can use any Visual Basic statement. The only difference between a function and a subprocedure is whether a value is returned when processing is completed. Functions return a value when processing is complete; subprocedures do not.

The Modules tab is not the only place where Visual Basic modules are found. You can place Visual Basic modules behind any form or report. They behave exactly like functions or subprocedures in a module library; they are just stored in a different place.

Done!

Generally, if a function or subprocedure is used only by a form or report, you store it behind the object. If it is to be used by more than one form or report, you store it in a module.

REVIEW

In this session, you learned the definition of programming and how Microsoft Access objects interact with the Visual Basic programming environment. You learned about database programming and the types of procedures used in Microsoft Access modules. You also learned about the Check Writer example used throughout this book. The following topics were covered:

- Programming is the name given to the process of creating instructions to accomplish a task.
- Visual Basic, or VBA, is the language used in Microsoft Access modules.
- Microsoft Access uses an event-driven, visual programming environment.
- Microsoft Access uses a file-server@ndbased database management system known as Jet to manage data. You can also create applications that work with the Microsoft Database Engine (MSDE) instead of with Jet, which then enables you to use the more powerful SQL Server when you are ready.
- The example used in this book is a working check writer, which is an electronic version of the checkbook you probably use all the time.
- Each module library can contain many procedures. Functions and subprocedures are the building blocks of modules.
- Whereas module libraries contain only Visual Basic procedures, form and report objects can also contain procedures embedded within the form or report object.

QUIZ YOURSELF

1. Define the term *programming*. (See "What is Programming?")
2. Name three reasons to use Visual Basic instead of macros. (See "Why Use the Visual Basic Language?")
3. What are the two internal database management systems that Microsoft Access contains? (See "Database Programming Is Incredibly Flexible.")
4. What is the difference between file/server and client/server database management systems? (See "Database Programming Is Incredibly Flexible.")
5. What are the main functions of the Check Writer example? (See "Using the Check Writer Example Database.")
6. Name the two types of procedures. (See "Modules, Subprocedures, and Functions.")

From Macros to Modules

Session Checklist

✔ Using Visual Basic versus macros

✔ Converting macros to Visual Basic

✔ Using the Command Button Wizard to create Visual Basic code

✔ Using the Visual Basic Editor

**30 Min.
To Go**

Many tasks can be carried out through the application's user interface along with some simple macros. However, there are some tasks that macros cannot perform. Visual Basic modules provide the most power and control over your application development environment.

When to Use Macros

Macros provide a quick and easy way to perform simple actions. The macro window provides a drop-down list of available commands and prompts you for the appropriate arguments for each command. You don't have to memorize complicated commands and arguments. In Access, some actions actually run faster in a macro than in a Visual Basic module. Here are some of the situations in which macros are a sensible solution:

- Opening and closing forms
- Running reports
- Deleting all the records in a table or updating all the values in a field

The macro mcr_OpenBankAccounts uses the OpenForm command to open the frm_BankAccounts form. Figure 2-1 shows the mcr_OpenBankAccounts macro in the Macro window.

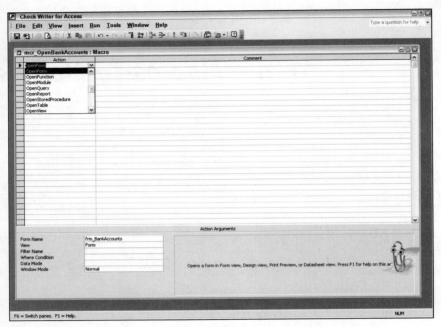

Figure 2-1   *Using the macro window to create a simple macro.*

Macros are most commonly used with command buttons. You can attach a macro to a command button on a switchboard, for example, for a quick and simple method of navigating to the various forms in your application. To attach a macro to a command button, you simply enter the macro name for its On Click property.

Figure 2-2 shows the cmdBankAccounts command button for the Check Writer switchboard. The mcr_OpenBankAccounts macro is associated with the command button's OnClick event. When the user clicks the Bank Accounts command button, the Open Bank Accounts macro runs to open the Bank Accounts form.

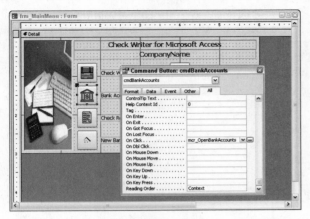

Figure 2-2 *Running a macro from a command button.*

When to Use Visual Basic

Although macros provide a simple way to perform many actions in an application, more sophisticated applications use Visual Basic as the tool of choice. Even though creating a Visual Basic procedure is more complex than creating a macro, Visual Basic provides a more robust set of commands and more control for handling any user and application errors that might occur in your application. Visual Basic is the best solution for the following situations:

- Creating your own functions
- Handling errors and displaying message boxes
- Integrating with other applications using automation (for example, Microsoft Word or Microsoft Excel)
- Calling Windows functions (for example, File Open and File Save dialogs)
- Stepping through a group of records in a table
- Manipulating the application's objects
- Passing variables to a procedure or function
- Displaying a progress meter

In a nutshell, Visual Basic makes your application more professional by providing better error handling and lots more horsepower.

**20 Min.
To Go**

Converting macros to Visual Basic code

Now that you see the advantages of using Visual Basic procedures, you may want to replace many of the macros in your existing applications with Visual Basic code. Even for an application of modest size, analyzing and rewriting each macro as equivalent Visual Basic code can be a daunting task.

Fortunately, Access provides a quick and easy solution for converting macros to Visual Basic code automatically. You can save a macro library either as a macro object or as a module. When you save a macro library as a module, Access automatically creates a module object for you in the Database window. This module contains a separate Visual Basic procedure for each macro in the original macro library.

To save a macro library as a module, select the macro in the macro objects tab of the Database window. Then choose File ⇨ Save As. The Save As dialog displays, as shown in Figure 2-3.

Figure 2-3 *Saving a macro as a module.*

In the Save As dialog, type a name for the new module and select Module for the As option. Then click the OK button. The Convert Macro dialog box displays, as shown in Figure 2-4.

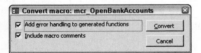

Figure 2-4 *Specifying the macro to module conversion options.*

Click to select the check boxes to include error handling and comments. Then click the Convert button.

During the conversion process, each new procedure displays in the Visual Basic Editor. When the process is finished, the Visual Basic Editor closes and the Conversion Finished message box is displayed. Click the OK button to close the message box. The new module is displayed in the Modules object window of the Database window. When Access names the new module, it adds the prefix *Converted Macro* – to the name you specified in the Save As dialog. Figure 2-5 shows the converted code for the mcr_OpenBankAccounts macro.

When the macro is converted to a module, the original macro library remains in the macro objects tab of the database container.

When you open the new module in Design view, the Visual Basic Editor displays the Visual Basic code for the new procedures. You can examine the Visual Basic code to see how it compares to the macro actions in the macro library. In fact, this is an excellent way to learn how to write Visual Basic code.

As you can see in Figure 2-5, Access creates a function called mcr_OpenBankAccounts. At the top of the function, Access inserts four comment lines. The comment lines here are simply used to display the name of the function. You can add additional comment lines here as appropriate.

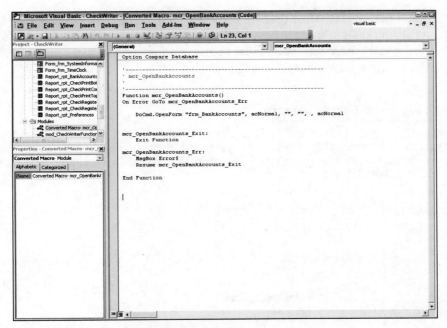

Figure 2-5 *The code for the converted macro.*

It is a good idea to add comment lines to the top of each function and procedure. You should include details about the purpose of the function or procedure and any special notes that may be necessary to understand the code.

When you specify in the Convert Macro dialog that you want to include error processing, Access automatically creates the OnError statement. The OnError statement is the first statement in a function or procedure. The OnError statement tells Access where to find the error processing code section if an error occurs when the code runs. The error processing section includes a statement to display an appropriate error message and the command to exit the procedure or function.

Error processing is covered in more detail in Session 16.

The statement beginning with DoCmd.OpenForm is the code equivalent to the OpenForm action in the macro. The DoCmd methods run Access actions from Visual Basic. Access actions include tasks like opening and closing forms and reports and setting the value of controls. The arguments for the macro's actions are converted to the parameters for the DoCmd method.

You can convert macros that are used in a form in the form's Design view by choosing Tools ⇨ Macro ⇨ Convert Form's Macros to Visual Basic. In addition to creating the Visual Basic code, Access will replace the macro name in the form with a reference to the new procedure.

Using the Command Button Wizard

Another easy way to learn how to write a Visual Basic procedure is to use the Command Button Wizard. The screens in this Wizard prompt you for the information Access needs to create the command button and its attached procedure. Figure 2-6 shows the Actions screen of the Command Button Wizard.

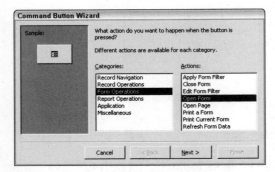

Figure 2-6   *The Command Button Wizard.*

When the Command Button Wizard is finished, you can view the procedure that it created for the command button. You can use this procedure as is, or you can use it as a starting point and modify it as necessary.

To view the command button's procedure, follow these steps:

1. Display the form in Design view.
2. Display the Property window for the command button.
3. Click the Builder button for the OnClick event property. The command button's procedure is displayed in the Visual Basic Editor.

Figure 2-7 shows the procedure for the cmdBankAccounts command button in the Visual Basic Editor.

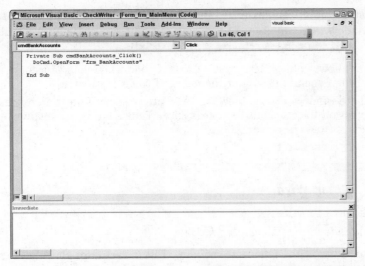

Figure 2-7 *The cmdBankAccounts command button's On Click procedure.*

Event procedures are covered in more detail in Session 4.

Understanding the Visual Basic Editor

10 Min. To Go

The Visual Basic Editor is the design tool provided with Access for creating and editing the Visual Basic code in your application.

Components of the Visual Basic Editor

The Visual Basic Editor has four basic areas:

- Menu bar (command bar)
- Toolbar
- Code window
- Immediate window

The menu bar helps you create new modules and procedures quickly. The toolbar contains buttons for the actions you use most often while working with Visual Basic code.

The code window is the most important area of the Visual Basic Editor. This is where you actually write the Visual Basic code.

You can resize, minimize, maximize, and move the code window. You can also split the window into two areas so that you can edit two procedures simultaneously. To split the window, choose Window ⇨ Split.

The Immediate window allows you to "test drive" a line of code while your procedure is still open. This is handy when you are unsure of the result of some expression.

To display the Immediate window, choose View ⇨ Immediate window. To test an expression, type **?** and the expression to test, and then press Enter. Figure 2-8 shows testing the result of subtracting 30 days from the current date.

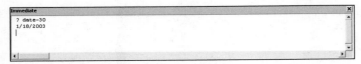

Figure 2-8   *Testing code in the Immediate window.*

You can also run a procedure in the Immediate window. This is useful for checking to see if the procedure works as expected. To test a procedure, type **?** and the name of the procedure to test. If the procedure requires arguments, be sure to specify them as well. Figure 2-9 shows testing the SpellNum procedure.

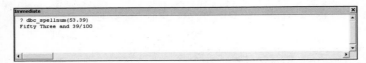

Figure 2-9   *Using the Immediate window to test a procedure.*

Writing code in the code window

While you are learning Visual Basic syntax, working in the code window can seem awkward compared to everything else you may have developed in your Access application. The Visual Basic Editor, however, has some built-in features to help you on your way to becoming a Visual Basic expert.

As you type each line of code in your procedure, on-screen help, called Auto List Members and Auto Quick Info, is displayed to guide you through the vast array of commands and options available for your procedure.

Auto List Members automatically displays when you type the beginning of a command. For example, when you enter DoCmd., a list of possible commands is displayed, as shown in Figure 2-10. You can either select one of the commands in the list or continue typing the command if you already know the one you want to use.

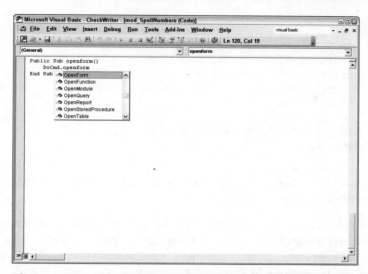

Figure 2-10 *Auto List Members help in the code window.*

Auto Quick Info help displays the options for the command you entered. The next parameter you need to enter is displayed in bold. As you specify each parameter and enter the comma separator, the next parameter is displayed in bold. Figure 2-11 shows the Auto Quick Info help for all the parameters of the Openform command.

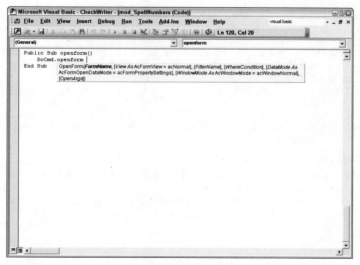

Figure 2-11 *Auto Quick Info help for the OpenForm command.*

Compiling procedures

After you create a procedure, you should compile it by choosing Debug ⇨ Compile. This action checks your code for errors and converts your Visual Basic code to a format that your computer can understand. If the compile process fails, a message box displays to advise you of the type of error that was encountered, and the offending line of code is highlighted in the code window.

 Access compiles all currently uncompiled procedures, not just the one you are currently viewing.

If you receive a compile error, you should immediately modify the code to rectify the problem. Then try to compile the procedure again.

 When your application is compiled, the Debug ⇨ Compile menu choice is disabled. Before implementing an application at the customer's site, you should make sure that your application is compiled. More information on distributing applications is available in Session 23.

Saving a procedure

While you are creating a procedure, you should save it often to avoid the loss of important code should there be any sudden hardware failure. To save the procedure, choose File ⇨ Save.

Done!

REVIEW

In this session, you learned how to use some of the built-in tools to create Visual Basic procedures automatically and how to use the Visual Basic Editor. These topics were covered:

- You can save a macro library as a module to automatically convert the macro actions to Visual Basic code.
- The Command Button Wizard automatically creates the Visual Basic procedure to run a command button's OnClick event.
- You can use the Immediate window to test your code.
- The Visual Basic Editor provides the Compile action for checking your code for errors.

You should now be familiar with some of the tools for creating Visual Basic code. But before you jump into writing your first program, you need to put some thought into the overall design for the program.

QUIZ YOURSELF

1. Name the situations where macros are a better solution than Visual Basic code.
   (See "When to Use Macros.")

2. Name the Access feature that automatically converts a macro to a module.
   (See "Converting macros to Visual Basic code.")

3. Name the Visual Basic statement that handles an error when a program runs.
   (See "Converting macros to Visual Basic code.")

4. Name the feature that allows you to quickly test a line of code. (See "Components
   of the Visual Basic Editor.")

5. How can you tell if your code is compiled? (See "Compiling procedures.")

System and Process Design, Testing, and Debugging

Session Checklist

✔ Designing your system

✔ Planning for programming

✔ Testing your programs

✔ Checking syntax and compiling

✔ Debugging, breakpoints, and the Immediate window

**30 Min.
To Go**

Before you begin any programming activities, you should have a firm understanding of the tasks you need to accomplish. System design is one of the first steps to building any computer application and encompasses hardware, networks, and software. With Microsoft Access, the first two are usually taken care of. As long as the computer system and network can run Microsoft Access, any program you create using Microsoft Access usually runs without any problems.

Because you have already created applications with tables, forms, reports, and possibly macros, you have already designed systems. This session reviews some basic design concepts and concentrates on taking a working set of forms and table designs and planning for the next step — programming. This session also introduces the concepts of testing and debugging Visual Basic programs.

Designing Your System

When you begin writing an application, you start with the most general of design goals and then get more and more specific. When the authors of this book decided to use a comprehensive example, they brainstormed for a representative application. We decided to use our award-winning Check Writer application, which we have used for previous versions of Microsoft Access, and to rewrite it using the ADO data access method used in Microsoft Access 2003.

Building an application is like building a house. You start by deciding you want a house. Next, you get more specific. You want a colonial, two stories high, and about 2,500 square feet in area. Then you decide how many rooms each floor will have and the dimensions and layout of each floor. Next, it's time to draw up some blueprints and order the materials. Only then can you start the building process.

As professional carpenters build the house, they constantly check to make sure everything is square by using a variety of tools including levels, chalk lines, and squares. Likewise, you use a variety of Visual Basic tools to ensure quality in your Microsoft Access application: the syntax checker, compiler, built-in debugger, Immediate window, and breakpoints.

When you build a Microsoft Access application, it costs much less than a house because no materials are involved, just labor. However, just because an application may be less expensive to build than a house, the up-front design time shouldn't be any less. Although you can always take down a wall in a house after it is built, you probably want to build it right the first time. It would be helpful if the house would tell you each time you made an error (such as making a door opening too small). The good news is that the built-in tools in Microsoft Access constantly give you this kind of feedback as you program your application.

You may not need a set of detailed blueprints to begin your system design using Microsoft Access, but you should create a set of specifications with increasing details. Your specifications should first address the general problem, then provide a set of details, and then offer a specification with even more details. The visual forms designer and user-friendly table-design environment of Microsoft Access make it a wonderful system-development environment. You can create prototypes as quickly as you can brainstorm features — and make changes as you go.

Because of this, you don't need to spend as much time designing your systems up front as you do with other less visual languages. However, the more time you spend discussing and defining your system before you start, the easier it will be to complete it successfully.

Building a computer application requires several distinct phases:

- General Design (also known as System Design)
- Detail Design
- Programming and Documentation
- Testing
- Debugging

General design

The overall system design is defined from a business point of view as opposed to a technical or computer outlook. A general design ordinarily takes just a few pages and lays out the most important aspects of the system. Major functions are mentioned by name only. Later all the details can be filled in. The output of the system (reports) should also be discussed because, generally, you can't create data designs or forms without knowing what information will ultimately be expected from the system.

When we first built the Check Writer application, we wanted to build an application that would closely resemble a process everyone used all the time. After deciding on a checkbook

Design Is a Never-Ending Process, Not Just a Phase

Designing anything is a fluid process. It never ends. You keep reviewing and working and reviewing. You start with an idea, refine it, discuss it further, add some new ideas, and continue changing it until you are satisfied with the result. This can occur during any of the phases of design. Sometimes, when testing a completed form, you realize you left out a very basic set of data items that may require you to create a new lookup table, rearrange the form, or even redesign portions of the entire application. Don't be discouraged if this happens. It is a normal part of development, and even the most experienced developers go through this process. In fact, sometimes it is better to prototype your first idea without even discussing it!

application, we moved to the next level and wrote a small group of bullets. We wanted to design a checkbook that worked like a manual checkbook and had the following features:

- A form to enter and edit bank account information
- Separate forms to enter and edit checks, deposits, and adjustments
- A Check Register listing all checks, deposits, and adjustments with a running balance
- A system to reconcile cleared checks
- A main menu to navigate among these functions

Detail design

After you have a general conceptual model of the system and a rough idea of what you want to build, you can get specific. For the purposes of this book, we assume that someone on your design team has the necessary business knowledge to produce detailed specifications of the system, regardless of the program being used. Detail design should include sketches of the forms and reports you think you need. From the form and report designs, you can lay out the raw data elements you require and then begin to create tables and relationships and normalize the data design. You can do this on paper or by using Microsoft Access as a prototyping tool.

A good place to start is with customers and their existing systems. In virtually every consulting job we have ever had, the customer is either automating a manual system that already exists on paper or on index-type cards, or he is creating a new system. If it is a new system, we are usually shown another company's system that is to be cloned. It is very unusual for a system to be developed with no basic template.

When building the Check Writer application, the very first thing our team did was to each get out our checkbooks and copy a check and the check register. We looked at five different examples that were all similar with a few minor differences. Bank names were in different places, one of the checks had a place for the payee's address, and the memo areas were a little different. Most of us had checks in small pocket-sized checkbooks, although one of our team members had a multipart check with the check itself on top and areas for the stub in the middle and on the bottom.

We decided that businesses would probably want the multipart check forms. After we had established this basic template, it was easy to come up with many of the print options, such as a choice among three kinds of check stock and the option to print check numbers if the paper didn't have preprinted numbers.

We decided to start with the most fundamental of needs — the check. We looked at the check and then used a table that we had already designed. The table consists initially of these data fields:

- CheckNumber
- CheckDate
- Payee
- PaymentAmount
- Memo

We then designed a simple form and moved the fields into position as shown in Figure 3-1. As you can see, with just this simple table and form, the application is already beginning to look like a check and could theoretically be used for data entry and reporting.

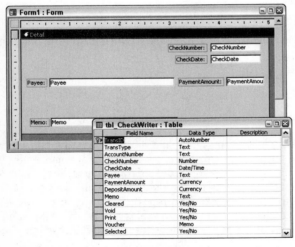

Figure 3-1 *The simple Check Writer table and form design.*

After we had the form design, we added some basic text, such as labels, for the bank account information — bank account number, bank name, bank address, and routing numbers. This led to a discussion about customers who had more than one bank account. We decided to add a bank account table and enable the Check Writer table and form to handle more than one bank account.

We not only had to design and create the Bank Account table and form, but we also had to add some additional fields to the Check Writer table. We added the AccountNumber field to the tbl_CheckWriter table and related the tbl_CheckWriter and tbl_BankAccounts tables. This enabled the Check Writer record to record the bank account number, allowing this record to be used for more than one bank account.

The Concentric Circle Approach to Development

Microsoft has always followed a philosophy of development that includes the design, programming, and testing of a set of core features followed by increasing functionality in phases. Microsoft develops a blueprint that includes small sets of features. First, the most fundamental features are developed. Next, this feature set can be distributed to customers for comments and testing. While one small team of developers is working on testing and debugging one of the feature sets, another team is working on programming the next feature set. Still another team is working on design refinement of the next set of features. This continues until Microsoft is ready to release the product. When it is ready, features that have not passed the testing criteria are simply removed.

The product can be released at many different times with different feature sets. Based on market dynamics and customer feedback, the product is either released or development continues. Think of a set of concentric circles that keeps getting bigger and bigger. At any time, the product could be released — but the longer development continues, the more features are added.

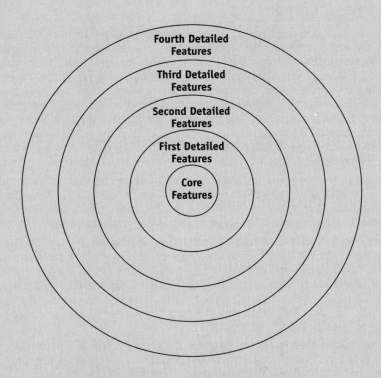

We then added a combo box to the Check Writer form to display all the bank accounts. This required us to add some Visual Basic code to change or filter bank accounts. At the same time, we discussed the fact that, although we had a form for checks, we needed other forms for balance adjustments.

Eventually, we realized that multiple forms are hard to navigate through, so we packaged all the forms into the tabbed dialog you see in the working example.

This process took several weeks of work and many prototypes. This is a normal part of development: analysis and design, programming, testing and debugging, refinement, and more design. It never really stops. You can continue to add more and more functionality. Our check register was developed using several different prototypes and, in fact, we started over several times before finding a design we really liked.

Eventually, you have a form that is as complete as it can be without macro or Visual Basic programming. Although a form can be used for simple data entry or display, it usually needs some sort of processing to complete the design. Error checking, calculations, moving data between tables, filling combo box row sources, filtering data, or building menus are just a few of the reasons you must write program code.

Planning for Programming

**20 Min.
To Go**

After you have designed the basic data entry objects on paper or used Microsoft Access to prototype your table, form, and report designs, you can turn your attention to adding process code. Having data entry forms without any programs behind them gives you very little flexibility. Adding Visual Basic code or macros behind Access forms gives you unlimited flexibility to handle errors, create calculations and formulas, add navigation (getting from one form to another), handle data interchange between tables, find records, and create flexible dialog boxes for printing. You may also want to have a splash screen, user-definable setup options, an About box, programmable security, and a menu system or switchboard. The best way to learn how to write the specific lines of code to accomplish a task is to find some code that does what you want and modify it to fit your tables and forms.

This book will give you plenty of examples. But before you start writing code, you must have an idea of what you want to write and where you want to write it. In Session 4, you learn about events. *Events* live behind forms, form controls, and form processes (before and after you insert, update, or delete records), and in other places as well.

When you begin to plan any Visual Basic coding, it is generally a good idea to start with data validation as the data is entered, on both a control-by-control basis and possibly before the record is saved. When you put validation code behind Before Update events, you can stop the data from actually being put into the control. You can display a message to require different input. If you put validation code behind After Update events, the data has already been accepted. You may be transferring the data to another control or storing it in a table other than the bound field of the control.

A lot of code is written to process numeric data or to follow business rules. These are the rules that the business dictates. For example, after a line item is entered into an invoice application, the subtotal is recalculated and the item is checked to see if it is taxable. If it is taxable, the taxable subtotal is recalculated and a calculation of Tax Rate × the Taxable Subtotal is added to the subtotal to calculate Total Owed. In the Check Writer example, voided checks must not be added to the running balance on the check register. The business rule determines what has to be designed, and then you add programming to implement the design.

After you have built a few applications, you also build your toolbox of routines. The more you build, use, discover, craft, or create, the easier it gets.

One way to jumpstart your development efforts is to purchase some of the low-cost libraries of preprogrammed utilities, interfaces, and source code repositories. Some of the best are the Total Access SourceBook, a library of Visual Basic code from FMS Corporation at www.fmsinc.com **and EZ Access Developer Tools, a library of interface designs and Visual Basic code from Database Creations (the authors of this book) at** www.databasecreations. com**. See the companion Web site for this book (**www.wiley.com/compbooks/ prague**) for links to demos of these and many other products, along with their Web sites for the latest product information.**

As you go through your design process and define tasks you can't accomplish with forms alone, you turn these tasks into business and process designs and eventually into Visual Basic designs. There are hundreds and even thousands of different types of Visual Basic statements, constants, variables, and constructs. Don't worry about trying to learn every one. Learn the ones you need for the type of programming you are doing. Pay special attention to the statements you use a lot and learn new ones as you need to.

Although only experience can teach you how to create algorithms (specific designs in a language), this book will show you many algorithms for a wide variety of situations.

Testing and Debugging Your Applications

Testing is the first step in a process that lets you ensure that your application is working as designed. Each time you move from form or report design or the Visual Basic Editor to running those same forms, reports, and Visual Basic code, you are testing your application. Each time you write a line of code and move to another line, you (or Access) is testing your code. Each time you change a property in a form or report and move your cursor to another property, you and Access are testing your form or report.

Testing is the process that ensures your application runs the way you designed it (or whether it runs at all). When you run an application that doesn't work, you have found a bug.

Fixing problems is known as *debugging***. This term dates back to the earliest electron tube computers. Legend has it that a moth shorted out a hardware circuit. Removing the moth was known as "debugging the system" — a phrase attributed to the late Admiral Grace Hopper, an early pioneer in computing.**

You may have already learned a lot about testing and debugging. When you run a report and no data appears, you have probably learned to check the report's Record Source property and to view the data in the query or table to see if the data source is the problem. If you run a form and you see #Name or #Error in individual controls, you have learned to check the Control Source of the control. Perhaps you have an incorrect reference to a table field or spelled something wrong. Maybe you have too many parentheses or have used a control name in a formula that uses the control name. Each time you run into a problem, you probably seek help from someone with more experience, or perhaps you look it up in a manual or research the syntax of the formula.

When you run forms and reports, Access may report an error if it finds something seriously wrong. When you create Visual Basic code, there are a wide variety of tools built into the editor to help you find the problem.

Syntax checking — the first step

When you type a line of code in Visual Basic, each character is evaluated against the known but limited set of valid Visual Basic commands. In Session 2, you learned about the Access Auto List Members and Auto Quick Info tools that help you enter code correctly. When you have completed entering each line of code, another built-in tool known as the *syntax checker* ensures that the line of code contains valid entries

Syntax is the name given to computer grammar. Figure 3-2 shows a statement typed incorrectly and the error message that is displayed as you try to leave the line. Although you can't tell this from the black-and-white figure shown here, the lines appear in different colors. The first line in Figure 3-2 appears in blue, which indicates a valid line of code. The second line is shown in green, which is used for comments. Red, used on the third line in the figure, indicates a line that has been flagged by the syntax checker and not yet corrected.

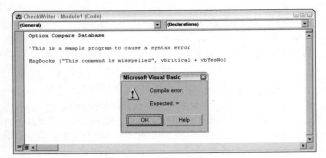

Figure 3-2   *The Microsoft Access syntax checker.*

 Unlike some other languages, Visual Basic lets you leave a line of code that has an error and fix it later. Sometimes, you need to add or change another line of code in order to fix a subsequent line.

Compiling procedures

After you create a subprocedure or function and want to make sure all your syntax is correct, you should compile your procedures by choosing Debug ➪ Compile *projectname* from the Visual Basic menu as shown in Figure 3-3. This action checks your code for errors and also converts the programs to a form your computer can understand. If the compile operation is not successful, an error window appears. This level of checking is more stringent than the single-line syntax checker. Variables are checked for proper references and type. Each statement is checked for all proper parameters. All text strings are checked for proper delimiters such as `'text string.'`

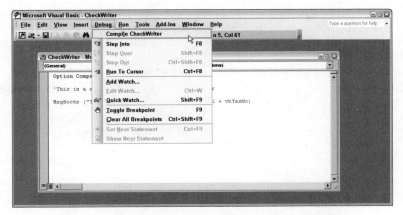

Figure 3-3 *Compiling the Visual Basic code in your database.*

Although your database is named a standard Windows name such as CheckWriter Access, there is a separate project name that Microsoft Access uses internally. You see this when you compile your database. When the database file is first created, the project name and the Windows filename are the same. The project name is not changed when you change the Windows filename. You can change the project name by selecting Tools ⇨ *projectname* Properties where *projectname* is the current internal project name.

When you compile your application, Access checks each and every uncompiled procedure and then converts each one to a form that can be run. If Access finds any errors, it stops and reports the error. It stops at the first error it finds. You must correct the error and then run the compile operation again.

Compiling your database does more that just make sure that you have no syntax errors. It ensures that object references are appropriate. The compiler can only check for language problems by first recognizing the Visual Basic statement and then checking that you specify the right number of options in the right order.

After you compile your program, you should also compact your database. Each time you make a change to your program, it stores both the changes and the original version. When you compile your program, it may double in size because the compiled and uncompiled versions of your code are stored. Compacting the database reduces its size by as much as 80 percent because this eliminates all previous versions internally.

Handling runtime errors

If you create a line of code that refers to a specific form, that form must already be opened. A previous line of code in a different procedure must open it. If the form is not already open when the program runs, an error occurs. You cannot determine a problem during the compile step because the compiler evaluates each procedure separately. It does not try to compare the logic between procedures or modules, and the code to open the form can be run from a variety of events. If the form has not been opened, however, when the program runs you get an error message.

When you get an error message, you want to respond to it. However, some errors are harder to understand than others, and some require you to instantly recognize the problem. For example, Figure 3-4 shows a simple program that declares and creates a text string variable and a numeric variable and then tries to assign the numeric variable the value of the text string. You probably already know that you can't put letters in a numeric field.

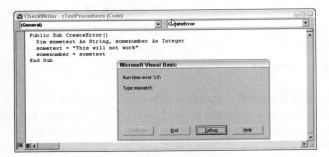

Figure 3-4   *A runtime error message.*

The error message in Figure 3-4 reports a `Run-time error '13'`, which happens to be a type mismatch. Unless you know the problem, how does this message help you? Without a great deal of experience, how do you then fix this type of problem? In fact, how do you determine what the problem is?

In the error dialog in Figure 3-4, you can see a button labeled Debug. Clicking the Debug button stops the program and places you on the offending statement. The program is in a state of limbo. All the values of temporary variables are intact, and you can view them to help you solve the error. Clicking the End button stops the program and prevents you from using any tools to check the problem.

Figure 3-5 shows the offending statement, highlighted by a yellow background. There are several tools you can now use to find your problem, and they are described next.

If you place your cursor over any variable in the highlighted area, you can see the current value. If you examine Figure 3-5, you can see the arrow in the left margin indicating the highlighted line is the currently running line of code. You can also see the rectangle containing the text `sometext = "This will not work"`, the current value of the variable named Text.

Although you can place your cursor on the running variable and determine the values, you may want to see the value of other variables as well. Sometimes, depending on how the program is structured, you can do this, but usually you are limited to the latest values created.

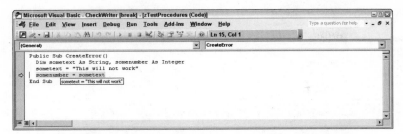

Figure 3-5 *Displaying the value from a running variable.*

Variables are user-defined values stored in memory. They are covered in detail in Session 6.

Using the Immediate, Locals, and Watches windows

**10 Min.
To Go**

There are several more tools that can help you debug a program. These include the Immediate, Locals, and Watches windows. You can display any or all of them as part of the Visual Basic editor window by selecting View ➪ Immediate Window, View ➪ Locals Window, or View ➪ Watch Window. The window you use depends on the severity of your problem and the mysteriousness of the error.

The Immediate Window is an area where you can run procedures, check the value of variables, check an expression, or run a single line of Visual Basic code. You can run a Visual Basic subprocedure by using the syntax Call *procedurename* where *procedurename* is a subprocedure or function. You can also run a function by placing a ? in front of the call and adding a variable for the return value such as ? x = *functionname*. You can check the value of any variable running in your program by placing a ? in front of the variable name.

Figure 3-6 shows you the values of the running variables. Here, in the Immediate window, you see that ? somenumber is entered and produces the value 0. Then on a separate line ? sometext is entered, and the text "This will not work" is displayed. This is the value of the variable named Text.

Another way to run a program is to display the procedure or function in the Visual Basic window, place your cursor on the first line, and then press F5 to run the entire procedure or function or F8 to step through the procedure or function one line at a time

You can use the Locals window to display all the active memory items in your running program. These include forms, modules, and variables. In Figure 3-6, you can see the Locals window in the bottom-left corner of the figure. Because only a simple module is running, you see only the reference to that object. If you were also running a form, you would see a reference to the form object along with a tree diagram that could be exploded to show each control on the form and the value of each control for the current record. This is important when you are debugging a module behind a form or report.

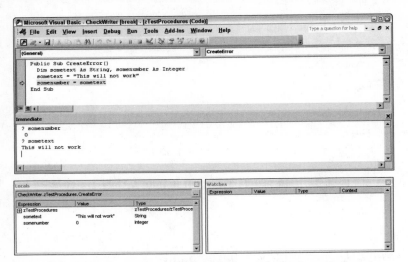

Figure 3-6 *Using the Immediate, Locals, and Watches windows.*

Generally, you start with just the module debugger and then, if necessary, move into the Immediate window. To view more variables, you might display the Locals window. There is also an advanced window known as the Watches window. Although detailed coverage of the Watches window is outside the scope of this book, the Watches window lets you set up specific values to watch for and then stops the program when a value is reached. For example, if you are expecting an incremental value to reach 500 by ones and it never does, you might set a Watch variable to see if it hits 100 rather than to randomly check the program when it runs. If the *watchpoint* (as the Watch variable is called) hits 100, the program stops and the line of code that the program is sitting on when the value reached 100 is highlighted. This is the same as a runtime error without the actual error.

When the program stops, there are other tools you can use to step through the program one line at a time. You can also move to previously executed lines to check your program logic. Besides the Watches window, you can stop your program at a specific point by using a breakpoint.

Creating a breakpoint

There is one final code-debugging tool that professional developers use: breakpoints. Whereas the Watches window watches for a specific value, *breakpoints* simply watch for a specific line to be executed and stop the program at that statement.

Professional developers often refer to running a program as *executing* it. You execute a program to start it. Either term is appropriate.

A breakpoint is often used to stop a running program before it causes an error. It checks all the variables and conditions of the objects before the error occurs.

To set a breakpoint, display your program in Design view and press the F9 function key or select the Toggle Breakpoint menu item from the Debug menu. Figure 3-7 shows a breakpoint on the line that sets the value of the variable Text in the simple program you have seen in this session. After you set the breakpoint, you can close the module and the program remembers the breakpoint until the database file is closed. When you run the program and that module is executed, the program stops on that line and displays the program at the breakpoint.

Figure 3-7 *Setting a breakpoint.*

After the program has run and stopped, you can use options on the Debug menu to control the execution. The Debug menu is discussed in the following section.

You can set as many breakpoints as you want, but more than one may be confusing unless you are trying to determine if a block of code is being run at all.

Using the Debug menu

Figure 3-8 shows the Debug menu. When there is a breakpoint, the code execution stops where the breakpoint is set. You will see a solid red circle and a yellow arrow in the margin. The red circle indicates the breakpoint and the arrow the current line.

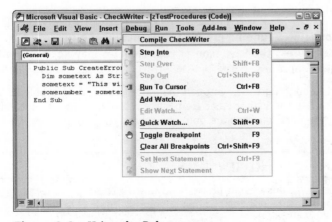

Figure 3-8 *Using the Debug menu.*

The Debug menu is broken into five sections. The first section lets you compile the application. You generally don't do this while the program is running.

The second section allows you to use four different methods to continue running your program one or more statements at a time:

Step Into	Run the next one line of code.
Step Over	Run the next line of code and all the code in any called procedures.
Step Out	Run the entire current procedure and then stop with the next line in the original called procedure.
Run to Cursor	Move your cursor to a later line and run all the statements between the current line and the line where the cursor is sitting.

The third section of the menu enables you to add or edit a watchpoint in the Watches window. You can also run a quick watch just to see the value of a variable, much like entering ? somevariablename in the Immediate window.

The fourth section lets you toggle a breakpoint on or off or clear all breakpoints. When you close a database file, all breakpoints are automatically cleared.

The menu choices in the fifth and final section are perhaps the most powerful. Set Next Statement lets you move the cursor to any line of code and run the program starting with that line. If you are trying to correct an error and keep getting it wrong, being able to go backwards is very important. Show Next Statement simply highlights the next statement without running it.

The Run menu also offers the following options to help you debug a program:

Continue	Continues running the program without stopping until the next error, breakpoint, or to the program's conclusion.
Break	Stops the program where it is running. You can also use Ctrl-Break to stop a running program and cause a manual break. If you accidentally create an endless loop, this will stop the program.
Reset	Stops the error process and lets you restart the program from any desired line of code.

 When you are debugging a running program and finally get a line of code corrected, be sure to press the Save icon or your changes may not be saved when you close the procedure.

By using the wide variety of debugging tools, you can diagnose your coding problems and quickly solve them. You can also use the Visual Basic Help system to help you understand the problem being reported, but generally errors are yours to solve.

Done!

REVIEW

In this session, you learned about various design phases and how to think properly about your program design. You learned how to use the various debugging tools to trap errors and fix them. The following topics were covered:

- Design is an ongoing process that contains many iterative phases.
- Development includes conceptual or general design, detail design, programming, testing, and debugging.
- You can use Microsoft Access itself to prototype your systems during design phases instead of using paper and pencil.
- Debugging is the name given to the process of finding problems with your systems and correcting them.
- Syntax is the name given to computer grammar. Access program statements follow rules of grammar similar to spoken language.
- Compiling checks all your program statements for correct syntax and translates your code into a form that Access can run quickly and efficiently.
- When a runtime error is displayed, you can use the Debug button to display the problem line.
- The Immediate, Locals, and Watches windows help you display your program variables.
- The Debug menu contains many options to help you run your program one line at a time to find and correct your errors.

QUIZ YOURSELF

1. Define the term *general design*. (See "Designing Your System.")
2. What is the *concentric circle* approach to development? (See "Detail design.")
3. Define the term *syntax*. (See "Syntax checking — the first step.")
4. What are the two main reasons to compile your programs? (See "Compiling procedures.")
5. When you get a runtime error, how do you display the offending line of code? (See "Handling runtime errors.")
6. What are some of the ways to watch your variables as your program runs? (See "Using the Immediate, Locals, and Watches windows.")
7. How can you stop your program anywhere you want and run it one line at a time? (See "Creating a breakpoint.")

Events — A Place to Run Your Code

Session Checklist

✔ Understanding events

✔ Responding to events

✔ Creating an event procedure

✔ Using an event procedure to validate data

✔ Understanding event sequences

**30 Min.
To Go**

Forms and reports are the objects that are most apparent to the users of your application. The text boxes, labels, and command buttons in the forms and reports provide the visual components that allow users to interact with the application. Although developing forms and reports constitutes a significant amount of the entire application development effort, a considerable amount of thought and planning (and a little code) are required to tie all these forms and reports together seamlessly.

Understanding Events

An event is a process that occurs whenever a user performs some action in a form or report. Microsoft Access is referred to as an *event-driven environment* because it can respond to actions like clicking a command button, opening a form or report, or updating data in a field. In an event-driven environment, the user has more control over the flow of the application. The user can update the fields on a form in any order, for example, or click any one in a set of buttons. Events provide a way to respond to actions that occur in an application. An event can occur when the user performs some action, such as clicking a button. An event can also occur in response to an action that the user does not perform directly, like the timer event that occurs when a form opens.

Every control you place on a form has a set of event properties. You can check the event properties available for a form, report, or control by displaying the property sheet. Figure 4-1 shows the list of events on the property sheet for the cmdBankAccounts command button.

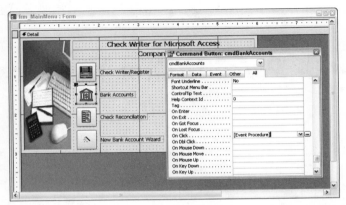

Figure 4-1   *The event properties for the cmdBankAccounts command button.*

Responding to Events

Event properties provide a way to respond to any of the actions a user might perform with a form, report, or control. You respond to an event by associating a macro or event procedure with a specific event property. The macro or event procedure contains the instructions that Access should perform whenever the associated event happens.

The cmdBankAccounts command button has an event procedure associated with its OnClick event property. The OnClick event occurs whenever the user selects the command button by clicking it with the mouse or by moving to the command button and pressing Enter. Whenever the cmdBankAccounts command button's OnClick event occurs, the event procedure runs automatically.

You learned how to associate a macro with a command button in Session 2.

An event procedure is a Visual Basic program that you create and associate with an event. Figure 4-2 shows the OnClick event procedure for the cmdBankAccounts command button. The cmdBankAccounts_Click procedure opens the frm_BankAccounts form.

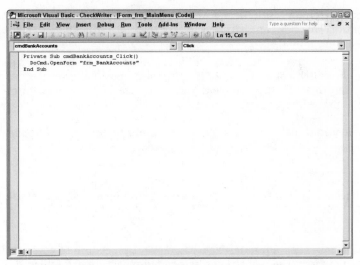

Figure 4-2　*The event procedure for the OnClick event of the cmdBankAccounts command button.*

Creating an Event Procedure

You can associate an event procedure with an individual control or with an entire form or report. To create an event procedure, follow these steps:

1. Open the form or report in Design view.
2. Select the control in the design window and display the property sheet.

To display the property sheet for the form or report, select the square at the top left of the design window.

3. Click the event property in the property sheet for the event that you want to respond to. For a command button, for example, select the OnClick event property.
4. Select Event Procedure from the event property's combo box. The Visual Basic Editor opens and automatically displays the first and last lines of the new event procedure.

There are two other methods for creating an event procedure: Choose Build Event from the shortcut menu, or click the Build button next to the event property and select Code Builder in the Choose Builder dialog.

When an event property has an associated event procedure, the text [Event Procedure] **displays next to the event property.**

When you create a new event procedure, Access automatically inserts the first and last statements for the procedure. This built-in feature acts as a template to help you create procedures quickly and easily.

The first statement in a procedure contains a good deal of information about its type and behavior. The `Private` keyword indicates that only this form or report can execute this procedure. The `Sub` keyword describes the type of event procedure. The third element of the procedure statement is the procedure's name.

The `Public` keyword makes the procedure available to any form or report in the application.

Session 1 discusses the difference between `Sub` and `Function` procedures.

Access automatically assigns an appropriate name to an event procedure to correspond with the associated event property. The name is the associated object's name followed by an underscore and the associated object's event. For example, the name for the cmdBankAccounts command button's `OnClick` procedure is `cmdBankAccounts_Click`.

When assigning a name for an event, Access converts a space in the control's name to an underscore.

Never change the name of an event procedure. The name maintains the connection between the control, the control's event, and the event procedure code. Likewise, never change the name of a control that has associated event procedures.

The last statement in the procedure is End Sub. This statement indicates the end of the procedure.

**20 Min.
To Go**

Running a Function for an Event

Event procedures are the recommended method of running Visual Basic code for an event. However, you can also associate a function with an event. Figure 4-3 shows the function associated with the txtBankAccountNumber text box in the frm_BankAccountsUnbound form.

In the frm_BankAccountsUnbound form, whenever the txtBankAccountNumber text box is updated, the dbc_SetEditedFlag function runs. The dbc_SetEditedFlag function is shown in Figure 4-4.

Figure 4-3   *Associating a function with an event.*

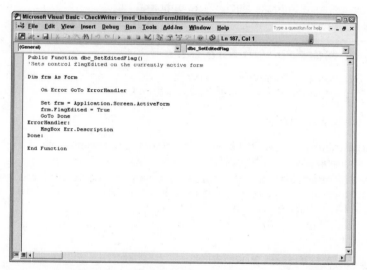

Figure 4-4   *A public function can be called by events in any form.*

The `dbc_SetEditedFlag` function changes the value of the `FlagEdited` field in the form to `True`. Notice that the `dbc_SetEditedFlag` function is declared as `Public`. This indicates that it can be executed by any event in any form. This function is stored in the Unbound Form Utilities module. By storing the function in a module, you can use it for multiple unbound forms in your application.

   You learn more about modules in Session 7.

To associate a function with an event, follow these steps:

1. Click the event property in the property sheet for the event that you want to respond to.
2. Enter an equal sign (=), followed by the function name and a pair of parentheses.

Entering the function name directly into the event property saves development time by eliminating the need for a separate event procedure for every control and event that needs to run it. Alternatively, you can call the function from an event procedure like this:

```
Private Sub BankAccountNumber_AfterUpdate()
    Dim x As Integer
    x = dbc_SetEditedFlag()

End Sub
```

To call the procedure using the event procedure method, you have to create an event procedure and write the same code for each field in the unbound form.

Using an Event Procedure to Validate Data

In most cases, you can use the Validation Rule property for a field to verify acceptable field values. By using an event procedure, however, you have much more power and flexibility available for data entry validation. You should use an event procedure when you need to validate data using any of these scenarios:

- You need to verify that multiple fields have been completed. For example, the user must enter a name and a Social Security number.
- You want to display a different error message for certain types of incorrect values. You might want to display one message if the value is below a certain amount and a different message if the value exceeds another amount.
- When you want to allow a potentially invalid entry and simply display a warning message.
- To validate the data against fields on other forms.

Figure 4-5 shows an event procedure for validating the field txtCheckDate in the frm_CheckWriter form.

The txtCheckDates_BeforeUpdate event compares the date entered to two possible scenarios. If the value of txtCheckDate falls into either scenario, a message appears and the user must enter a different Check Date in order to continue.

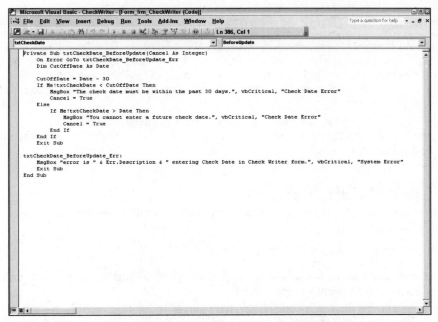

Figure 4-5 *Displaying separate error messages for types of incorrect values.*

In the first scenario, the event checks to see if the value of txtCheckDate is within the past 30 days. In order to test this condition, the procedure performs the following steps:

1. The CutoffDate variable is calculated as the current date minus 30 days.

> **The** Date **keyword refers to the current date.**

2. The CheckDate is compared to the CutoffDate. If the CheckDate is before the CutoffDate, the message box displays.

3. If the CheckDate is before the CutoffDate, the Cancel variable is set to True. Setting Cancel to True causes Access to stop processing the update.

> **Notice that the** BeforeUpdate **event receives the** Cancel **variable as a parameter. When an event procedure includes** Cancel **as a parameter, this indicates that you can cancel the event in process.**

The Else portion of the txtCheckDate_BeforeUpdate procedure tests the second scenario. This scenario checks to see if the value of txtCheckDate is a future date. If the value of txtCheckDate is greater than the current date, a different error message displays and the event is cancelled.

Understanding the Order of Events

You have learned that forms, reports, and controls have many associated event properties. You have also learned that the user's actions can trigger these events. It is extremely important to note, however, that a single action can trigger multiple events. These events are processed in a prescribed sequence. Understanding this sequence is fundamental to creating effective event procedures.

When the user clicks a field, for example, the Enter event occurs followed by the GotFocus event. If you create event procedures for both of these events, you must be aware of which event occurs first.

Events for updating data in controls

When the user updates data in a control and then moves to another control, the order of events is as follows:

BeforeUpdate ⇨ AfterUpdate ⇨ Exit ⇨ LostFocus

If the BeforeUpdate event is cancelled, either through its Validation Rule or through its event procedure, no other events are triggered.

If, after updating the data in a control, the user moves to another record, the form's BeforeUpdate and AfterUpdate events also occur.

Events for deleting records

The order of events for deleting a record is:

Delete ⇨ BeforeDelConfirm ⇨ AfterDelConfirm

When a user attempts to delete a record, Access automatically displays a confirmation message. If the user cancels the deletion, none of the events occurs.

Events for opening a form

When a form opens, the following events occur:

Open ⇨ Load ⇨ Resize ⇨ Activate ⇨ Current

The Current event also runs whenever the user moves to another record or to a new record.

Events for creating a new record

When the user creates a new record, these events occur:

Current ⇨ BeforeInsert ⇨ AfterInsert

Events for closing a form

These events occur when a form closes:

Unload ⇨ Deactivate ⇨ Close

Working in an event-driven environment is confusing at first. After you become familiar with events and how they are processed, however, you will find many opportunities to use them to your advantage as you strive to make your application run as smoothly and efficiently as possible.

REVIEW

In this session, you learned how events allow the user to control the flow of the application. The event-driven environment used by Access allows you to create event procedures that perform specific instructions in response to the user's actions. The following topics were covered:

Done!

- Forms, reports, and controls have many associated event properties.
- An event property can contain a macro, a function, or an event procedure.
- Event properties occur in a prescribed order.
- You can use an event procedure to accept or reject an update to a control or form.

QUIZ YOURSELF

1. How do you determine what events are available for a control on a form or report? (See "Understanding Events.")

2. What event is triggered when the user selects a command button? (See "Responding to Events.")

3. Name the three components of the first line of a procedure. (See "Creating an Event Procedure.")

4. When should you use an event procedure instead of the Validation Rule property when validating data entered by a user? (See "Using an Event Procedure to Validate Data.")

5. When data in a control is updated, which event occurs first: Exit or AfterUpdate? (See "Events for updating data in controls.")

Friday Evening
Part Review

1. Define the term *database management system*.
2. Is the Visual Basic window a separate window or part of Microsoft Office Access 2003?
3. What are the two types of procedures and what is the difference between them?
4. What are VBA, Jet, and MSDE?
5. True or false: You should use a macro to handle application errors.
6. For which of the following situations are macros a sensible solution?
   a. Creating functions
   b. Calling Windows common dialogs
   c. Integrating with Word or Excel
   d. Opening a form from a command button
7. When you begin typing a command in the code window, the built-in feature _____ automatically displays a list of commands.
8. You know your application is compiled when
   a. the "Compile Complete" message box displays.
   b. the Debug→Compile menu choice is disabled.
   c. the code in the code window changes to green.
   d. the computer speaker beeps.
9. What are the five major steps of development?
10. Why is compiling important and what should you do after you compile your program?
11. What are the names of the three windows that help you debug a program?
12. What is the difference between a watchpoint and a breakpoint?
13. The _____ lists the events that are available for a form.
14. True or false: An event procedure is a special type of macro.

15. The first statement of the event procedure for the cmd_BankAccounts command button's OnClick event procedure is:

    a. Private Sub cmd_BankAccounts_Click()

    b. On Error GoTo cmd_BankAccounts_Err

    c. Function cmd_BankAccounts_Click()

    d. Dim strName as String

16. You must use an event procedure to validate data in which of the following scenarios?

    a. The check amount must be greater than zero.

    b. You must enter the check date.

    c. The check amount must be less than $500 and the check amount must be greater than zero.

    d. The check date cannot be in the future.

17. What statement allows you to declare a variable?

18. Why should you use the Option Explicit statement at the beginning of every procedure?

19. What are the keywords used to make a variable known to your entire program or just to a specific procedure?

20. Which of the following are valid Visual Basic variable types?

    a. Integer

    b. Text

    c. Number

    d. Long

☑ Friday

☑ **Saturday**

☐ Sunday

Part II — Saturday Morning

Part III — Saturday Afternoon

Part IV — Saturday Evening

PART

II

Saturday
Morning

Declaring and Understanding Variables and Using Naming Conventions

Session Checklist

✔ Types of variables

✔ Declaration of variables

✔ Public and private variables

✔ Naming conventions

**30 Min.
To Go**

When you create programs in any computer language, you must create temporary storage areas known as variables. Unlike data fields, which are stored permanently in tables in your database file, variables are stored in memory and are active only while your program is running. They are called variables just as x in the algebraic expression $x = 5 + 9$ is called a variable. The value within the variable changes or varies based on the expression.

Variables can be used to store numbers, dates, text strings, Boolean (yes/no) values, control names, or data values. Variables can be used to store the value of a control or the name of a form. There are variables at every object level in Microsoft Access. You can store the value of any object including control names in forms or reports, table field names, or the names of tables, queries, forms, or reports. You can use a variable for the name of a database or even a Windows filename. Anytime you need a temporary storage area, you can create a variable and assign a value to it.

Creating and using variables is a two-step process. First, you give the variable a name and assign it a type (data type, object type, and so on). Then you assign it a value.

In this session, you learn how to declare variables and assign values to them. You also learn how to make variable values available to one module or to your entire program. The session covers some of the standard naming conventions for objects and variables used by professional developers and some alternative object naming guidelines.

Using Variables

One of the most powerful concepts in programming is the variable. A *variable* is a temporary storage location for some value and is given a name. You can use a variable to store the result of a calculation, or you can create a variable to make the value of a control available to another procedure.

To refer to the result of an expression, you create a name to store the result. The named result is the variable. To assign an expression's result to a variable, you use the = operator. Following are some examples of calculations that create variables:

```
counter = 1

counter = counter + 1

today = Date()
```

Naming variables

Every programming language has its own rules for naming variables. In Visual Basic, a variable name must meet the following conditions:

- It must begin with an alphabetical character.
- It must not contain an embedded period or type-declaration character.
- It must have a unique name — one not used elsewhere in the procedure or in modules that use the variables.
- It must be no longer than 255 characters.
- It must not contain spaces. Field names can contain spaces, but it is not recommended.

Although you can make up almost any name for a variable, most programmers adopt a standard convention for naming variables. Some common practices include the following:

- Using uppercase and lowercase characters to represent multiple words, as in TotalCost.
- No spaces. Do not create a field named Total Cost.
- Using all lowercase characters, as in counter. Although this contradicts the first bullet, it is also a practice of some programmers.
- Preceding the name with the data type of the value. A variable that stores an integer type number might be called intCounter or int_counter. This type of naming convention is used by some professional programmers so religiously that, in our opinion, it sometimes makes code harder to read.

When you need to see or use the contents of a variable, you simply use its name. When you specify the variable's name, the computer program goes into memory, finds the variable, and gets its contents for you. This procedure requires, of course, that you remember the name of the variable.

Declaring variables

Declaring a variable before assigning anything to it sets up a location in the computer's memory, ahead of time, for storing a value for the variable. Later in this session, you learn about the Dim statement used to declare (or *dimension*) variables.

Visual Basic, like many other programming languages, allows you to create variables as the program runs without first defining their data type. In the Counter = 1 example, the Counter variable was not declared before the value 1 was assigned to it. Because you assign an integer to the variable named Counter, the variable is implicitly (automatically) declared as an integer data type.

The amount of storage allocated for the variable depends on the type of data that you plan to store in the variable. More space is allocated for a variable that will hold a currency amount (such as $1,000,000) than for a variable that never will hold a value greater than, say, 255.

Even though Visual Basic does not require that you declare your variables before using them, it does provide various declaration commands. Getting into the habit of declaring your variables is good practice. Declaring a variable assures that you can assign only a certain type of value to it — always a number or always characters, for example. You can attain real performance gains in Visual Basic by *predeclaring* (known as *explicitly naming*) variables. For purposes of maintenance, most programmers like to declare their variables at the top of the procedure.

Although Visual Basic does not require initial declaration of variables, you should avoid using undeclared (implicitly named) variables. If you do not declare a variable, the code may expect one type of value in the variable when it actually contains another type. If, in your procedure, you set the variable TodayIs to Monday, but later you change the value for TodayIs to a number (such as TodayIs = 2), the program generates an error when it runs because the first value set was a string. More important, this change slows down the running of the program each time the variable is used because the program must validate the type of data in the variable rather than simply expecting a specific, predetermined type (such as text or date).

Using the Option Explicit statement

At the top of your Visual Basic module (either the module behind a form or report or a standard module object) in the Declarations section, you should always enter the text **Option Explicit** as shown in Figure 5-1. This tells Visual Basic that you want the compiler to report an error for any variable that is not explicitly declared.

Why would you want to do this? Because Access and Visual Basic can automatically assign a data type the first time you assign a value, why bother to make sure you define every variable? Aside from the danger of potential errors when you assign different data type values, the answer is speed. Access runs a Visual Basic program much faster if Option Explicit is used once at the top of each module and all your variables are declared.

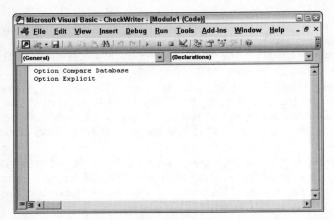

Figure 5-1   *Using the Option Explicit statement with the Declarations section of your module.*

    You can go to the Declarations section of a module while you are creating an event procedure in a form by selecting declarations from the Procedure combo box. Another way to move to the Declarations section is to select (General) in the Object combo box. Figure 5-1 shows the Module window combo boxes.

Using the Dim statement

To declare a variable, you most often use the Dim statement. When you use the Dim statement, you must supply the variable name that you assign to the variable. The format for the Dim statement is

```
Dim variablename [As type]
```

Figure 5-2 shows the Dim statement for a simple procedure named VariableTest. As you can see in the figure, the displayed Message Box is shown below the Visual Basic window. The vbInformation + vbOKOnly displays the informational icon and the single OK button.

This program declares two variables, assigns values to them, and uses them in a message box. The message box is shown running below the Visual Basic window in Figure 5-2. The message box is shown concatenating (joining together) string text, string variables, and numeric variables. You can also see the open Immediate window where the Call statement is used to run the program to display the message box.

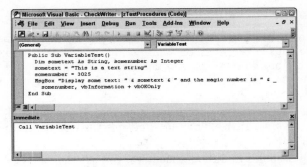

Figure 5-2   *A simple Dim statement for a simple program.*

The `Dim` statement declares two different variables, each with a different data type. The first part of the declare statement, `Dim sometext As String`, declares a variable named `sometext` and assigns a `String` data type to the variable. Notice the comma following the declaration and that a second variable named `somenumber` is declared and assigned the numeric `Integer` data type.

You could have used two separate statements like the following:

```
Dim sometext As String
Dim somenumber As Integer
```

You could have also declared the variables like this:

```
Dim sometext As String,  somenumber As Integer
```

Sometimes it is easier to declare multiple variables on one line, but the statement is easier to read if each variable is declared on its own line.

Notice that the variable name follows the `Dim` statement. In addition to naming the variable, you should use the optional `As` clause to specify a data type for the variable. The data type is the kind of information that is stored in the variable: `String`, `Integer`, `Currency`, and so on.

If you don't have the `As` clause, the default data type is known as `Variant`. A `Variant` data type can hold any type of data but requires Access to figure out what type of data is put into it. If you use `Variant` data types or don't declare your variables, you slow down your application.

When creating variables, you can use uppercase, lowercase, or mixed-case characters to specify the variable or call it later. Visual Basic variables are not case-sensitive. Therefore, you can use the `TodayIs` variable again and again without having to worry about the case that you used for the name when you created it; `TODAYIS`, `todayis`, and `tOdAyIs` all refer to the same variable. Visual Basic automatically changes any explicitly declared variables to the case that was used in the declaration statement or the last entered reference (`Dim` statement).

Making variables available to the entire application

When you use the Dim statement to declare a variable in a procedure, you can refer to that variable only within that procedure. This is known as a *private variable* or one declared in a procedure that is known only in the procedure where it is declared and used. Other procedures, even if they are stored in the same module, do not know anything about the private variable.

You can also declare variables in the Declarations section of a module. This enables all the procedures in the module to access the variable. Procedures outside the module in which you declared the variable, however, cannot read or use the variable.

To declare a variable for use by procedures in different modules, you use the Public statement.

The Public statement

To make a variable available to all modules in the application, use the Public keyword when you declare the variable. Figure 5-3 illustrates using the Public keyword to declare a variable. Notice that the statement is in the Declarations section of the module. Public variables must be declared in the Declarations section of the module.

Figure 5-3 *Declaring a public variable.*

Although you can declare a public variable in any module, it seems logical to declare public variables only within the module that will use them the most. The exceptions to this rule are true global variables that you want to make available to all procedures across modules and that are not specifically related to a single module. You should declare global variables in a single standard module so that you can find them easily.

You declare global variables by entering **Global variablename** in the Declarations section of a module. The variable is then known to the entire application. You can set the value anywhere.

If for any reason Access crashes, the value in a global variable is lost.

You cannot declare a variable as public within a procedure. It must be declared in the Declarations section of a module. If you attempt to declare a variable as public, you receive an error message.

In a standard, report, or form module, you can refer to a public variable from a different form or report module. To access the value of a public variable from another module, you must qualify the variable reference, using the name of the form or report object. `CheckWriter.somevariable`, for example, accesses a form named **Check Writer** and obtains the value of the variable `somevariable`.

The Private statement

The declarations section in Figure 5-2, shown earlier, shows the use of the `Dim` statement to declare variables. You could substitute the text `Private` instead of `Dim`. Technically, there is no difference between `Private` and `Dim`; however, using `Private` at the module (Declarations) level to declare variables available to all procedures is a good idea. Declaring private variables does the following things:

- Contrasts with `Dim`, which must be used at the procedure level, distinguishing where the variable is declared and its scope (module versus procedure).
- Contrasts with `Public`, the other method of declaring variables in modules, making your code easier to understand.

When you declare a variable, you use the `As` clause to assign a data type to the variable. Data types for variables are similar to data types in a database table definition.

Working With Data Types

The main reason to declare any variable is to save internal resources. Saving resources, in turn, makes programs run more quickly and efficiently. When a program knows the variable type, it can process the data faster because it has limited options for handling the data, as well as an enhanced capability to validate each value assigned to the variable. If you don't declare the variable name or fail to specify the data type (no `As` parameter), the variable is internally defined as a variant. A variant is a data type, too. It means the variable can handle any type of data. If you rely on using an undeclared variant for a variable when you could have used an integer, for example, you waste 14 bytes of memory for every variable you use.

When you declare a variable, you also can specify the data type for the variable. All variables have a data type. The type of variable determines what kind of information can be stored in the variable.

A *string variable* — a variable with a data type of string — can hold any values ranging from A–Z, a–z, and 0–1, as well as formatting characters (#, -, !, and so on). Once created, a string variable can be used in many ways. It can compare its contents with another string, pull parts of information out of the string, and so on. If you have a variable defined as a string, however, you cannot use it to do mathematical calculations. Conversely, you cannot assign a number to a variable declared as a string.

Table 5-1 describes the main data types that Visual Basic supports.

Table 5-1   *Data Types Used in Visual Basic*

Type	Range	Storage
Boolean	True or false	2 bytes
Byte	0 to 255	1 byte binary data
Currency	−922,337,203,685,477,5808 to 922,337,203,685,477,5807	8-byte number with fixed decimal point
Decimal	+/−79,228,162,514,264,337,593,543,950,335 with no decimal point; +/−7.9228162514264337593543950335 with 28 places to the right of the decimal; smallest non-zero number is +/0.0000000000000000000000000001.	14 bytes
Date	01 Jan 100 to 31 Dec 9999	8-byte date/time value
Double	−1.79769313486231E308 to −4.94065645841247E−324	8-byte floating-point number
Integer	−32,768 to 32,767	2-byte integer
Long	−2,147,483,648 to 2,147,483,647	4-byte integer
Object	Any object reference	4 bytes
Single	negative values: −3.402823E38 to −1.401298E − 45 positive values: 1.401298E −45 to 3.402823E38	4-byte floating-point number
String (variable-length)	0 to approximately 2,000,000,000	10 bytes plus length of string
String (fixed-length)	1 to approximately 65,400	Length of string
Variant (with numbers)	Any numeric value up to the range of Double	16 bytes
Variant (with characters)	0 to approximately 2,000,000,000	22 bytes plus length of string
User-defined (using Type)	Same as Range of its data type	Number required by elements

Most of the time, you use the string, date, integer, currency, or double data types. If a variable always contains whole numbers between –32,768 and 32,768, you can save bytes of memory and gain speed in arithmetic operations if you declare the variable an integer type.

When you want to assign the value of an Access field to a variable, make sure that the type of the variable can hold the data type of the field. Table 5-2 shows the corresponding Visual Basic data types for Access field types.

Table 5-2   *Comparative Data Types in Access Tables and Visual Basic Variables*

Access Table Field Data Type	Visual Basic Variable Data Type
AutoNumber (Long Integer)	Long
AutoNumber (Replication ID)	—
Currency	Currency
Computed	—
Date/Time	Date
Memo	String
Number (Byte)	Byte
Number (Integer)	Integer
Number (Long Integer)	Long
Number (Single)	Single
Number (Double)	Double
Number (Replication ID)	—
OLE object	Array of bytes
Text	String
Yes/No	Boolean

 If a variable may have to hold a value of Null, it must be declared as variant. `Variant` **is the only data type that can accept Null values.**

Now that you understand variables and their data types, you're ready to learn how to use them in writing procedures.

Using Standard Naming Conventions

As you can imagine, you can use quite a few variables in a program. This can make it difficult to remember what all your variables are used for. The same is true of objects in your

Access databases, such as tables, forms, and reports. As the number of objects and variables increases, so does the inherent complexity of the programs that use those objects and variables.

Part of the solution to this problem is to use descriptive names for both objects and variables. This is only part of the solution, however. The other part involves using some sort of standard naming convention so that you can immediately understand the type of data referred to by a variable or an object name.

For professional developers, adhering to a standard makes it easier to maintain other developer's programs. In development projects with multiple programmers, naming conventions can make it easier to understand what each object or variable is used for, the data type of a variable, or other critical information needed to properly code and debug a program efficiently.

However, for a casual or power user or even the novice developer, adhering to naming conventions can be a less than productive experience. Whereas naming conventions are supposed to make programs easier to read and maintain because they are instantly clear to the Visual Basic developer, they can do the exact opposite.

In this portion of the session, you learn about the standard naming conventions that most professional developers use, and you see some alternatives to using them.

Figure 5-4 shows two Microsoft Access database containers. The database container on the left uses a standard naming convention prefix. The database container on the right uses no special naming convention for the table objects. Which do you think is easier to read?

Figure 5-4 *Object naming conventions. The database container on the left uses a standard naming prefix.*

There are several competing naming conventions used for Microsoft Access. One is the Leszynski Naming Conventions (LNC), developed by Stan Leszynski (www.kwery.com), and the other is the Reddick Naming Conventions developed by Greg Reddick. The tables in the remaining portion of this session provide an overview of these standards. If you want to see the entire, detailed list of naming conventions, you can view the file ReddickNamingConventions.pdf on the companion Web site for this book at www.wiley.com/compbooks/prague.

Both of these naming conventions suggest using prefixes for several different types of Microsoft Access items:objects (tables, queries, forms, reports, data access pages, macros, modules), table fields, form and report controls, ADO and DAO recordset objects, and variables.

Microsoft Access database object naming conventions

These two standard Access naming conventions suggest using leading tags also known as *prefixes*. This means that the naming convention precedes the standard business name, as in tblCheckWriter.

 In the example files in this book, we use object naming conventions with an underscore between the prefixes and the object name. We did not use the prefixes for the table fields, control names, or variables. Our belief is that there is enough to understand in the example without also having to concentrate on the naming conventions.

The standard Microsoft Access object names are shown in Table 5-3.

Table 5-3 *Object Naming Conventions*

Prefix	Object	Example
tbl	Table	tblBankAccounts
qry	Query	qryCheckWriterDisplay
frm	Form	frmCheckWriter
rpt	Report	rptCheckRegister
mcr	Macro	mcrAutoexec
mod	Module	modFileUtilities
cls	Class Module	clsBankAccount
fsub	Subform	fsubCheckRegisterDetails
rsub	Subreport	rsubCheckPrintContinuous

Microsoft Access table field naming conventions

**10 Min.
To Go**

Another portion of the naming conventions covers fields in tables. Figure 5-5 shows the Check Writer table modified to use these prefixes. Table 5-4 shows these table field naming conventions.

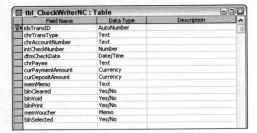

Figure 5-5 *Table field naming conventions.*

Table 5-4 *Table Field Naming Conventions*

Prefix	Object
idn	Autonumber (Random)
idr	Autonumber (Replication ID)
ids	Autonumber (Sequential)
bin	Number (Binary)
byt	Number (Byte)
cur	Currency
dtm	Date/Time
dbl	Number (dbl)
hlk	Hyperlink
int	Number (Integer)
lngz	Number (Long)
mem	Memo
ole	OLE Object
sng	Number (Single)
chr	Text (Character)
bln	Yes/No (Boolean)

Microsoft Access form/report control naming conventions

Another area covered by naming conventions is control names on forms on reports. These are used whenever you are naming a control on a form or report. Table 5-5 shows these conventions.

Table 5-5　*Form/Report Control Naming Conventions*

Prefix	Object
frb	Bound Object frame
cht	Chart (Graph)
chk	Check Box
cbo	Combo Box
cmd	Command Button
ocx	ActiveX Custom Control
det	Detail (section)
gft[*n*]	Footer (group section)
fft	Form footer section
fhd	Form header section
ghd[*n*]	Header (group section)
hlk	Hyperlink
img	Image
lbl	Label
lin	Line
lst	List Box
opt	Option Button
grp	Option Group
pge	Page (tab)
brk	Page break
pft	Page Footer (section)
phd	Page Header (section)
shp	Rectangle
rft	Report Footer (section)
rhd	Report Header (section)
sec	Section

Continued

Table **5-5**   *Continued*

Prefix	Object
sub	Subform/Subreport
tab	Tab Control
txt	Text Box
tgl	Toggle Button
fru	Unbound Object Frame

Microsoft Access Visual Basic variable naming conventions

The final major area covered by the standard Access naming conventions is Visual Basic data variables. Table 5-6 shows these conventions.

Table **5-6**   *Visual Basic Data Variable Naming Conventions*

Prefix	Object
bln	Boolean
byt	Byte
ccc	Conditional Compilation Constant (#xxx)
cur	Currency
dtm	Date
dbl	Double
err	Error
int	Integer
lng	Long
obj	Object
sng	Single
str	String
typ	User-Defined Type
var	Variant

There are many more tags defined by the standard naming conventions. In fact, there are close to one thousand different tags. Professional developers use these standards to varying degrees. Some ignore them for anything but data variables, whereas others ignore them completely. Some developers try their best to follow them religiously. You have to make your own decisions about whether to follow these conventions.

Are naming conventions really necessary in Access?

The human mind is a wonderful thing. It can provide wondrous creative solutions to problems. It can turn manual nightmares into automated algorithmic processes. But give the human mind something just a little foreign and processing slows to a crawl as the brain's disruptive subroutine circuitry is invoked with a nearly endless loop. Having to filter out the characters that precede the business names makes it much more difficult to read and understand the purpose of the application.

The same could be true for variable and field naming in tables. Imagine if written English words required naming conventions. Perhaps all predicates could be prefixed with pre, verbs with vrb, nouns with nou, adverbs with adv, adjectives with adj, and so on. The sentence below:

```
The Quick Brown Fox Jumps Over The Big Computer
```

would become

```
preThe adjQuick adjBrown nouFox vrbJumps advOver preThe adjBig nouComputer
```

Although the sentence can be read, it is more difficult to understand than the first sentence because you first must filter out the prefixes. Only in rare instances is the meaning or content of a word so questionable that it needs a label. Our experience is far more important than our need to explicitly understand sentence structure or grammar.

How does a professional developer know that zip codes, phone numbers, and Social Security numbers are almost always defined as text strings? Fields like Salary, Total Expense, or Amount Paid are obviously currency or numeric data types, whereas Date of Birth or the Last Sale Date is probably always stored as a date data type. This simply takes experience and common sense. This same experience or training enables us to read a sentence with the correct understanding of words, intonation, and grammar.

The bottom line is that sometimes less is more. You have to program in a style that suits you and your environment. Although naming conventions can be good, consistency is always better. If you are investing in a set of naming conventions, check a few simple things:

1. Do they make sense? Does it seem that common sense dictated them rather than some committee whose sole purpose was to get something on paper through compromises, endless debate, and finally exhaustion and frustration?

2. Are they endorsed by an international board such as ISO or even Microsoft? Notice the main Microsoft Access sample file named Northwinds.mdb does not use any naming conventions.

Done!

REVIEW

In this session, you learned about variables and how to define them. You learned the difference between public and private variables and how to use both of them. Finally, you learned about the standard naming conventions that professional developers use. The following topics were covered:

- Variables are temporary storage because the value within the variable changes or varies based on the expression.
- Variables can be used to store numbers, strings, control names, or data values. Variables can also be used to store the value of a control or the name of a form.
- Every programming language has its own rules for naming variables.
- You should always use Option Explicit at the beginning of a module to tell Visual Basic that you want the compiler to report an error for any variable that is not explicitly declared.
- You define a variable with the Dim statement, and you use the As clause to specify the data type for the variable.
- There are public and private variable types.
- Professional developers usually use some type of standard naming convention.

QUIZ YOURSELF

1. Define the term variable. (See "Using Variables.")
2. What are the most important rules for naming variables? (See "Naming variables.")
3. Why is the Option Explicit statement important to have in every module? (See "Using the Option Explicit statement.")
4. Why would you use the public variable definition instead of Dim? (See "Making variables available to the entire application.")
5. What are some of the variable data types? (See "Working with Data Types.")
6. Should you use naming conventions? (See "Are naming conventions really necessary in Access?")

6

Logical Constructs — Loops, Decisions, Choices, and Quick Exits

Session Checklist

✔ Understanding logical constructs

✔ Handling single conditions (`If...Then...Else...End If`)

✔ Handling multiple conditions (`Select Case...Case...End Select`)

✔ Creating repetitive loops (`Do...Loop`)

✔ Creating loops that count (`For...Next`)

✔ Constructs that remember (`With...End With`)

**30 Min.
To Go**

Logical constructs are a certain class of Visual Basic statements that control the way a program runs. Generally, programs run one statement after another in the order they appear. Logical constructs are used to make the program run in the order that makes sense for the business purpose. Logical constructs include

- Conditional processing (single condition decision making)
    ```
    If...Then...Else...End If
    ```
- Conditional processing (multiple-condition decision making)
    ```
    Select Case...Case...End Select
    ```
- Repetitive looping
    ```
    Do...Loop
    For...Next
    ```

Using logical constructs, you make the program respond to values in your variables to run or skip one or more statements or run a group of statements repeatedly. In this session, you learn the three types of logical constructs and how to create counters and variables that react within these constructs.

Each of these logical constructs requires specific syntax to operate correctly. Generally, there is an opening statement, statements in the middle, and a closing statement, also known as an *end* statement. Sometimes the syntax makes sense, like starting a conditional statement with If and ending with End If. Select Case starts a multiple-condition, decision-making construct, whereas End Select completes it.

Repetitive looping is a little different. A Do statement ends with a Loop, and a For statement ends with Next. This session explains all these differences.

Conditional Processing

One of the real powers of a programming language is the capability to have a program make a decision based on some condition. Often, a program in Visual Basic performs different tasks based on some value. If the condition is True, the code performs one action. If the condition is False, the code performs a different action.

Procedures are evaluated to see if they are True or False. For example, suppose you code the following:

```
If CheckAmount > 200 Then
    Call largedollarprocedure
  Else
    Call smalldollarprocedure
Endif
```

The first part of the expression checks to see whether the value of the variable CheckAmount is greater than 200. If it is, the expression evaluates to True, and the code after Then is run up to the Else clause. If the expression does not evaluate to True, the line of code within the Else clause is run. In this example, a False condition (actually not True) occurs if the value of CheckAmount is less than or equal to (<=) 200.

This procedure is similar to walking down a path and coming to a fork in the path; you can go to the left or to the right. If a sign at the fork points left for home and right for work, you can decide which way to go. If you need to go to work, you go to the right; if you need to go home, you go to the left. Conditional processing of code works the same way. A program looks at the value of some variable and decides which set of code should be processed.

When writing code, you must control which actions execute. You may write some statements that execute only if a certain condition is True.

An application's capability to look at a value and, based on that value, decide which code to run is known as *conditional processing*.

The If...Then...Else...End If statement

The If...Then and If...Then...Else constructs enable you to check a condition and, based on the evaluation, perform a single action. It is a binary evaluation. With an If...Then...Else statement, there are only two choices — one or the other. You can have one or more statements after both the Then and the Else clauses. In fact, it is possible to have no statements after one or both conditions, but it would be easier to eliminate the clause. For example, you do not have to include an Else statement with an If...Then construct.

Here is the general syntax of the If...Then...Else statement:

```
If test_expression Then
    code statements here (test_expression = true)
Else
    code statements here (test_expression = not true)
End If
```

The If...Then...Else **construct does not require an** Else **statement. You can have just an** If Then **condition that, if met, runs the statements to the** End If **and skips any processing within the construct if the condition is not met.**

Figure 6-1 shows a conceptual diagram of an If...Then...Else condition:

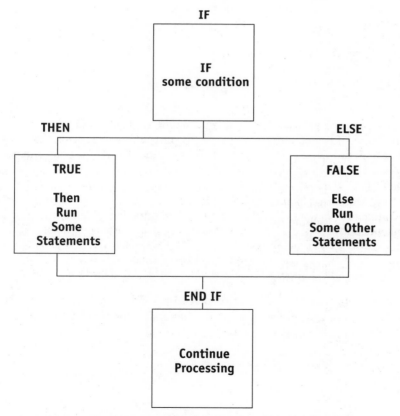

Figure 6-1   *A conceptual diagram of an If...Then...Else statement.*

The condition must evaluate to True or Not True. The reason we say True and Not True is that just because something is True doesn't mean the opposite is necessarily False. The condition can evaluate to Unknown if one of the values is null or blank. You must make sure when you use an If...Then...Else statement that the condition you use has a binary selection (one or the other).

If the condition is True, the program moves to the next statement in the procedure and runs each statement between the Then and any Else statement, or if there is no Else statement, to the End If. If the condition is Not True (or False), the program skips to the statement(s) following the Else statement and then continues to the End If statement. Once the End If statement is reached, processing continues normally to the next logical construct.

Figure 6-2 shows the OnClick event subprocedure code from the Print button on the frm_DialogBankPrint form. The procedure is used to handle user selections to determine where a report prints and which records or which report prints. Notice the If... Then...Else statement.

```
CheckWriter - Form_frm_DialogBankPrint (Code)
cmdPrint                              Click

Private Sub cmdPrint_Click()

Dim ReportDest As Integer

    'Hide the Report Print Dialog
    Me.Visible = False

    If Me![Type of Output] = 1 Then
        ReportDest = acPreview
    Else                        ' Destination is printer
        ReportDest = acNormal
    End If
```

Figure 6-2   *A simple If...Then...Else condition.*

The If statement checks the value of the Type of Output control on the frm_DialogBankPrint form. If the condition Me![Type of Output] = 1 is True, the value of ReportDest is set to acPreview (Print Preview). If the value of Me![Type of Output] is anything other than 1, the Else condition is met and the value of ReportDest is set to acNormal (the default printer).

Remember, the Else statement is optional. You can use Else to test for a second condition when the If statement evaluates to False. When the If statement is True, the program executes the statements between the If statement and the Else statement. When the If statement evaluates to False, the program skips to the Else statement, if it is present. Then, if the Else statement is True, the program executes the next statement. If the Else statement is False, the program skips to the statement following the End If statement.

You can also use the Not operator to check for conditions that are expected to be False, as in the following example. Generally, the most common condition is first, which makes the code easier to read.

```
If Not CheckType = 'Deposit' Then
    Process Checks
Else
    Process Deposit

End If
```

This is also equivalent to

```
If CheckType <> 'Deposit' Then ....
```

Nesting If...Then...Else statements

You can put an If...Then...Else statement within another If...Then...Else statement, which is known as *nesting*. For example, the code in Listing 6-1 shows an example of a nested If...Then...Else statement.

Listing 6-1   *A Nested If...Then...Else Statement*

```
If ClassType = "Elementary School" Then
    If Grade Between 1 and 3 Then
        'Process something for grades 1-3
      Else
        'Process something for other elementary grades
    End If
  Else
    'Process Middle and High School
End If
```

The first If statement checks the value of the variable ClassType to see if it is equal to "Elementary School". If the condition is True, the next statement is run. This is another If statement that checks to see if the value of Grade is Between 1 and 3; if this is True, the grade 1–3 process runs. If the value of ClassType is "Elementary School" and the value of Grade is not Between 1–3, the statements after the Else are run.

If the value of the variable ClassType is not "Elementary School", processing moves to the corresponding Else statement and the process for middle and high school is run. Because these are just comments, you would substitute the real statements in place of or after the comments.

When creating nested constructs, it is a good idea to first type the constructs themselves along with any End statements, and then enter some comments about what each If or Else statement does. This is known as *pseudocoding*. You can then enter the code to be run after the comments and leave the comments in place.

 You can nest any logical construct within another logical construct.

Suppose you had to test for five different conditions. You could write a set of If...Then...Else statements like this:

```
If Salary Between 0 and 20000 Then
  'Do Some Processing (0-20000)
End If
If Salary Between 20001 and 40000 Then
  'Do Some Processing (20001-40000)
End If
If Salary Between 40001 and 60000 Then
  'Do Some Processing (40001-60000)
End If
If Salary Between 60001 and 80000 Then
  'Do Some Processing (60001-80000)
End If
```

```
If Salary Not Between 0 and 80000
   'Do Some Other Processing (Not Between 0-80000)
End If
```

However, this code would be very inefficient because each condition would be tested for — even if only one condition or the first condition is met. Better, but more complex code, is shown here:

```
If Salary Between 0 and 20000 Then
   'Do Some Processing (0-20000)
Else
   If Salary Between 20001 and 40000 Then
      'Do Some Processing (20001-40000)
   Else
      If Salary Between 40001 and 60000 Then
         'Do Some Processing (40001-60000)
      Else
         If Salary Between 60001 and 80000 Then
            'Do Some Processing (60001-80000)
         Else
            'Do Some Other Processing (Not Between 0-80000)
         End If
      End If
   End If
End If
```

However, this code is complex to write and maintain. Even though processing stops after a condition is satisfied, the nested If statements can get very complicated.

When you have many conditions to test, a better approach is to use the Select Case construct.

The Select Case...End Select construct

In addition to If...Then statements, Visual Basic offers a command for checking more than one condition. You can use the Select Case construct to check for multiple conditions. Figure 6-3 shows a conceptual diagram of a Select Case statement.

SYNTAX ▶ The Case statement contains the opening Select Case statement, an unlimited number of Case *test_expression* clauses, a potential Case Else clause, and finally, an End SelectSelect statement. Here is the general syntax of the Case statement:

```
Select Case test_expression
   Case expression value1
       code statements here (test_expression = value1)
   Case expression value2
       code statements here (test_expression = value2) ...
   Case Else
       code statements (test_expression = none of the values)
End Select
```

Notice that the syntax is similar to that of the If...Then statement. Instead of a condition in the Select Case statement, however, Visual Basic uses a test expression. Then each Case statement inside the Select Case statement tests its value against the test expression's value. When a Case statement matches the test value, the program executes the next line or lines of code until it reaches another Case statement or the End Select statement. Visual Basic executes the code for only one matching Case statement.

Figure 6-4 again shows the OnClick event subprocedure code from the Print button on the frm_DialogBankPrint form. The procedure is used to handle user selections to determine where a report prints and which records or which report prints. Notice the Select Case statement.

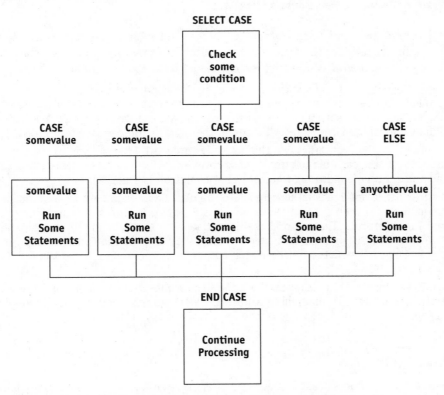

SELECT CASE

Check some condition

CASE somevalue	CASE somevalue	CASE somevalue	CASE somevalue	CASE ELSE
somevalue Run Some Statements	somevalue Run Some Statements	somevalue Run Some Statements	somevalue Run Some Statements	anyothervalue Run Some Statements

END CASE

Continue Processing

Figure 6-3   *A conceptual diagram of a Select Case statement.*

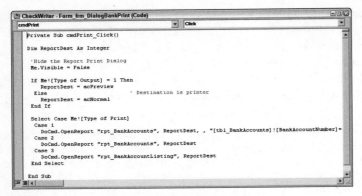

```
CheckWriter - Form_frm_DialogBankPrint (Code)
cmdPrint                                            Click

Private Sub cmdPrint_Click()

Dim ReportDest As Integer

    'Hide the Report Print Dialog
    Me.Visible = False

    If Me![Type of Output] = 1 Then
        ReportDest = acPreview
    Else
        ReportDest = acNormal          ' Destination is printer
    End If

    Select Case Me![Type of Print]
    Case 1
        DoCmd.OpenReport "rpt_BankAccounts", ReportDest, , "[tbl_BankAccounts]![BankAccountNumber]="
    Case 2
        DoCmd.OpenReport "rpt_BankAccounts", ReportDest
    Case 3
        DoCmd.OpenReport "rpt_BankAccountListing", ReportDest
    End Select

End Sub
```

Figure 6-4   *A simple Select Case statement.*

If more than one `Case` statement matches the value of the test expression, only the code for the first match executes. If other matching `Case` statements appear after the first match, Visual Basic ignores them.

In Figure 6-4, the `Select Case` statement looks at the value of the control `Type of Print` and then checks each `Case` condition. If the value of `Type of Print` is 1 (Current Bank Account), the `Case 1` statement evaluates to True, and the Bank Account report prints but limits the value to the current record through the report's filter parameter.

An `If...Then...Else` construct can theoretically run every `If` condition in a group of statements. It must test each branch until one is satisfied. A `Select Case` statement will stop testing and running conditions when the first condition is True.

If `Type of Print` is not 1, Visual Basic goes to the next `Case` statement to see whether `Type of Print` matches the next test value, which is 2. If this is True, the Bank Accounts report is run for all records. There is no `Case Else` clause, so theoretically, if the value of `Type of Print` is not 1, 2, or 3, no statements within the `Select Case` construct are run. Each `Case` statement is evaluated until a match occurs or the program reaches the `End Select` statement.

The `Case Else` statement is optional. The `Case Else` clause is always the last `Case` statement of `Select Case`. You use this statement to perform some action when none of the `Case` values matches the test value of the `Select Case` statement.

Repetitive Looping

Another very powerful process that Visual Basic offers is *repetitive looping* — the capability to process a group of code over and over. The statement or group of statements is processed continually while or until some condition is met.

Visual Basic offers two types of repetitive-looping constructs:

Do...Loop   Generally used to process data

For...Next   Used when you know the exact number of repetitions

The Do...Loop statement

**10 Min.
To Go**

You use the Do...Loop statement to repeat a group of statements while a condition is True or until a condition is True. This statement is one of the most common commands that can perform repetitive processes.

SYNTAX ▶

The Do...Loop statement has the following format:

```
Do [While | Until condition]
    code statements [for condition = TRUE]
    [If some additional condition Then Exit DO]
    code statements [for condition = TRUE]
Loop [While | Until condition]
```

Notice that the Do...Loop statement has several optional clauses. The While clause tells the program to execute the code inside the Do...Loop as long as the test condition is True. When the condition evaluates to False, the program skips to the next statement following the Loop statement.

The Until clause works in just the opposite way; the instructions in the construct execute as long as the condition is False. Where you place the While or Until clause determines whether the code inside Do...Loop executes.

The Do While may never run any statements if the condition is not initially True, while the Do Until always runs the loop at least once.

You use the Exit Do statement to terminate Do...Loop immediately. The program then skips to the next statement following the Loop statement. Figure 6-5 shows a conceptual diagram of the Do...Loop. As long as the condition of the Do...Loop is True and any condition to run the Exit Do remains False, the loop executes over and over again.

Generally, inside the loop you process records in a table, recordset, or dynaset. Figure 6-6 shows the Clear Marks OnClick event from the frm_CheckWriter form. This code is used to change the value of the Print field to False in the Check Writer table for all records.

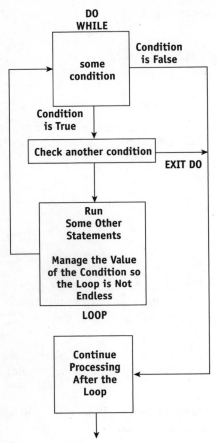

DO
WHILE

some
condition

Condition
is False

Condition
is True

Check another condition

EXIT DO

Run
Some Other
Statements

Manage the Value
of the Condition so
the Loop is Not
Endless

LOOP

Continue
Processing
After the
Loop

Figure 6-5   *A conceptual diagram of a Do... Loop statement.*

```
CheckWriter - Form_frm_CheckWriter (Code)

cmdClearMarks                                    Click

    Private Sub cmdClearMarks_Click()
    Dim cnn As ADODB.Connection
    Dim CheckTB As New ADODB.Recordset
    Dim SQLStmt As String

        On Error GoTo ErrorHandler
        RunCommand acCmdSaveRecord
        Set cnn = CurrentProject.Connection
        Set CheckTB = New ADODB.Recordset
        CheckTB.CursorType = adOpenKeyset
        CheckTB.LockType = adLockOptimistic
        SQLStmt = "SELECT Print FROM tbl_CheckWriter WHERE [AccountNumber] = '" & Me![BankAccount] & "'"
        CheckTB.Open SQLStmt, cnn, , , adCmdText

        Do Until CheckTB.EOF
          CheckTB![Print] = False
          CheckTB.Update
        CheckTB.MoveNext
        Loop
        |
        CheckTB.Close
        Set CheckTB = Nothing

        Me.Refresh
        GoTo Done
    ErrorHandler:
        MsgBox Err.Description
    Done:
    End Sub
```

Figure 6-6   *A simple Do Until loop.*

The first part of Figure 6-6 uses some ADO statements to set up and open a recordset of all records in the tbl_CheckWriter table for the specific bank account open in the frm_CheckWriter form. The Do loop in the middle of the figure runs through all the records.

 Although you haven't learned ADO yet or how to create or process a recordset, the code in Figure 6-6 is described so that you can follow it. The important part is the loop construct syntax (and not the ADO) in this example.

The Do statement is typical of a loop that processes recordset data. Generally, you want to start at the top of the recordset defined in the SQL statement and process all the records. In this example, CheckTB is the name of the recordset, and the Do Until CheckTB.EOF statement runs the loop until the CheckTB recordset reaches the end of the file.

The next line, CheckTB![Print] = False, sets the value of the current record to False. The line CheckTB.Update actually updates the value of Print in the Check Writer table. Without the Update method, the change would not be saved.

When you create a loop, you must set up code to manage coming out of the loop. There are two ways to do this. You can use an Exit Do statement or change the condition at the top of the loop that the Do clause is repetitively checking.

The final statement inside the loop CheckTB.MoveNext moves the record pointer of the recordset to the next record. When the last record has been processed, the value of the .EOF (end of file) marker is set to True. This causes the loop to terminate, as the Do Until CheckTB.EOF condition is satisfied. The statements after the Loop statement are then executed. This closes the open recordset.

The While and Until clauses provide powerful flexibility for processing Do...Loop in your code. Table 6-1 describes the various alternatives for using the While and Until clauses and how they affect the processing of code.

Table 6-1 *Repetitive Looping Using Do...Loop with the While and Until Clauses*

Pseudocode	Purpose of Do...Loop

Do	Code starts here
	If condition Then
	Exit Do
	End If

Loop	The code always runs at least once. The code has some conditional statement (If...Then) that, if True, runs the Exit Do statement. The Exit Do statement allows the user to get out of Do...Loop. If that statement were missing, the code inside the loop would run forever.
Do	While condition code starts here for the condition on the Do While line being True

Continued

Table 6-1   *Continued*

Pseudocode	Purpose of Do...Loop
Loop	The code inside the Do While loop runs only if the condition is True. The code runs down to the Loop statement and then goes back to the top to see whether the condition is still True. If the condition is initially False, Do...Loop is skipped; if the condition becomes False, the loop is exited when the code loops back to the Do While line. Exit Do is not needed for this purpose.
Do	Until *condition* *code starts here* *for the condition on the* *Do Until line being* *False*
Loop	This code works the opposite way from Do While. If the condition is False (not True), the code begins and loops until the condition is True; then it leaves the loop. Regardless if the condition is True, the loop and its code are run at least once even if the Until condition is True.
Do	*Code starts here for* *the condition on the* *Do While line being* *TRUE*
Loop While *condition*	This code always runs at least once. First, the code is executed and reaches the Loop While line. If the condition is True, the code loops back to process the code again; if not, the code loop ends.
Do	*Code starts here for* *the condition on the* *Do Until line being* *FALSE*
Loop Until *condition*	This code works similarly to the preceding code. The code always runs at least once. When the code reaches the Loop Until line, it checks to see whether the condition is True. If the condition is True, the code drops out of the loop. If the condition is False, the code loops back up to redo the code.

The For...Next statement

The For...Next construct is another method for the Do...Loop construct. You can use For...Next when you want to repeat a statement a specific number of times. In the previous example shown in Figure 6-6, rather than process the recordset until .EOF, you can count the number of records in the recordset and then process that many records. This code might look like Figure 6-7.

Notice the differences between the Do...Loop and this For...Next code. First, several variables are defined. NumRecs holds the total number of records, and Counter holds the number of the record being processed. The variable NumRecs is set to the recordset variable for the number of records (CheckTb.RecordCount).

The loop is executed by running through the recordset from record number 1 to record number *n*, where *n* is the number of records counted by the RecordCount method.

This example uses a default Step clause of 1. You actually do not need the Step clause if you are using the default value. The Step clause, followed by an increment, lets you process the loop in a nonsingle step amount. For example, if the start number is 1, the end number is 100, and you want to increment the counter by 10 each time, you use step 10. Although the loop would be executed only 10 times, the value of the counter would be 1, 11, 21, and so on, instead of 1, 2, 3, and so on.

Figure 6-7   A simple For... Next loop.

SYNTAX ▶ Here is the general syntax of the For...Next statement:

```
For counter = start number To end number [Step increment]
    Some code goes here
    [If somecondition is True Then Exit For]
    Other code can continue here after the Exit for
Next [counter]
```

At the start of the For...Next loop, the program initializes the value of the counter variable RecNum to 1; then it moves on and executes each statement. Whenever the program encounters the Next statement, it automatically increments the counter variable by 1 and returns to the For statement. The program compares the value of RecNum with the value in NumRecs. If the test is True, the code executes again; otherwise, the program exits the loop.

You can execute the same basic code with a Do While or Do Until loop by managing the counter yourself just as you manage the recordsets. The following example shows equivalent loops using For...Next and Do While loops:

Do While Loop

```
Dim Counter As Integer

Do While Counter <= 20
    Some process goes here
    Counter = Counter + 1
Loop
```

For Next Loop

```
Dim Counter As Integer

For counter = 1 To 20
    Some process goes here
Next Counter
```

Constructs That Remember: With ... End With

You should understand one additional construct that can simplify large amounts of coding and can process form data very fast. We hope that you are familiar with form and control referencing. To reference a specific property on a form, you might code something like this:

```
Forms!CheckWriter!CheckAmount.Visible = True
```

If you have a number of different properties to set or methods to run, you must reference the form over and over again, like this:

```
Forms!CheckWriter!CheckAmount.Visible = True
Forms!CheckWriter!CheckAmount = 0
Forms!CheckWriter!Void.Visible = False
Forms!CheckWriter!Memo = ""
```

This is an incredibly inefficient way to reference controls. Each time you run a statement that references a form, Access has to find that form in the list of all forms in your database. Believe it or not, it starts at the top alphabetically and looks at each one until it finds the one you are referencing. If you are looking for the forms that begin with the letter A versus forms that begin with the letter Z, you can actually see the difference on a slower machine when you have a lot of forms.

There is a better way: Define a form type variable and then use the variable to reference the controls, like this:

```
Dim frmControl As Form
Set frmControl = Forms!CheckWriter
frmControl!CheckAmount.Visible = True
frmControl!CheckAmount = 0
frmControl!Void.Visible = False

frmControl!Memo = ""
```

By using the previous code, the form variable is set and referenced only once. Each time you refer to `frmControl` (or any name you use), Access knows where to find the form in the list. In effect, you are creating an index, and you will see a big performance gain throughout your programs.

The best way to reference forms, however, is to use the `With...End With` construct:

```
With Forms!CheckWriter
  !CheckAmount.Visible = True
  !CheckAmount = 0
  !Void.Visible = False
  !Memo = ""
End With
```

As you can see, you specify the form variable in the `With` statement and just precede each control with the ! symbol. Everything within the `With....End With` construct references the value of the `With` clause.

Done!

REVIEW

In this session, you learned about logical constructs that are used to make a program run in the order that makes sense for the business purpose. Logical constructs include conditional processing and repetitive looping. The following topics were covered:

- Logical constructs refer to a certain class of Visual Basic statements that control the way a program runs.
- An application's capability to look at a value and, based on that value, decide which code to run is known as conditional processing.
- `If...Then...Else` statements are used to process binary conditions.
- `Select Case` statements are used to process multiple conditions.
- `Do While` or `Do Until` loops let you perform repetitive processing.
- `For Next` loops allow processing with counter variables.
- Any logical construct can be nested within another construct.
- The `With` construct can speed up processing when referencing form variables.

QUIZ YOURSELF

1. Define the term *logical construct*. (See the beginning of the session.)

2. Name two types of conditional processing. (See "Conditional Processing.")

3. Can you run one If statement within another? (See "Nesting If...Then...Else statements.")

4. When would you use an If-Then over a Select Case? (See "The Select Case...End Select construct.")

5. What are the two types of repetitive loops? (See "Repetitive Looping.")

6. What's the difference between a Do While and a Do Until? (See "The Do...Loop statement.")

7. What type of looping construct includes an automatic counter variable? (See "The For...Next statement.")

8. How do you speed up processing when using referenced form variables? (See "Constructs That Remember: With...End With.")

Procedures, Modules, and Class Modules

Session Checklist

✔ Understanding procedures

✔ Working with modules

✔ Using class modules

✔ Creating and running procedures

**30 Min.
To Go**

Y ou have seen in previous sessions how event procedures expand the capabilities of your Access application. Event procedures are just one of several available types of procedures. Whereas event procedures run automatically in response to some action in a form or report, subprocedures and function procedures provide another way to process actions in your application.

Understanding Subprocedures

A *subprocedure* is a series of programming statements that carries out some action. Subprocedures begin with the `Public Sub` keywords and end with the `End Sub` statement. They can receive arguments, but they cannot return a value. The following is an example of a subprocedure:

```
Public Sub IsWeekday(dtmDateToCheck As Date)
  If Weekday(dtmDateToCheck) = vbSaturday Or _
Weekday(dtmDateToCheck) = vbSunday Then
      MsgBox dtmDateToCheck & " is not a weekday.", vbInformation
  Else
      MsgBox dtmDateToCheck & " is a weekday.", vbInformation
  End If
Exit Sub
End Sub
```

Event procedures are also declared with the Sub...End Sub **statements. They are a special type of subprocedure because they are associated with a form's or a report's event properties.**

The IsWeekday subprocedure receives the DateToCheck argument. An *argument* is simply a value that the procedure needs in order to process the procedure statements. The IsWeekday subprocedure displays a message indicating whether DateToCheck is a weekday or not.

If the procedure does not have any arguments, leave the parentheses empty. For example, the following procedure declaration statement doesn't have any arguments:

```
Public IsWeekday()
```

Understanding Function Procedures

Function procedures are similar to subprocedures. They are composed of a series of statements that perform some action, and they, too, can receive arguments. Unlike subprocedures, however, they can return a value.

Function procedures begin with the keywords Public Function and end with the End Function statement. If the function receives arguments, the argument declarations are enclosed by parentheses following the Function keyword. The beginning statement ends with the declaration of the function's return value. The following is an example of a function procedure:

```
Public Function CalcTax(curPurchaseAmt As Currency, dblTaxRate As Double)
As Currency
    CalcTax = Round(curPurchaseAmt * dblTaxRate, 2)
Exit Function
End Function
```

The CalcTax function receives two arguments: one for the amount of the purchase, and one for the current tax rate. The keywords As Currency at the end of the function declaration statement indicate that the function returns a currency value. The CalcTax function calculates the tax amount for the amount purchased based on the supplied tax rate. The function returns the calculated tax amount to the procedure that called it by assigning the result of the calculation to the function name (CalcTax).

Access provides numerous built-in procedures for common operations, such as working with date/time data, string manipulation, and conversion between data types. Some examples of these built-in procedures include

- Round(): Rounds a number to the specified number of decimal places.
- IsWeekday(): Returns the position in the week for the specified date.
- Now(): Returns the current date and time.
- Left(): Returns the specified number of characters in a string starting from the first letter.

Consult Microsoft Visual Basic Help for a complete list of all the available built-in procedures.

Understanding Modules

**20 Min.
To Go**

Before you can create a subprocedure or function procedure, you need to understand modules. A *module* is an Access object that stores a collection of procedures. There are four types of Access modules: form modules, report modules, standard modules, and class modules.

Form and report modules

All the event procedures for a form or report are stored in a *form module* or *report module*. When you create the first event procedure for a form or report, Access automatically creates the form or report's module.

To view a form or report's module, open the form or report in Design view. Then choose View ➪ Code. The module displays in the Visual Basic Editor. Figure 7-1 shows the module for the frm_MainMenu form.

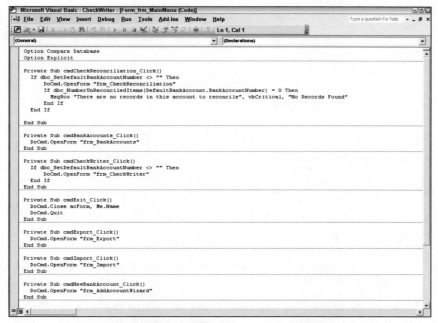

Figure 7-1   *Viewing the module for a form.*

Form and report modules provide a way to keep all the code that pertains only to an individual form in one place. Although form and report modules usually contain only event procedures, you can also add subprocedures and function procedures as well.

Standard modules

Standard modules enable you to store procedures that you want to use in any form and report in your application. Standard modules are stored in the Modules tab of the Access database window.

To view the procedures in a module, select one of the modules listed on the Modules page and click the Design button. The module displays in the Visual Basic Editor. Figure 7-2 shows the mod_UtilityFunctions module.

Figure 7-2   *Viewing a standard module in the Visual Basic Editor.*

The mod_UtilityFunctions module contains some common procedures that you can use throughout the Check Writer application. These procedures include

- dbc_CheckNum(): Generates the next check number for the Check Writer form.
- dbc_IsLoaded(): Determines whether the specified form is currently open.

Although the dbc_CheckNum function is associated with the Check Writer form, the dbc_IsLoaded function can be used in any form, report, or query in any application.

Keep generic procedures together in one module so that you can easily import the module into other applications as needed.

Class modules

Class modules allow you to create new custom objects for your application. For most applications, the built-in user-interface objects provide the framework for just about anything you need to build. After you start developing more sophisticated applications, however, you may want to build your own objects.

Class modules are stored on the Modules tab of the Access database window along with standard modules. The icon that displays on the Modules page for class modules is different from the one that displays for standard modules. Figure 7-3 shows a Modules page that includes both standard and class modules. The cls_Setup module is a class module, whereas the other modules in the list are standard modules.

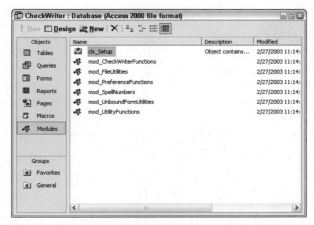

Figure 7-3 *The Modules tab displays different icons for standard and class modules.*

To view the procedures in a class module, select one of the modules listed on the Modules page and click the Design button. The module displays in the Visual Basic Editor. Figure 7-4 shows the cls_Setup class module.

You use the cls_Setup class module to work with application setup objects. You can use this object in any application where you might want to include company information and default data values. You can use this class module in any application because it does not include references to any specific form or report in the application.

To see how the cls_Setup class module works, open the form called frm_CompanySetup in the Check Writer database. The frm_CompanySetup form displays data from the table tbl_CompanySetup. Figure 7-5 shows the code for the frm_CompanySetup form's OnLoad event.

When the frm_CompanySetup form loads, the GetSetup function in the cls_Setup class module displays the values for each of the form's controls.

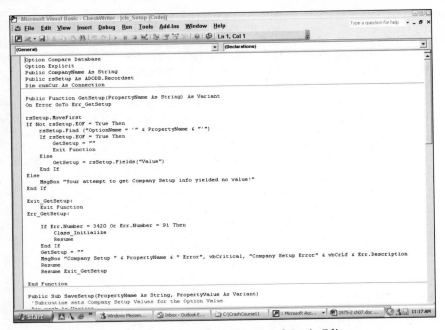

Figure 7-4 *Viewing a class module in the Visual Basic Editor.*

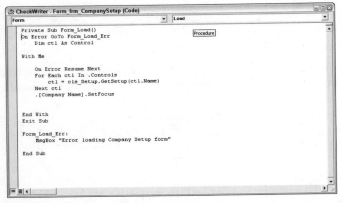

Figure 7-5 *Using a class module to display setup information.*

Creating a New Module

To create a new standard module, follow these steps:

1. Click the Modules object button in the Database window.
2. Click the New toolbar button.

The Visual Basic Editor opens and creates a new module named Module1. Figure 7-6 shows the new module Module1.

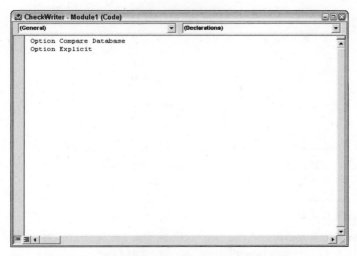

Figure 7-6 *A new module in the Visual Basic Editor.*

When you create a new module, the Code window automatically displays these two statements: Option Compare Database and Option Explicit. These two statements are optional, but it's good practice to include them. The Option Compare Database statement tells Access what the sort order should be when comparing data for strings. The Option Explicit statement forces you to declare all variables used in the procedures in this module.

There are two advantages to including the Option Explicit **statement in your modules: it speeds up execution of the module code, and it makes the code easier for others to read later on.**

Each module is composed of a declarations section and a separate section for each procedure. The two combo boxes at the top of the Code window help you locate a section in the module. Figure 7-7 shows the available sections in the mod_UtilityFunctions module.

When you create a new module, the Declarations section is created automatically. The two Option statements are always placed at the beginning of the Declarations section. The Declarations section can also include any variables that you want to be available to all procedures in the current module, or to any module in the application.

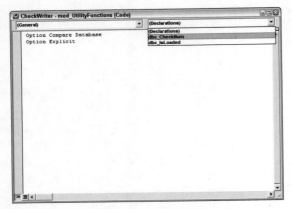

Figure 7-7 *Using the combo boxes to locate a section in a module.*

10 Min.
To Go

Creating a New Procedure

After completing the declarations section of the new module, you are ready to create a procedure. Follow these steps to create a procedure called ShowMessage:

1. Choose Insert ⇨ Procedure from the Visual Basic Editor menu. The Add Procedure dialog box displays, as shown in Figure 7-8.

Figure 7-8 *Creating a new procedure.*

2. Type **ShowMessage** for the new procedure's name. Select the Sub option for the Type and the Public option for the Scope.

3. Click OK. The new procedure displays in the Code window.

The new procedure should look like the one in Figure 7-9.

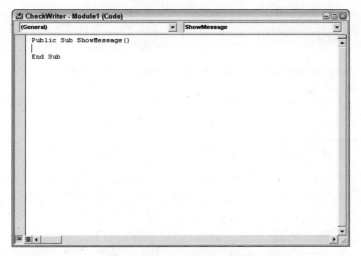

Figure 7-9　*A new procedure in the Code window.*

You enter the statements for the procedure between the Sub and End Sub statements. Enter the following statements for the ShowMessage procedure:

```
Dim MsgTxt As String
MsgTxt = "Running the ShowMessage procedure."
Beep
MsgBox MsgTxt, vbInformation, "ShowMessage Procedure"
```

The completed procedure should look like Figure 7-10.

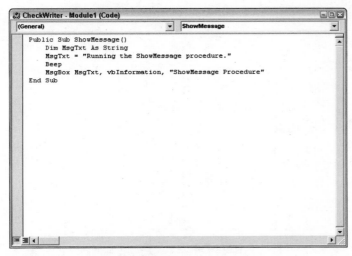

Figure 7-10　*The ShowMessage procedure.*

To see how the ShowMessage procedure works, you can run it from the Visual Basic Editor. To run the ShowMessage procedure, open the Immediate window. Then type **ShowMessage** and press Enter. When ShowMessage runs, it beeps and then displays the message.

You should always compile your procedures before running them.

Using a Procedure in a Form

After you have created a procedure, you can use it in any form, report, or query. To use the procedure in a form or report, you simply enter the procedure name as a statement or part of a statement in one of the event procedures. When entering the procedure name, also be sure to include the procedure's arguments inside the parentheses.

The OnOpen event for the Check Writer form calls the dbc_IsLoaded function stored in the mod_UtilityFunctions module. The following code shows the section of the code for the Check Writer form's OnOpen event:

```
If dbc_IsLoaded("frm_CheckReconciliation") Then
    Me![BankAccount] = [Forms]![frm_CheckReconciliation]![BankAccount]
Else
    Me![BankAccount] = DLookup("[DefaultBankAccountNumber]", "[tbl_Preferences]")
End If
```

When the OnOpen event procedure calls the dbc_IsLoaded function, it passes the name of the form to check, frm_CheckReconciliation, as an argument. When the dbc_IsLoaded function runs, it checks to see if the frm_CheckReconciliation form is open. If the form is open, the function returns True; otherwise, it returns False. Figure 7-11 shows the code for the dbc_IsLoaded function.

Figure 7-11 *Receiving a parameter in a procedure.*

The dbc_IsLoaded function receives the parameter MyFormName. MyFormName is used to specify the name of the object you want to check — the frm_CheckReconciliation form, in this case. The dbc_IsLoaded function calls the built-in function SysCmd to check the status of the object specified in MyFormName.

Using a Procedure in a Query

You can use function procedures in a query because they return a value. You can include function procedures in queries to convert data or to calculate expressions. You can include either a built-in function like Left, Date, or Now, or you can include one of your own functions. To use a function in a query, you simply pass the column name as the argument for the function. Figure 7-12 shows a query that calls the Date function.

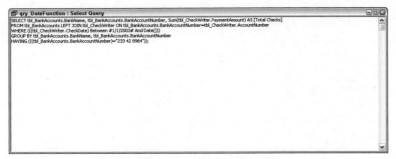

Figure 7-12   *Calling a function from a query.*

Done!

REVIEW

This session discussed working with procedures and modules. The following topics were covered:

- The two types of procedures are subprocedures and function procedures.
- Function procedures return a value. Both subprocedures and function procedures can receive arguments.
- Procedures are stored in modules.
- Class modules are used for creating custom object definitions. All other procedures are stored in standard modules.
- You can call function and subprocedures from forms and reports. In a query, you can only call function procedures.

Quiz Yourself

1. Name the component of a subprocedure that tells you that the procedure needs a value from another program. (See "Understanding Subprocedures.")

2. What is the difference between a subprocedure and a function procedure? (See "Understanding Function Procedures.")

3. Name the Access object used to store procedures. (See "Understanding Modules.")

4. Name the four types of modules. (See "Understanding Modules.")

5. Name two reasons why you should include the Option Explicit statement in your procedures. (See "Creating a New Module.")

Access Architecture

Session Checklist

✔ Working with the objects of the Application layer

✔ Understanding the Jet database engine

✔ Interfacing with external applications

✔ Viewing objects in the Object Browser

✔ Creating a database library

✔ Calling Windows API functions

30 Min. To Go

The examples you have seen in the previous sessions demonstrate only a fraction of the many properties and methods available in Visual Basic for Applications. Gaining an understanding of Access architecture can help you choose the most efficient methods and properties to use when you write procedures and functions in your own Access applications.

Understanding Microsoft Access Architecture

Microsoft Access consists of two fundamental structural components: the Application layer and the Microsoft Jet database engine. The Application layer provides the framework for creating and displaying the user interface objects in an application. The Microsoft Jet database engine provides data management services for the application.

An alternative component to the Jet database engine, Microsoft Data Engine 2000, is used with Microsoft Access Projects.

More information on Microsoft Data Engine 2000 is provided in Session 29.

Understanding the Application layer

The Application layer of the Microsoft Access architecture refers to the objects that you can see in an Access application — in other words, the user interface. When you create a new form, report, or data access page in the Access Design window, you are adding a new object to the Application layer of the database.

Actually, when you work with the database container in Access, you are actually working with the built-in Application layer of Microsoft Access itself. The database container is a user-interface object that organizes your application's objects into each of the seven Access database categories: tables, queries, forms, reports, pages, macros, and modules. The database container also provides the Design and Open tools for working with the objects in your application.

Although you can use the Application layer to create tables and queries, they are not considered to be part of the Application layer. Tables and queries are part of the collection of objects called *data access objects*. Data access objects are managed by the Jet database engine.

Managing data with the Jet database engine

The Microsoft Jet database engine is a database management system that stores data in and retrieves data from a database. The Jet database engine handles the following functions. It can

- Open a database
- Create or modify a database structure
- Browse, create, or edit data
- Control multi-user updates
- Create and synchronize replicas
- Restrict access through security settings

The Jet database engine is the gatekeeper between the Application layer in your application and your application's data. Figure 8-1 illustrates the relationships between the architectural components in Microsoft Access.

The data component of the Jet database engine refers to the file that contains the data accessed from the Application layer. The data files used throughout most of the examples in this book are Microsoft Jet database — .mdb — files. But the Jet database engine can also access data from external ISAM databases or ODBC databases. Some examples of ISAM databases include dBase, Microsoft Excel, and Paradox. The Jet database engine can access Microsoft SQL Server or Oracle databases through ODBC.

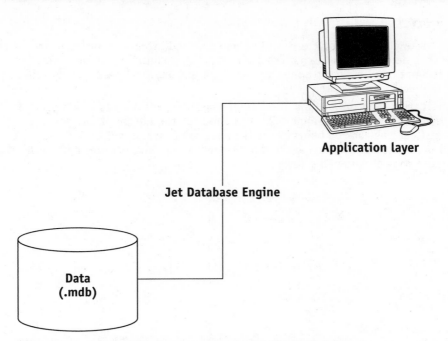

Application layer

Jet Database Engine

Data (.mdb)

Figure 8-1 *The architectural components of Microsoft Access.*

Jet database format

Jet databases are stored in the Indexed Sequential Access Method (ISAM) format. Data is stored in 4K file chunks called *pages*. A page can contain one record or several records depending on the length of the record.

Data definition

When you create and modify tables, queries, indexes, and relationships in Access, Jet stores these table and query designs in the database file. When you apply referential integrity to relationships, it is Jet that enforces these rules as users enter data.

Data retrieval

The Jet query engine enables you to use Access to visually create queries for adding, editing, or deleting data in your application. As Jet processes the Access query, it first converts it to SQL. You can also access data in VBA code using a special data access language called ActiveX Data Objects (ADO).

ActiveX Data Objects are covered in Session 10.

Multi-user access

Most likely, the applications you create will be implemented in workgroup situations. At one time or another, depending on the nature of the workgroup's business environment, two users may attempt to edit the same information simultaneously. Jet handles this situation by locking the record being edited.

As an alternative to record locking, Jet also provides the capability to lock a page of records. In Access, if you choose Tools ⇨ Options and click the Advanced tab, you see a check box that controls locking behavior for the database (see Figure 8-2). By default, the Open Databases Using Record-Level Locking is checked. If you uncheck this option, Jet locks the entire page of data being edited.

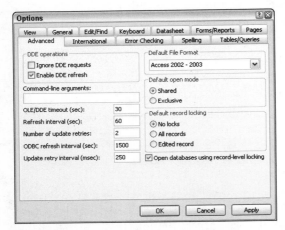

Figure 8-2 *Setting database-locking behavior.*

Remember that a page can contain one or more records. When Jet locks a page that contains multiple records, all the records on the page are locked, even though only one of the records is being edited.

In multi-user environments, the locking mode for the database is determined by the setting specified by the first user who opens the database. If the first user who opens the database has record-level locking turned on, all subsequent users open the database with record-level locking, regardless of their individual settings.

Experiment with setting this option for each application in each user environment. Page locking generally provides better performance. However, it increases the incidence of collisions — that is, multiple users attempting to edit data located on the same page.

Replication

The replication feature of Jet provides a method for distributing your database to other users. You can use replication to distribute your tables, queries, forms, reports, and application code. An entire database or just specific objects in the database can be replicated to a laptop, to other workstations on the network, or to another standalone computer. This feature goes well beyond making a simple copy of the database because changes are, through Jet, easily synchronized back to the master database.

Designing, distributing, and maintaining replicas are complex processes beyond the scope of this book.

Security

Access provides two models of security for controlling access to the database: share-level and user-level. The share-level model simply applies a single password to the entire database. With user-level security, you can restrict access to specific objects for each individual user of the database. When you implement either security model into your database, it is Jet that grants or denies permission to the database and/or its objects.

You learn how to implement security in Session 28.

The Visual Basic procedures that you create, modify, and execute as part of the Application layer use the built-in Access objects and collections of objects referred to as the Access object model.

Navigating the Microsoft Access object model

Microsoft Office Access 2003 is a system of objects and collections of objects referred to as the *object model*. These Access objects and object collections are accessible to Visual Basic procedures and functions. Having a thorough understanding of the Microsoft Access object model is fundamental to creating efficient Visual Basic programs.

20 Min. To Go

The object model describes the hierarchical organization of the objects and object collections in Microsoft Office Access 2003. At the top of the hierarchy in the object model is the Application object. Figure 8-3 shows you the Microsoft Office Access 2003 object model.

Working with the Application object

The Application object refers to the currently active Access database and contains all the Access database's objects and collections of objects. The Application object contains a number of properties and methods that you can use in Visual Basic to affect the behavior of the entire Access database application. You can use the MenuBar property, for example, to display a custom menu bar throughout the database. The following example illustrates using the MenuBar property:

```
Application.MenuBar = "CheckWriterMenu"
```

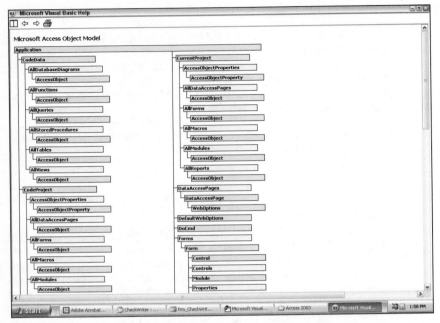

Figure 8-3 *The Microsoft Office Access 2003 object model.*

You set this property to the name of a menu bar that you previously created. You can redisplay the built-in Access menu bar by setting the MenuBar property to a zero-length string. The following example illustrates redisplaying the Access menu bar:

```
Application.MenuBar = ""
```

The Quit method is another handy Application method; you can use Quit to close the database, as illustrated in the following example:

```
Application.Quit
```

You can attach this Visual Basic statement to the Exit command button on your main switchboard form to give users a quick and easy way to close the database and Microsoft Access.

 You can redisplay the Access built-in toolbar manually by pressing Ctrl+F11.

The Application object also has the capability to interact with other applications that support Automation. Most applications that support Automation, called *Automation servers*, expose an Application object. The Application object reveals its collection of objects to other applications.

You can use the Application object to open an Access object from another application. The following example shows the Visual Basic code for setting up an object variable in Excel to point to an instance of an Access application.

```
Dim appAccess As New Access.Application
```

In addition to setting up a variable to point to the instance of the Automation server, the New keyword actually starts the application.

After you have created an Access Application object, you can use the object to open an Access database. The following statement illustrates opening the CheckWriter database:

```
appAccess.OpenCurrentDatabase ("C:\CrashCourse\CheckWriter.mdb")
```

When you open the Access database, you expose all the database's objects. This enables you to write Visual Basic code to open any of the objects stored in the database. The following example uses the Application object's DoCmd method and its OpenForm method to open the frm_CheckWriter form:

```
AppAccess.DoCmd.OpenForm "frm_CheckWriter"
```

Setting a reference to an external application

Before you can implement Automation code in Excel, you must first set a reference to the Microsoft Access 11.0 Object Library. In Microsoft Excel, to create a reference to Microsoft Access, open the Microsoft Visual Basic window by choosing Tools ⇨ Macro ⇨ Visual Basic Editor. In the Microsoft Visual Basic window, choose Tools ⇨ References to access the References dialog box shown in Figure 8-4.

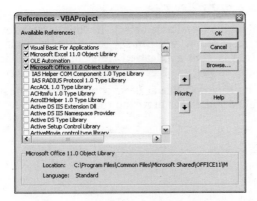

Figure 8-4 *Setting a reference to an Automation server.*

In the References dialog box, you specify all the references that your application needs for using Automation or any other library database. To select or deselect a reference, click its check box.

To create a reference in Access, first create a new module or open any existing module in your application database. When the module opens in the Microsoft Visual Basic window, choose Tools ⇨ References to display the References dialog box.

After you set a reference to an Automation server, you can begin working with any of the application's objects. As you create your Automation code, the Auto List Members help feature displays a drop-down list of available methods and properties for the selected `Application` object. Figure 8-5 shows the list of available objects for Microsoft Word.

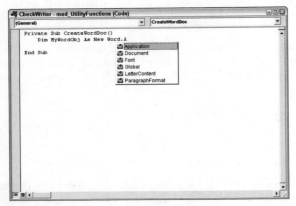

Figure 8-5 *When an Automation server is referenced, its objects are immediately available in Auto List Members help.*

Viewing object properties in the Object Browser

The Object Browser enables you to browse through all available objects in your application to see their properties, methods, and events. In addition, you can see the procedures and constants that are available from object libraries in your application. You can use the Object Browser to find and use objects that you create, as well as objects from other applications.

You can display the Object Browser from the Microsoft Visual Basic window by choosing View ⇨ Object Browser from the menu. Figure 8-6 illustrates browsing the objects of the Word library in the Object Browser window.

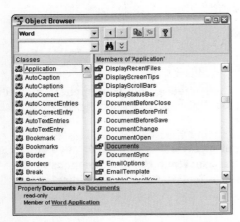

Figure 8-6 *Viewing objects and properties in the Object Browser.*

The Project/Library list displays a list of the names of the references you have included in your application. When you select one of the libraries, a list of classes available in the library displays in the left pane of the Object Browser. When you select one of the classes, a list of the class members displays in the right pane of the Object Browser. The Details pane at the bottom of the Object Browser displays specific information about the class or member you selected.

 For help on any of the classes and members in the Object Browser, choose the Help button.

Referencing database libraries

In addition to referencing Automation Server object libraries, you can reference other types of object libraries and incorporate them into your application.

A *database library* is used for databases that hold Visual Basic routines that provide utility across several Access applications. A database library is a standard Access database and usually has either an .mda or an .mde extension. These databases are built the same way typical application databases are built and contain the usual Access application objects (such as forms, queries, and tables). Figure 8-7 shows the Modules tab of the CheckWriterLibrary.mda.

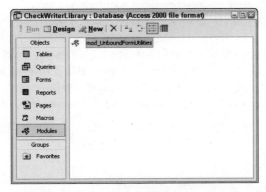

Figure 8-7   *The Modules tab for a database library.*

The CheckWriterLibrary.mda database library contains a single module named mod_UnboundFormUtilities. The mod_UnboundFormUtilities module contains several functions for working with unbound forms. Figure 8-8 shows the list of available functions in the mod_UnboundFormUtilities module.

The unbound form functions in the CheckWriterLibrary.mda database library are completely generic. They can be used with any Access application that includes unbound forms because they do not refer to any specific table name or form name.

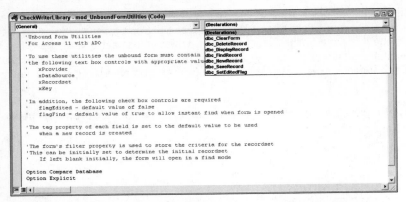

Figure 8-8 *Viewing the available functions in a database library.*

Database libraries may contain procedures that are customized for a particular business, or they may contain a standard toolset that you have developed for use with any Access application. You could simply import from these databases the specific objects that you need in the new application you are creating. Referencing these special databases, however, is a better alternative for the following reasons:

- If you keep a single version of the reusable code, it is far simpler to maintain or add to later.
- At runtime, Access doesn't load the library into memory until a function in your application calls a function or procedure in the library database.

 Circular references are not allowed. You cannot establish a reference from YourAccountingLib.MDA to YourMathLib.MDA and also establish a reference in YourMathLib.MDA to YourAccountingLib.MDA. A library can reference another library, but both cannot reference each other at the same time.

To establish a reference in the CheckWriter.mdb to the database library CheckWriterLibrary.mda, follow these steps:

1. Open any module window in CheckWriter.MDB.
2. Choose Tools ⇨ References to display the References dialog box.
3. Click the Browse button in the References dialog box.
4. In the Files of Type box, select Microsoft Office Access Databases (*.mdb).
5. Locate the library database CheckWriterLibrary.mda.
6. Click OK.

You should see your library database name in the list of available references in the References dialog box, as shown in Figure 8-9.

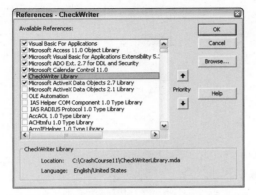

Figure 8-9 *Referencing a database library.*

If your library contains a procedure with a name that is also found in another referenced library, a call to this procedure invokes the first library in the references list that contains the procedure name. If you find that the correct procedure is not being called, you can move your library higher on the list of referenced libraries or rename the procedure so that conflicts do not occur.

 You should take care in naming library procedures to reduce the risk of collisions with other libraries. Use a naming convention that has a good chance of being unique.

When you select the drive, folder, and filename for a library, the application continues to look for a library with that name in that specific drive and folder. Keep this in mind when you distribute your application and plan ahead for runtime error recovery if the file is moved or deleted.

The procedures in a database library that you want to expose to applications must be declared as public procedures and must be stored in standard modules. An application cannot directly access class modules stored in a database library. However, the functions and procedures in the library can call class methods within the library. Although your library procedures can call private procedures within the library, the application database cannot access those private procedures.

Calling functions in Dynamic Link Libraries

**10 Min.
To Go**

As you gain experience developing Access applications and libraries, sooner or later you'll need a function that resides in a Windows Dynamic Link Library (DLL) or some third-party DLL. It is quite common today to find Access applications containing calls to the Windows Application Programming Interface (API) to take advantage of the power provided by the API.

Most applications include some kind of process that requires the user to specify the folder location and name of a file. This might occur in an import or export process, for example. Or, you might use it to reattach a broken library reference. Figure 8-10 shows the Import Data Dialog form in the CheckWriter database.

Figure 8-10   *A typical import dialog box.*

In the Import Data Dialog form shown in Figure 8-10, the user can either enter the path and filename for the file that contains the data to import, or she can select the folder icon to the right of the path name text box. When the user selects the folder icon, the File Open dialog box displays, as shown in Figure 8-11.

Figure 8-11   *Using the File Open dialog box to select a file to import.*

Instead of forcing the user to remember and manually enter the folder name and filename, you can provide the same familiar File Open dialog box that Windows and Windows applications (like Microsoft Access) use. By calling a DLL, you can incorporate the Windows File Open dialog into your application.

To use functions contained in DLLs, you declare the functions to Visual Basic. You use the Declare statement for this purpose. Declare alerts Visual Basic that the module contains a DLL and establishes the functions from the DLL that the application plans to use along with the function arguments and argument types that the DLL functions expect as parameters. This information enables Visual Basic to check at compile time that your function is calling the function with the proper parameters and parameter types.

The following `Declare` statement is specified in the CheckWriter.mdb General Declarations section of the mod_FileUtilities module to declare the common dialog `GetFileInfo` function for opening a file:

```
Declare Function GetFileInfo Lib "msaccess.exe" Alias "#56" (FSI As FileSelInfo, _
    ByVal fOpen As Integer) As Long
```

In the preceding `Declare` statement, `GetFileInfo` is the name of the function being declared. The statement also specifies that it is contained in the DLL named `msaccess.exe`.

In this example, you are actually referencing the Microsoft Access application itself, msaccess.exe, as a DLL. If the user is running our application, you can be sure that the reference exists.

The `Alias` argument specifies that `#56` is the actual name of the function in `msaccess.exe`. In your code, you call the function with the name `GetFileInfo`, but when the code runs, the DLL runs the function named `#56` in the DLL.

The parentheses contain the arguments expected by the `GetFileInfo` function. In this case, the function expects a `FileSelInfo` structure to be passed into it. You need to declare this structure before the reference to it in the `Declare` statement. Figure 8-12 shows the entire General Declarations section of the mod_FileUtilities module.

```
CheckWriter - mod_FileUtilities (Code)
(General)                                              (Declarations)

Option Compare Database
Option Explicit

Type FileSelInfo
    hwndOwner As Long
    strApp As String * 255
    strTitle As String * 255
    strButton As String * 255
    strFile As String * 4096
    strDir As String * 255
    strFilter As String * 255
    lngIndex As Long
    lngView As Long
    lngFlags As Long
End Type

Declare Function GetFileInfo Lib "msaccess.exe" Alias "#56" (FSI As FileSelInfo, ByVal fOpen As Integer) As Long
```

Figure 8-12 *Declaring an API function to display the File Open dialog box.*

The final `As Long` indicates to Visual Basic that `GetFileInfo` returns a value of type `Long`. Alternatively, you can specify this return type as follows:

```
Declare Function GetFileInfo& Lib "msaccess.exe" Alias "#56" (FSI As FileSelInfo, _
    ByVal fOpen As Integer)
```

Note the use of the & symbol at the end of the function name to designate the return type.

You can specify the arguments as `Optional`, `ByVal`, `ByRef`, or `ParamArray` to indicate the means of passing the arguments to the function, and each variable specified can also designate a type. Note that the variables specified in the `Declare` statement need not match those used in the actual call to the function, but the variables used in the call must match the type specified by position.

If you use `Optional` to specify an argument that may be passed to the function or omitted, you must designate the type of the argument as `Variant` and specify all remaining arguments as `Optional`.

`ByVal` causes the variable's value to be passed to the function instead of to the variable's address. If an argument is designated as `ByVal`, the function cannot modify the argument variable (with the exception of `String` arguments). Read on for more information on modifying String arguments.

`ByRef` causes the variable's address to be passed to the function. Argument variables passed in this manner can be modified by the called function. This is the manner in which you pass a variable to receive a return value other than that passed by the function's `As Type` specifier. In other words, some functions pass back a value indicating the success of the function execution in the function's `As Type` return value, but they also return other values into variables passed `ByRef`. If you don't specify an argument-passing method, the `ByRef` method is assumed.

The `ParamArray` specification can only be used as the last argument specifier and implies an `Optional` array of `Variant` elements. You may pass any number of arguments in place of this argument specification.

If a function does not require any arguments, you need only specify the parentheses with nothing inside of them.

Indicate the type of the argument after the argument name by using `As Type`, where `Type` can be any of the valid Visual Basic types, a user-defined structure as used in the `GetOpenFileName` function, an object type, or the generic type `Object`. If you use `ByVal` in front of a `String` type, Visual Basic passes a C-Type string, that is, a reference to a null-terminated string. This type of argument can be modified by the calling function.

Take a look at the dbc_OpenFile function in the CheckWriter.mdb mod_FileUtilities module. Figure 8-13 shows the code for the dbc_OpenFile function. The function first sets up a string variable with the filters that appear in the File of Type drop-down list in the Open File dialog box. These are the file types that are listed in the directories that the user can choose from in the File Open dialog box.

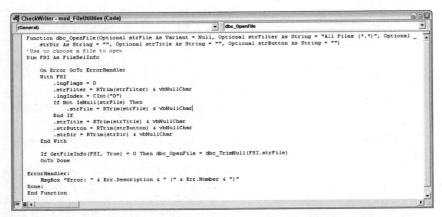

Figure 8-13 Calling an API function to display the File Open dialog box.

Next, the members of the variable FSI declared as a FileSelInfo structure are given values before the actual call to the GetOpenFileName function. The strTitle structure property, for example, is assigned to the strTitle member of GetFileInfo to display a custom title in the File Open dialog box when it appears. Note that each assignment is concatenated with the vbNullChar constant. Most API functions require that structure members be separated by a null-terminator character.

When the FileSelInfo structure has been set up for the call, the actual call to GetFileInfo is made to open the File Open dialog box. The address of the filename chosen by the end user is returned in the strFile member of FileSelInfo. Because, as noted above, the strFile points to a null-terminated string, the dbc_TrimNull function strips the null character at the end of the filename. Stripping the null character is necessary for the filename to be recognized as a valid filename within the Access application. The resulting string is passed back to the caller of GetFileInfo. This filename contains the full path of the file.

Win32 API calls and calls to other DLLs can be very valuable in your Access applications. Of course, you have to know the API functions and their syntax before using them successfully in your application, and some are easier to use than others. If you do decide to use a Win32 API call, you can pick up its declaration statement, structure declarations, and constant declarations from the Win32API.txt file that ships with the Access 2003 Developer Extensions. It is very handy documentation for understanding how to declare and call the available functions.

Done!

REVIEW

In this session, you learned about the components of the architecture of Access. The architectural design of Access makes its functionality accessible to other applications. The following topics were covered:

- The Application layer is the component that contains the visual objects of your application.
- The Jet database engine is the component that retrieves and manipulates the data needed by your application.
- The Access Object Model is a hierarchical system of objects and object collections.
- You can use the Application object to display a custom menu bar for your application.
- As an Automation server, Access objects can be displayed from other applications.
- References tell Access where to find a library database. You choose Tools ⇨ References in the Microsoft Visual Basic window to view and work with the list of references for your application.
- Windows API functions add a lot of functionality to your application, but you need to become skilled in how to declare them properly, how to call them, and how they return their values to your application.

QUIZ YOURSELF

1. Name the two basic components of Access architecture. (See "Understanding Microsoft Access Architecture.")

2. Describe how Access handles changes being made to the same record by different users at the same time. (See "Managing data with the Jet database engine.")

3. What Visual Basic statement opens Access from another application, such as Microsoft Excel. (See "Working with the Application object.")

4. When is it a good idea to create and reference an .mda file? (See "Referencing database libraries.")

5. Where can you look for help on using Windows API functions in your application? (See "Calling functions in Dynamic Link Libraries.")

Working with Data Programmatically

Session Checklist

✔ Viewing SQL Statements

✔ Creating SELECT, UPDATE, and DELETE SQL Statements

✔ Using SQL statements in procedures

✔ Using ADO to retrieve data

✔ Creating procedures to validate data

✔ Updating calculated fields from fields in a recordset

**30 Min.
To Go**

By now, you are familiar with using fields on forms and reports to display and update data in a table. At some point, however, you will work with data in a table that is not available in the form's record source. The Visual Basic language provides a rich set of powerful commands that enable you to retrieve and update data programmatically. This session provides an overview of SQL and ADO — the Visual Basic tool sets you can use to manipulate data in local and remote databases.

What Is SQL?

SQL is a programming language used to retrieve and manipulate data in databases. Like the Visual Basic language, it has a unique set of commands and syntax that you must follow. Many procedures that you write for working with recordsets utilize Structured Query Language (SQL) statements to retrieve data from a database, add new data to a database, or update records in a database. You are familiar with building queries using the Access Query Designer. When you use the Query Designer, you create the query graphically by pointing and dragging tables and fields to the Design view workspace. What may not be apparent to you, however, is that as you select each table and field, Access is simultaneously building a structured query language (SQL) statement.

To view the SQL statement that Access creates, choose View ⇨ SQL View from the Query menu. Figure 9-1 shows the SQL statement for the Check Writer Display query.

Figure 9-1   *Viewing the SQL view of an Access query.*

The Check Writer Display query retrieves fields from the Check Writer table. The query has a filter that limits the result to include only the records where the Bank Account Number matches the BankAccount field in the Check Writer form. The example in Figure 9-1 utilizes the four most common SQL commands. Table 9-1 shows each command and explains its purpose.

Table 9-1   *Four Common SQL Keywords*

Keyword	Purpose in SQL Statement
SELECT	This keyword starts a SQL statement. It is followed by the names of the fields selected from the table or tables (if more than one is specified in the FROM clause/command). This is a required keyword.
FROM	This keyword specifies the name(s) of the table(s) containing the fields specified in the SELECT command. This is a required keyword. If more than one table is used, specify a JOIN type (known as a Table Expression).
WHERE	This keyword specifies any condition used to filter (limit) the records to be viewed. This keyword is used only when you want to limit the records to a specific group on the basis of the condition.
ORDER BY	This keyword specifies the order in which you want the resulting dataset (the selected records that were found and returned) to appear.

The SELECT statement

The SELECT command is the one you use most often. The syntax for the SELECT statement includes the keywords SELECT, FROM, WHERE, and ORDER BY. This powerful statement performs the following functions:

- Retrieves specific fields or all fields
- Can retrieve the fields from one or more tables
- Includes all the rows from the table or uses a filter expression to limit the rows to be included
- Sorts the rows by a specific field or fields

The SELECT keyword

The SELECT keyword must be the first word in the statement and precedes the list of field names that you want to include in the query. A comma separates each field name in the list. Optionally, each field name can be preceded by the table name where it is found, followed by a period.

When retrieving fields from multiple tables, always include the table name prefix. In fact, if a field name appears in multiple tables and you do not include the table name, you get an error when you run the query.

The SELECT statement for the Check Writer Display query includes 13 fields. The first field name in the list is CheckWriter.TransID. Brackets around the table and field names are optional if the name does not include any spaces. For example, the same item could be coded as [CheckWriter].[TransID].

If you want to retrieve all the fields from a table, you can use an asterisk (*) in place of the field name list. The Check Writer Display query could be coded like this:

```
SELECT * FROM tbl_CheckWriter
```

Specifying SELECT predicates

When you create a SQL SELECT statement, several predicates are available for the SELECT clause:

- ALL
- DISTINCT
- DISTINCTROW
- TOP

The predicates are used to restrict the number of records returned. They can work in conjunction with the WHERE clause (actually in SQL terminology the WHERE *condition*) of a SQL statement.

The ALL predicate selects all records that meet the WHERE condition specified in the SQL statement. If you do not specify the keyword ALL, all records are returned by default.

Use the DISTINCT predicate when you want to omit records that contain duplicate data in the fields specified in the SELECT statement. For instance, if you create a query and want to look at both the company name and the products that the customer purchased, without considering the number of products in a single category, the SELECT statement is as follows:

```
SELECT DISTINCT AccountNumber, Payee
```

If two checks were issued to Acme Vending from Account Number 233 42 8964 (one on 3/15/2003 and one on 3/22/2003), only one appears in the result set. The DISTINCT predicate tells Access to show only one record if the values in the selected fields are duplicates (that is, same payee and same account number). Even though two different records are in the tbl_CheckWriter table for the payee, only one is shown. DISTINCT eliminates duplicates based on the fields selected to view.

The DISTINCTROW predicate is unique to Access. It works much like DISTINCT, with one big difference: It looks for duplicates on the basis of all fields in the table(s), not just the selected fields. For instance, if multiple checks were issued to a payee in the tbl_CheckWriter, you could use the predicate DISTINCTROW in this SQL statement:

```
SELECT DISTINCTROW AccountNumber, Payee
```

In this example, many check writer records are displayed. DISTINCTROW looks for duplicates across all fields selected for the query. If any field is different (in this case, the description), both records are displayed in the result set.

The TOP predicate is also unique to Access. It enables you to restrict the number of records returned to the TOP <number> of values. For instance, the following SELECT statement displays the first five check writer records:

```
SELECT TOP 5 PaymentAmount FROM tbl_CheckWriter
```

You can use the TOP predicate in conjunction with the ORDER BY clause to answer some practical business questions. This example uses the TOP predicate with the ORDER BY clause:

```
SELECT TOP 5 PaymentAmount FROM tbl_CheckWriter ORDER BY PaymentAmount DESC
```

This example returns a list of the five highest payments in the check writer. In other words, the query lists all the payment amounts and orders them by their amounts in descending order. It then picks only the first five amounts in the ordered list.

The TOP predicate has an optional keyword, PERCENT, that displays the top number of records on the basis of a percentage rather than a number. To see the top two percent of your check writer payments, use a SELECT statement like this one:

```
SELECT TOP 2 PERCENT PaymentAmount
```

The FROM keyword

You use the FROM keyword, as you may have guessed, to list the table names for the fields listed for the SELECT clause. This keyword is required and always follows the SELECT clause.

If the query includes fields from more than one table, you must include a join type expression in the FROM clause. The join type expression tells Access how the tables relate to one another. There are three join type keywords:

- INNER JOIN. Combines the records from two tables where the values in the joined fields in both tables match.
- LEFT JOIN. Includes all records from the table in the left side of the clause even if no records from the table on the right side match.
- RIGHT JOIN. Includes all records from the table in the right side of the clause even if no records from the table on the left side match.

The following is an example of the FROM clause syntax using a join type expression:

```
FROM <left side table name> <join type> <right side table name> ON <left side join field>
= <right side join field>
```

The following is an example of a query using a RIGHT JOIN clause:

```
SELECT tbl_CheckWriter.*, tbl_BankAccounts.BankName

FROM tbl_BankAccounts RIGHT JOIN tbl_CheckWriter ON
tbl_BankAccounts.BankAccountNumber = tbl_CheckWriter.AccountNumber;
```

In this example, the query retrieves all fields from the tbl_CheckWriter table and just the BankName field from the tbl_BankAccounts table. The RIGHT JOIN clause tells Access to match the BankAccountNumber field in the tbl_BankAccounts table with the AccountNumber field in the tbl_CheckWriter table. Because the join type is RIGHT JOIN, all tbl_CheckWriter rows are retrieved, even if the AccountNumber field does not match any of the values in the BankAccountNumber field in the tbl_BankAccounts table.

The WHERE keyword

The WHERE keyword is optional. If you include it, it always follows the FROM clause. You can use it as a filter to limit the rows that the query retrieves.

The WHERE clause always begins with the WHERE keyword followed by some condition that must be met. The condition is an expression that evaluates to either True or False. It includes a field name from one of the tables included in the FROM clause followed by a test expression. An example of a query using a WHERE clause might look something like this:

```
WHERE ((tbl_CheckWriter.TransType = 'Check') AND (tbl_CheckWriter.Payee =
'Random House'))
```

In this example, the test expression involves comparing the values in the field name TransType to the value 'Check'. In this case, the WHERE clause includes two test expressions joined by the AND operator. The second test expression compares the values in the field Payee with the value 'Random House'. The AND operator tells Access that both of these expressions must evaluate to True for the record to be included in the result.

The ORDER BY keywords

The ORDER BY keywords are also optional. When used, they always appear at the end of the SQL statement. You can use these keywords to sort the query results.

The ORDER BY clause always begins with the ORDER BY keywords followed by the field names by which to sort. The following is an example of an ORDER BY clause:

```
ORDER BY tbl_CheckWriter.CheckDate;
```

In this example, the query results are sorted by CheckDate in ascending order. To sort the results in descending order, use the DESC keyword. For example:

```
ORDER BY tbl_CheckWriter.CheckDate DESC;
```

The semicolon at the end of the SQL statement tells Access that there are no more keywords to process. If you omit it, however, Access inserts it for you.

The DELETE statement

Another SQL command that you use quite often is the DELETE command. The syntax for the DELETE command includes the keywords DELETE, FROM, and WHERE. You use the DELETE command to remove records from one or more of the tables listed in the FROM clause that satisfy the WHERE clause. The following is an example of a delete query:

```
DELETE tbl_CheckWriter.* FROM tbl_CheckWriter;
```

In this example, all rows are deleted from the tbl_CheckWriter table.

The UPDATE statement

You can use the UPDATE statement to change the data in a field for many records simultaneously. The syntax for the UPDATE statement is a little different from the SELECT and DELETE statements. The keywords for this statement are UPDATE, SET, and WHERE. Figure 9-2 shows an example of a DELETE statement.

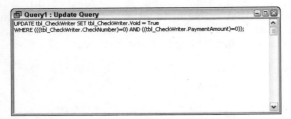

Figure 9-2   *An UPDATE statement changes many rows simultaneously.*

The SQL statement in this example changes the value in the Void field to True if any rows in the tbl_CheckWriter table have a zero in the CheckNumber field and if the PaymentAmount field is also zero.

> **The** DELETE **and** UPDATE **statements do not return any records.**

Using SQL statements in procedures

You can use SQL statements in procedures. For example, you can use a SQL statement to set the RecordSource property for a subform. Figure 9-3 shows the code for the AfterUpdate event of the Recon Display option group in the Check Reconciliation form.

Figure 9-3 *Using a SQL statement in a procedure to set the RecordSource for a form.*

The Recon_Display_AfterUpdate procedure checks the value of the Recon Display option group. The procedure sets the RecordSource property for the frm_CheckReconciliation-RegisterSubform subform based on the selected Recon Display option. If the Uncleared Only option is selected (Option value 1), the SQL statement filters the RecordSource to include only the records that have Cleared values set to False or 0, and where the AccountNumber matches the BankAccount field in the frm_CheckReconciliation form. If the All Transactions option is selected (Option value 2), the SQL statement filters the RecordSource only on the AccountNumber field.

Instead of attempting to write your SQL statement from scratch in a procedure, you can use the Query Design window to create and test the query. You can then switch to SQL view for the query, copy the SQL statement to the clipboard, and paste it into your procedure.

Creating Procedures to Validate Data

In Access, it is simple to display or update the data for a field in a form. You simply drag one of the fields from the field list to the Design view of the form. When the form runs, it displays the current value for the field. If the user changes the value, Access automatically stores the new value in the field.

In many cases, however, you want to validate the data the user entered against other values that are already stored in the form's table. For example, if the user is creating a new account in the frm_BankAccounts form, you need to check to make sure that the new account number does not already exist in the tbl_BankAccounts table. If the account number is a duplicate, you should display an error message to the user and cancel the update.

To validate the new account data, you must check all the records in the table to see if the new account already exists. There is no built-in function that you can enter into the ValidationRule property to span multiple records in a table automatically. You must write your own procedure.

Note Because the BankAccountNumber field in the tbl_BankAccounts table is the primary key, Access does not allow a duplicate entry for this field. You could omit the validation procedure and let Access accept or reject the new account. However, this might be annoying to the user entering the data because Access does not perform the check until the user has completed all the information for the new record and attempted to save it.

You use a field's BeforeUpdate event to validate potential new data. Figure 9-4 shows the BeforeUpdate event for the BankAccountNumber field. This event combines the use of a SQL statement along with some special VBA commands called ADO commands.

```
CheckWriter - Form_frm_BankAccounts (Code)
BankAccountNumber                              BeforeUpdate

Private Sub BankAccountNumber_BeforeUpdate(Cancel As Integer)
    On Error GoTo ErrorHandler
        Dim cnn As New ADODB.Connection
        Dim rst As New ADODB.Recordset
        Dim Response As Integer

    If IsNull(Me![BankAccountNumber]) Or Me![BankAccountNumber] = " " Then
        Response = MsgBox("Bank Account Number Must Be Entered!" & vbCrLf & "Do You Want to Cancel the Entry?", _
            vbYesNo + vbCritical, "Missing Bank Account Number")
        If Response = vbNo Then
            Cancel = True
            GoTo Done
        Else
            Me.Undo
            Cancel = True
            GoTo Done
        End If
    Else
        If (Me![BankAccountNumber] <> Me![BankAccountNumber].OldValue) Or IsNull(Me![BankAccountNumber].OldValue) Then
            cnn.Open CurrentProject.Connection
            rst.Open "SELECT * FROM tbl_BankAccounts WHERE [BankAccountNumber] = """ & Me![BankAccountNumber] & """", _
                cnn, adOpenForwardOnly, adLockOptimistic
            If Not rst.EOF Then
                Response = MsgBox("Duplicate Bank Account Number!" & vbCrLf & "Do You Want to Cancel the Entry?", _
                    vbYesNo + vbCritical, "Duplicate Bank Account Number")
                If Response = vbYes Then
                    Me.Undo
                End If
            End If
            rst.Close
            Set rst = Nothing
        End If
    End If
    GoTo Done
ErrorHandler:
    MsgBox Err.Description
Done:
```

Figure 9-4   *Using a procedure to validate data.*

Understanding ADO

The BankAccountNumber_BeforeUpdate procedure checks to make sure that the new data entered into the BankAccountNumber field does not already exist in the tbl_BankAccounts table. This procedure uses a SQL statement along with some VBA code. The VBA code consists of a special set of commands called *ActiveX Data Objects (ADO)*. ADO commands are used to retrieve and manipulate data in tables and queries within a procedure.

You have seen how easy it is to work with Access databases whether they reside on your local desktop or on a remote server. As a powerful client/server development tool, Access makes it just as easy to connect to non-Access databases such as Oracle and SQL Server. ADO is a simple, powerful command set designed specifically to work with non-Access databases.

Earlier versions of Access include the Data Access Objects (DAO) data access interface. Improvements in data access technology have taken Access to new levels as a client-server development tool. ADO, a refinement of DAO, represents these improvements and provides a simpler, more powerful array of data access tools.

Visual Basic currently supports DAO. However, Microsoft does not plan to provide any future DAO enhancements. All new features will be incorporated only into ADO. You should use ADO for any new development projects.

Declaring ADO variables

The first step in creating an ADO procedure is to declare ADO object variables. The Dim statement in this example declares ADO object variables for the connection and the recordset.

DAO and ADO share some data types. Because both ADO and DAO have a recordset type, you must precede the variable name with the appropriate class. When you are referring to a DAO recordset, you use the DAO.Recordset data type. ADO recordsets are referred to as type ADODB.Recordset.

The ADO Recordset object provides the Open method to retrieve data from a table or query. The Open method has four parameters: Source, ActiveConnection, CursorType, and LockType. The Source parameter is the name of the data source to open. The Source parameter in this example is a SQL statement to retrieve the tbl_BankAccounts record that matches the new bank account number on the Check Writer form. The ActiveConnection parameter refers to a predefined connection to the database. A connection is a communication line into the database. You use CurrentProject.Connection to refer to the currently active Microsoft Access database connection — the Check Writer database in this example. The Open method runs the query specified in the SQL statement and assigns the record or records resulting from running the query to the ADO recordset variable.

You can make a recordset updatable by using the CursorType and LockType parameters. The CursorType and LockType properties determine how ADO can access and modify the recordset.

Table 9-2 describes the recordset properties you can set.

Table 9-2   *Recordset Properties*

ADO CursorType	**ADO** LockType	**Description**
adOpenForwardOnly	adLockReadOnly	You can only scroll forward through records. This improves performance in situations where you do not need to update, as when you are finding records and printing reports.
adOpenDynamic	adLockOptimistic	Additions, changes, and deletions by other users are visible, and all types of movement through the recordset are allowed.
adOpenStatic	adLockReadOnly	A static copy of a set of records that you can use to find data or generate reports. Additions, changes, or deletions by other users are not visible.

If you don't specify a `CursorType` or `LockType`, ADO automatically creates the recordset as an `adOpenForwardOnly`/`adLockReadOnly` type recordset. This type of recordset is not updatable. If you need to make changes to the data in the recordset, you must understand the various `CursorType`/`LockType` combinations and how they affect the capabilities of a recordset.

 The `adOpenForwardOnly` cursortype is the most efficient option when you are opening a recordset to simply find a record.

When you use ActiveX Data Objects, you interact with data almost entirely by using Recordset objects. Recordset objects are composed of rows and columns, just like database tables. When the recordset has been opened, you can begin working with the values in its rows and columns.

If the recordset is opened as an updatable recordset, that is by using the `adOpenDynamic` cursortype and `adLockOptimistic` locktype, the recordset opens in Edit mode automatically.

Working with recordsets

After the recordset is open, you can begin working with the data that it contains. Before you use the data in any of the recordset's fields, however, make sure that the recordset contains records. When a recordset opens and the recordset contains a record or records, the current record is the first record. If the recordset contains no records, the property EOF is True. Because the SQL statement in the example for this topic is based on the table's unique key, you know that the first record in the recordset is the only record.

In this example, the statements between the `If` and `End If` statements perform the validation:

```
If Not rst.EOF Then
    Response = MsgBox("Duplicate Bank Account Number!" & vbCrLf & _
"Do You Want to Cancel the Entry?", _
vbYesNo + vbCritical, "Duplicate Bank Account Number")
    If Response = vbYes Then
        Me.Undo
    End If
End If
```

 If you attempt to manipulate data in a recordset that contains no records, a runtime error occurs.

The validation code tests the rst recordset to see if it is *not* at the end of the file. If the recordset does contain data (the recordset status is *not* at the end of the file), the SQL statement found a match on the new account number data — an undesirable result. An error message displays to notify the user of the duplicate entry, and the update is cancelled.

 If the recordset status is EOF, the SQL statement did not find a match and the procedure does nothing. The update is not cancelled.

Opening a connection for a non-Jet database

When developing in a client/server environment, you must establish connections to many different database systems, such as Oracle or SQL Server. When you open a connection for these external databases, you must use a connection string that is appropriate for the data source. The connection string is different for each database provider. The following is an example of a connection string for a SQL Server database:

```
CurConn.Open "DSN=pubs;uid=sa;pwd=;database=pubs"
```

This connection string opens the pubs database (the example database supplied with SQL Server). Each of the four parameters in this connection string is separated from the others by a semicolon. The DSN parameter refers to the data source name of the database. The pubs data source name contains the drive letter and directory for the location of the database. Most external databases require a user ID and password to gain access. The uid and pwd parameters contain these values. The database parameter refers to the actual name of the database in SQL Server.

Session 29 has more information about working with client/server databases.

Closing ADO object variables

The two statements after the End If statement are basic housekeeping statements that you should always use when working with objects:

```
rst.Close
Set rst = Nothing
```

The Close method tells Access that you are finished working with the object. If you work with the object later on in the procedure, you must code another Set statement to reopen the object. Assigning Nothing to an object variable releases all the system and memory resources associated with the object.

10 Min.
To Go

Using a Procedure to Update Unbound Fields

When a field on a form is bound to a field in a form's recordsource, Access automatically displays the value in the field. When the user opens the form, Access displays the current value of the field stored in the table. When the user updates the value in the bound field, Access automatically stores the new value in the table.

Many times, you need to display some data on a form that is not available using any of the fields in the form's recordsource. In most well designed databases, the table that the form is bound to contains one or more fields acting as foreign-key fields to another table. For example, the tbl_CheckWriter contains a BankAccountNumber field. The tbl_CheckWriter does not include any other information about the bank account for an individual account number. The information for an individual Account Number is stored in the tbl_BankAccounts table. On the frm_CheckWriter form, however, you want to display the associated bank's name and the ABA number for the account number record displayed in the form.

When the user selects a Bank Account in the Bank Account finder combo box in the Check Writer form, the Bank Name and ABA number display for the selected Bank Account. You use a field's AfterUpdate event to search for the new data. Figure 9-5 shows the AfterUpdate event for the BankAccount field.

```
CheckWriter - Form_frm_CheckWriter (Code)

BankAccount                                    AfterUpdate

    Private Sub BankAccount_AfterUpdate()
    Dim rst As New ADODB.Recordset
    Dim SQLstmt As String

        On Error GoTo ErrorHandler

        SQLstmt = "SELECT * FROM tbl_BankAccounts WHERE [BankAccountNumber] = """ & Me.BankAccount & """"
        rst.Open SQLstmt, CurrentProject.Connection, adOpenForwardOnly, adLockReadOnly
        With Me
            .BankName = rst!BankName
            .BankAccountNumber = rst!BankAccountNumber
            .ABANumber = rst!ABANumber
            If .TabControl.Value <> 0 Then
                .TabControl.Pages(0).SetFocus
            Else
                TabControl_Change
            End If
        End With
        rst.Close
        Set rst = Nothing
        GoTo Done

    ErrorHandler:
        MsgBox Err.Description
    Done:
```

Figure 9-5   *Updating unbound fields in a procedure.*

The BankAccount_AfterUpdate procedure opens a recordset to find the bank account information for the bank account number selected in the BankAccount combo box. The procedure fills in the form's unbound fields BankName, BankAccountNumber, and ABANumber using the fields in the recordset. In addition to setting the values for the unbound fields, the procedure also changes the active tab on the form's tab control.

Notice that the statements to update the unbound fields are within a With Me...End With statement. The With statement enables you to perform a series of statements on a specified object without respecifying the name of the object. The Me object in the statement simply refers to the form object attached to the current procedure. The code to update the unbound fields can be coded like this:

```
Forms!frm_CheckWriter.BankName = rst!BankName
Forms!frm_CheckWriter.BankAccountNumber = rst!BankAccountNumber
Forms!frm_CheckWriter.ABANumber = rst!ABANumber
```

Using the With statement, you can refer to the form object once instead of referring to it over and over for each statement in the procedure.

> The With statement offers developers a handy shortcut for referring to an object multiple times in a procedure. In addition, the With statement executes faster than each object reference executes individually.

Updating a Calculated Field Programmatically

A calculated field refers to an unbound field that displays the result of a mathematical expression or an aggregate value. A simple calculated field in a form might show the difference between two fields displayed on the form. For example, an invoice form might show a Total Sale Amount field and a Total Payment Amount field. A third calculated field might show the Total Amount Due — Total Sale Amount minus Total Payment Amount. A calculation like Total Amount Due is simple to define. You just enter the expression as the controlsource for the unbound field.

Calculated fields that display an aggregate value, however, usually cannot be defined using a simple expression or formula. The aggregate amount that you want to display might span many rows in the form's recordsource. Alternatively, the aggregate amount might be calculated from some other table in the database. For example, the Check Reconciliation form displays items that remain uncleared in two calculated fields. The Checks and Payments field displays the total of the payment amounts in the Check Writer that have not been cleared. The Deposits and Credits field displays the total of the deposit amounts in the Check Writer that have not been cleared.

The calculations to total the Checks and Payments and Deposits and Credits fields are performed in the frm_CheckReconciliationRegisterSubform form. When the user selects the Cleared check box in the subform, the Cleared_AfterUpdate procedure executes. Figure 9-6 shows the procedure for the Cleared_AfterUpdate event.

Figure 9-6 *Updating calculated fields in a procedure.*

The Cleared_AfterUpdate procedure issues a SQL statement to sum up the PaymentAmount fields in the tbl_CheckWriter table for the transactions with an account number that matches the account number on the Check Reconciliation form. The SQL statement only includes payment amounts greater than zero, transactions that are not cleared, and transactions that are void. The same SQL statement also counts the number of transactions being summed. The procedure opens the recordset using the SQL statement and updates the form's Uncleared Checks field with the recordset's SumPmtAmt amount (the sum of the Payment Amounts) and the ChecksPayments field with the recordset's NumPmts amount (the transaction count).

The procedure issues a second SQL statement to sum up the DepositAmount fields in the tbl_CheckWriter table for the transactions with account numbers that match the account numbers on the Check Reconciliation form. The SQL statement includes only deposit amounts greater than zero and transactions that are not cleared. The same SQL statement also counts the number of transactions being summed. The procedure opens the recordset using the SQL statement and updates the form's Uncleared Deposits field with the recordset's SumDepAmt amount (the sum of the Deposit Amounts) and the DepositsCredits field with the NumDep amount (the transaction count).

Use the Nz() function when working with recordset fields to convert Null values to a zero-length string. If you attempt to update a field using a Null value from a recordset field, you may receive an Invalid Use of Null **runtime error.**

Determining the Number of Records in a Recordset

To display the number of records that meet a certain condition, you can use a procedure to count the records and display the result in an unbound field on a form. For example, the Check Reconciliation form might display the total number of uncleared transactions in the tbl_Checkwriter table for the selected bank account. Figure 9-7 shows the procedure for calculating the number of unreconciled transactions in the tbl_CheckWriter table.

```
CheckWriter - mod_CheckWriterFunctions (Code)
(General)                                          dbc_NumberUnReconciledItems

Public Function dbc_NumberUnReconciledItems(dbc_DefaultBankAccountNumber) As Integer
Dim rst As New ADODB.Recordset

    On Error GoTo ErrorHandler

    rst.Open "SELECT AccountNumber FROM tbl_CheckWriter WHERE AccountNumber = """ & _
            dbc_DefaultBankAccountNumber & """ AND [Cleared] = False", CurrentProject.Connection, _
            adOpenStatic, adLockReadOnly
    If rst.EOF Then
        dbc_NumberUnReconciledItems = 0
    Else
        dbc_NumberUnReconciledItems = rst.RecordCount
    End If
    rst.Close
    Set rst = Nothing
    GoTo Done
ErrorHandler:
    MsgBox Err.Description
Done:

End Function
```

Figure 9-7   Determining the number of records in a recordset.

The dbc_NumberUnReconciledItems function determines how many transactions have not been cleared for the default bank account. The function opens a recordset using a SQL statement to retrieve the tbl_CheckWriter rows with an AccountNumber that matches the default bank account numbers that have not been cleared. When the recordset opens and it contains no records (EOF is True), the function returns zero as the number of unreconciled items. Otherwise, the function returns the value of the recordset's RecordCount property as the number of unreconciled items. The RecordCount property is a Long value that indicates the number of records in the recordset.

When you need to use the RecordCount **property, use either the Keyset or Static cursortype.** RecordCount **returns -1 for the ForwardOnly cursortype. Depending on the data source,** RecordCount **may not return the actual count for a Dynamic cursortype.**

Done!

REVIEW

This session provided information on how to use procedures to retrieve information from a database. You learned how to create SQL statements and how to use them with the ADO object model. The following topics were covered:

- Access queries are actually stored as SQL statements, and you can view them by selecting View ⇨ SQL View from the Query Design window menu.
- The SELECT statement retrieves a set of records from one or more tables and, optionally, can filter and sort the set of records.
- If the SELECT statement uses more than one table, you must include a join type in the FROM clause.
- The DELETE statement removes one or more records from a table.
- The UPDATE statement changes the values for one or more fields in a table.
- You can use a SQL statement in a BeforeUpdate event to validate data.
- In procedures like the BeforeUpdate event procedure, you use ADO to send a SQL statement to a database and to access the recordset it returns.
- RecordCount is a handy property for determining the number of records that meet a condition.
- A recordset can automatically sum the values stored in many rows using an aggregate SQL statement.

QUIZ YOURSELF

1. How can you view the SQL statement for an Access query? (See "What Is SQL?")
2. Name four keywords used in a SELECT statement. (See "The SELECT statement.")
3. Name two SQL statements that do not return any records. (See "The UPDATE statement.")
4. What property indicates that a recordset contains no records? (See "Working with recordsets.")
5. Which is the most efficient recordset cursortype to use when performing a search? (See "Declaring ADO variables.")

Adding, Updating, and Deleting Records Using ADO

Session Checklist

✔ Using a `NotInList` event procedure to add a new record

✔ Saving changes to a recordset

✔ Locking records for update

✔ Handling update errors

✔ Minimizing update conflicts

✔ Navigating throughout a recordset

✔ Deleting a record

30 Min. To Go

I n Session 9, you learned how to retrieve data from a table with a procedure using ADO code. This session expands on that topic to show you how you can also add, change, and delete data in a table. Manipulating data using a procedure may seem intimidating at first. However, the power that these command sets give you to develop a full-featured, multi-user application makes it well worth the investment of effort to become familiar with them.

Adding a Record to a Table

You can create a Visual Basic procedure to add a record to a table programmatically. To use ADO to add a new record to a table, use the `AddNew` method. Figure 10-1 shows the ADO procedure for adding a new payee to the Payees table.

```
CheckWriter - Form_frm_CheckWriter (Code)
Payee                                    NotInList

Private Sub Payee_NotInList(NewData As String, Response As Integer)
Dim rst As New ADODB.Recordset
Dim Answer As Integer

    On Error GoTo ErrorHandler

    Answer = MsgBox("This Payee is not on file. Add it to the Payees list?", _
            vbQuestion + vbYesNo, "New Payee")
    If Answer = vbNo Then
        Response = acDataErrContinue
    Else
        Response = acDataErrAdded
        rst.Open "tbl_Payees", CurrentProject.Connection, adOpenKeyset, adLockOptimistic
        With rst
            'Add new payee to tblPayees table
            .AddNew
            !Payees = NewData
            .Update
        End With
        rst.Close
        Set rst = Nothing
    End If
    GoTo Done
ErrorHandler:
    MsgBox Err.Description
Done:

End Sub
```

Figure 10-1   *Adding a new record to a table using ADO.*

When the user enters a payee name in the Check Writer form that does not appear in the combo box list of payees, the Payee_NotInList procedure runs. The message box prompts the user to confirm whether to add the new payee to the Payees combo box list. If the user selects Yes, the ADO code runs to add the new payee to the Payees table.

The NotInList **event executes only if the** LimitToList **property for the combo box is set to** Yes.

Using the AddNew method

The AddNew method creates a buffer for a new record. You assign values to fields in the recordset by coding a separate statement for each field assignment. The field assignment statements are always coded between the AddNew statement and the Update statement. As each field assignment statement runs, the new field information is copied into the buffer.

Completing the new record

The Update method, when used with the AddNew method, moves the information from the buffer to the end of the recordset. With ADO, however, you can omit the Update method. When you move to a new record in ADO or close the recordset, the changes are saved automatically. It is a good idea, however, to include the Update statement so that others who read the code later on understand that the update section of the code is complete.

To cancel any pending updates in ADO, you use the CancelUpdate method. After an Update method has executed, however, you cannot issue the CancelUpdate method. You cannot undo any changes after they have been saved.

Making a recordset updatable

To add, change, or delete records in a recordset, the recordset must be updatable. You can make a recordset updatable by setting specific properties for the recordset before opening it using the Open method. The CursorType property, in conjunction with the LockType property, determines whether changes can be made to the recordset. The adOpenKeyset cursortype is the only updatable cursortype available for Jet databases.

Session 9 discusses all the available cursortypes.

Table 10-1 describes the locktypes available for recordsets. The LockType determines which type of lock to place on the record to prevent other users from modifying the record you are about to update.

Table 10-1   *Recordset LockTypes*

ADO LockType	Description
adLockReadOnly	Read only. No changes allowed.
adLockPessimistic	Locks the record immediately upon editing.
adLockOptimistic	Attempts to lock the record when the record is saved.
adLockBatchOptimistic	Used for updating records in batch mode.

The adLockReadOnly locktype is used with the adOpenForwardOnly and adOpenStatic cursortypes when you are simply querying data. For updatable recordsets, use the adLockPessimistic and adLockOptimistic locktypes most of the time.

If you specify an invalid CursorType/LockType combination for a Jet database, Jet automatically opens the recordset using a valid LockType for the specified CursorType. Valid CursorType/LockType combinations for Jet databases include: adOpenForwardOnly/adLockReadOnly, adOpenKeyset/adLockOptimistic, **and** adOpenStatic/adLockReadOnly.

Using the adLockPessimistic locktype is called *pessimistic locking*. With pessimistic locking, the record is locked as soon as an edit occurs. The disadvantage of this method is that the record stays locked until the record is saved. Other users cannot edit the record until the record is saved. If your procedure must execute many statements before the update is complete, the record might be unavailable to others for a long time.

Using the Update method, moving to another record, or closing the recordset saves the changes.

Optimistic locking, using the `adLockOptimistic` locktype, does not lock the record until the record is saved. This approach minimizes the amount of time the record is unavailable to other users.

With both optimistic and pessimistic locking, an error occurs if a record cannot be locked. In multi-user applications, multiple users might attempt to change the same record at the same time. Your procedures must be able, at least, to attempt to resolve editing conflicts rather than just drop to a default error message.

Handling lock errors

20 Min. To Go

You can include a special error-handling section in your procedure to handle the errors that can occur when updating a recordset. With Jet databases, the three most common error codes that can occur are listed in Table 10-2.

Table 10-2 *Common Locking Error Messages*

Code	Message	Description
3218	Could not update. Currently locked.	The record is already locked by another user.
3197	The database engine stopped because you and another user attempted to change the same data at the same time.	Another user has already started editing the record.
3260	Couldn't update. Currently locked by <user> on machine <machine name>.	The record is already locked by another user.

Listing 10-1 shows an example of an ADO error-handling routine for managing locking errors.

Listing 10-1 *Handling Locking Errors*

```
Proc_Sql_Err:
Dim Response As Integer, LockCount As Integer,  RndCtr As Integer
Dim I As Integer

Const MULTIUSER_EDIT As Integer = 3197
Const RECORD_LOCKED As Integer = 3218

Select Case CurConn.Errors(0).SQLState
   Case MULTIUSER_EDIT   'someone else already changed the data

      Response = MsgBox("This record was changed by another" _
             & "user. Save anyway?", vbYesNo + vbQuestion
      If Response = vbYes Then
           Resume
        Else
        Resume Proc_Exit
```

```
        End If

Case RECORD_LOCKED
    ' The record is locked.
    LockCount = LockCount + 1
    ' If more than 2 retries, then ask the user what to do
    If LockCount > 2 Then
        Response = MsgBox("Could not complete update due to " _
                    & Err.Description & " Retry?", vbYesNo + _
                    vbQuestion)
        If Response = vbYes Then
            LockCount = 1
        Else
            Resume Proc_Exit
        End If
    End If

    ' Yield to Windows.
    DoEvents
    ' Delay a short random interval, making it longer each
    ' time the lock fails.
    RndCtr = LockCount ^ 2 * Int(Rnd * 3000 + 1000)
    For I = 1 To RndCtr
    Next I
    Resume                  ' Try the edit again.
Case Else                   ' Some other kind of error
    MsgBox "Error " & CurConn.Errors(0).SQLState & ": " _
            & Err.Description, vbOKOnly, "ERROR"
    Resume Proc_Exit


End Select
```

The Proc_Sql_Err error-handling routine evaluates the type of error that occurred and attempts to resolve it. The SQLState property of the active connection's current error returns the error number for the error. The Case statement in the routine compares the SQL error to two different SQL error conditions.

Instead of using error numbers in your code, such as 3218, 3197, and 3260, you can use constants to make them easier to understand.

If the error was due to a multi-user error (MULTIUSER_EDIT), another user already changed the data before this update could be completed. The message box prompts the user to decide how to resolve this. If the user selects Yes to retry, the code returns to the Update statement and executes it again. If the user selects No, the code jumps to the exit routine for the procedure canceling the update.

If the error was due to a failed lock problem (RECORD_LOCKED), another user has locked the current record. The statements in this branch of the routine attempt to automatically retry the update after waiting a short time. The DoEvents and the For Next loop tick off some time, thereby making the procedure "wait" before returning to retry the Update statement. The error routine keeps track of how many times the retry process has occurred. If a third attempt occurs, the message box prompts the user to decide if further retry attempts should be made.

Error-handling programs are covered in more detail in Session 16.

Locking multiple records

When you lock a record for a Jet-based recordset, more than one record may actually be locked. In a Jet database, issuing a lock on a recordset locks a section of records in a table called a page. A *page* consists of approximately 4K of data. If the size of the current record in a table is less than 4K, contiguous records are also locked until the total size of the locked records reaches the page size.

Jet also enables you to lock a single record. Locking an individual record is called *record-level locking*. In Access, you can choose Tools ➪ Options, click the Advanced tab, and control locking behavior for the database. By default, Open Databases Using Record-Level Locking is checked. If you uncheck this option, Jet locks the entire page of data being edited.

Remember that a page can contain one or more records. When Jet locks a page that contains multiple records, all the records on the page are locked, even though only one of the records is being edited.

To turn on record-level locking, select the option Open Databases Using Record-Level Locking in the Tools ➪ Options window under the Advanced tab. Figure 10-2 shows the Options window.

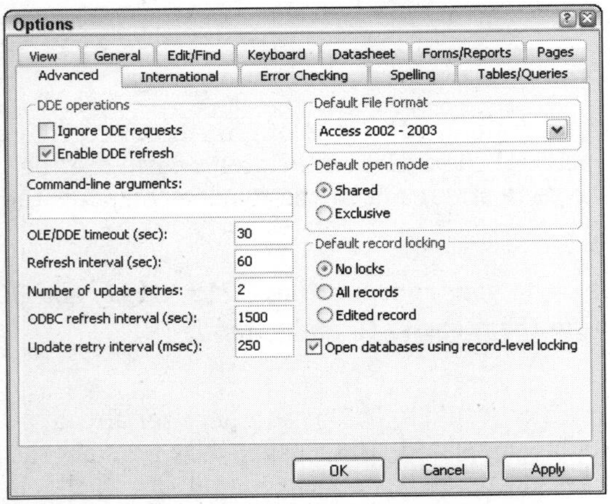

Figure 10-2   Setting the record-level locking feature.

To use *page-level locking* (locking an entire page of records), clear the Open Databases Using Record-Level Locking check box.

Using page-level locking generally provides better performance. However, in an application where many simultaneous updates occur, you can imagine how often locking conflicts can occur. The likelihood is probably high that two users will attempt to update records within 4K of each other at the same time. If you have included a good error routine for conflict resolution, your users probably won't get any update rejection messages. However, the system does slow down as it makes each retry attempt.

Adding Multiple Records

One of the goals of a well-designed application is to make data entry quick and easy for the end user. In addition to providing ordinary data entry screens where users add and maintain database data, just about every application provides some sort of process for handling a group or batch of transactions simultaneously. In the Check Writer example, the Recurring Payments form provides a process for issuing multiple checks. When the user selects a payment frequency and bank account in the Recurring Payments form, a list of recurring, already-defined payments displays. The user can select one or more recurring payment items to process in the list. Selecting the Process button creates the checks for all the items the user selected in the list. Figure 10-3 shows the ADO procedure for processing the recurring payments.

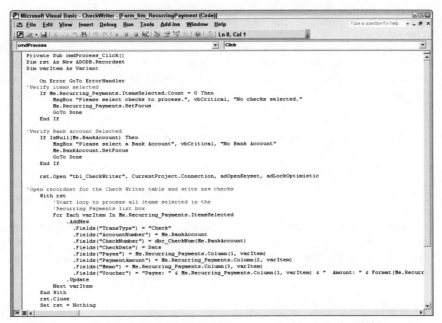

Figure 10-3   *Adding a batch of records.*

When the user clicks the Process button in the Recurring Payments form, the cmdProcess_Click procedure executes. The procedure first validates that the user has selected at least one item in the Recurring_Payments list box and that the user has selected a bank account in the BankAccount combo box. The procedure opens a recordset called rst. The new records for the tbl_CheckWriter are added to rst. The With rst statement starts the block of code where the new Check Writer records are created. The For Each statement is used to perform the statements that follow on only the items that the user selected in the Recurring_Payments list box. The ItemsSelected property of the list box identifies which items are selected. The statements between For Each and Next execute one or more times until all the selected items have been processed. The .AddNew statement creates a new blank record in the recordset. The statements that begin with the word `.Fields` update the fields in the new record with the following information:

- `TransType` is set to `"Check"` because the transaction is a payment.
- `AccountNumber` is set to the bank account selected on the Recurring Payments form.
- `CheckNumber` is set to the next available check number as returned by the `dbc_CheckNum` function.
- `CheckDate` is set to the current date.
- `Payee` is set to the payee name in the Recurring_Payments list box.
- `PaymentAmount` is set to the payment amount in the Recurring_Payments list box.
- `Memo` is set to the memo information in the Recurring_Payments list box.
- `Voucher` is set to a concatenation of the information above.

The `.Update` statement copies all the new records in the `rst` recordset into the tbl_CheckWriter table.

This example illustrates using a recordset's `Fields` collection to update the value of each field name. The syntax for working with a recordset's `Fields` collection is:

```
<recordsetname>.Fields(<field name (in quotes)>)
```

These statements could also have been coded like this:

```
<recordsetname>!<field name>
```

as in:

```
rst!TransType
```

You should use caution, however, in using the `Fields` collection when working with a recordset. If you misspell a field name, ADO attempts to add the field to the underlying table structure when the procedure executes the `Update` method.

Updating a Record

Changing a record in a table is very similar to adding a new record. To update a field in a table using ADO, you simply assign a new value to the field you want to update. Figure 10-4 shows the ADO procedure for changing the `LastBankStatementDate` and `LastBankStatementBalance` fields in the tbl_BankAccounts table.

The frm_CheckReconciliation form is an unbound form. The fields to update using the form's Bank_Balance field are located in the tbl_BankAccounts table. You must use a procedure to update the tbl_BankAccounts fields because the tbl_BankAccounts table is not bound to the form.

Figure 10-4 *Updating a record using ADO.*

When the user enters the Bank Balance amount in the Check Reconciliation form, the Bank_Balance_AfterUpdate procedure executes. This procedure changes the values for the LastBankStatementDate and LastBankStatementBalance fields in the tbl_BankAccounts table. The LastBankStatementDate field in the tbl_BankAccounts table is set to the current date. The LastBankStatementBalance is set to the amount entered in the Check Reconciliation form's Bank_Balance field.

When the Update method runs, the changes to the tbl_BankAccounts table are saved.

> **With ADO, a recordset automatically opens in Edit mode. You do not explicitly code an `Edit` method. In order to edit the fields in a recordset, however, the recordset must be updatable.**

Moving between recordset records

10 Min. To Go

Before you edit a record in a recordset, make sure that the recordset contains records and that you are on the correct record. In the Bank_Balance_AfterUpdate procedure (refer to Figure 10-3), the search criteria specified that the procedure's SQL statement produced a recordset containing a single record based on the tbl_BankAccount's primary key — BankAccountNumber. Many recordsets, however, contain any number of records.

If a recordset contains no records, the beginning of file (BOF) and end of file (EOF) properties are True. When you open a recordset that contains one or more records, the first record in the recordset automatically becomes the current record, and the BOF and EOF properties are both False.

Listing 10-2 shows some of the methods you can use to move around in a recordset.

Listing 10-2 *Navigating a Recordset*

```
Public Sub Moving_Methods()
    Dim PayeeTB As New ADODB.Recordset

    PayeeTB.Open "tbl_Payees", CurrentProject.Connection, adOpenStatic, adLockReadOnly
    If Not PayeeTB.EOF Then
        With PayeeTB
```

Continued

Listing 10-2 *Continued*

```
        .MoveFirst
        MsgBox "Payee is " & !Payees, vbInformation
        .MoveNext
        If Not .EOF Then
            MsgBox "Payee is " & !Payees, vbInformation
        End If
        .MovePrevious
        MsgBox "Payee is " & !Payees, vbInformation
        .MoveLast
        MsgBox "Payee is " & !Payees, vbInformation
    End With
End If
PayeeTB.Close
Set PayeeTB = Nothing
Exit Sub
End Sub
```

The Moving_Methods procedure uses the MoveFirst, MoveNext, MovePrevious, and MoveLast methods to move around in a recordset that contains multiple records. Notice that after the MoveNext statement, the code checks the status of the EOF property. When the EOF property is True, an error occurs if you try to access data from the recordset or attempt to move forward in the recordset.

Before moving backward in the recordset, make sure that the cursortype you specified for the recordset supports backward movement.

Updating Multiple Records

The frm_CheckWriter form includes a check box called Print Check to mark a check for printing later on. The user can view and then mark each check to print. The Print button on the Check Writer form opens the dialog called frm_DialogCheckPrint for printing checks. The dialog includes an option to print marked checks. When the user selects this option, the Print button on the dialog prints all the marked checks. The Print Check check box for the check in the Check Writer remains checked after printing. Leaving this field checked allows the user to reprint the marked checks if the printing process somehow fails. To clear the Print Check field for the checks that have been printed, the user can view each check in the Check Writer and clear the Print Check check box. Or, the user can select the Clear Print Marks to automatically uncheck all checks marked for printing. Figure 10-5 shows the ADO procedure for clearing the Print Check field for multiple records in the tbl_CheckWriter table.

The cmdClearMarks button in the frm_CheckWriter form executes the cmdClearMarks_Click procedure. The cmdClearMarks_Click procedure saves the current Check Writer record.

For procedures that are launched from data entry forms that may contain pending changes, it is a good idea to explicitly save the record before executing any code that updates the form's data.

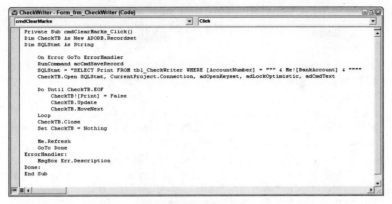

Figure 10-5   *Updating multiple records.*

Next, the cmdClearMarks_Click procedure opens a recordset containing all the Print field values in the tbl_CheckWriter table. If the recordset contains records, the statements within the Do loop execute. The statements within the Do loop set the value for the Print field to False for each record in the recordset. After the recordset is closed, the Me.Refresh statement updates the data in the Check Writer form to reflect the changes in the table.

Deleting a Record

You can use ADO to delete a record in a table. To delete a record, you use the Delete method. Listing 10-3 shows the ADO procedure for deleting a bank account.

Listing 10-3   *Using ADO to Delete a Record*

```
Public Sub Delete_Click()
 On Error GoTo Delete_Err
Dim BankTB As New ADODB.RecordSet, Response As Integer

 Response = MsgBox("Are you sure you want to delete this Bank" & _
Account?", vbQuestion + vbYesNo)
 If Response = vbYes Then
    BankTB.Open "SELECT * FROM BankAccounts WHERE " & _BankAccountNumber = """ & _
Me!BankAccountNumber _
               & """", CurrentProject.Connection, adOpenKeyset, adLockOptimistic
    If Not BankTB.EOF Then
       With BankTB
          .Delete
       End With
    End If
    BankTB.Close
    Set BankTB = Nothing
End If
 Exit Sub

Delete_Err:
    MsgBox ("Error is " & Err.Description)
Exit Sub
End Sub
```

When you are writing SQL statements, you must use two sets of double quotation marks to represent a single set of double quotation marks. For example, "...WHERE [LastName] = """ & CustName & """"

When you use the Delete method, you do not precede it with the Edit method or follow it with the Update method. After the Delete method executes, the record is permanently deleted from the recordset.

When you delete a record, the record remains the current record in the recordset. However, if you try to retrieve any data from the record, an error occurs. After you move to another record, you cannot move back to the deleted record.

When writing code to delete a record in a table, make sure that no records in any other table are related to the current record. In a well-designed database, relationships between tables are protected using *referential integrity*. Figure 10-6 shows the relationship defined between the tbl_BankAccounts and tbl_CheckWriter tables.

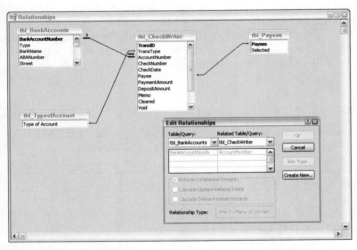

Figure 10-6   *Enforcing referential integrity in Access.*

Figure 10-6 illustrates that AccountNumber values in the tbl_CheckWriter table must match the values in the BankAccountNumber field in the tbl_BankAccounts table. In other words, you cannot delete a row in the tbl_BankAccounts table if its account number exists in the tbl_CheckWriter table.

Some programmers do not use the Access Relationships window to define referential integrity relationships for their databases. Instead, they simply use Visual Basic code to validate the integrity of the tables before deleting a record. Listing 10-4 shows the Delete_Click procedure rewritten with code to check referential integrity.

Listing 10-4 *Checking Referential Integrity*

```
Public Sub Delete_Click()
 On Error GoTo Delete_Err
Dim BankTB As New ADODB.RecordSet, Dim CheckTB As New ADODB.RecordSet, Response As Integer

  Response = MsgBox("Are you sure you want to delete this Bank" & _
      Account?", vbQuestion + vbYesNo)
  If Response = vbYes Then
     CheckTB.Open "SELECT TransID FROM tbl_CheckWriter WHERE AccountNumber = """ & _
       Me!BankAccountNumber & """", _
                 CurrentProject.Connection, adOpenForwardOnly, adReadOnly
     If Not CheckTB.EOF Then
        MsgBox "You cannot delete this record because there are related records in the
Check" & _
             Writer.", vbCritical, "Delete Error"
     Else
  BankTB.Open "SELECT * FROM BankAccounts WHERE " & _BankAccountNumber = """ & _
      Me!BankAccountNumber  & """", _
        CurrentProject.Connection, adOpenKeyset, adLockOptimistic
     If Not BankTB.EOF Then
        With BankTB
           .Delete
        End With
     End If
       BankTB.Close
       Set BankTB = Nothing
     End If
     CheckTB.Close
     Set CheckTB = Nothing
  End If
  Exit Sub

 Delete_Err:
     MsgBox ("Error is " & Err.Description)
 Exit Sub
 End Sub
```

The `Delete_Click` procedure in Listing 10-4 opens a recordset called `CheckTB` consisting of the TransID values in the tbl_CheckWriter that have AccountNumber values that match the Bank Account Number displayed in the form. If the `CheckTB` recordset contains records (not EOF), that means that deleting the current bank account would violate referential integrity. If referential integrity is violated, the procedure displays an error message and exits. If the `CheckTB` recordset does not contain any records, the procedure continues to delete the bank account record.

Using Visual Basic code to protect the database's referential integrity is a valid technique. However, this technique by itself does not prevent a user from opening the bank accounts table directly and accidentally deleting a record. Defining referential integrity in the Relationships window protects referential integrity during any delete event — directly in a table or through Visual Basic code.

The downside of using built-in referential integrity, however, is that when a delete event triggers a referential integrity violation, Access displays its own error message. This is desirable when working directly in a table. It is less desirable, however, for an Access error message to display from code running in a form. Therefore, it is a good idea to implement both techniques — using built-in referential integrity and Visual Basic code. If you do so, the database is protected from all sides and you have the added control of displaying your own error message.

Done!

REVIEW

The ADO command set provides powerful capabilities for building Access applications. Although these concepts may represent some of the more challenging topics presented in this book, you use them in just about every application you develop. This session included the following topics:

- The AddNew method adds a new record to a recordset.
- The Update method saves pending changes to a recordset.
- The Update method is optional but highly recommended.
- The Open method includes parameters for opening an updatable recordset.
- With pessimistic record locking, the record is locked as soon as you edit it.
- With optimistic record locking, the record is not locked until you update it.
- Page-level locking can lock multiple records, whereas record-level locking locks an individual record.
- You can use error-handling routines to resolve locking conflicts.
- The Delete method deletes a record from a recordset.
- With ADO, you can update or delete multiple records automatically.

QUIZ YOURSELF

1. What method is used to save the changes to a recordset? (See "Completing the new record.")
2. Name the two ADO properties that determine if a recordset is updatable. (See "Making a recordset updatable.")
3. Which locking scheme locks the record as soon as you edit it? (See "Making a recordset updatable.")
4. Name four methods for moving through the records in a recordset. (See "Moving between recordset records.")
5. How is the Delete method different from the methods used to add or edit a record? (See "Deleting a Record.")
6. What process protects related data in a database? (See "Deleting A Record.")
7. What property identifies the selected items in a list box? (See "Updating Multiple Records.")

PART

II

Saturday Morning
Part Review

1. Define the term *logical construct*.
2. What are some of the classes of logical constructs?
3. What is a nested statement?
4. What is the difference between `Do While` and `Do Until`?
5. True or false: The procedure declaration `Public IsWeekday()` does not have any arguments.
6. What kind of procedures return a value?
7. Which of the following is true: Using the `Option Explicit` statement in a module
   a. slows down code execution.
   b. automatically declares the procedure's variables.
   c. runs the procedure's error processing statements when an application error occurs.
   d. speeds up code execution.
8. A subprocedure cannot be called from which of the following objects?
   a. Form
   b. Report
   c. Query
   d. Module
9. Which of the following are considered part of the Application layer?
   a. Tables
   b. Queries
   c. Forms
   d. All of the above
10. True or false: The page size of a Jet database is 4K.

11. UsefulFunctions.mda is an example of what type of database?
    a. Access project
    b. Library
    c. ISAM
    d. None of the above

12. Name an application process that typically calls a DLL.

13. Which of the following is not performed by the SELECT command?
    a. Retrieve specific fields or all fields.
    b. Retrieve the fields from one or more tables.
    c. Change the values in a group of rows in a table.
    d. Sort the rows by a specific field or fields.

14. True or false: The Update statement returns a group of records.

15. In ADO, a _____ is a special object variable that you use to refer to the records in a table.

16. True or false: ADO was designed to work only with SQL Server databases.

17. True or false: When making changes to an ADO recordset, the Update statement is unnecessary.

18. Locking a record as soon as an edit occurs is called _____.

19. Which one of the following ADO lock types does not allow changes to the recordset?
    a. adLockReadOnly
    b. adLockOptimistic
    c. adLockPessimistic
    d. adLockBatchOptimistic

20. If you do not specify a type for an ADO recordset, which default type is automatically applied?
    a. dbOpenReadOnly
    b. dbOpenStatic
    c. dbOpenDynaset
    d. dbOpenForwardOnly

PART

III

Saturday Afternoon

Navigating an Application Using Switchboards, Custom Menus, and Keyboard Events

Session Checklist

✔ Creating an application switchboard

✔ Adding functionality to the switchboard

✔ Adding custom menus to your application

✔ Using keyboard events

**30 Min.
To Go**

E very application should provide an easy way for users to navigate to other components of the application. One way that you can do this is to create a user interface that provides access to other forms or functions within the application. These types of interfaces are normally called switchboards. A *switchboard* is actually a type of menu system. One type of switchboard is a form-based switchboard, which consists of a set of buttons that enables users to access other forms and functions in the application.

Another method for navigating an application is through the use of a customized menu system. You can create a custom menu bar, similar to the one used in Microsoft Access, to provide access to the various components of your application.

In this session, you learn how to create a basic application switchboard and add navigation links to the switchboard. You also learn how to create your own menu system. In addition, you see how you can add keyboard events to help users navigate through the switchboard or menu system without using a mouse.

Creating a Custom Application Switchboard

An *application switchboard* is typically a form that enables a user to navigate to other components of the application. You can even create a main switchboard that brings the user to additional switchboards, such as a data entry switchboard, a reports switchboard, or a utility switchboard. A switchboard can contain several different types of objects, including labels, text boxes, tabs, list boxes, buttons, or ActiveX controls. Controls you add to a switchboard can perform several types of functions, including the following:

- Opening a form
- Printing a report
- Running a query
- Running a macro, function, or subroutine

Figure 11-1 shows the application switchboard for the Check Writer application, named frm_MainMenu. This form is displayed automatically when the user starts the application. It consists of nine buttons that, when clicked, open other forms contained within the application. One of the buttons is also used to close the application. Other fields on the form are used to display a product logo, application title, and company name.

Figure 11-1   *The Check Writer application switchboard.*

Creating a simple custom switchboard is easy. Just follow these steps:

1. Create a new form and work in the Design view of the form.
2. Set the form so that it doesn't show scroll bars or record selectors.
3. Create the title and subtitle by adding text and label fields to the form. You can manually enter titles and other information to be displayed on the form, or you can set the record source to point to a table or query that contains the information you want to use. For example, with the frm_MainMenu switchboard, the record source is set to the tbl_Preferences table. This enables you to display the company name as entered in the Company Name field on the Setup form.
4. Add a company logo or other graphics, as desired, by inserting a graphic or unbound object frame onto the form. In the Check Writer switchboard, the graphic located to the left of the form also serves as a link to display the About box. You accomplish this by adding the following code to the graphic's OnClick event.

    ```
    DoCmd.OpenForm "frm_About"
    ```
5. Add a command button for each major function of the application to which you want to give users access. Set these up in some organized manner so that it's easy for users to locate and navigate items on the form.

Each command button should contain code to execute a specific function. For example, the New Bank Account Wizard performs the following when its button is clicked:

```
Private Sub cmdNewBankAccount_Click()
  DoCmd.OpenForm "frm_AddAccountWizard"
End Sub
```

This is an example of a simple button: it opens the AddAccountWizard form when the button is clicked. Other buttons may contain more advanced functions such as error checking and lookup functions. As you can see in Listing 11-1, the OnClick event of the Check Reconciliation button contains more advanced functions.

Listing 11-1 *The OnClick Event for the Check Reconciliation Button*

```
Private Sub cmdCheckReconciliation_Click()
    If cls_Setup.GetSetup("Default Bank Account Number") <> "" Then
        DoCmd.OpenForm "frm_CheckReconciliation"
      If dbc_NumberUnReconciledItems(cls_Setup.GetSetup("Default Bank Account Number")) =
0 Then
        MsgBox "There are no records in this account to reconcile", vbCritical, "No
Records Found"
      End If
    End If
Exit Sub
```

Adding intelligence to switchboard buttons

Although you can program buttons simply to open a form or perform a function, you can also create buttons with more intelligence behind them. This includes adding error handling, opening recordsets, or performing other actions before a form is opened.

You learn more about using error handling in Session 16.

Take a look at Listing 11-1 again. When the user clicks the Check Reconciliation button, the code checks the DefaultBankAccountNumber field in the tbl_Preferences table to make sure a default account number has been entered. If it has, the form opens and displays transactions for this account.

```
Public Function dbc_NumberUnReconciledItems(dbc_DefaultBankAccountNumber) As Integer
Dim rst As New ADODB.Recordset

  On Error GoTo ErrorHandler
  rst.Open "SELECT AccountNumber FROM tbl_CheckWriter WHERE AccountNumber = " & Chr(34) &
dbc_DefaultBankAccountNumber & Chr(34), CurrentProject.Connection, adOpenStatic
  If rst.EOF Then
    dbc_NumberUnReconciledItems = 0
  Else
    rst.MoveLast
    dbc_NumberUnReconciledItems = rst.RecordCount
  End If
```

```
    rst.Close
    GoTo Done
ErrorHandler:
    MsgBox Err.Description
Done:

End Function
```

A second check is also made to determine if transactions exist for the default bank account. If there are no transactions to reconcile, a message box is displayed alerting the user that there are no records to reconcile.

Building a Custom Menu

Another way to add navigation to your application is to build a customized menu bar. You can add commands to the menu that are appropriate for your application. You can even use a custom menu bar with a switchboard to provide users with an alternative method for selecting items normally displayed on a switchboard.

Figure 11-2 shows the Check Writer switchboard with a custom menu bar. Notice that this menu bar replaces the default menu bar normally displayed with a form. Each of the five choices on the menu bar (File, Forms, Reports, Utilities, and Help) consists of a drop-down menu that is displayed when the menu option is selected. You can view this form by opening the form named frm_MainMenuwithBar from the Check Writer sample application included on the companion Web site.

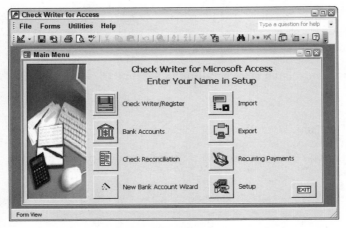

Figure 11-2   *A switchboard with a custom menu bar.*

Adding a custom menu to a form is fairly easy. There are two ways to create custom menus in Access:

- Use the Access CommandBar object.
- Use macros.

In Access 2.0 and Access 95, the only way to create menus was by using macros.

Creating custom menu bars

You can create the custom menu bar shown in Figure 11-2 by first creating the top-level menu consisting of five elements: File, Forms, Reports, Utilities, and Help.

1. Create the top-level menu by choosing View ➪ Toolbars ➪ Customize. The Customize dialog box is displayed, as shown in Figure 11-3.

Figure 11-3   *The Customize dialog box.*

The Customize dialog box contains three tabs:

- **Toolbars:** Displays all the toolbars, including built-in toolbars and custom toolbars. You can use this tab to create new toolbars or edit existing bars.

- **Commands:** Lists commands sorted by category that you can add to your menu and toolbars.

- **Options:** Provides various options for personalizing menu bars and toolbars.

2. To create a new menu bar, select New from the Toolbars tab of the Customize dialog box. A dialog box appears asking you to provide a name for the custom menu bar. In this example, the custom menu bar is named CheckWriter.

After you create the menu bar, a small, gray rectangle appears in the center of the screen. This represents the new menu bar you have created. The name of the new menu bar also appears at the bottom of the Customize menu list.

3. Before you begin adding functions or commands to this bar, you need to decide which type of menu bar you want to create. To do this, select the menu bar you created from the Toolbars tab of the Customize dialog box and click the Properties button. The Properties dialog box is displayed, as shown in Figure 11-4.

Figure 11-4 *The Toolbar Properties dialog box.*

You can choose from three types of bars:

- **Menu Bar:** Used for drop-down menus of commands containing text and, optionally, pictures.
- **Toolbar:** Used for button bars containing only pictures.
- **Popup:** Used either for drop-down menu lists or shortcut menus; this type can contain pictures and text.

4. For this example, you want to create a menu, so choose the Menu Bar option. Several other options are available when you select this option. Select the options you want to apply to your menu. If you do not want the user to have the option of customizing your menu or other options, you may want to clear some of these options. Click the Close button when finished.

20 Min. To Go

Adding a submenu to a custom menu bar

Most menu commands are placed on submenus. It is very rare for a top-level menu to do anything but display a submenu. The submenu contains the actual menu item that, when clicked, runs the desired action, such as opening a form or printing a report.

To create a submenu, follow these steps:

1. Display the Customize dialog box by right-clicking the top-level menu bar you created and selecting Customize from the shortcut menu.
2. Click the Commands tab and select the New Menu choice from the bottom of the Categories list box.
3. Select the New Menu item in the Commands area, and then drag and drop it from the Customize dialog box to your new menu bar. The text New Menu appears on the menu bar.
4. Click it again, and a rectangle appears around the name. This is the submenu. Figure 11-5 shows the custom menu bar with the new submenu. You can change the name of the new submenu by right-clicking it and entering a name in the Name area. If you are following along with this example, rename New Menu to **Help**.

Figure 11-5 *The main menu bar.*

Repeat this process for each submenu you want to add to your menu bar. After you have finished adding submenus, you can add commands to the submenus.

 After you add submenus to a menu bar, you cannot change it to a toolbar or pop-up menu.

Adding commands to a submenu

You can add commands to a custom menu bar by dragging pre-existing commands to the menu bar or by adding any of your tables, queries, forms, reports, or macros to the menu bar. You can also add your own ActiveX controls to a menu bar. If you add your own items, you may need to add functionality behind them. Using a pre-existing command completes all the necessary actions and options for you. However, unless you are planning to use an action found on one of the Access menus, you should create your own menus by first creating a new command bar and making it a menu bar, as discussed in the previous section.

 With the Customize dialog box open, you can add commands from other menus by simply clicking the menu on the menu bar or toolbar or by clicking the shortcut menu that contains the command you want to copy or move. Use the Ctrl key when selecting a command to copy the command.

After you have defined the blank submenus on the menu bar, you can drag controls to them. For example, you might want to display the About dialog box in your Help submenu. To do this, follow these steps:

1. Choose View ➪ Toolbars ➪ Customize to open the Customize dialog box and then click the Commands tab.
2. Select All Forms from the Categories list.
3. Select frm_About from the Commands list and drag it over the Help submenu. Notice that a gray box appears below the Help submenu text. Drop the item in this area to have it displayed under the Help submenu.

 If you move or copy a command to a built-in menu (for example, the Edit menu), the command appears on that menu in all views that have that menu.

Figure 11-6 displays the custom menu bar with the About form added to the Help submenu.

Figure 11-6 *The main menu bar with a submenu.*

If you simply drop the item on the menu bar, it appears as a command on the main menu bar. You must place the item in the gray box beneath a submenu if you want the item to be accessible from the submenu.

By default, the form name is used as the name of the menu item. You can change the name by right-clicking the menu item and entering a new name in the Name field of the shortcut menu.

When the user selects About from the Help menu, Access opens the About form. Access automatically opens the form because any time you add an existing object to a submenu, Access assumes the object should be opened and adds the appropriate open action to the command. If you want to perform some other action, you must change the On Action property in the Properties dialog for the selected item. The following section covers this process in detail.

Setting properties for menu items and commands

Each command or item you add to a submenu has its own shortcut menu that enables you to further customize the item. You can display the shortcut menu by right-clicking the item you want to modify. Several options are available, such as the capability to delete the command, add graphics to the command, add a hyperlink, or edit properties for the command. These options provide you with the flexibility to control how your menu items behave.

After you have added an item to your menu, follow these steps to display the properties dialog and add a graphic to the menu item:

1. Display the Customize dialog box. If it is not open, right-click the menu bar and select Customize from the shortcut menu. You can also open the Customize dialog by clicking the arrow displayed to the right of the menu bar. Select Add or Remove Buttons and then select Customize. You can only make changes to menu bar items if the Customize dialog is displayed.

2. Right-click the item you want to modify to display its shortcut menu.

3. To add a graphic to appear next to the item, select the Change Button Image option, as shown in Figure 11-7.

4. Select a graphic from the ones displayed.

You can create your own image and add it to a command by copying the image to the clipboard and selecting the Paste Button Image option from the shortcut menu.

If you select the Begin a Group menu item, Access places a horizontal separator line before the menu item.

You can further customize each item by changing its properties. The Properties form for a command or menu item is displayed when you click Properties from a menu item's shortcut menu (refer to Figure 11-7). The Properties dialog box is displayed in Figure 11-8.

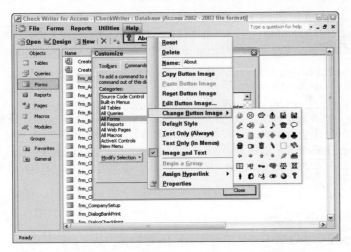

Figure 11-7　*Adding a graphic to a submenu item.*

Figure 11-8　*Customizing properties for a control.*

Changing the caption changes the text displayed on the menu. In Figure 11-8, notice that an ampersand (&) is added in front of the word About. This defines the hot key for this command and allows the user to press the letter *A* after selecting the Help menu to display the About form.

> **To define a hot key for the menu item, add an ampersand in front of the letter you want to use as the hot key.**

If you set up an AutoKeys macro list, you can specify the action behind the shortcut text. Notice the Ctrl+A in the Shortcut Text box. In an autoexec macro, this key combination would be set to open the About form. AutoKeys are explained in more detail later in the section "Using AutoKeys."

If you assign a set of actions to a key combination that is already being used by Access (for example, Ctrl + C is the key combination for Copy), the actions you assign this key combination replace the Access key assignment.

You can also define ScreenTip text for the control by entering text in the ScreenTip text box.

The most important option in the Properties dialog box is normally the On Action option. This enables you to specify a VBA function or macro that should run when the menu item is selected. If you selected a predefined menu item, this may already be completed for you.

The other options let you choose the Help filename and entry point if you click Help while selecting the menu. The Parameter entry is used to specify optional parameters when calling a VBA function.

10 Min.
To Go

Attaching the menu bar to a form

After you have completed your custom menu bar, you can attach the menu bar to a form by following these steps:

1. Open the form in Design view.
2. Display the Property sheet for the form by selecting the Properties icon from the tool bar or by choosing View ⇨ Properties.
3. As shown in Figure 11-9, you select the Menu Bar property and choose a menu bar from the list. When you display the form in Form view, notice that the only menu bar that displays is the custom menu bar.

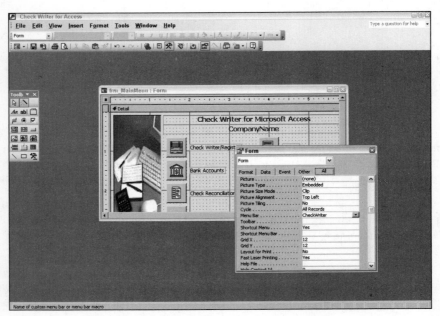

Figure 11-9   *Choosing a menu bar to display with a form.*

You can specify a menu bar to be displayed with a form using VBA code behind the form. The following code displays the CheckWriter menu bar each time the Preferences form is opened.

```
Forms!frm_Preferences.MenuBar = "CheckWriter"
```

To display the built-in menu bar for a form, you set the MenuBar property to a zero-length string (" "):

```
Forms!frm_Preferences.MenuBar = ""
```

You can also specify a custom menu bar to use as the global menu bar for your application. The custom menu bar replaces the built-in menu bar in all windows of your application, except where you have specified an alternative menu bar by using the StartupMenuBar property.

The easiest way to set a global menu bar is by using the Menu Bar option in the Startup dialog box, as shown in Figure 11-10. You display this dialog box by choosing Tools ⇨ Startup.

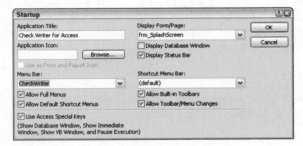

Figure 11-10 *Setting a custom menu bar as the global menu bar.*

You can also set the StartupMenuBar property, as well as other startup properties, by using code. If you use your own custom properties, before you attempt to set a property be sure that the property exists for the Database object. If it does not exist, you must add it.

There are two ways you can set startup properties using code:

- Create a macro named AutoExec and use the RunCode action to execute a VBA procedure that sets the properties. An AutoExec macro is automatically executed after a database is loaded.
- Add code to the Open event of a splash screen or other startup form in your database to set the startup properties. This method is preferable to using a macro because most database applications use some type of startup form. However, it is much easier to use the Startup Option if the property you want to set is displayed there.

Using Keyboard Events

Because forms are a core part of most applications, you must understand the different form and control events available to you. This can help you learn which events control certain tasks, enabling you to control the behavior of your forms.

Microsoft Access traps for about 30 form events, each of which has a specific purpose. Some of these events include keyboard events, which are the focus of this section. Trapping for these types of events is often used to control what action occurs when a user presses a specific key combination. Using keyboard events is helpful when you are building applications where the user is not relying solely on using a mouse, such as in a point-of-sale application.

You can use three types of key events within your application:

KeyDown   Occurs when the user presses a key or key combination

KeyUp   Occurs when the user releases a key or key combination

KeyPress   Occurs when the user presses and releases a key or key combination

 These key events apply only to forms and controls on forms, not controls on reports.

 Keyboard characters for key events are passed as ASCII. You can determine the ASCII equivalent for each key by viewing the Character Set listing in Microsoft Access VBA Help.

Using KeyUp and KeyDown events

You use the KeyDown and KeyUp events to set actions when a key or key combination is pressed or released. These events use the following syntax. Notice two arguments are used with this event: KeyCode and Shift.

```
Sub controlname_KeyDown(KeyCode As Integer, ByVal Shift As Integer)
```

As an example, the frm_Main Menu form in the Check Writer sample application contains the following KeyDown event code:

```
Private Sub Form_KeyDown(KeyCode As Integer, Shift As Integer)
If KeyCode = vbKeyF6 Then   'F6 Key
  MsgBox "This is an example of a KeyDown event"
End If
KeyCode = 0
End Sub
```

When the user presses the F6 key, designated by the KeyCode vbKeyF6, a message box is displayed. The KeyCode is then set to 0. There is a separate KeyCode constant for each key on the keyboard. A list of these keys is found in Microsoft Access VBA Help.

The previous code displays the message box if the user presses F6, Ctrl+F6, Shift+F6, or Alt+F6. Suppose you want the message box to display only if the user presses the Ctrl+F6 key combination. In this case, you revise the KeyDown event to the following:

```
Private Sub Form_KeyDown(KeyCode As Integer, Shift As Integer)
If KeyCode = vbKeyF6 And Shift=acCtrlMask Then   'Ctrl F6 Key
```

```
    MsgBox "This is an example of a KeyDown event"
End If
KeyCode = 0
End Sub
```

The Shift argument checks for the state of the Ctrl, Shift, and Alt keys at the time of the event. By including a check for this, you can determine the key combination used and the action to take. The following constants are used for each of these special keys:

acCtrlMask   Constant for the Ctrl key

acShiftMask   Constant for the Shift key

acAltMask   Constant for the Alt key

Each Shift argument is assigned a separate value. For example, the value for Ctrl is 2, whereas the value for Ctrl+Alt is 6. You can view the Access Help for a list of values for each special key type used in the Shift argument.

You can use the arguments for the KeyDown, KeyPress, **and** KeyUp **events, in conjunction with the arguments for the** MouseDown, MouseUp, **and** MouseMove **events to make your application work smoothly for both keyboard and mouse users.**

In some cases, you may want to control what does not happen when the user presses a specific key or key combination. For example, in Microsoft Access, whenever the F11 key is pressed, the database container is displayed. You can stop your users from being able to access the database container by adding the following code behind a form's KeyDown event:

```
Private Sub Form_KeyDown(KeyCode As Integer, Shift As Integer)
If KeyCode = F11 Then   'F11 Key
KeyCode = 0
End If
End Sub
```

This automatically sets the KeyCode to 0 when the F11 key is pressed, so the F11 key event, in essence, becomes disabled.

Using the KeyPress event

The KeyPress event occurs when the user presses and releases a key or key combination that corresponds to an ANSI code while a form or control has the focus. The event can involve only printable characters, such as the Ctrl key combined with a character from the standard alphabet or a special character, and the Enter or Backspace key. The syntax of this event is as follows:

```
Private Sub Form_KeyPress(KeyAscii As Integer)
```

Unlike the KeyUp and KeyDown events, the KeyPress event does not indicate the physical state of the keyboard. Instead, it indicates the ANSI characters that correspond to the key or key combination that is pressed. Because it handles only ANSI keys, you can use the Chr and Asc functions to convert the KeyAscii argument between an ASCII character and the equivalent ANSI character. For example:

```
fkey=Chr(KeyAscii)
KeyAscii=Asc(fkey)
```

If you want to use a keyboard event for a nonprinting character, such as the function keys or navigation keys, you should use the KeyDown **or** KeyUp **event.**

KeyPress **interprets the uppercase and lowercase of each character as separate key codes and, therefore, as two separate characters.**

If you hold down a key, the KeyPress **event occurs repeatedly.**

Understanding the KeyPreview property

You can use the KeyPreview property to create a keyboard-handling procedure for a form. This enables you to specify whether form-level keyboard events are invoked before a control's keyboard events. The KeyPreview property is set to False (No) by default. With this setting, only the active control receives keyboard events. If the KeyPreview property is set to True (Yes), as shown in Figure 11-11, the form receives the keyboard event first, and then the active control receives the keyboard event.

Figure 11-11 *Setting the KeyPreview property.*

Using AutoKeys

You can assign an action to a specific key or key combination using an AutoKeys macro group. When the user presses the key or key combination, Access performs the action. AutoKeys are useful if you want to perform an action behind shortcut keys you have used in custom menu bars or toolbars. Selecting the shortcut key on the bar automatically performs a specific action.

 If you assign an action to a key combination that Access is already using, the action you assign to the key combination replaces the Access key assignment.

You can create an AutoKeys macro by performing the following steps:

1. Create a new macro.
2. In the Macro Name column, type the key or key combination to which you want to assign an action or set of actions.
3. Add the action(s) you want the key or key combination to carry out.
4. Save the macro group with the name **AutoKeys**.

The new key assignments are in effect as soon as you save the macro group and are available each time you open the database. You can select one of several types of key assignments for the Macro Name field. Table 11-1 lists the types of key assignments you can use.

Table 11-1   *Key Assignments for Macros*

Key Code	Key Assignment
^B or ^3	Ctrl+any letter or number key
{F3}	Any function key
^{F3}	Ctrl+any function key
+{F3}	Shift+any function key
{INSERT}	Ins
+{INSERT}	Ctrl+Ins
{DELETE} OR {DEL}	Del
^{DELETE} OR {DEL}	Ctrl+Del
+{DELETE} OR {DEL}	Shift+Del

Figure 11-12 shows the properties for a submenu item located on a custom menu bar. Notice that a shortcut has been set up for this item. When the user presses Ctrl+A, you want the About form to open.

If you haven't set up an AutoKeys macro with this key combination defined, nothing happens when the user presses the key combination. To make it work, add the following macro name and action to the AutoKeys macro as shown in Figure 11-13.

Figure 11-12   *A shortcut key for a submenu item.*

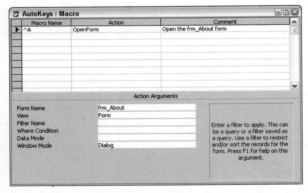

Figure 11-13   *Adding a macro name to the AutoKeys macro group.*

Done!

REVIEW

In this session, you learned that it's important to provide users with a means for navigating an application. These specific topics were covered:

- You can add navigability in two ways: by creating switchboards and by creating custom menu bars.
- You can use keyboard events behind various forms in an application to control certain actions, including the overall behavior of the form.

QUIZ YOURSELF

1. What are two ways to provide navigation for your application? (See "Creating a Custom Application Switchboard" and "Building a Custom Menu.")

2. What types of functions can be performed from switchboards? (See "Creating a Custom Application Switchboard" and "Adding intelligence to switchboard buttons.")

3. How can you create a custom menu bar? (See "Building a Custom Menu.")

4. How do you create and enable a shortcut key on a menu or submenu? (See "Setting properties for menu items and commands.")

5. How can you make a custom menu bar the global menu bar? (See "Attaching the menu bar to a form.")

6. What are the three types of keyboard events? (See "Using Keyboard Events.")

7. How can you prevent the database container from being displayed when the user presses F11? (See "Using KeyUp and KeyDown events.")

8. Why are AutoKeys macro groups used? (See "Using AutoKeys.")

Using Unbound Forms

Session Checklist

✔ Defining unbound forms

✔ Examining record locking and the functionality of unbound forms

✔ Using ADO programming for unbound forms

✔ Creating a simple unbound form

**30 Min.
To Go**

This session covers the use and programming associated with unbound forms. These types of forms require a significant amount of programming and provide a good foundation for learning how to connect to data sources programmatically, as well as how to work with the properties and methods of an Access form.

What Are Unbound Forms?

Access makes it easy to create a form and bind it to a record source. It might be worthwhile to repeat that last sentence: *Access makes it easy to create a form and bind it to a record source*. Many Access features work behind the scenes to simplify form design and form use, not only for the developer, but for the end user as well. With little training, a user can create a completely functional form bound to a table or query. The user then has the capability to add, edit, or delete records, as well as to navigate between records. Access provides wizards with which users can build the forms. It doesn't get much easier. But these forms are all bound forms. A *bound form* is a form tied directly to a record source that provides a constant connection and open view of the underlying data. Bound forms are simple to build, but they are not always the best approach to use when the application is running.

An *unbound form* is a form that does not have a constant connection and open view of the underlying data. It can behave like a bound form, but instead of maintaining a constant connection, it retrieves one record at a time programmatically. In other words, VBA code behind the form controls the retrieval and saving of data. The code has to do a lot more than that, and these capabilities are covered later in this session.

Why Use Unbound Forms?

There are several reasons to use unbound forms:

- You can use them to solve record-locking conflicts.
- They request the minimal amount of data, thereby improving performance.
- You can include a means to cancel the changes to a record in case the user changes his or her mind.
- You can include a means for the user to confirm saving a record.
- You can programmatically perform a record validation before the record is saved.
- All record changes are under the control of code rather than Access or the property setting of a bound form.
- Unbound forms are required for transaction processing.

With all these great reasons, why wouldn't you want to use unbound forms? First, a lot of code is required to duplicate the functionality of a bound form. You need to handle not only data retrieval and saving, but also navigation, error checking, data validation, and so on. It is also difficult to provide continuous forms or a datasheet view, which a bound form can easily do.

Consider these facts about using unbound forms: When you use unbound forms, you have to handle functions that are automatic with Access bound forms. These functions include record locking, the functions that connect the form to a data source, reading and writing of data, and searching for data.

Record locking

Using an unbound form can limit the time a record is locked. For a bound form, the record is locked from the time the user first makes a change in the first field until the time the record is saved. This may take a few seconds or several minutes. For unbound forms, the record is locked only for the split second it takes to update it. When the unbound form saves a record, you should check whether the record was changed since you first retrieved it. This is necessary if the record was not locked when it was loaded onto the form.

 It makes sense to design the form based on the bound record source so that controls relating to the fields can easily be added to the form. Then, after you design the form layout, remove the record source and add the necessary code to make the form work.

Functionality

When using an unbound form, you need to create code to handle the following functions because you can't rely on Access to do this:

- Connecting to the record source
- Selecting/finding a record or records from a record source
- Loading up the controls on the form with data
- Retrieving the record(s)
- Editing a record
- Saving a record
- Adding a new record
- Deleting a record
- Moving among multiple records, including going to the first record, last record, next record, and previous record
- Undoing changes made to the record before it is saved

These functions are the basic ones; in this session, you use ADO to learn about them.

It is always good programming practice to make your code as modular and flexible as possible. Therefore, the code you create for the previous functions must be as generic as possible so that you can reuse it. To do that, you put the general functions into a module rather than into the class module associated with the form. This enables the general functions to be shared by other unbound forms without repeating them in each form. Code specific to a form should be located with the form. This also minimizes the code behind the form, which allows it to load more quickly.

Although you can create a generic form to use for different record sources, this task is beyond the scope of this session. To keep things simple, this session covers recordsets with only one key field.

Programming for Unbound Forms

You can find the code for this section in the module mod_UnboundFormUtilities and the form frm_BankAccountsUnbound in the sample application.

The unbound form functions

The module mod_UnboundFormUtilities contains several of the functions required to make an unbound form work, including the following:

dbc_NewRecord	Adds a new record
dbc_SaveRecord	Saves the current data on the form to a new or existing record
dbc_FindRecord	Finds a set of records meeting a criteria
dbc_DisplayRecord	Retrieves and displays a selected record

dbc_DeleteRecord	Deletes a record
dbc_ClearForm	Clears all fields on the form contained in the record source
dbc_SetEditedFlag	Is called by a field on the form when it is updated

Most of these functions require a form parameter to be passed, which is the form that calls the function and contains the data.

The unbound form references

To use the aforementioned functions, the unbound form must contain the following text box controls loaded with the appropriate values to tell the functions which data to connect to and to identify the key field. These controls are subsequently referred to as the form's *X controls*:

| xProvider | xRecordset |
| xDataSource | xKey |

In Sessions 9 and 10 you learned about ActiveX Data Objects (ADO). These objects are used here to connect to the data sources. To simplify the code for this session, these functions are limited to a single key field. The key field(s) can be retrieved from an ActiveX Data Objects Extensions (ADOX) table definition, but you don't want to use ADOX here. Instead, you want to provide for maximum flexibility in case you connect to a non-Jet database. The only reference needed is for the object ADODB, which is the standard object for the ActiveX Data Objects library.

In addition, the unbound form must contain the following check box controls:

| flagEdited | The default value of False, used to determine if the user has changed any data. |
| flagFind | The default value of True, used to allow instant Find when the form is opened. Used with the Find function to determine whether search criteria were entered. |

The controls on the form that relate to fields in the record source must be named with the same name as the fields. To handle default values on the form, you cannot use the default value property because the unbound controls automatically display that value. Instead, you put any default values in the control's Tag property, which is a property Access doesn't use.

You also use the form's Filter property to store the criteria for the recordset. This can be set to determine the initial recordset or just left blank.

Each function is discussed in detail because each is an important part of understanding unbound forms and record handling with ADO. Some of the code is also discussed in detail as necessary, but the discussion is not repeated for the same code in other functions.

Adding a new record

To add a new record to the recordset as specified by the form's X controls, you must establish a connection to the recordset. The New Record function does this after it first checks to see if any data has been changed or entered on the form (see Listing 12-1). The form's `flagEdited` control is used for this.

Listing 12-1   *The New Record Function*

```
Public Function dbc_NewRecord(frm As Form)
'Adds a new record

Dim strConnection As String
Dim cnn As New ADODB.Connection
Dim rst As New ADODB.RecordSet
Dim fld As ADODB.Field
Dim ctl As Control
Dim vartemp As Variant

    On Error GoTo ErrorHandler

    'reset find flag if set
    frm.FlagFind = False

    'Check to see if data has been changed
    If frm.FlagEdited Then
        If MsgBox("Do you want to save your changes", _
            vbYesNo) = vbYes Then
            dbc_SaveRecord frm
        Else
            frm.FlagEdited = False
        End If
    End If

    'Open connection
    cnn.Open frm.Controls("xProvider") & _
        frm.Controls("xDataSource")

    'Open recordset with no records
    rst.Open "Select * From " & frm.Controls("xRecordset") & _
        " Where True;", cnn, adOpenStatic

    'Iterate through controls on form that match fields in
    'recordset
    For Each ctl In frm

        'if error the field is not on the form
        On Error Resume Next
        Err = 0
```

Continued

Listing 12-1 *Continued*

```
            vartemp = rst.Fields(ctl.Name).Name
        If Err = 0 Then
            On Error GoTo ErrorHandler
            'if control enables then set default value from tag
            '   and set focus if tab index 0
            If ctl.Enabled Then
                If IsNull(ctl.Tag) Then
                    ctl.Value = Null
                Else
                    ctl.Value = ctl.Tag
                End If
                If ctl.TabIndex = 0 Then ctl.SetFocus
            End If
        End If
    Next
GoTo Done

ErrorHandler:
    MsgBox Err.Description
Done:

End Function
```

The flag works similarly to the Access form's `Dirty` property. Whenever a value in a field on the form has changed, the flag is set to `True`. This is done by adding the function call `dbc_SetEditedFlag()` to the `AfterUpdate` event property for all the controls on the form that are part of the recordset.

If data has been entered or changed, the New Record function displays a message asking the user whether he or she wants the record saved. If so, the `dbc_SaveRecord` function is called first before a new record is added.

Adding a new record is a three-step process:

1. Clear the fields on the form, set them to their default value, and set focus to the first field.
2. Allow the user to enter the data.
3. Save the record.

Step 1 is accomplished by the remaining section of the New Record function. Control is then passed to the user. When the user clicks a Save button, the record is saved using the `dbc_SaveRecord` function.

Note that the `dbc_NewRecord` function iterates through the controls on the form that are enabled and that also have corresponding fields in the recordset. This prevents controls on the form that don't contain data from being cleared.

After the user clicks a Save button, the form's `On Click` event for that button should call the function `dbc_SaveRecord`, passing it the name of the form containing the data.

Refer to the code for this function in the sample file in the module mod_UnboundFormUtilities on this book's companion Web site.

The function first checks to see if the form has been edited. If not, the function simply exits. Otherwise, it opens a connection to the recordset. It does this not to retrieve any records, but simply to determine the type of the key field so that a criteria string can be created. The criteria string is used to search the recordset for a record with the same key field. This is necessary so the function can determine whether to update an existing record or create a new record.

If it is a new record, the function uses the AddNew method and iterates through the controls on the form that match the fields in the recordset. It then creates a record with the new data. If a record exists with the same key field, these fields are copied to the recordset, and the record is updated. The fields are also checked to see if any field is an Auto Increment type and whether it is enabled. If it is, the field value is not updated.

For simplicity, the example does not deal with checking the existing record to see if another user has changed the record since it was last retrieved. This code should be added for a multi-user system.

After the record has been successfully saved, the user is informed and flagEdited is reset.

Finding records

You can find records using the function dbc_FindRecord. This function is based on the capability to enter criteria on the form in any field control. The function works in two passes as determined by the control flagFind on the form. If this flag is True, the form contains the criteria to do the find. If it is False, the form is cleared so the user can enter the criteria. A message is displayed telling the user to enter the criteria and to click the Find button again to retrieve the records.

You can set the default value of this flag to True so that when the form is opened, the user can start entering criteria right away. After the function is finished, the resulting criteria are stored in the Form's filter property for later use. The function checks to see if the current record has been saved before clearing the form out for the criteria.

Refer to the code for this function in the sample file in the module mod_UnboundFormUtilities on the companion Web site. There is an option set by a constant named AllowAllRecords that, when set, retrieves all records from the recordset if no criteria are specified. If set to False, the user is warned that no criteria are entered and no records are retrieved.

The heart of this function's operations is creating a criteria string. It provides a very flexible mechanism for the user to find a record. Any combination of fields on the form can be used, and the function creates a criteria using AND logic between all the fields selected. For example, in our sample application, you can enter a state and all records for that state are retrieved. If a user knows an account or a bank, he or she can enter those as well. The trick to making the criteria string is to find the fields on the form that the user has filled in and then to look up the types of the fields in the recordset to determine how to format the criteria string.

For text fields, you must enclose the search value in quotes; for dates, you must enclose the search value with a pound (#) sign. For numbers, no delimiter is needed. To create the criteria string, the recordset is opened without retrieving any records. This is done with the `Where` clause equal to `False`. The code then cycles through all the controls on the form that match the field names. If the control value is not a zero-length string or is not null, the field name and the field value are added to the criteria string.

When all the controls have been checked, the recordset is opened with the criteria. If the record count is not zero, the criteria string is stored in the forms `Filter` property and the first record is displayed on the form.

The actual retrieval of the data and populating of the form is done with the `dbc_DisplayRecord` function. Refer to the code for this function in the sample file in the module mod_UnboundFormUtilities. Because only one record is retrieved at a time, the `DisplayRecord` function gets only one record based on the record source, the filter property of the form, and the record number passed as an argument to the function. The function returns the current number of recordsets based on those parameters. This information is useful when you want to fill in a control on a form such as the total number of records.

Before processing, this function checks to see if the user has changed any data on the form. If data has been entered and changed and not saved, as determined by the `flagEdited` control, the user is prompted to save the record.

The connection to the data is opened using the X controls and the `Filter` property of the form, if it exists. The function then moves to the specified record based on the argument `intRecord`. As in previous functions, the code iterates through the controls on the form that match a field in the recordset, and the code, thereby, populates the control.

Deleting records

The `dbc_DeleteRecord` function has a flow similar to the previous functions. It first prompts the user to confirm the deletion; next, it opens the recordset and moves to the record based on the argument `intRecord`. It then uses the `Delete` and `UpdateBatch` methods to carry out the delete action.

It is up to the VBA code in the calling form to determine what to do next. In our sample application, the calling form displays the first record of the current recordset after the deletion is complete.

How to Create a Simple Unbound Form

**10 Min.
To Go**

In this section, you use the sample Check Writer application and a form to work with the Bank Accounts table. The form name is frm_BankAccountsUnbound, and it can be found in the sample application on this book's companion Web site.

Figure 12-1 shows the frm_BankAccountsUnbound form in Normal view.

This form contains almost all the features you need to add, edit, delete, and find records. The form footer contains a series of buttons to provide these functions and more. The Undo button enables the user to redisplay a record after changes have been made but before the Save button is clicked. The Print button opens another form in the application, which is a dialog box providing choices about what to print. Finally, the Done button closes the form and, if the record wasn't saved, prompts the user to save it.

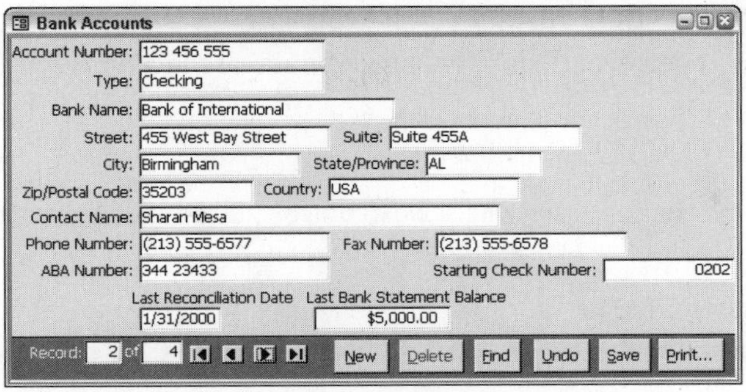

Figure 12-1   *An unbound form in Normal view.*

When dealing with an unbound form, the changes to the record are not saved until the Save button is clicked.

The record navigation buttons found in a bound Access form are re-created here. The Access record navigation buttons cannot be used because the form is not bound to a record source. There are also controls to show the user the current record number as well as the total number of records.

Because of the unique functions created to handle unbound forms (described in the previous section), this form needs to have some special controls that are invisible to the user. These are shown on the form with red text in the upper-right portion of the form (see Figure 12-2). The `Visible` property of these controls is set to `False` so they cannot be seen when the user is using the form.

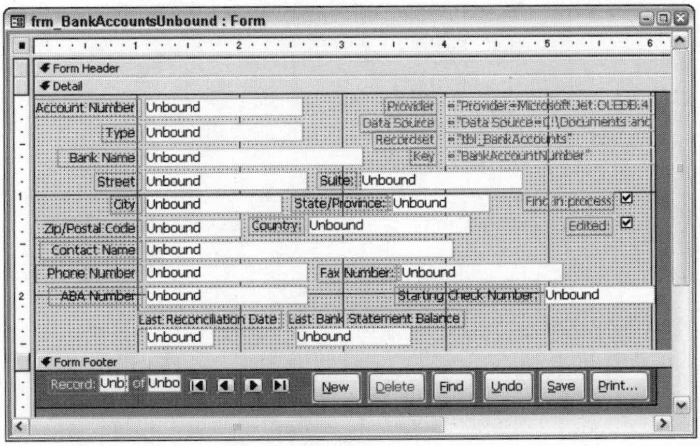

Figure 12-2   *An unbound form in Design view.*

On the top-right of the form are four controls referred to previously as the X controls. They are named and must be set to the appropriate values to work. The values that follow are used in our sample application and are put in the control source property:

xProvider ="Provider=Microsoft.Jet.OLEDB.4.0;"

xDataSource = (Set on form's open event based on current database location)

xRecordset ="tbl_BankAccounts"

xKey ="BankAccountNumber"

The unbound form also contains the following check box controls, also hidden, located on the right side of the screen.

flagEdited with default value of False

flagFind with default value of True

The form's remaining controls have no Control Source property set, and the form has no Record Source property set. You can optionally include a filter for the form with the Filter property. Each of the fields that you use from the recordset needs a control on the form with the same name as the recordset field name. Default values for the fields, if needed, are set in the Tag property, not the default property. Also, the controls for the fields need to have an entry for the After Update event property. This is a call to the function dbc_SetEditedFlag() to set the flagEdited control when the field value has changed.

This form has a minimum amount of code. Most of the code is in the module mod_UnboundFormUtilities. The code behind the form falls into two categories: form subroutines (see Listing 12-2) and button subroutines (see Listing 12-3). When the form loads, it displays the first record based on the X controls and the filter. When the form closes, the flagEdited control is checked to see if data has changed on the form; if the data has changed, the function prompts the user to save the form.

Listing 12-2   *Form Subroutines*

```
Private Sub Form_Load()
    Me.tbxRecordCount = dbc_DisplayRecord(Me, 1)
    If Me.tbxRecordCount > 0 Then Me.tbxRecordNumber = 1
    Me.FlagFind = False
End Sub

Private Sub Form_Unload(Cancel As Integer)
Dim Answer As Integer
    If Me.FlagEdited Then
        Answer = MsgBox("Do you want to save your changes?", vbYesNoCancel)
        If Answer = vbCancel Then Cancel = True
        If Answer = vbYes Then dbc_SaveRecord Me
    End If
End Sub
```

Each button has a subroutine. These subroutines use calls to the general functions as described in the previous sections. Also referenced frequently are the controls tbxRecordNumber and tbxRecordCount, which are text box controls containing information about the current record number and the total number of records. These are referenced by almost all the subroutines to keep track of the location in the current recordset.

Listing 12-3   *Button Subroutines*

```
Private Sub cmdDelete_Click()
    If Not IsNull(Me.tbxRecordNumber) Then
        dbc_DeleteRecord Me, Me.tbxRecordNumber
        Me.tbxRecordCount = dbc_DisplayRecord(Me, 1)
        Me.tbxRecordNumber = 1
    End If
End Sub

Private Sub cmdDone_Click()
    On Error Resume Next
    DoCmd.Close acForm, Me.Name
End Sub

Private Sub cmdFind_Click()
    Me.tbxRecordCount = dbc_FindRecord(Me)
    If Me.tbxRecordCount > 0 Then Me.tbxRecordNumber = 1
End Sub

Private Sub cmdFirst_Click()
    Me.tbxRecordCount = dbc_DisplayRecord(Me, 1)
    Me.tbxRecordNumber = 1
End Sub

Private Sub cmdNew_Click()
    Me.tbxRecordCount = Null
    Me.tbxRecordNumber = Null
    dbc_NewRecord Me
End Sub

Private Sub cmdPrevious_Click()
    If Me.tbxRecordNumber > 1 Then
        Me.tbxRecordCount = dbc_DisplayRecord(Me, Me.tbxRecordNumber - 1)
        Me.tbxRecordNumber = Me.tbxRecordNumber - 1
    End If
End Sub

Private Sub cmdNext_Click()
    If Me.tbxRecordNumber < Me.tbxRecordCount Then
        Me.tbxRecordCount = dbc_DisplayRecord(Me, Me.tbxRecordNumber + 1)
        Me.tbxRecordNumber = Me.tbxRecordNumber + 1
    End If
End Sub

Private Sub cmdLast_Click()
    Me.tbxRecordNumber = dbc_DisplayRecord(Me, Me.tbxRecordCount)
End Sub

Private Sub cmdSave_Click()
    dbc_SaveRecord Me
End Sub

Private Sub cmdUndo_Click()
    If Me.FlagEdited And Me.tbxRecordNumber > 0 Then
```

Continued

Listing 12-3 *Continued*

```
        dbc_DisplayRecord Me, Me.tbxRecordNumber
        Me.FlagEdited = False
    End If
End Sub

Private Sub cmdPrint_Click()
    DoCmd.OpenForm "yBank Print Dialog"
End Sub
```

Done!

REVIEW

A lot of good reasons exist to use unbound forms, but some very strong reasons also exist not to use them. These topics were covered:

- Unbound forms can improve performance significantly, but they also require a lot of development time.
- When using unbound forms, you need to duplicate in code the functionality that Access provides with bound forms.
- ADO provides the necessary functionality to program unbound forms.

QUIZ YOURSELF

1. What is the difference between a bound and unbound form? (See "What Are Unbound Forms?")
2. When should you use unbound forms instead of bound forms? (See "Why Use Unbound Forms?")
3. What are the precautions for record locking for unbound forms? (See "Record locking.")
4. What functions need to be programmatically added to an unbound form to achieve the same functionality as an Access bound form? (See "Programming for Unbound Forms.")
5. Why would you use ADODB rather than ADOX as the data object for unbound forms? (See "The unbound form references.")

Programming Check Box, Option Group, Combo, and List Box Controls

Session Checklist

✔ Handling true/false selections with a check box

✔ Programming option control groups

✔ Working with combo and list boxes

✔ Handling items not in a combo/list box listing

✔ Selecting and handling multiple choices in list boxes

**30 Min.
To Go**

Learning to program check box, option group, combo box, and list box controls gives you a powerful and flexible arsenal of interfaces. With a little ingenuity, creativity, and programming knowledge, you can make the forms that use these controls more robust and dynamic. You can use these controls, alone or in conjunction with others, to collect data, control how your forms look, and limit or expand options and choices.

Handling True/False Selections with a Check Box

You have, most likely, already used check box, option button, or toggle button controls when you are recording Boolean data types. For yes/no or true/false information, these controls offer ideal simplicity and effectiveness. When coupled with code, they become even more useful and, in fact, very powerful tools. The examples in this session focus on the check box control. You can easily apply the same technique to an option button or a toggle button.

Figures 13-1 and 13-2 show the frm_CheckWriter form from the Check Writer database. The figures show two instances of the same form. There is a Void check box on the bottom left of both forms. The form in Figure 13-1 has the Void check box cleared, whereas the form in Figure 13-2 has the box checked and includes a large gray shaded stamp that reads VOID across the face of the check. Because the Void check box could easily be missed as the user navigates from record to record, the form was designed with the stamp as a visual cue for the user.

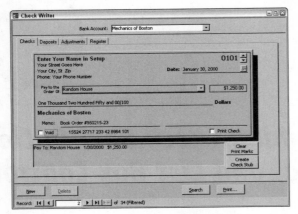

Figure 13-1   *A view of the frm_CheckWriter form with the Void check box cleared.*

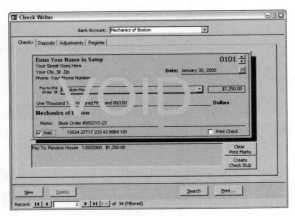

Figure 13-2   *A view of the frm_CheckWriter form with the Void check box selected and the VOID stamp visible.*

By definition, a check box, option button, or toggle button can be only true or false, giving the controls either a positive or negative state. Additionally, because of their unusually small size, these options can be very easily overlooked. Using additional visual cues, such as the VOID stamp, makes the controls more effective. This is especially vital for important information such as whether a check is void.

This check box serves two functions. Just as you mark a check as voided in a real checkbook, you can do the same in the Check Writer sample program. On the frm_CheckWriter form, the Void check box is bound to a field also named Void. This is used to store information about whether the current check record is voided in the table. This control is no different from any other bound control. Figure 13-3 shows how the form looks in Design view. Selecting the check box marks the record as being voided. The code in the `After Update` event of the check box displays the VOID stamp across the check to indicate that the check has been voided.

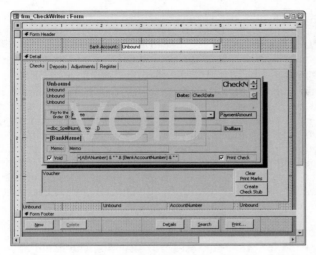

Figure 13-3　*The Design view of the frm_CheckWriter form showing the check box and the VOID stamp.*

The code in Listing 13-1 shows the After Update event of the Void check box. It determines whether the transaction type is a check and what the value of the check box is. The VOID stamp becomes visible if the transaction is a check and the Void field is True. To turn the VOID stamp on, the code initiates a With statement and references the CodeContextObject property. By using the With statement, we reduce the need to reference the object multiple times. In this case, it is the frm_CheckWriter form, which eliminates the need to refer explicitly to each control.

Listing 13-1　*The After Update Event for the Void Check Box*

```
Private Sub Void_AfterUpdate()

    On Error GoTo ErrorHandler

    With CodeContextObject
        If (.[TransType] = "Check" And (.Void = False Or IsNull(.Void))) Then
            .[Void Stamp].Visible = False
        End If
        If (.[TransType] = "Check" And (.Void = True And Not IsNull(.Void))) Then
            .[Void Stamp].Visible = True
        End If
    End With

    GoTo Done

ErrorHandler:
    MsgBox Err.Description
Done:
End Sub
```

The code shown in Listing 13-1 uses two If...Then statements. Both of them work the same way; each determines the transaction type of the record. The void status applies only to checks and not to deposits or adjustments. In the first condition, if the transaction is a check and the Void field equals False or is null, the VOID stamp's visible property is set to False. This means it is not displayed. The second If...Then statement checks for the check transaction but checks for a True value, verifies that the field is not null in the Void field, and sets the VOID stamp's visible property to True. This causes the stamp to be displayed.

A key point to remember when using this technique is that, whether because of a visual cue such as the VOID stamp or for another reason, the status of a particular field may change as you navigate from record to record. Because the value may change, the form must respond accordingly. One record may be voided and the next may not be. It is, therefore, vitally important to check the status and have the form display the correct visual cue as you move from record to record. This is done in the form's On Current event. Reviewing the code in the On Current event, you see the exact same code as in the After Update event of the Void check box. As the user moves from record to record, the On Current event fires and checks the transaction and the Void field. The VOID stamp displays appropriately.

This particular example displays a visual cue. You could use the same technique and different code for other purposes. For example, you could have a field named Locked, and you could have code that locks the form based on a particular field. Your creativity is the key to the many ways these controls and techniques can be used.

Programming Option Group Controls

What if you want to have more than a simple True or False value available? The individuality of a check box can be limiting. For instance, you may want the user to choose one of six different values instead of just two. This is where an option group is effective. Whereas a check box can be tied to a single field (making it a True/False value), an option group gives you more flexibility.

Toggle buttons, option buttons, or check box controls can be used separately or as part of a group, as shown in Figure 13-4. The top half of the figure shows two sets of controls. The controls change state when they are active and inactive. When used independently, these controls can represent a two-state Yes/No or True/False data type. When used as a group, these controls become a single entity of an option group in which each option selected now represents a numbered value.

Technically, a Boolean field has three states, yes/true, no/false, and null. For the purposes of this session, we treat a null value in a Boolean field as false or no. In your programming, there may be instances where you must differentiate between a value of no/false versus a null value. Remember a null value indicates no value. This could mean, for instance, that the user chose not to check the option or that it was not applicable. This can, in itself, be an important piece of data.

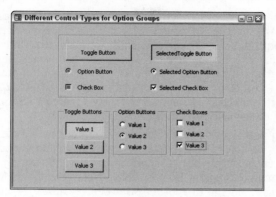

Figure 13-4 *Examples of an option group and the different control types.*

The bottom half of Figure 13-4 shows three separate option groups. In this example, each option group has only three choices. You could just as easily have four, five, or more. The option group, as a whole, can have only one value associated with it and is bound to a single field. Each option group in the example is toggled among one of the three choices. These controls can be very useful and effective when you need to provide several options but want to tie the selection value to a stored field to produce an action. The Check Writer program provides many examples of option groups, two of which are presented here.

An option group functions as just that — a group. Within the option group, you can have any number of values to select from. However, you cannot select multiple items in the option group. The group can hold or store only a single value returned by the different options.

Figure 13-5 shows the frm_DialogCheckPrint form. This form opens when you click the Print button on the frm_CheckWriter form and is what the user sees when printing out a check. Several options and conditions are available based on the choices, and the form works like this: The user clicks the Print button on the frm_CheckWriter form. The Print dialog box opens and the user is presented with options, the first of which is Check Type. There are three alternating toggle buttons for the Check Type options: Check stock with the check on top, check stock with the check on the bottom, or a continuous sheet of checks.

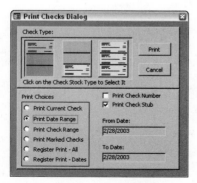

Figure 13-5 *The Print Checks dialog for the Check Writer program showing two option groups.*

Beneath the Check Type section is the Print Choices section. Here, the user can choose between printing the current check, a range of checks based on the date, a range of checks by check number, checks marked for printing, or printing the register for all transactions or for a specific date selection. Notice that as you change from one option to the next in the Print Choices section, additional controls appear and disappear to prompt you for more input. In addition, the user can choose whether to print check numbers on the printout and whether to print the check stub. When the selections have all been made, the user clicks the Print button to initiate the printing of the selected check(s) or register.

Two separate option groups are being used on this form. The first is under Check Type, where toggle buttons are used to indicate which style of checks to use. The second group uses option buttons that offer six different print choices from which to select. Changing the print choices to either Print Date Range or Register Print — Dates causes two fields to appear on the form: From Date and To Date. Moving to another print choice causes the controls to disappear.

 Notice the use of pictures on the Check Type toggle buttons. In the CheckWriter sample, bitmap images of check styles are created and placed on the buttons. Adding images to buttons is an excellent way to make a form and interface more user-friendly.

The code shown in Listing 13-2 illustrates this use of the option group. The initial lines of code set the Visible property of several controls to False. When you use the frm_DialogCheckPrint form and make certain choices in the option group for Print Choices, additional controls appear and disappear. These conditional controls are set to be invisible in the first eight lines of code. Why? To "reset" the interface as the user moves from option to option, thereby eliminating the need for extensive lines of code to determine which option was selected last. All the controls that could be affected by any of the choices are set to invisible. This makes the previously selected value irrelevant; the remaining code determines what current value is selected and proceeds from there.

Listing 13-2   *The After Update Event of the Option Group for Print Choices*

```
Private Sub Type_of_Print_AfterUpdate()
  With Me
    ![From Check].Visible = False
    ![To Check].Visible = False
    ![From Check Text].Visible = False
    ![To Check Text].Visible = False
    ![From Date].Visible = False
    ![To Date].Visible = False
    ![From Date Text].Visible = False
    ![To Date Text].Visible = False
    If ![Type of Print] = 2 Or Me![Type of Print] = 6 Then
      ![From Date].Visible = True
      ![To Date].Visible = True
      ![From Date Text].Visible = True
      ![To Date Text].Visible = True
    End If
    If ![Type of Print] = 3 Then
      ![From Check].Visible = True
      ![To Check].Visible = True
```

```
            ![From Check Text].Visible = True
            ![To Check Text].Visible = True
        End If
    End With
```

Working with Combo and List Boxes

The combo box and list box are the only Access controls that enable you to see multiple columns (or fields) of data in a single listing. These two can be very useful because of this feature. Figure 13-6 shows a combo box used in the frm_CheckWriter form. At the top of the form is a combo box listing the available bank accounts that can be selected. Clicking the drop-down arrow shows a listing of the Bank Name, Account Type, and Account Number. This example also illustrates how a combo box can be extended beyond a simple selection control. When you select a different bank account, the form is updated to display transaction records that apply only to that account.

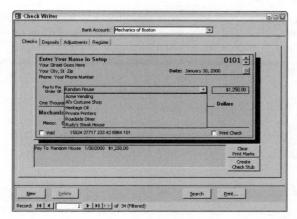

Figure 13-6   *A Combo Box used in the frm_CheckWriter form.*

Understanding the differences between combo boxes and list boxes

Table 13-1 is a comparison of combo and list boxes and their related features. Figure 13-7 is an example of a form with combo boxes and a list box.

Table 13-1   *Combo Box and List Box Feature Comparison*

Feature	Combo Box	List Box
Size/Space	When not selected by the user, compresses to the height of a single field.	Has the size and dimensions that you assign. Displays more than one row of information and is always open.

Continued

Table 13-1   *Continued*

Feature	Combo Box	List Box
Typing	Allows for fill-in-as-you-type feature. For instance, as you type **A**, it goes to the first instance of A in the column. If you then type **B**, the first instance of AB comes up. This continues until no more matches can be made.	Typing a letter brings you to the first item that starts with that letter. If you type **A**, the focus moves to the first instance of A. If you then type **B**, the focus moves to the first instance of B, disregarding the previously typed A.
Choice	You can choose from the list or enter a value not in the listing, depending on which setting you choose in the Limit to List property.	You can select only the items in the list.
Selection	Allows for only one selection.	Gives you different levels of selection, from a single selection to multiple selections.

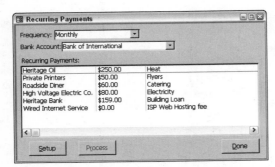

Figure 13-7   *An example of a form with combo boxes and a list box.*

Both the combo box and list box are powerful controls because they can display more than just a single field of data. You can define multiple columns for a single record or row and bind that to a particular field. These controls become vastly more useful as you learn more about using their properties.

Figures 13-8 and 13-9 show the property sheet dialog box for a combo box and a list box, respectively. Notice that in addition to the universal properties such as Name and Control Source, these two controls also have other similar properties. It is important that you have a solid understanding of these properties because they dramatically affect how your controls work. As the examples show, you can programmatically set these properties to greatly affect the appearance and function of the control. Please refer to the on-line help in Access for a full listing of each and every property as it relates to combo and list boxes.

Figure 13-8　*Property sheet dialog box for a sample combo box.*

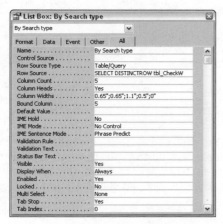

Figure 13-9　*Property sheet dialog box for a sample list box.*

In addition to the common properties that list boxes and combo boxes share, each has some properties unique to that interface. Table 13-2 shows the additional properties associated with a combo box.

Although Access uses a zero-based numbering system when referencing the columns in VBA code, when referencing the bound column, it uses a one-based system. This means that if you want to reference the first column in the Bound Column property of the control, you enter 1. To reference the same column in code, you enter 0.

Table 13-2 *Additional Properties for Combo Boxes*

Property	Description
List Rows	A value representing the number of rows of the list to show when the combo box is activated.
List Width	A separate value from the Width property of the control. The List Width can be narrower or wider than the actual width of the control. This is set in conjunction with the Column Widths property. Note that unless you specify the column widths, the default value of the control width is used. This means that if you have multiple columns and want to make them wide enough to adequately display the information, you must enter values for the columns. Otherwise, your columns are truncated unless they are set in this property.
Limit To List	A Yes/No value that determines if the item entered must match an existing item in the list or if other entries can be entered and accepted.

A list box has one additional property associated with it: Multi Select, a property that indicates whether to allow multiple selections. There are three possible settings: None, Simple, or Extended:

None	No multiple selections can be made.
Simple	Multiple selections are allowed. Clicking the row or pressing the Space bar on the keyboard selects and deselects a row.
Extended	Multiple selections are allowed. You select rows by clicking the row while pressing the Shift key. You can extend the selection by clicking the first row and using the mouse or arrow keys to select contiguous rows. Additionally, holding down the Ctrl key and clicking a row enables you to select or deselect that row.

Populating the controls

By referencing the Row Source Type and Row Source properties of either the combo box or list box in your VBA code, you can affect the information displayed. This gives you the capability to dynamically change the data source listed, the order (sorting), and which fields or columns to list.

For this example, refer to Figure 13-10, which shows the yCheck Search Dialog form that opens when you click the Find button on the Check Writer screen.

The yCheck Search Dialog form enables you to choose different types of searches based on the criteria. The Type of Search section lists five different options. Notice how the option group in this instance is used to control the display of the list box. As you change the type of search (for example, Checks By Check Number to Checks By Payee), the list box changes its display. You then scroll up and down until the desired row or record is displayed. Double-clicking closes the yCheck Search Dialog dialog form and opens the selected record. You can also select the desired record with a single click and click the OK button. This closes the form and takes you to the selected transaction.

Figure 13-10   *The yCheck Search Dialog form showing an option group and list box.*

This operates by changing the Row Source property of the list box, depending on which option is chosen for the search type (option group). Also notice that the type of information is not only changing, but the column widths also change to accommodate the differences in the information displayed. This example illustrates the dramatic effects gained by manipulating the Row Source and Column Widths properties programmatically.

Listing 13-3 is a partial code listing of the processes that occur in the After Update event of the option group and how these processes affect the list box display.

Listing 13-3   *After Update Event of the Type of Search Option Group*

```
Private Sub Type_of_Search_AfterUpdate()
    Me!Keyword.Visible = False
    With Me
      ![By Search type].RowSource = ""
      Select Case ![Type of search]
        Case 1
          Forms!frm_CheckWriter.TabControl.Pages("Checks").SetFocus
          ![Search Text].caption = "Select the Check Number to Search For"
          ![By Search type].ColumnCount = 5
          ![By Search type].ColumnWidths = ".65 in;.65 in;1.1 in;0.5 in;0 in"
          ![By Search type].BoundColumn = 5
          ![By Search type].RowSource = "SELECT [tbl_CheckWriter].[CheckNumber],
                  [tbl_CheckWriter].[CheckDate], [tbl_CheckWriter].Payee,
                  [tbl_CheckWriter].[PaymentAmount],[tbl_CheckWriter].[TransID] AS Amount
                  FROM [tbl_CheckWriter] WHERE (([tbl_CheckWriter].[TransType]='Check') and

[tbl_CheckWriter].[AccountNumber]=[Forms]![frm_CheckWriter]![BankAccountNumber])
                  ORDER BY [tbl_CheckWriter].[CheckNumber]"
        Case 2
          Forms!frm_CheckWriter.TabControl.Pages("Checks").SetFocus
          ![Search Text].caption = "Select the Payee Record to Search For"
          ![By Search type].ColumnCount = 5
          ![By Search type].ColumnWidths = "1.1 in;.65 in;.5 in;.65 in;0 in"
```

Continued

Listing 13-3   *Continued*

```
        ![By Search type].BoundColumn = 5
        ![By Search type].RowSource = "SELECT [tbl_CheckWriter].[Payee],
            [tbl_CheckWriter].[CheckDate],[tbl_CheckWriter].[CheckNumber],
            [tbl_CheckWriter].[PaymentAmount] As Amount,[tbl_CheckWriter].[TransID]
    FROM
            [tbl_CheckWriter] WHERE (([tbl_CheckWriter].[TransType]='Check') and

[tbl_CheckWriter].[AccountNumber]=[Forms]![frm_CheckWriter]![BankAccountNumber])
            ORDER BY [tbl_CheckWriter].[Payee],[tbl_CheckWriter].[CheckDate]"
```

This snippet of code performs several tasks. In this case, the example shows the code
for values 1 and 2 and for the options Checks By Check Number and Checks By Payee, as
they appear in the form. These are the values of the options in the option group. Analyzing
the code, you see that the settings for the list box are based on the case value. The code
changes the Caption property of the label control to correctly describe the type of search.
From there, the number of columns is set to five in the Column Count property.

In conjunction with the Column Count, the Column Widths property is set to display
the data appropriately, varying the width size as needed. Note that in this case, the *bound
column* — the column that has its information saved to the field — does not change. You are
not required to keep the same bound column. As a matter of practice, you may find it easier
to keep the bound column the same within a given control even when changing the row
source. Finally, the Row Source is updated. In the first case, the source is set to a SQL
string. In the second, it refers to a query (ChecksByPayee) instead.

**Changing any of the preceding properties causes the control to be reset and
requeried for each change. This can cause major performance problems each
time you set a property, especially if you are using a complex query or the
source tables are large. Therefore, the trick is to set the** Row Source **to be a
blank value. The control is requeried more quickly because there is no** Row
Source. **This is done with the following line of code:**

```
![By Search type].RowSource = ""
```

Then, after setting all the other properties, set the Row Source **property with
the query name or SQL string you wish to use.**

You have seen how you can use an option group to change the display of a list box. The
code examples shown in Listings 13-4 and 13-5 from the Check Writer program take the
concept further and illustrate some simple ways that you can create dynamic, interactive
forms.

Listing 13-4 uses the After Update event of a combo box to affect the data and the form
display. The frm_CheckWriter form's Bank Account combo box changes or filters records for
the form based on the selection of the user.

Listing 13-4　*The After Update Event of the Bank Account Combo Box*

```
Private Sub BankAccount_AfterUpdate()
Dim rst As New ADODB.Recordset

  On Error GoTo ErrorHandler

    rst.Open "SELECT * FROM tbl_BankAccounts WHERE [BankAccountNumber] = " & Chr(34) &
             Me.BankAccount & Chr(34), CurrentProject.Connection, adOpenForwardOnly

    With Me
        .BankName = rst!BankName
        .BankAccountNumber = rst!BankAccountNumber
        .ABANumber = rst!ABANumber
        If .TabControl.Value <> 0 Then
            .TabControl.Pages(0).SetFocus
        Else
            TabControl_Change
        End If
    End With
    rst.Close
    GoTo Done

ErrorHandler:
  MsgBox Err.Description
Done:
End Sub
```

This is a simple but very significant code listing. In this case, the form is being set to filter for check transactions for only a particular bank account. Without having to do a filter on the form, you have set it up so that, with a simple selection from a combo box, the user can change the record source for the entire form. This is an extremely user-friendly way of setting up filters for your forms. You can filter the records on a form with a minimum of code and without the user having to go through menu items.

Handling items not in the list

One of the most versatile properties of the combo box is its capability to handle nonlisted items. The property Limit to List and the event On Not In List work together to dictate how the control handles instances where the text entered in the combo box does not match the list.

The Payee combo box of the frm_CheckWriter form has been set up to illustrate how you can give the end user the ability to update the listing as new information is encountered. In this example, the Payee combo box allows you to select from a pre-existing list of payees. The property Limit to List has been set to No, which allows the user to enter a name that is not listed.

However, to provide a more robust interface, the property in our example has been set to Yes to force only listed items to be selected. In addition, the code shown in Listing 13-5 is added to the On Not In List event that runs when a value that is not listed has been entered. The code prompts the user to see if he/she wishes to add the nonlisted payee to the listing for future use. If No is returned, the code ends. Otherwise, if Yes is returned, it adds the record.

Listing 13-5   *The On Not In List Event Code for the Payee Combo Box*

```
Private Sub Payee_NotInList(NewData As String, Response As Integer)
Dim cnn As ADODB.Connection
Dim PayeeTB As New ADODB.Recordset
Dim Answer As Integer

    On Error GoTo ErrorHandler

    Answer = MsgBox("This Payee is not on file. Add it to the tblPayees list?", _
            vbQuestion + vbYesNo, "New Payee")
    If Answer = vbNo Then
        Response = acDataErrContinue
    Else
        Response = acDataErrAdded
        Set cnn = CurrentProject.Connection
        PayeeTB.CursorType = adOpenKeyset
        PayeeTB.LockType = adLockOptimistic
        PayeeTB.Open "tblPayees", cnn, , , adCmdTable
        With PayeeTB
            'Add new payee to tblPayees table
            .AddNew
            !tblPayees = NewData
            .Update
        End With
        PayeeTB.Close
        Set PayeeTB = Nothing
        cnn.Close
        Set cnn = Nothing
    End If
    GoTo Done
ErrorHandler:
    MsgBox Err.Description
Done:
End Sub
```

Listing 13-5 involves a very simple situation in which the Payees table consists of a single field. In most cases, your tables have more fields, including some that may require input from the user before the record can be created. You may want to expand this example even further by opening a data entry form for the user to populate the entire record and then updating the list.

**10 Min.
To Go**

Selecting and handling multiple choices

Unlike a combo box or an option group, a list box has the unique capability to allow for multiple selections, or what Access refers to as the MultiSelect property. The MultiSelect property can have one of three variations: None, Simple, or Extended. The difference between Simple and Extended is that with Simple, the user selects the row by clicking the mouse. Extended allows you to select records by using the Shift or Ctrl key and clicking each row. You can select a contiguous group of rows by clicking the first and last row while holding down the Shift key. The Ctrl key enables you to select rows in any order.

The Recurring Payments module has a list box that is set up with the `MultiSelect` property set to `Extended`, as shown in Figure 13-11. The code in the `On Click` event of the Process button cycles through all the selected rows and creates checks for each record selected.

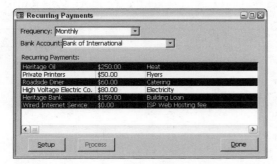

Figure 13-11　*The Recurring Payments form with a MultiSelect list box.*

You should be aware of several key properties when dealing with the `MultiSelect` property.

`ListCount`	An integer value indicating the total number of items in the list. box.
`ListIndex`	A zero-based value assigned to each row. You can use this to determine which row is selected.
`SelectedProperty`	A property that you can use to determine if a particular item in the list box is selected. A True/False value indicates whether a row is selected.
`ItemsSelected`	A collection of variants that indicate the row of items selected in a list box. This collection is used with other properties to enable you to retrieve data from specific rows and columns in the list box.

 These properties are also available for a combo box.

On the frm_RecurringPayments form, the user can set up multiple recurring payments. First, each payment considered a recurring payment must be set up. This works by clicking the Setup button. The user is then presented with a form that creates new payment listings. Each payment must be entered and set up here first before it can be used on the frm_RecurringPayments form. When the time comes for the checks to be created, the user simply selects from the Recurring Payments list box and marks the items to be processed. After all the items have been marked, the user clicks the Process button to create the checks.

The code for referencing the columns refers to a variable, varitem. Remember that referring to a particular column requires you to pass the row and the column because you are referring to a row that is represented by varitem.

Listing 13-6 is the partial listing of the On Click event code for the Process button.

Listing 13-6   *The On Click Event for the Process Button*

```
Dim rst As New ADODB.Recordset
Dim varItem As Variant

    On Error GoTo ErrorHandler
'Verify items selected
    If Me.Recurring_Payments.ItemsSelected.Count = 0 Then
        MsgBox "Please select checks to process.", vbCritical, "No checks selected."
        Me.Recurring_Payments.SetFocus
        GoTo Done
    End If

'Verify Bank Account Selected
    If IsNull(Me.BankAccount) Then
        MsgBox "Please select a Bank Account", vbCritical, "No Bank Account"
        Me.BankAccount.SetFocus
        GoTo Done
    End If

    rst.Open "tbl_CheckWriter", CurrentProject.Connection, adOpenKeyset,
adLockPessimistic

'Open recordset for the tbl_CheckWriter table and write new checks
    With rst
        'Start loop to process all items selected in the
        'Recurring Payments list box
        For Each varItem In Me.Recurring_Payments.ItemsSelected
            .AddNew
                .Fields("TransType") = "Check"
                .Fields("AccountNumber") = Me.BankAccount
                .Fields("CheckNumber") = dbc_CheckNum(Me.BankAccount)
                .Fields("CheckDate") = Date
                .Fields("Payee") = Me.Recurring_Payments.Column(1, varItem)
                .Fields("PaymentAmount") = Me.Recurring_Payments.Column(2, varItem)
                .Fields("Memo") = Me.Recurring_Payments.Column(3, varItem)
                .Fields("Voucher") = "Payee: " & Me.Recurring_Payments.Column(1, varItem) &
"  Amount: " & Format(Me.Recurring_Payments.Column(2, varItem), "Currency") & "  Date: "
& Date & vbCr & vbLf & Me.Recurring_Payments.Column(3, varItem)
            .Update
        Next varItem
    End With
    rst.Close

    MsgBox "Checks Created Successfully.", vbExclamation, "Process Status"

    DoCmd.Close acForm, Me.Name
    GoTo Done
```

```
ErrorHandler:
    MsgBox Err.Description
Done:

End Sub
```

The code starts by first declaring the variables for the procedure. Next, the code does standard checks to verify that items have indeed been selected and that a bank account was selected. Then the code starts processing the selections. The CheckTB recordset is opened using ADO code. You are opening a recordset based on the tbl_CheckWriter table because this is where the data is populated. A loop is initiated and it goes through all the items in the `ItemSelected` collection. For each of the rows retrieved from the collection, the check information is populated. This first saves the transaction as a check, then saves the account number and date. The Payee, Amount, and Memo fields are populated by referring to the other columns in the list box.

Information is concatenated into the Voucher field. This is done by building a string and setting the field to it:

```
.Fields("Voucher") = "Payee: " & Me.Recurring_Payments.Column & _
(1, varItem) & "  Amount: " & Format(Me.Recurring_Payments. & _
Column(2, varItem), "Currency") & "  Date: " & Date & vbCr & _
vbLf & Me.Recurring_Payments.Column(3, varItem)
```

This example uses the `ItemsSelected` property to process the selected rows. Alternatively, you could use the `ListCount`, `ListIndex`, and `SelectedProperty` to loop through and check each value to determine if a particular row was selected.

Concatenating strings

In the previous section, you were introduced to a piece of code that concatenated or built a string. This string was then used to populate the Voucher field of the check, thereby eliminating the need to retype the data in the string. Concatenation is a technique that you should master. It enables you to build a string of separate pieces of data that you can then store in a field. Additionally, you can use it to build SQL statement strings or text strings for message box displays.

The key component of concatenation is the ampersand (&) or the plus (+) sign. You can use these to join two separate statements. The key difference between the two operators is that the plus operator can only join text data together. The ampersand enables you to join text data as well as nontext data. In addition, the ampersand converts nontext data to text.

 If you must use the plus operator for nontext data, you can convert the data to a text format. For example, the function `CStr()` converts the string to a text data type.

```
= "Today's Date Is: " + Cstr(Date())
```

The following two examples show how to concatenate two strings of data. The first takes the First Name and Second Name strings and creates a resultant Names string that is a single text string. Note that three items are actually being added together in the example: First Name, a space, and Last Name. A space must be added because no spaces are automatically added when you concatenate. You must take proper spacing into consideration. Otherwise, the example's result could be "JohnDoe" with no space.

```
[First Name] = John
[Last Name] = Doe
Concatenate: [First Name] & " " & [Last Name]

Resultant: "John Doe"
```

The next example starts like the previous example but is a little more sophisticated. It joins several strings of text and field references, including calling a function.

```
[First Name] = John
[Last Name] = Doe
[Amount] = 3,299.50

Concatenate: "Pay To: " & [First Name] & " " & [Last Name] & _
        "      " & Format$(Date(),"mm/dd/yyyy") & "    " & _
        Format$([Amount], "Currency")"

Resultant:  "Pay To: John Doe 11/09/1999    $3,299.50"
```

The frm_CheckWriter form has a Create Check Stub button on the bottom. The code in Listing 13-7 builds a string of text by concatenating several pieces of data into the Voucher string. This is done by determining if the Voucher field is empty. If it is, the code then sets the voucher. If the existing Voucher field is not blank, the user is prompted with a message box asking whether to overwrite the existing stub information. If the response is Yes, the code overwrites the existing stub with the concatenated string of data. The concatenated string is the following line:

```
Me![Voucher] = "Pay To: " & Me![Payee] & "    " & _
        Me![CheckDate] & "    " & Format$(Me![Amount], _
        "Currency")
```

Listing 13-7   *The On Click Event Code of the Create Check Stub Button*

```
Private Sub cmdCreateCheckStub_Click()
Dim Response As Integer
  If IsNull(Me![Voucher]) Then
        Me![Voucher] = "Pay To: " & Me![Payee] & "    " & Me![CheckDate] & "    " &
Format$(Me![Amount], "Currency")
    Else
        Response = MsgBox("Do you want to overwrite the Check Stub?", 36, "Create Stub")
        If Response = vbYes Then
            Me![Voucher] = "Pay To: " & Me![Payee] & "    " & Me![CheckDate] & "    " &
Format$(Me![Amount], "Currency")
        End If
    End If
End Sub
```

Done!

REVIEW

In this session, you learned about the check box, option group, combo box, and list box controls. You also learned how to programmatically manipulate the information displayed and associate events to the controls. The following topics were covered:

- Populating the option controls
- Using code to change the row source properties of the combo box and list box
- Handling items not in the list
- Writing code to handle instances in which the text entered in the combo box is not an item in the list
- Selecting and handling multiple choices
- Using the list box to choose multiple selections
- Creating a dynamic form using these controls and going beyond data entry
- Using the controls to change the look, operation, and function of forms
- Concatenating data to build a string

QUIZ YOURSELF

1. Which interface would be the most appropriate to use in the following situation?
   a. You want to have a Posted field and lock the form on records marked as Posted and unlock the form for records not marked as Posted. (See "Handling True/False Selections with a Check Box.")
   b. You want the user to be able to select multiple items on a list. (See "Understanding the differences between combo boxes and list boxes.")
   c. You want a control that lists multiple items. You want to have the first column be bound to a field called ItemNumber, and you want the user to be able to type a partial item number and have it pull up the closest match. (See "Understanding the differences between combo boxes and list boxes.")

2. Which main characteristic differentiates a combo box from a list box? (See "Understanding the differences between combo boxes and list boxes.")

3. The Item Not In List property is available for which control? Detail the general steps you would take to handle a situation where the item is not in the list. (See "Handling items not in the list.")

4. What is concatenation and why is the concept of concatenation so important in programming? (See "Concatenating strings.")

5. What is the ItemSelected property/collection and how is it used in list boxes? (See "Selecting and handling multiple choices.")

Programming Subforms and Continuous Forms

Session Checklist

✔ Understanding subforms

✔ Creating subforms

✔ Specifying the subform control's form

✔ Linking master and child forms

✔ Referencing controls in subforms

**30 Min.
To Go**

Subforms give you great flexibility when you are displaying and entering data, especially when using data found in more than one table and with one-to-many relationships. Continuous forms let you display many records from one table at the same time and still use editing- and data-searching techniques as well as calculated columns and totals. In this session, you see several examples of how to use subforms and continuous forms to display data.

What Is a Subform?

A *subform* is simply a form within a form. It lets you use data from a one form within another form. For example, in the Check Writer example, the main frm_CheckWriter form displays the check register in a subform in a continuous form view. A *subform control* is simply a container for displaying another form. The form view displayed within the subform control depends on the view of the form used in the subform.

There are three basic types of form views:

- **Datasheets:** Display multiple records using one line per record.
- **Forms:** Display one record on a form.
- **Continuous forms:** Display multiple records on a form.

Creating a Subform

Any of the three form views can be displayed within a subform. The form inside the subform control can display the same data in a different view, or it can display totally different data. Figure 14-1 shows the frm_BankAccounts form. This form displays one record at a time. The frm_CheckWriter form in your `CheckWriter.mdb` sample file is a tabbed dialog box that displays several tabs, including one with a continuous subform.

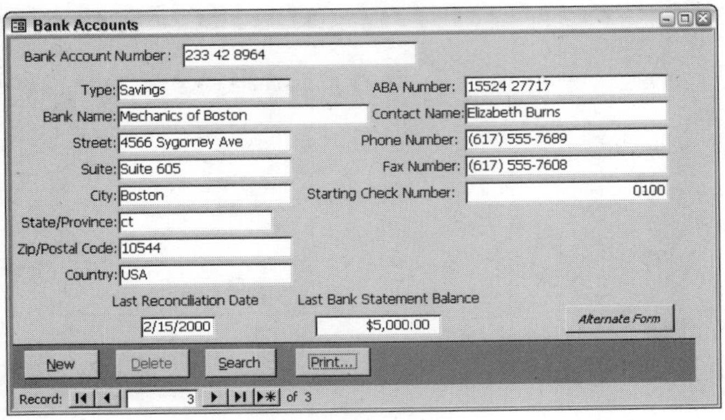

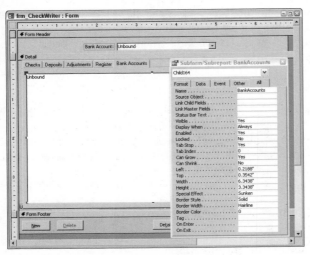

Figure 14-1   *The Bank Accounts form.*

Suppose you want to display the bank account information in this tabbed dialog box. The best way is to add a new tab and a subform. Including a subform on your form enables you to display your data in multiple formats including one record at a time or many records at a time. Figure 14-2 shows this process. First a new tab control page is added to the tab control in the frm_CheckWriter form. Then a subform control is added to the tab page and named Bank Accounts.

Figure 14-2   *Adding a subform to a form.*

> **You can add a subform to any form, and you can add more than one subform to a form. A subform can even contain a subform, but you are limited to two levels deep.**

Selecting the subform's control Source Object

After you place a subform control onto a form, you must tell the control which form will be displayed within it. To do this, you use the Source Object property. In this example, select the frm_BankAccounts form from the list of forms displayed in the control's Source Object property. The Bank Accounts form displays controls used to store data for each bank account.

After you select the Source Object, the form itself, showing all the controls, is displayed within the Subform control. You can see this in Figure 14-3.

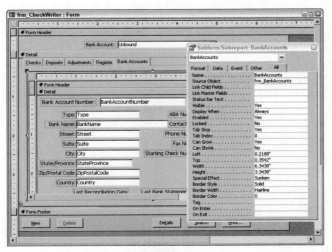

Figure 14-3   *Selecting the Subform control's Source Object property.*

You can edit the form and change anything by working through the Subform control.

> **Remember, if this form is used by another subform or displayed by itself in another part of your application, changing it here changes it in every other place it is used. You are not working with a copy, but the original version of the form.**

After you have set the Source Object property of the subform, you are finished if all you want to do is display the form. However, you can perform many other functions with subforms. One function is to limit the records displayed in the subform to match a record displayed in the main form.

You might want to link the Bank Accounts form displayed in the subform to the combo box displayed in the main Check Writer form.

Linking the subform to the main form record

When you create a subform, you can link the main form to it by a common field or expression. The subform then displays only records that are related to the main form.

When you create a subform, if Microsoft Access finds a predefined relationship or a match between a primary key and a foreign key, the Link Child Fields and the Link Master Fields properties of the subforms show the field names that define the link. You should verify the validity of an automatic link. If the main form is based on a query, or if neither of the conditions just listed is true, Access cannot match the fields automatically to create a link.

The Link Child Fields and Link Master Fields property settings must have the same number of fields and must represent data of the same type. In this example, as you can see in Figure 14-4, the BankAccountNumber field is found in both the tbl_CheckWriter and tbl_BankAccounts tables. The BankAccountNumber field name placed in the Link Child Fields entry area is from the tbl_BankAccounts table found in the frm_BankAccounts subform. The BankAccountNumber field name placed in the Link Master Fields entry area is from the tbl_CheckWriter table found in the frm_CheckWriter form.

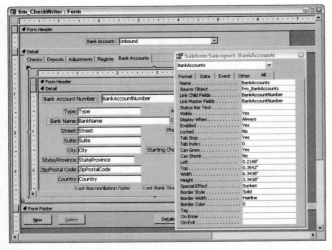

Figure 14-4 *Linking the subform to the main form.*

Although the data must match, the names of the fields or controls can differ. For example, the BankAccountNumber field in the subform could be linked to the AccountNumber field in the frm_CheckWriter form because they contain the same value.

In this example, the relationship is one-to-one because the Bank Accounts form displays only one record at a time.

When you select a bank account from the combo box in the main form, you are changing the displayed bank account. As the BankAccountNumber field changes in the main form, an internal filter in the subform control is applied to display only records in which the BankAccountNumber in the Check Writer or Check Register value matches the value of BankAccountNumber.

Working with Continuous Form Subforms

The greatest advantage of subforms is their capability to show the one-to-many relationship. The main form usually represents the *one* part of the relationship; the subform represents the *many* part. An example of this is found in the Check Register form. The form frm_CheckWriterRegisterSubform is a continuous form, as shown in Figure 14-5.

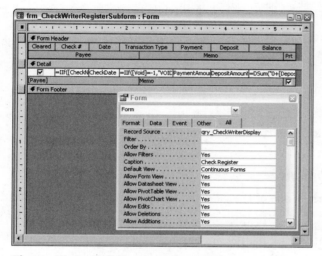

Figure 14-5   *Building a continuous form.*

You can see in the property window that Default View is set to Continuous Forms. Notice that the detail section contains two rows of controls. This is one of the benefits of a form over a datasheet. A datasheet is limited to one row of largely unformatted data. The continuous form can contain controls with different background colors and fonts, combo boxes, check boxes, and even command buttons.

When you use the form as a subform, you simply embed it within a form just as you do with a datasheet or form view. Figure 14-6 shows this form within the Register tab of the frm_CheckWriter form. Notice that there is also an unbound OLE object frame containing the image of the ledger. This is just used as a background and does not affect the subform control.

In Figure 14-6, you can see that the Source Object property of the subform control is set to the form frm_CheckWriterRegisterSubform and the common field AccountNumber is used as the Link Master Fields and Link Child Fields properties.

When this form is run, all the records in the continuous form are displayed from the selected bank account. This is filtered by the link to the Account Number field. Without this link, all the records in the Check Writer table would be displayed.

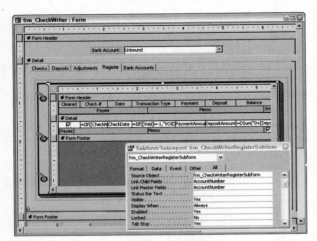

Figure 14-6   *Linking the subform control to the main form.*

**10 Min.
To Go**

Referencing controls in subforms

The frm_CheckWriterRegister form is one of the more interesting forms in the application because it includes some unique calculations in the controls. As you can see in Figures 14-5 and 14-6, there are several calculated controls.

The Check Register displays data from the tbl_CheckWriter table, which includes check, deposit, and adjustment data. Each is a little different. The Check # control contains a formula that displays a check number if the line is a check, and if it is a deposit or adjustment, it displays a blank. The control does this by checking for the value of the check number and, if it is 0, the control assumes this is not a check..

```
=IIf([CheckNumber]=0," ",[CheckNumber])
```

The transaction type is set to either Check, Deposit, or one of an unlimited user-defined set of adjustments. If the transaction is a check and is Void, the word VOID is placed in front of the transaction type to indicate that it is not included in any totals:

```
=IIf([Void]=-1,"VOID-" & [TransType],[TransType])
```

The last calculated control named Balance calculates a running total for the check register. This uses a calculation that looks at the transaction ID (TransID) field and sums all of the records for the current transaction and all previous transactions.

```
=DSum("0+[DepositAmount]-[PaymentAmount]","tbl_CheckWriter","[TransID] <=
[Forms]![frm_CheckWriter]![frm_CheckWriterRegisterSubform].Form![TransID]
and [AccountNumber]=[Forms]![frm_CheckWriter]![BankAccount] and Void <>
True")
```

The calculation must start with 0+. If it doesn't, the calculation fails because there is no starting point.

Notice that the calculation uses the reference for the TransID within the subform control's form. This requires the special notation

```
Forms![frm_CheckWriter]![frm_CheckWriterRegisterSubform].Form![TransID]
```

which uses the format

```
Forms![main form name]![subform control name].Form![subform control]
```

After the subform control is referenced, a .Form reference is used to move internal focus to the subform control's form where controls on that form can now be referenced.

Some people might argue that the calculation is in error. Because the calculation uses the TransID field (which is an auto number), it does not group transactions together by date. For example, because the autonumber field increments sequentially, if after entering all your checks for the previous week, you realize that you forgot one, you can enter the check with the date (that might be last week). But this transaction appears with the next batch of transactions because the sort (or DSUM filter) is only by the TransID field.

Done!

REVIEW

In this session, you learned about subforms, which enable you to display a form within a form. Using subforms, you can display one record or many records using a datasheet or continuous form view. The following topics were covered:

- A subform is simply a form within a form.
- You can create a subform control on any form and specify another form using the subform control's Source Object property.
- You can link a subform to a main form using the Link Child Fields and Link Master Fields properties.
- To have the subform control automatically fill in the linking properties, you must have single field relationships already specified.
- Using continuous forms enables you to display one-to-many relationships.
- You can reference controls in the subform's form by adding the .Form control reference after the subform control.

QUIZ YOURSELF

1. Define the term subform. (See "What Is a Subform?")
2. Name the three types of forms that can be displayed with a subform. (See "What Is a Subform?")
3. Which property allows the subform control to display another form? (See "Selecting the subform's control Source Object.")

4. Which properties allow you to link a subform and a main form? (See "Linking the subform to the main form record.")

5. Which type of data do you need to create a link between a form and subform? (See "Linking the subform to the main form record.")

6. How do you reference a control on a subform? (See "Referencing controls in subforms.")

Programming Tabbed Controls

Session Checklist

✔ Using tabbed controls

✔ Using tabbed controls versus using multipage forms

✔ Programming tabbed controls

**30 Min.
To Go**

The ubiquitous use of tabbed controls by the Microsoft Office suite and the Windows operating system indicates both the popularity and effectiveness of these controls. Using tabbed controls in your applications can improve the user's experience and enhance your application in many ways. Programming the controls enables you to expand the capabilities of a form and, in turn, your application.

Why Use Tabbed Controls?

Why have tabbed controls gained so much popularity? Foremost, tabbed controls are user friendly. Because they are now a Windows standard, users have become accustomed to seeing them. You can set them up to group information or functions in an organized and logical manner, which enables you to make effective use of space on a form.

In addition to their inherent ease of use, tabbed controls are simple to program, and you can manipulate them in many different ways. From a developmental viewpoint, tabbed controls give the programmer an excellent tool. You can manipulate a tabbed control's pages, the look of the tabbed control itself, and its properties. All these features explain why tabbed controls have become so popular and effective. Figure 15-1 shows a tabbed control in the main Frm_CheckWriter form of the sample Check Writer program.

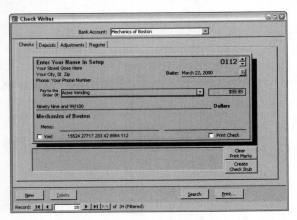

Figure 15-1 *The Frm_CheckWriter form illustrating the tabbed control.*

You can use tabbed controls for many reasons, ranging from aesthetics to functionality. Whether you want to standardize a look and feel for your program or to increase functionality by segregating your data and controls, tabbed controls are a great tool for your programming toolbox. Use a tabbed control in any of the following situations:

- To incorporate a standard Windows look and feel.
- To break up your data into logical groups or functions, each on its own tab.
- To make effective use of desktop space.
- To tie the controls to the same record source so that you don't have to create multiple separate forms for numerous controls that won't fit on a single form.

You can, of course, use tabbed controls in other ways. With a few exceptions, you are limited only by your imagination as to how you use tabbed controls. You can perform many tasks by using controls, but some limitations also exist. The following list describes some of the advantages and limitations of using tabbed controls:

Advantages:

- **Using multirow capability:** You can set the MultiRow property setting to choose the number of tabbed rows you want to use.
- **Controlling the form's appearance:** You can have the tabbed control *morph* from Tabs, Buttons, or None. Use the None setting if you want to create a multipage form with little programming required.
- **Using graphics on the tabs:** You can display both a bitmap picture and text on the tabs. Remember that visual cues such as graphics or icons can enhance the user's experience.
- **Controlling the display of pages:** You can programmatically control the display of the tabs during runtime so that you can hide and unhide pages. Use this feature if you want to make certain data or functions on specific pages accessible under different circumstances.
- **Ordering the pages:** You can programmatically control the order of pages.

- **Layering controls:** You can place additional controls on top of a tabbed control. This lets you "float" a control on top that is visible on all pages — not just one.
- **Adding Subforms:** You can place subforms in the tabbed control. In fact, you can even have different subforms on each page of the tabbed control.

Limitations:

- **Adding or deleting pages during runtime:** Although you can hide or unhide pages during runtime, you cannot add or delete pages. You can add or delete pages only in Design view.
- **Nesting tabbed controls:** You cannot embed one tabbed control within another. You are only able to "float" it.
- **Changing the text orientation:** You cannot change the orientation of the text. You can have the text on the tabs only horizontally.

Tabbed Controls versus Multipage Forms

Tabbed controls are really a variation on a multipage form. You may be familiar with this concept from earlier versions of Access or from other applications. A *multipage form* is one in which you use a page break to split a single form into multiple sections. Splitting the form enables you to extend the area available on the form because you are limited in the area that you can display on the screen. Remember, a well-designed form does not cram too many controls in one area. You should space controls appropriately for readability, functionality, and aesthetics.

Using multiple page breaks enables you to split a form into different sections. A tabbed control is an extension of the multipage concept. It makes it easier to develop and manipulate a single form that can be tied to a single record source. In addition, because you are using the form in this manner, you have more room to work. It's now fashionable and practical to use tabbed controls. They just make life easier.

This session concentrates on using the tabbed control as opposed to the multipage format. Should you want an additional challenge, try using the multipage format at some point. However, after you have wrestled with that format for a time, we're sure you'll agree that the tabbed control makes development faster and easier.

Keep in mind that you can still use multipage forms to create a single form containing a number of controls. However, using a tabbed control is a better alternative for several reasons.

First, a tabbed control is a container for multiple pages (see Figure 15-2). Each page is its own separate entity and has properties pertaining to it, as well as controls that are a part of that particular collection. At the same time, the controls and properties can be referenced as if they were a part of the form. Thus, each control that is part of the page collection of the tabbed control is also a part of the form's collection. This unique situation makes it tremendously easy to put controls on a page of a tabbed control and bind it to a field from the form's record source. You can also reference all the controls as if they were right on the form itself and not as if they were embedded within another control.

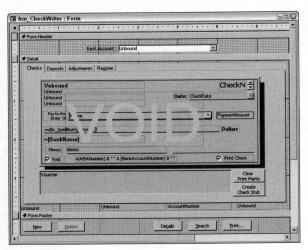

Figure 15-2 *Design View of the Frm_CheckWriter form illustrating the tabbed control.*

Second, if you set up a multipage form and use page breaks, you must program navigation buttons to move from page to page. Multipage forms have no built-in navigation buttons to do this. This can be a major task if you have a large form and must account for differences going from one page view to another. The tabbed control eliminates the need for this by giving you two means of moving from one page to the next using tabs or buttons.

In addition, on a multipage form, you must design each section correctly to prevent a "jumping" effect caused by differences in the section sizes and the placement of common controls from one page to the next. Otherwise, controls and the page seemingly move about because not everything is positioned or sized properly.

Third, a form's length is limited to only 22 inches. This is a major problem in Access 2.0 and Access 95. How do you create a single form that has room for multiple controls if it exceeds 22 inches when you place them all? The solution in earlier versions of Access was to use subforms. A tabbed control makes the size limitation a moot point. You can have numerous pages in a tabbed control that, if put together, easily extend beyond 22 inches.

All in all, tabbed controls are simply the descendents of multipage forms. This does not make multipage forms entirely useless. You may find that creating a multipage form for simple situations is a better solution than using a tabbed control. However, there are few instances where a tabbed control would not be a better solution than a multipage form.

20 Min. To Go

Programming a Tabbed Control

Programming a tabbed control can extend the functionality of the control several times over. After you understand which properties can be manipulated and how they can be manipulated, you can affect a tabbed control during runtime and create a more powerful interface.

A tabbed control can be viewed as a container that holds the controls for a particular page. Each page can then be considered as a collection of controls on that page. The advantage is that the controls on the page are also a part of the collection of controls on the form. You can reference the controls on the page just as you would a control on a form. Working with a control on your tabbed control now becomes like working with any other control on a form.

Tabbed control properties and methods

As with any Access control, you can programmatically affect many properties of a tabbed control. Table 15-1 lists the properties that pertain to tabbed controls.

Table 15-1   *Tabbed Control Properties*

Property Name	Function	Set at Runtime
MultiRow	Allows you to have multiple rows of tabs. The default is No. If you set this property to No and the tabs exceed the width of the control, Access adds a scroll bar and truncates the widths as necessary.	No
Style	Allows you to choose between Tab, Buttons, or None.	Yes
TabFixedHeight	Allows you to choose the height of the tabs. If the value is set to 0, the height is high enough to display the caption and picture.	Yes
TabFixedWidth	Allows you to choose the width of each tab. If you set the value to 0, each tab is wide enough for its contents. If there are multiple rows of tabs, the width of the tab is adjusted so that each row's total width is equal to the control width.	Yes
Picture	Allows you to display a bitmap graphic alongside the text of the caption on a particular tab. If you want only the graphic, you can enter in a space for the caption text.	No
On Change	Allows you to set and assign a macro or code that is processed when the user changes from tab to tab. Especially useful when you want to run code that reacts to going from tab to tab.	No
Page Index	Allows you to indicate the position of the tab or page in relation to all the other tabs.	Yes
Visible (tabbed control page)	Allows you to hide and unhide a particular tab or page of the tabbed control.	Yes

Tabbed control styles

Tabbed controls provide three different styles that you can choose from to determine the appearance of your tabs: Tabs, Buttons, or None. The default is Tabs (which was illustrated earlier in Figure 15-1). Figures 15-3 and 15-4 illustrate the changing appearance of the same tabbed form if you choose Buttons or None, respectively.

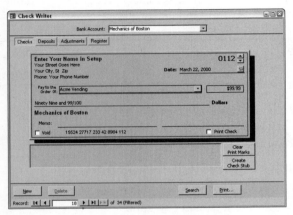

Figure 15-3   *The Frm_CheckWriter form using the Buttons style for tabs.*

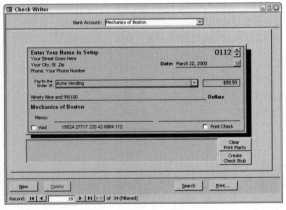

Figure 15-4   *The Frm_CheckWriter form with the tab style property set to None.*

Choosing a style type is primarily an aesthetic choice; however, sometimes one style is preferable to the others regardless of the look. If you are designing a tabbed control with multiple pages, using the Tabs style is the best choice. The look is clean and the operation is intuitive for the end user. This is especially true if you are using the MultiRow property to have more than one row of tabs. Multirowed buttons would look cluttered and messy.

If your design calls for only two or three pages, using buttons to navigate the forms may be a better choice. In this case, buttons may be just as intuitive and aesthetically pleasing as tabs.

At first, selecting None as the style may seem to be a redundant choice considering this is, after all, a tabbed control. However, there are times when you may want to set up multiple pages without any tabs or buttons. One excellent example is when you are creating a wizard-like interface. In the case of a wizard form such as AddAccountWizard, a tabbed control is used to set up each page of the wizard. Because a wizard has a specific order in which the information must be presented, you don't want to give the user free access to move from page to page randomly.

Giving such freedom in a wizard would present problems if the user went through the wizard in the wrong order. Specific buttons to move forward and backward are provided as the means of navigating from one page to the next. This lets you add conditional checks at each point to make sure that the data entered on a page is valid. In this case, it is better to remove all tabs and buttons as navigational tools. More important, using a tabbed control to set up the wizard makes designing the form easier.

 Session 25 contains more information on creating wizard-type forms.

Changing the style programmatically

One nice trick is to use code to change the style programmatically during runtime. For example, suppose that certain users should have access to the Deposits page of the form only. You do not want the user to be able to create checks or view the check register. When the user opens the form Frm_CheckWriterLimitedFunctionality, he or she is prompted to enter one of two IDs: Supervisor or User. If the user enters Supervisor, he or she sees the normal Frm_CheckWriter form. All the tabs are present. If the user enters User, he or she sees only the Deposit page of the tab. Note also that no tabs appear.

If you view the same form in Design view, you can see that it is identical to the Frm_CheckWriter form except for the code in the On Open event that determines the user and his or her access level. If the user enters an ID of User, only the Deposits page of the tabbed control is displayed. In addition, the tabbed control is set to display None as the style. This prevents the user from seeing and accessing other pages. If the ID entered is Supervisor, the user sees the form normally, with all the tabs visible.

The code for changing the look of the tab is very straightforward. It is simply a matter of setting the tab's Style property. You can have one of three settings: Tabs (0), Buttons (1), or None (2). You can view this at the end of the On Open event's code, as seen here:

```
If InputBox("Please enter in either Supervisor or User", "Log In") = "User" Then
        Me.TabControl.Style = 2
        Me.TabControl.Pages(1).SetFocus
End If
Me.TabControl.Visible = True
```

The beginning of the code has a line that sets the tabbed control to not visible. This prevents the user from seeing the form open with all the tabs initially and then seeing the tabs disappear after he or she has entered the logon ID. The code provides prompts for an ID by using the InputBox function. If the entry is "User", the tabs are turned off by setting the style to 2. The focus is then set to the tabbed control's page 1. Note that the pages are indexed starting from zero.

Showing and hiding pages

Another excellent technique is to control whether the individual pages of the tabbed control are visible. This allows you incredible control over how the tabbed control appears as well as access to specific tab pages. In this case, rather than hiding all the tabs, only specific ones are hidden. This can be done by setting the Visible property of the page. On the bottom of the form Frm_CheckWriterLimitedFunctionality, a new button, Hide Tabs, has been created. This button lets the user enter the name of the tab and the code, and then it hides that particular tab page. The code works in the following manner:

```
Private Sub btnHideTabs_Click()
    Dim TabName As String

    TabName = InputBox("Enter the tab name you wish to hide.", "Hide Tabs")

    With Me.TabControl
        .Pages(0).Visible = True
        .Pages(1).Visible = True
        .Pages(2).Visible = True
        .Pages(3).Visible = True
    End With

    Select Case TabName

        Case "Checks"
            Me.TabControl.Pages("Checks").Visible = False

        Case "Deposits"
            Me.TabControl.Pages("Deposits").Visible = False
        Case "Adjustments"
            Me.TabControl.Pages("Adjustments").Visible = False
        Case "Register"
            Me.TabControl.Pages("Register").Visible = False
        Case Else
            MsgBox "No valid tab name entered.", vbCritical, "Tab Name Error"
    End Select

End Sub
```

First, all the tabs are set to Visible. The code then uses the InputBox function to let the user enter a tab name. A Select Case statement is used to determine which tab to make not visible. Note that in this example, the control name of the tab page is used rather than the index page number.

Using either technique to limit access to specific tabs can provide security. Of course, these two types of security are very simplistic. However, coupled with other techniques, they can be an important element of a fully secured application.

**10 Min.
To Go**

Using the On Change event

Sometimes, you may want to affect an event as the user goes from tab to tab. This is where the On Change event of the tabbed control comes into use. In the Frm_CheckWriter form, for example, as the user moves from tab to tab the On Change event is run. Because each tab of the form is set for different types of transactions, as the user moves from tab to tab only those records pertaining to the particular tab on which the user is positioned are displayed. Thus, when you are on the tab for checks, you see only check transactions. When you are on the tab for deposits, you see only deposits. Here is the code for the tabbed control's On Change event in the Frm_CheckWriter form:

```
Private Sub TabControl_Change()
 Dim CurConn As ADODB.Connection
 Dim CheckTB As New ADODB.RecordSet
 Dim FindCrit As String

    Set CurConn = CurrentProject.Connection

    On Error GoTo ErrorHandler
    With Me
        Select Case .TabControl.value
            Case 0 'Checks
                .Filter = "[TransType] = 'Check'"
                .FilterOn = True
                .Requery
            Case 1 'Deposits
                .Filter = "[TransType] = 'Deposit'"
                .FilterOn = True
                .Requery
            Case 2 'Adjustments
                .Filter = "[TransType] <> 'Deposit' AND [TransType] <> 'Check'"
                .FilterOn = True
                .Requery
            Case 3 'Register
                DoCmd.RunCommand acCmdSaveRecord
                .frm_CheckWriterRegisterSubform.Requery
                If Not IsNull(.[TransID]) Then
                    .frm_CheckWriterRegisterSubform.SetFocus
                    .frm_CheckWriterRegisterSubform.Form![TransID].Enabled = True
                    .frm_CheckWriterRegisterSubform.Form![TransID].SetFocus
                    DoCmd.FindRecord Forms! _
                        [Check Writer Limited Functionality]![TransID]
                End If
                .frm_CheckWriterRegisterSubform.Form![Memo].SetFocus
                If (Not IsNull(.[TransID])) Then
                    .frm_CheckWriterRegisterSubform.Form![TransID].Enabled = False
                End If
        End Select
        Select Case Me.TabControl.value
            Case 0, 1, 2
                .NavigationButtons = True
                .New.Visible = True
                .Delete.Visible = True
                .btnDetails.Visible = False
                'Move to the matching Check Writer item pointed to in Register
                If IsNull(![TransID]) Then
                    DoCmd.GoToRecord acActiveDataObject, , acLast
                Else
                    FindCrit = "TransID = " & Me![TransID]
                    Set CheckTB = Forms![Check Writer Limited Functionality] _
                        .RecordsetClone
                    CheckTB.Find FindCrit
                    If Not CheckTB.EOF Then
```

```
                    Forms![Check Writer Limited Functionality].Bookmark = _
                        CheckTB.Bookmark
                End If
                CheckTB.Close
                Set CheckTB = Nothing
            End If

        Case 3
            .NavigationButtons = False
            .New.Visible = False
            .Delete.Visible = False
            .btnDetails.Visible = True
        End Select
    End With
    GoTo Done

ErrorHandler:
    If Err.Number = 2105 Then
        New_Click
        Resume Next
    End If
Done:
End Sub
```

The code uses two `Select Case` statements to change the tabbed control and the information it displays. Each statement checks for the page that the control is on. The first is used to change records to be filtered for that particular tab. So for the Checks tab, which has an index of 0, the filter is set to display only transactions of checks. For the Deposits tab, which has an index of 1, the filter is set to display only deposit transactions. This is done for each of the four tabs.

The second Select Case `select case` statement makes the additional navigation buttons visible. It then checks to see if a particular Trans ID has been entered in the Trans ID field and moves to that record. This is done for instances where a particular record has been selected in the Check Register. Otherwise, the last record is selected. If the tab is the Register tab, the Delete and New navigation buttons become invisible.

Done!

REVIEW

In this session, we discussed how to program tabbed controls and when to use a tabbed control instead of a multipage form. The following topics were covered:

- Tabbed controls can be extremely useful in creating a user-friendly interface. As a developer, you will find them very easy to set up and manipulate.

- A tabbed control is unique in that it can be viewed as a container for pages on a form. Each page, in turn, has its own properties that can be manipulated to act as a collection for controls on that page or tab. At the same time, the controls on the page are also a part of the control collection for the form.

- If you understand the properties of a tabbed control, you can program it. You can change its looks by choosing various styles. You can also affect changes as you move from tab to tab to reflect the particular tab you are on.

QUIZ YOURSELF

1. Why are tabbed controls so effective? (See "Why Use Tabbed Controls?")

2. If you wanted to make a particular button on the main form visible on page 0 and not visible when you move from page 0 to page 1, what technique would you use? (See "Tabbed control properties and methods" and "Changing the style programmatically.")

3. You can determine which page of the tab you are on by referencing which property? (See "Tabbed control properties and methods.")

4. Can tabbed controls contain a subform? (See "Programming a Tabbed Control.")

5. What technique can you use to make some tabs or pages visible and others not visible? (See "Showing and hiding pages.")

Message Boxes and Error-Handling Programs and Techniques

Session Checklist

✔ Using the Access Message Box function

✔ Understanding different types of errors

✔ Handling errors

✔ Understanding the Error and Err collections

**30 Min.
To Go**

I n this session, you learn about two of the most frequently used elements of application programming: communicating with the user using the message box and the handling of errors.

The Message Box Function

Probably one of the most commonly used functions is the MsgBox function. It is frequently used because it provides an easy way for VBA code to communicate with the user. Not only does it display a message, but it can also return a selection from the user. The selection is limited to a predefined set of buttons, but in most cases, these buttons are all you need. The syntax of this function follows:

YNTAX ▶

```
MsgBox(prompt[, buttons] [, title] [, helpfile, context])
```

When called, this function displays the string expression prompt in a dialog box. This string expression can be up to 1,024 characters and can include the string constant vbCRLF to start a new line.

The buttons parameter is an optional numeric expression that does more than just display a set of buttons. It also determines the icon that is displayed, which button is the default button, and the modality of the message box. When a form opens as a modal form, you must first close the form before you can move <u>focus</u> to another object.

The list of button sets is shown in Table 16-1. You can use the value or, to make your code more readable, use the constant.

Table 16-1 *MsgBox Button Values and Constants*

Value	Button Set	Constant
0	OK	VbOKOnly
1	OK, Cancel	VbOKCancel
2	Abort, Retry, Ignore	vbAbortRetryIgnore
3	Yes, No, Cancel	VbYesNoCancel
4	Yes, No	VbYesNo
5	Retry, Cancel	VbRetryCancel
6 – 15	Not used	

To choose an icon, you add another value to the button value. Note that these values represent bits in a binary number. This allows them to be added and to be mutually exclusive of each other. Icon values are shown in Table 16-2.

Table 16-2 *MsgBox Icon Values and Constants*

Value	Icon	Constant	Image
0	No icon		
16	Critical message	VbCritical	
32	Warning query	VbQuestion	
48	Warning message	VbExclamation	
64	Information message	VbInformation	
80, 96, 112, 128, 144, 160, 176, 192, 208, 224, 240	Not used		

You can also select which button is the default by adding another number to the Button argument. Table 16-3 shows the values for the button defaults.

Table 16-3   *Constants for Setting Button Defaults*

Value	Button is default	Constant
0	First button	vbDefaultButton1
256	Second button	vbDefaultButton2
512	Third button	vbDefaultButton3
768	Fourth button	vbDefaultButton4

By default, the message box is *Application modal*, which means the user must respond to the message box before continuing within the current application. If you add a value of 4096 (the constant is vbSystemModal), the message box is *System modal*, which means all applications are suspended until the user responds to the message box.

A few other options are also available, as shown in Table 16-4.

Table 16-4   *Values and Constants for Other MsgBox Options*

Value	Action	Constant
16384	Adds a Help button to the message box	vbMsgBoxHelpButton
65536	Makes the message box window the foreground window	VbMsgBoxSetForeground
524288	Right-aligns the text	vbMsgBoxRight
1048576	Makes text appear as right-to-left reading on Hebrew and Arabic systems	vbMsgBoxRtlReading

As an example, suppose that you want a Yes/No button combination with a Help button and a Warning icon, and you want the No button to be the default. The button value should be

```
VbYesNo + VbExclamation + vbDefaultButton2 + vbMsgBoxHelpButton
= 4 + 48 + 256 + 16384 = 16,692
```

The optional Title argument is a string expression displayed in the title bar of the dialog box. When this is omitted, the application name is displayed in the title bar.

If your application displays a Help button, you should enter values for the two parameters HelpFile and Context. The HelpFile is a string expression that contains the name of the Help file. The Context argument is a numeric expression that is the help context number assigned to the appropriate help topic. If you don't have a Help button, you can press the F1 button for the same effect. Clicking the Help button calls the Microsoft Help Workshop or Microsoft HTML Help Workshop application. It loads the custom Help file specified by the HelpFile string and displays the Help topic specified by the Context parameter.

Refer to the Microsoft Access online Help topics *HelpContextID* and *HelpFile Properties* to get more information. Clicking the Help button does not cause the MsgBox to close or return a value.

The MsgBox function can return a value that represents the button you clicked. The return values are listed in Table 16-5.

Table 16-5 *MsgBox Return Values and Constants*

Value	Description	Constant
1	OK	vbOK
2	Cancel	vbCancel
3	Abort	vbAbort
4	Retry	vbRetry
5	Ignore	vbIgnore
6	Yes	vbYes
7	No	vbNo

For an example of how to use the Msgbox function, refer to Listing 16-1. This subroutine comes from the form frm_BankAccountsUnbound in the sample Check Writer application. The subroutine is called when the form is closed or unloaded. If the control FlagEdited is True, the user has changed or entered data on the form and did not save the data. So if FlagEdited is true, a message box appears that reads Do you want to save your changes? The function is called with the vbYesNoCancel value set for the buttons, so three buttons are displayed: Yes, No, and Cancel. The function returns a value for the user selection, and it is assigned to the variable Answer. If Answer contains the value associated with the Cancel button, the Cancel variable is set to True and the form does not close. If Answer contains the value associated with the Yes button, the function uf_SaveRecord is called to save the data. Otherwise, the No button was pressed, so the form continues to close.

Listing 16-1 *An Example of Using the MsgBox Function*

```
Private Sub Form_Unload(Cancel As Integer)
Dim Answer As Integer
    If Me.FlagEdited Then
        Answer = MsgBox("Do you want to save your changes?", _
vbYesNoCancel)
        If Answer = vbCancel Then Cancel = True
        If Answer = vbYes Then uf_SaveRecord Me
    End If
End Sub
```

There are at least 90 calls to the MsgBox function within the sample Check Writer application, and this is typical of the number of times you will use the function. Be sure to use the powerful features that this function provides to communicate with your users.

EZ Extensions from Database Creations, Inc. (www.databasecreations.com), includes a customizable message box that can be used to replace the Access message box. It is compatible with the Access message box, plus it provides for the use of user-defined icons, allows different fonts and font sizes to be used, enables text alignment to be changed, and can be further customized by the user to include different font colors, background colors, and so on.

Errors

**20 Min.
To Go**

Assuming that you get past the syntax checking using the VBA Editor and you also get past the errors that Access finds when you compile your application, the only remaining errors that can occur happen at runtime. Runtime errors occur for many reasons. When they do, one of the following happens:

- A fatal error occurs, causing the application to crash.
- An untrapped error occurs, causing the Access error dialog box to appear.
- A handled error occurs, and your code takes care of the problem.
- An unknown application error occurs that does not cause an Access error.

Types of errors

A fatal error is a nonrecoverable error that causes an application to crash. This error generally occurs as a result of an operation outside the Access environment, so Access cannot handle it; therefore, your code is not able to handle it. Fatal errors generally occur when a Windows API is called. Windows API calls are calls from your application to a procedure in a Windows library. An example of this type of call is retrieving the screen resolution. You have to go to Windows to get this kind of information. You cannot do much about fatal errors in your Access VBA program; so in this section, we concentrate on the types of errors you can control.

The Access error dialog box appears for untrapped errors (see Figure 16-1). This can be good for development because problems can be traced to the specific line of code that caused the error. When the Debug button is clicked, the VBA window opens and highlights the guilty line of code. Usually, this is not the kind of result you want your application's end users to experience. By using an error handler, you can still alert the user to the error, but the user doesn't have to worry about the problem because the code either works around the error or corrects the problem.

As mentioned earlier in the bulleted list, the last type of error is the unknown application error. This is a logic error in the code. No error notification occurs because the program is working the way it was coded. The problem is that the code is performing the wrong function. This is often the most difficult type of error to discover. You can handle an unknown application error in either of these two ways:

- Test, test, test
- Check the results programmatically by redundantly checking the result

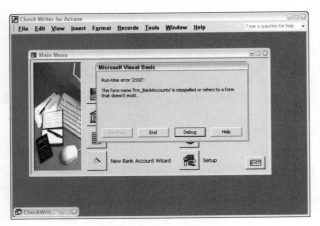

Figure 16-1   *The Access error dialog box.*

For a simple example to show how you can check the result, imagine a spreadsheet of numbers. Create a column that contains a subtotal on each row that is the sum of all the numbers in a given row. Then total the subtotals to get the total for all the numbers. Now, to check that result, create a new row that sums the numbers in each column with a sub-total for each column. The total of these subtotals should equal the first total. If it doesn't, you have an error condition, and you must take some action.

This type of error checking is very application-specific, so it cannot be discussed in general terms. This session, therefore, deals only with the errors that Access can detect. The Check Writer application contains much application-specific error checking code that is described throughout this book.

The elements of error handling

Access and ADO provide four basic programming elements for error handling:

- Errors collection
- Err object
- VBA Error statements
- Error event

When Access detects an error, most of the time an object is created for the error. The two types of error objects in Access are based on whether the error was detected by ADO or Access. The Errors collection is part of the ADO object model. The Err object is part of the Access object model. In addition to these two elements, Access has an Error event that is triggered when an error occurs with a form or report.

The Errors collection

When an error occurs in an ADO object, an Error object is created in the Errors collection of the Connection object. These are referred to as *data access errors*. When an error occurs, the collection is cleared and the new set of objects is put into the collection. Although the collection exists for one error event only, the event could generate several errors. Each of these errors is stored in the Errors collection. The Errors collection is an object of the Connection object, not ADO.

The Errors collection has one property, Count, which contains the number of errors or error objects. It has a value of 0 if there are no errors. Each Error object has a few properties, including Description, HelpContext, HelpFile, Number, and Source. When there are multiple errors, the lowest-level error is the first object in the collection and the highest-level error is the last object in the collection.

When an ADO error occurs, the VBA Err object contains the error number for the first object in the Errors collection. Check the Errors collection to see whether additional ADO errors have occurred. (See Listing 16-3 later in this session for an example of the ADO Errors collection.)

The Err object

The Err object is created by VBA. When an error occurs, information about that error is stored in the Err object, which contains information about only one error at a time. When an error occurs, the Err object is cleared and updated to include information about that most recent error.

The Err object has several properties, including Number and Description. The Err object also has two methods: Clear to clear information from the Err object, and Raise to simulate an error.

When an error occurs relative to the Jet database engine or ADO, you need to refer to the Errors collection to get more information.

VBA error statements

The two basic VBA statements for handling errors are On Error and Resume. The On Error statement enables or disables error handling. There are three forms of the On Error statement:

- On Error GoTo *label*
- On Error GoTo 0
- On Error Resume Next

The On Error GoTo *label* statement enables an error-handling routine. The label is the one for the error-handling routine. When this statement is executed, error handling is immediately enabled. When an error occurs, execution goes to the line specified by the *label* argument, which should be at the beginning of the error-handling routine.

To disable error handling, use the On Error GoTo 0 statement. This statement also resets the properties of the Err object.

The On Error Resume Next statement ignores the line that causes an error and continues execution with the line following the line that caused the error. No error-handling routine is called. This statement is useful if you want to ignore errors. You can also use it if you want to check the values of the Err object immediately after a line at which you anticipate an error will occur and then handle the error within the procedure rather than in an error handler.

You return to the main procedure from an error handler using the Resume statement. If you do not want to resume execution in case of an error, the Resume statement is not necessary. In that case, all you need to do is exit the procedure.

As with the On Error statement, the Resume statement has three forms:

- Resume or Resume 0
- Resume Next
- Resume *label*

The Resume or Resume 0 statement returns execution to the line at which the error occurred. This statement is used, typically, when the user must make a correction. This might occur if you prompt the user for the name of a file to open, and the user enters a filename that doesn't exist. You can then force the execution of the code back to the point where the filename is requested.

When your error handler corrects or works around the problem that caused the error, the Resume Next statement is used. It returns execution to the line immediately following the line at which the error occurred.

If you need to continue execution at some other place besides the line that caused the error or the line after the line that caused the error, you should use the Resume *label* statement. It returns execution to the line specified by the *label* argument.

**10 Min.
To Go**

The Error event

Access provides for an Error event with forms and reports. This event is triggered when an error occurs on a form or report, and it gives you a good way to trap an error when VBA code is not running. You create an event procedure for the On Error event to trap these errors. The procedure looks like one of the following depending on whether it was a form or report:

```
Private Sub Form_Error(DataErr As Integer, Response As Integer)
'Insert error handler here
End Sub

Private Sub Report_Error(DataErr As Integer, Response As Integer)
'Insert error handler here
End Sub
```

These subroutines have two arguments: DataErr and Response. DataErr is the error code returned by the Err object when an error occurs. Note that the Err object isn't populated with information after the event occurs. You need to use the DataErr argument to determine which error occurred. The second argument, Response, should contain either one of the following constants:

AcDataErrContinue	Ignores the error and continues without displaying the default Access error message.
AcDataErrDisplay	Displays the default Access error message. (This is the default.)

When you use `AcDataErrContinue`, you can supply a custom error message or handler in place of the default error message.

Error-handling procedures

There are obviously numerous ways to deal with errors within forms, reports, and code. Each form and report, as well as each function and subroutine, can and probably should have an error-handling routine. It is normal for a good part of the development effort to be devoted to error handling. As you look through the various components in the sample Check Writer application, you see numerous instances of error-handling routines. Probably the most common routine is shown in Listing 16-2.

Listing 16-2   *The Error-Handler Structure*

```
Function SampleCode
'Dim statements here

    On Error goto ErrorHandler
    'insert functional code here
    Goto Done

ErrorHandler:
    'error handler code here
    Msgbox err.description
    'either enter a resume statement here or
        ' nothing and let the function end
Done:
    'insert clean-up code here
End Function
```

The `On Error` statement enables the error handler; if an error occurs, execution continues on the line after the label `ErrorHandler`. This label can be any valid VBA label. The error-handler code deals with the error and then either resumes execution back in the body of the procedure or just exits the function or subroutine. The inclusion of the `Msgbox` statement in the error handler is a typical way of informing the user of what happened.

When an error occurs in a called function or subroutine that doesn't have an enabled error handler, VBA returns to the calling procedure looking for an enabled error handler. This process proceeds up the calling tree until one is found. If none is found, execution stops with an Access error message displayed.

Creating an error-handling routine

When an error occurs within an application, you have a few choices:

- Ignore the error and resume execution
- Programmatically correct the problem causing the error and resume execution

- Request that the user correct the problem and resume execution
- Inform the user of the problem and continue execution
- Inform the user of the problem and stop execution

In this section, we create a section of code for a generic error handler that informs the user of the problem. We do this by exploring the Error and Err objects that contain the information about the error.

Listing 16-3 contains an error handler that can be used in a procedure that deals with an ADO connection. When an error occurs, the code following the label ErrorHandler runs. The code first checks to see if the Error object contains any items. If there are items, it checks to see if the error is the same as the Err object; if so, the error is an ADO error and the variable strMessage contains the descriptions of all the errors in the Errors collection. If it is not an ADO error, the error is from VBA and the single Err.Description value is displayed. This error handler is used in the form frm_BankAccountsUnbound in our sample application.

Listing 16-3   *A General Error Handler*

```
Dim cnn As New ADODB.Connection
Dim errX As ADODB.Error
Dim strMessage As String

    On Error goto ErrorHandler

    'insert code here

    GoTo Done

ErrorHandler:
    If cnn.Errors.Count > 0 Then
      If err.Number = cnn.Errors.Item(0).Number Then
         'error is an ADO Connection Error
         For Each errX In cnn.Errors
            strMessage = strMessage & err.Description & vbCrLf
         Next
         MsgBox strMessage, , "ADO Error Handler"
      End If
    Else
        'error is a VBA Error
        MsgBox err.Description, , "VBA Error Handler"
    End If
Done:
```

Other Ideas

In designing your application, you can expand its error-handling capabilities in many ways. However, a full discussion is beyond the scope of this book. Consider the following ideas to get you started:

- Create a user-defined error. If something goes wrong with data within your application or an operation the user has chosen, you can use the Raise method of the Err object to cause an error to occur and run your standard error handler. The range 513–65535 is available for user-defined errors and is used with the Raise method as an argument.
- Create a standard error handler called from multiple procedures.
- Record errors in a log. Create a table to store errors as they occur. You can then keep a history of errors for further refinement of your application design or to see trends within problems.
- Instead of just displaying an error message, provide for a printed problem report that can be forwarded to the appropriate technical support group. You can also automatically e-mail an error message to a technical support organization.

Done!

REVIEW

In this session, you learned about the MsgBox function, as well as how to handle error conditions in an application. The following points were discussed:

- One of the most commonly used functions is the MsgBox function. It provides an easy way for your VBA code to communicate with the user both by displaying a message and returning a decision made by the user.
- Having an error handler can alert the user to a problem and prevent the application from crashing.
- Error handlers can also take some action to either work around the error or correct the problem and prevent any user intervention.
- You should devote a good part of your development effort to handling errors.

QUIZ YOURSELF

1. Why is the MsgBox function one of the most commonly used functions? (See "The Message Box Function.")
2. What four things might possibly happen when a runtime error occurs? (See "Errors.")
3. When and why do fatal errors occur? (See "Types of errors.")
4. How would you reduce the likelihood of an application error? (See "Types of errors.")
5. What are the two different types of error objects? When is each type used? (See "The elements of error handling.")
6. When would you use Resume or Resume 0 in your code? (See "VBA error statements.")
7. What type of error would occur if the err.number property returned a 600? (See "Other Ideas.")

PART

III

Saturday Afternoon
Part Review

1. True or false: A Switchboard is a type of menu system.
2. True or false: The Switchboard Manager must be used to create a switchboard.
3. True or false: You can create a custom menu bar by using the Access 2002 Commandbar object or by creating a macro.
4. True or false: KeyUp, KeyDown, and KeyRight are all three types of keyboard events.
5. Which of the following is/are true for unbound forms?
   a. They do not have a constant connection and open view of the underlying data.
   b. They retrieve one record at a time.
   c. They improve performance.
   d. Record changes are under control of code.
   e. All of the above.
6. True or false: When you use unbound forms Access automatically handles record locking.
7. List three functions you need to include on an unbound form to make it functional.
8. List two reasons why you would not want to use unbound forms.
9. When is it preferable to use an option group over a check box?
10. True or false: A ComboBox allows you to have multiple selections.
11. Which properties are unique to combo and list boxes?
    a. Controlsource
    b. rowsource
    c. font size
    d. after update
    e. column width
    f. bound column
    g. multi selection

12. You want to run code that occurs when a user selects an item that is not listed. What event do you use?

    a. After Update

    b. Before Update

    c. In List

    d. Not In List

13. What are the three different types of form views?

14. True or false: A subform must be linked to a main form.

15. Name the most compelling reason to use a continuous form instead of a datasheet.

16. What are the properties that are used to link data between a subform to a form?

17. List three reasons why you should use a tabbed control.

18. To run a procedure as the user changes from tab to tab, you would use which event?

    a. After Update

    b. On Click

    c. On Change

    d. On Tab Click

19. True or false: You can only set the Visible property for the tab control as a whole.

20. What are the three types of tab styles you can use?

PART

IV

Saturday Evening

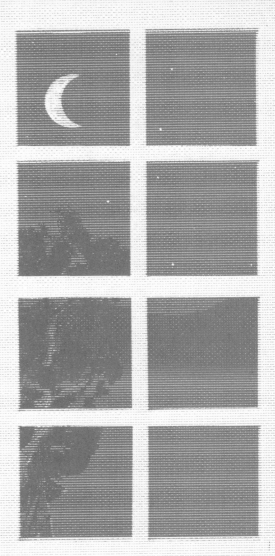

Importing and Exporting Data

Session Checklist

✔ Understanding the basic concept of importing and exporting data

✔ Creating import/export specifications

✔ Programming an import interface

✔ Programming an export interface

**30 Min.
To Go**

I t is becoming standard that applications be able to communicate with one another in some way. Whether it is to bridge two separate programs, move data from a legacy program to a newer one, or to share data across different platforms, the power to import and export data is a vital and important function. Therefore, one of the main functions of any good database program is its capability to import and export data.

Fortunately, Access has a powerful built-in wizard that walks you through doing an import or export. Plus, with the power of VBA, you can design interfaces to give your end-users a more intuitive means of processing external data.

Importing and Exporting

Access has built-in import and export capabilities that are powerful, flexible, and simple to use. You can import to and export from another database, a spreadsheet, or a SQL database that supports ODBC. In fact, Access enables you to directly import to or export from numerous popular off-the-shelf databases and spreadsheets. Access also allows you to exchange data with standard text files, further expanding its flexibility. Table 17-1 lists the formats that you can import to and export from.

Table 17-1 *File Formats Supported by Access*

Data Source	Version/Format
Microsoft Access databases	2.0, 7.0/95, 8.0/97, 9.0/2000
Microsoft Access Project	9.0/2000
dBASE	III, III+, IV, and 5
	7.0 — Linking requires Borland Database Engine 4.x or later
Paradox	3.x, 4.x, 5.0
	8.0 — Linking requires Borland Database Engine 4.x or later
Microsoft Excel Spreadsheet	3.0, 4.0, 5.0, 7.0/95, 8.0/97, 9.0/2000
Lotus 1-2-3 Spreadsheet	.wks, .wk1, .wk2, .wk3, and .wk4
Microsoft Exchange	All versions
Delimited text files	All character sets
Fixed-width text files	All character sets
HTML	For lists; 3.x for lists and tables
XML	
SQL tables, Microsoft FoxPro, and all other data sources that support ODBC	Visual FoxPro 2.x, 3.0, 5.0, and 6.x (only for import)

Importing data

With Access, you can do two types of importing: a true import (where the data is copied into the database) and a linked table. In a true import of the data, the information is copied into the existing database and becomes part of the database. The data can become a new table or the data can be appended to an existing table. A linked table means the information remains external and is never truly incorporated into the database.

Which method is the best? The answer depends on several factors. You should import the data into the database in the following situations:

- Performance is your main goal. Local tables provide the best performance. Access is optimized to work with local data in an Access format.
- The incoming data need not be shared with other database applications. The data from the table will not be accessed from other external applications.

- The information contained in the table is not updated frequently, or this is a one-time update of the data.
- You are converting from one format to another and no longer need to maintain the older (legacy) format.

Consider using Access's linking feature in these situations:

- Your application structure has the data tables in a database that is separate from the application database.
- You need to be able to update and also keep the original data available to other applications.
- The information is frequently updated from other applications.
- The file size of the database exceeds the 1GB capacity of Access's limit for local tables.

Issues related to importing data

Importing data is actually a very simple process. The complexity lies not in bringing the data into Access, but rather, in making sure the data gets updated properly in the local tables. Importing data can be broken into the following major steps:

1. Organize the data.
2. Format the data.
3. Map the data.
4. Append the records.

The following sections take a closer look at each of these steps.

Organizing the data to import

How you gather and organize the data depends on which database platform you use. If the database is another Access database, you can either import an entire table or parts of the table. Should you need to import a part of a table, you can use a query and import the results of the query. You can also pull information from multiple tables into a single query and then import that result.

What information you gather and the tables from which you gather that information are totally dependent on what you need to import into the current database. First, gather the information or data that you need to import from the appropriate tables. After the information has been gathered, you can format it.

Formatting the data

Because of Access's capability to read many different types of file formats, the first step in importing data is to get the data file in a format that Access can read. This depends on the external program from which the data is coming.

If you are working with other Access databases, you don't need to convert the data. Even if the data is coming from another database, Access can read directly from such sources as FoxPro, dBASE, and Paradox. In addition, it can read directly from spreadsheet programs like Excel and Lotus.

What if the data is coming from a nonstandard platform? For instance, what if you are using a legacy MS-DOS–based system, a mainframe, or a once-popular-but-presently-obscure format such as Btrieve. In these cases, you must output the data into a format that Access can read. In most cases, this means exporting the data from the external application into a text file.

Text files can have many different formats, but they fall into two essential groups: delimited and fixed-width. In a *delimited text file*, the fields are separated by some character, and each individual record is on a separate line. Separator characters (*delimiters*) can be any of the standard ones such as a comma, semicolon, space, or tab. Additionally, nonstandard text formats sometimes use other characters that can be defined. With a delimited file, it is unnecessary to define the field widths, as you see in Figure 17-1. Each line is considered a separate record and as you read the lines from left to right, each instance of the delimiter indicates a new field.

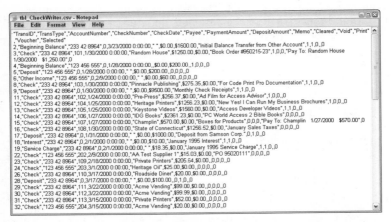

Figure 17-1 *A sample of a delimited text file that uses a comma to separate the fields. Note the first line contains the field names.*

A *fixed-width file* does not use any type of delimiter to separate the fields. In this format, each record is also on a separate line. However, the text file is formatted so that the widths of the fields are defined as part of the file. Simply put, the data is formatted so that the fields are lined up in a columnar structure. Figure 17-2 shows an example. The figure contains data that is identical to the data shown in Figure 17-1 but in a fixed-width format. The column widths determine the size of the fields, and the data for that field must fit within the column.

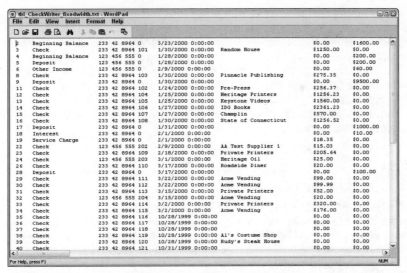

Figure 17-2 *A sample of a fixed-width text file. Notice the columnar formatting of the text. Each column indicates a separate field.*

Mapping the data

Mapping is the process of matching up field for field and table for table. Obviously, if the information you are importing does not have to be appended to existing tables, this issue is moot. However, in most cases, you will want to populate existing tables.

Consider three issues when mapping data to existing tables: matching, definition, and order. The first issue involves matching the correct fields and tables. This requires knowing the definition, function, or purpose of a field and table. Just imagine the old school book exercise in which you have two columns of names and identifiers and you must match the correct names from one column to the correct identifier in the other column. The fields and tables from your external source may have different names, but the content itself matches existing fields and tables. For example, the external table may refer to a field as PayToName, whereas your internal table has a field named Payee. The function of each, in both cases, is the name of the Pay To or Payee on a check transaction.

The second issue to consider during the mapping process is field definition. This goes one step deeper into the structure of the fields and tables. In this step, you go beyond the superficial names of the fields and compare the fields' data types, length, and other characteristics. You must take great pains to make sure that you properly reconcile the definition of the fields and tables. Compare a list of each field's definitions on both sides and make sure that you are bringing the information across correctly. The following is a list of the field properties you should take into consideration during an import.

Data type	Check the number, text, date, and so on.
Field length	Reconcile differences in field size or risk losing data.
Validation rules	Consider any validation rules that apply to the field.

The final step in mapping is the order in which the information is imported and updated. Your database is most likely a normalized relational database. This means that you have table relationships established and, thus, your data must be populated in a specific order. For example, you probably want to update the BankAccounts table before you import and update the Check Writer table because the Check Writer table has a foreign key that ties back to the BankAccounts table. Therefore, you must update in the proper order. If you have enforced referential integrity in your relationships, you get errors if you attempt an import in the wrong order. Referential integrity requires that the parent record exist before you can create a record that references it.

Consider the following points as you import your data:

- Update lookup tables first. Even if you have not established a relationship, it's good practice to update the lookup tables first.
- Update parent tables before you update any child tables.
- If you are importing a table that has an autonumber field as the primary key, make sure that when you append to the table, the numbers are not automatically renumbered by Access. If they are renumbered, the rippling effect requires that related information be updated accordingly.

Appending the data

After you gather the data, put it in a format that Access can recognize and read. After you have outlined how the data will be mapped, the actual process of appending or writing the imported data is fairly painless and straightforward. You do, however, have two different approaches to take in importing the data into your database: using queries or using ADO. The methodology is discussed later in this session in "Methods for Importing/Exporting."

**20 Min.
To Go**

Issues related to exporting data

The process for exporting data is almost identical to that of importing data. It requires similar steps to organize the data to format, map, and finally export or write the data to the external file. Again, because Access supports popular database and spreadsheet applications, you can export to many formats directly. In addition, as with the import function, you can export to both SQL ODBC-compliant databases or to text files.

Here are the steps for exporting data:

1. Collect the data.
2. Format the data.
3. Map the data.
4. Export the records.

The following sections look more closely at each of these steps.

Collecting the data to export

You can use either a query or VBA code to process the existing data and create a recordset with the information you want to process in the export procedure. Access enables you to export the data in various formats. The formats supported for an export are the same as those supported for data importing (refer to Table 17-1).

Formatting the export data

As with importing, Access supports many formats when exporting. Which format you export to depends on the external program to which you are exporting. Again, you can choose to export to another Access database, other databases such as dBASE and Paradox, any database that supports ODBC, or to a common spreadsheet program such as Excel or Lotus.

Mapping the data

In mapping the data to be exported, you must consider the same factors as you do during an import. This is especially true when you are exporting to a text file. You must set up every aspect of the export file.

In many cases, you do not have control over external programs and must export your data to follow a specific format set by that program. In these cases, you map your data as part of the export process. Start by first matching the data from the two sources, field for field and table for table. Make sure that you give the exported file the correct field names as defined by the structure of the external program. One of the nice features of Access is its capability to automatically define the first line of the text file as the field names.

Next, make sure that the field definitions are correct. Define text fields appropriately. In many cases, you must convert or redefine your fields' basic properties. Neither the delimited nor fixed-width formats contain information about the field definitions. You must format the information appropriately prior to writing the text file. Be sure to check the following properties:

Data type	Check the number, text, date, and so on.
Field length	Reconcile differences in field size or risk losing data.
Validation rules	Make sure you consider any validation rules that apply to the field.

The order in which you export the information is important. Should the external program to which you export require the data to be formatted in a specific order, take that into consideration as part of the export process.

Import/Export Processes

Access has several ways to import and export data. Which process you use depends on how much control you want to give the end user. For a quick and easy setup, you can use the Access Import/Export wizard to do the work for you. However, if you want to create your own interface, use some of the built-in methods available and write the appropriate code to process the interface.

Import/export specification

Access has a very useful feature that enables you to create importing and exporting specifications for text files. This is a great utility with which you can create a single specification that you can use over and over on both delimited or fixed-width text files.

Here are instances when you would use the specification file:

- To automate the import/export process.
- To import the information from multiple text files to the same tables.
- To export the data to the same text file.

An import or export specification is stored with a default name: *filename*_ImportSpec or *filename*_ExportSpec. The specification is stored in the database and is an Access system object. To create a specification file, you can use either of the Import Text or Export Text wizards. The wizard creates a listing of information that is critical to the import or export process, such as the format of the file, field mappings, field properties, and so on. Initiate the import wizard by choosing Get External Data from the File menu and then choosing Import. After you select a text file, the wizard opens. An Advanced button appears in the lower-left corner of the screen. Clicking the Advanced button opens the form shown in Figure 17-3.

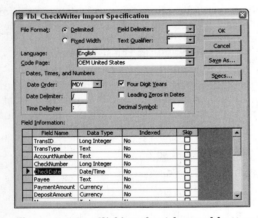

Figure 17-3   *Clicking the Advanced button in the Access Import/Export wizard opens the Import Specification dialog box.*

 You can use the wizard only on text files where the specific format of the file is not known. Access databases and other recognized standard formats do not allow you to use import/export specifications.

As you look at the figure, notice that the main information for how the file is formatted is displayed. There are check boxes that indicate the file format (Delimited or Fixed Width). Choosing Delimited enables Field Delimiter and Text Qualifier fields. The Field Delimiter field enables you to choose which character is the delimiter character. The Text Qualifier field defines whether text strings are enclosed with a single or double quote or no quotes at all.

You can also indicate which language and code page to use. The Code Page option lets you choose the character set to use. Additionally, you can also define how date and time fields are formatted to ensure proper reading of the files. Set the order in which the days, months, and years are arranged and indicate if the data includes four-digit years. You can also enter the delimiter character for both date and time data types.

Defining date fields is very important if you are importing information from different countries because the standard month, day, year format common to the U.S. is different from the day, month, year format of many European countries.

When you have selected the File Format options, you can then start to enter the field information. Enter each field on a separate line. Start by entering the field name. In many of the files you export or import, the first line can be used to store the field name. You can enter this information manually and define the field properties in the File Format options. Enter the name of the field followed by its data type (such as text, currency, number, and so forth). You can then determine if the field should be an indexed field. This indicates to Access whether an index of that field should be created during the import.

As an alternative to creating a specification file within Access, you can also define a file type by creating a Schema.ini **file. A** Schema.ini **file operates by providing Access with the specifics of a particular data source. In this manner, you can provide a detailed specification file for all parameters of the data source. Using the** Schema.ini **file is a very advanced technique for automating the import/export process that you will want to learn later. Creating a** Schema.ini **file, however, is beyond the scope of this book.**

Methods for importing and exporting

After the main pieces of information are obtained, the Start Import button (see Figure 17-4) initiates the import process. In reviewing the code (shown in Listing 17-1), you see that the import is done using one of three Access methods: TransferDatabase, TransferSpreadsheet, or TransferText. You can use these methods for importing and exporting to and from Access.

The TransferDatabase method

YNTAX ▶

TransferDatabase enables you to import or export. The method has the following syntax:

```
DoCmd.TransferDatabase [transfertype], databasetype, databasename[,
objecttype], source, destination[, structureonly][, saveloginid]
```

Note that when you use the TransferDatabase method for importing tables, a new table is created with the data. This method does not append the data to an existing table. Its arguments are defined as follows:

Transfertype	It can be one of the three constants: `acExport`, `acImport`, or `acLink`.
Databasetype	The name of the type of databases that Access recognizes: Microsoft Access Jet 2.x Jet 3.x dBASE III dBASE IV dBASE 5 Paradox 3.x Paradox 4.x Paradox 5.x Paradox 7.x ODBC databases
Databasename	The full name and path of the file

ObjectType	One of the following constants:
	
	`acTable`
	`acQuery`
	`acForm`
	`acReport`
	`acMacro`
	`acModule`
	`acDataAccessPage`
	`acServerView`
	`acDiagram`
	`acStoredProcedure`

Source	The name of the object to be imported
Destination	The name of the object in the destination file
Structureonly	A Boolean value to indicate whether to import just the structure or both the data and its structure
Saveloginid	A Boolean value to indicate whether to save the login identification and password for connecting to ODBC databases

The TransferSpreadsheet method

SYNTAX ▶

The `TransferSpreadsheet` method enables you to import or export from standard spreadsheet files that Access supports.

```
DoCmd.TransferSpreadsheet [transfertype][, spreadsheettype], tablename,
filename[, hasfieldnames][, range]
```

The arguments are defined as follows:

Transfertype	It can be one of the three constants: `acExport`, `acImport`, or `acLink`

Spreadsheettype	The name of the types of databases that Access recognizes. The types include the following: acSpreadsheetTypeExcel3 acSpreadsheetTypeExcel4 acSpreadsheetTypeExcel5 acSpreadsheetTypeExcel7 acSpreadsheetTypeExcel8 acSpreadsheetTypeExcel9 acSpreadsheetTypeLotusWK1 acSpreadsheetTypeLotusWK3 acSpreadsheetTypeLotusWK4 acSpreadsheetTypeLotusWJ2 — Japanese version only
Tablename	The name of the Access table you want to import the data into or the name of the table from which you want to export the data
Filename	The full name and path of the file
Hasfieldnames	A Boolean value to indicate whether the first row of the spreadsheet contains the field names
Range	An expression indicating the cell rows to import. This is an import option only.

The TransferText method

SYNTAX ▶

TransferText is the method to import from text or HTML files.

```
DoCmd.TransferText [transfertype][, specificationname], tablename,
filename[, hasfieldnames][, HTMLtablename][, codepage]
```

The arguments are defined as follows:

Transfertype	It can be one of the following constants: acExportFixed acExportHTML acExportMerge acImportDelim acImportFixed acImportHTML acLinkDelim acLinkFixed acLinkHTML
Specificationname	The name of an import or export specification file you have created in Access
Tablename	The name of the Access table into which you want to import the data or the name of the table from which you want to export the data
Filename	The full name and path of the file

`Hasfieldnames`	A Boolean value to indicate whether the first row of the spreadsheet contains the field names
`Htmltablename`	The name of the table or listing in an HTML file to which you want to import or link
`Codepage`	A value indicating the character set to use

Creating an Import Interface

**10 Min.
To Go**

Certainly, you can let your application use the built-in Import wizard that Access provides. However, to provide a better experience for the end user, you can create an interface form for this purpose. The end user does not have to understand all the intricacies of file formats if you offer him a well-designed form. This also gives you more control over which files are imported and how the file data is processed.

Parts of an import interface

All import utility interfaces share similar basic characteristics. Figure 17-4 shows an example of a simple import form. This import utility enables Check Writer users to import information from external sources into the program. The user opens this form by clicking the Import button on the main menu. This form illustrates the components needed in a basic import form. The user is prompted for the information to import (Payee Listing, Bank Account Information, or Bank Transactions). Next, the user can select the file from which to import by using the Open File button. The user then enters the file's path and name into the text box. Alternatively, the user can manually enter the path and filename directly into the text box. After entering the filename, the user can process the data by clicking Start Import.

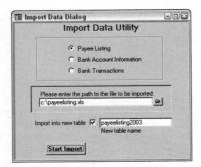

Figure 17-4   *The import utility used to import data in the Check Writer program.*

When you review the Import Data Dialog box, the basic components of an import are evident. An option group lets the user choose the type of information to import. There is an entry for the file's path and name and a button to initiate the import process.

This is an oversimplified example, but all the basic components of an import utility are present. In your use of this interface design, you may add more advanced features. For instance, you can expand it further to allow user control over which fields from the data file to import. This example imports all the information and uses the code and import specification to selectively remove unnecessary information.

Initiating and completing the import process

The import methods shown earlier in the section "Methods for importing and exporting" are all illustrated in the preceding import example. After the user determines the main parameters — which data to import and which file to import from — he or she clicks the Start Import button to initiate the process. When you review the code, you see that the following steps occur. The code first verifies that all the necessary parameters are being provided. Then it determines which data is being imported: payee, bank account, or transactions. This is done with a select case statement that references the ChooseDataType option group on the form. Next, the code analyzes the file selected and bases the import on the format type of the file: Access, Excel, or text file. After the format has been determined, the import is completed using the appropriate Access method: TransferDatabase, TransferSpreadsheet, or TransferText.

The entire import process occurs in the On Click event of the StartImportButton. The initial import occurs for the Payees table. The code in this example illustrates several points. First, the code verifies that it has all the necessary information to do the import. Next, it starts the import by using a Select Case statement to determine which data type is being imported. You see this in Listing 17-1. In the first Case, Payee information is processed. You then see another nested Select Case statement. It's used to determine which file type and, therefore, which of the three methods, to use for importing.

Listing 17-1   *The On Click Event of the Start Import Button*

```
Private Sub cmdStartImport_Click()
Dim rst As New ADODB.Recordset
Dim strNewTableName As String
Dim strExistingTableName As String
Dim strFileType As String

    On Error GoTo ErrorHandler

'check a filename was entered
    If IsNull(Me.selFileName) Then
        MsgBox "You must enter the path and filename.", vbExclamation, "Error"
        Me.selFileName.SetFocus
        GoTo Done
    End If

'if new table was checked, verify tablename entered
    If Me.Newtable = True And IsNull(Me.TableName) Then
```

Continued

Listing 17-1 *Continued*

```
        MsgBox "You must enter the new tablename.", vbExclamation, "Error"
        Me.TableName.SetFocus
        GoTo Done
    End If

    DoCmd.Hourglass True
    DoCmd.SetWarnings False

'Check data type and setup variables
    Select Case Me.ChooseDataType
        Case 1
            strExistingTableName = "tbl_Payees"
        Case 2
            strExistingTableName = "tbl_BankAccounts"
        Case 3
            strExistingTableName = "tbl_CheckWriter"
        Case Else
            MsgBox "You must select a data type.", vbExclamation, "Error"
            Me.ChooseDataType.SetFocus
            GoTo Done
    End Select

    If Me.Newtable = True Then
        strNewTableName = Me.TableName
    Else
        strNewTableName = "tbl_Temp"
        On Error Resume Next
        DoCmd.DeleteObject acTable, "tbl_Temp"
        On Error GoTo ErrorHandler
    End If

'Check for a valid file type and import into temporary table or new table
    strFileType = Right$(Me.selFileName, 3)
    Select Case strFileType
        Case "mdb"
            DoCmd.TransferDatabase acImport, "Microsoft Access", Me.selFileName, acTable,
strExistingTableName, strNewTableName
        Case "xls"
            DoCmd.TransferSpreadsheet acImport, acSpreadsheetTypeExcel97,
strNewTableName, Me.selFileName, True
        Case "txt", "csv"
            DoCmd.TransferText acImportDelim, , strNewTableName, Me.selFileName, True
        Case Else
            MsgBox "You did not select a correct file type.  Choose *.mdb, *.xls, *.txt,
or *.csv"
            GoTo Done
    End Select

'If new table selected then done otherwise append data
    If Me.Newtable = False Then
        'Run append query from temp table to new table
        DoCmd.RunSQL "INSERT INTO " & strExistingTableName & _
            " SELECT tbl_Temp.* " & _
            " FROM tbl_Temp"
        DoCmd.DeleteObject acTable, "tbl_Temp"
```

```
    End If

'display message that import is completed
    MsgBox "Import Completed.", vbExclamation, "Import Status"
    GoTo Done

ErrorHandler:
    MsgBox Err.Description
Done:
    DoCmd.SetWarnings True
    DoCmd.Hourglass False
    Application.Echo True


End Sub
```

In addition to this code, another process is going on. On the form, the user is given the option of importing the table as a new table or importing it into existing tables. In the first instance, importing is done from an Access database. The `TransferDatabase` method, when used to import tables, imports the entire table. You can't import just the data using this method. Therefore, this code imports the table and then uses VBA code to process it. The code, in this case, is used to process the payees' information. It opens up two recordsets. The first is for the imported table and the second is for the local Payees table. It then loops through the newly imported table, and for each record, it creates a new record for that payee in the Payees table. The import table for the Bank Accounts table uses an append query instead.

Note that in the `TransferText` method, lines of code used for each reference import specification files that have been set up in advance. To view the specifications, select the Get External menu item, select Import, click the Advance button, and then click Specs. This gives a listing of all the available specification files. To view one, select and open it.

After the import has been completed, any temporary tables are deleted and a message displays telling you that the import was successful. The example shows you many of the ways you can affect the data during the import process. You can affect it during the creation of the import specification. You can manipulate it after it is in a table, during the append query, or through VBA code during the ADO updates.

Creating an Export Interface

You can create an export interface similar to an import interface. The goal is again to either simplify the export process or give the user more control over the export of the data. You can perform the export using the same techniques as you used for the import.

Parts of an export interface

The ExportChecks form in the Check Writer database is an example of an export interface. The main elements are all represented, as shown in Figure 17-5. An option group enables you to select what type of information is being exported: Payee Listing, Bank Account Information, or Bank Transactions. Note that choosing Bank Transactions makes additional options visible. The user selects the account and the date range of the transactions he or she wishes to process. All the available transactions are then listed.

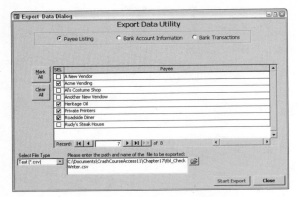

Figure 17-5 *Example of the Export utility in the Check Writer database.*

The user has the option of selectively choosing which records to export. This is an example of providing a multilevel selection. The user can choose which type of data and the specific groups of records — grouped, for example, by bank account and with a date range. The user can also select the records from that data source to export. After the user selects the records and enters the filename and path, he or she clicks the Start button to initiate the export process. Similar to the import process, the what, where, and how must be collected. Any export interface requires input regarding which information is to be exported, which of the records to import, where they are to be exported to, and how.

Coding the export procedure

The Start button's On Click event (see Listing 17-2) on the Export form starts the export process by verifying that the necessary components have been supplied. The user must select the type of data to export, which records to export, and where to export to.

Listing 17-2 *The On Click Event of the Start Export Button*

```
Private Sub cmdStartExport_Click()
Dim strQueryName As String

    On Error GoTo ErrorHandler

'check for filetype
    If IsNull(Me.selFileType) Then
        MsgBox "You must enter a file type.", vbCritical, "Error"
        Me.selFileType.SetFocus
        GoTo Done
    End If

'check for path and filename
    If IsNull(Me.selFileName) Then
        MsgBox "You must enter in the path and filename.", vbCritical, "Error"
        Me.selFileName.SetFocus
        GoTo Done
    End If

'check for selected records
```

```
    Select Case Me.SelectType
        Case 1
            strQueryName = "qry_ExportPayees"
            If DCount("*", strQueryName) = 0 Then
                MsgBox "You have not selected any Payee records to export.", vbCritical,
"Error"
                GoTo Done
            End If
        Case 2
            strQueryName = "qry_ExportBankAccounts"
            If DCount("*", strQueryName) = 0 Then
                MsgBox "You have not selected any Bank Account records to export.",
vbCritical, "Error"
                GoTo Done
            End If
        Case 3
            strQueryName = "qry_ExportTransactions"
            If DCount("*", strQueryName) = 0 Then
                MsgBox "You have not selected any Transactions to export.", vbCritical,
"Error"
                GoTo Done
            End If
    End Select


    DoCmd.Hourglass True

'turn off warnings to avoid prompts for updates
    DoCmd.SetWarnings False

'If file exists, delete it
    If Dir(Me.selFileName) <> "" Then
        Kill Me.selFileName
    End If

'exports selected records to separate table and initiates method

    Select Case Me.selFileType
        Case "Access (*.mdb)" 'Access database
            If Nz(Me.selTableName) = "" Then
                MsgBox "You must enter a table name for an Access Export"
                GoTo Done
            Else
                DoCmd.TransferDatabase acExport, "Microsoft Access", Me.selFileName,
acTable, strQueryName, Me.selTableName
            End If
        Case "Excel (*.xls)"  'Excel spreadsheet
            DoCmd.TransferSpreadsheet acExport, acSpreadsheetTypeExcel9, strQueryName,
Me.selFileName, True
        Case "Text (*.csv)"   'text file
            DoCmd.TransferText acExportDelim, , strQueryName, Me.selFileName, True
    End Select

    MsgBox "Export Completed Successfully."
    GoTo Done
```

Continued

Listing 17-2 *Continued*

```
ErrorHandler:
    MsgBox Err.Description
Done:
    DoCmd.Hourglass False
    DoCmd.SetWarnings True
End Sub

Private Sub Form_Load()
    SetMarks False
End Sub

Private Sub FromDate_AfterUpdate()
    Me.Subfrm.Requery
End Sub
```

The usual verification is done. Note that the code uses a Dcount function to quickly count whether any records have been selected for each of the data types. It presents an error message if no records have been selected. Additionally, if the extension is .mdb for an Access database, the system checks for a valid table name to be entered. The code then starts a Select Case statement to determine the type of data being processed. For each one, a make-table query is run. This creates a new query for just the selected data. Next, a nested Select Case statement is used to determine which format to export to based on what is entered for the filename and its extension. Then, the appropriate code is used to export the data using one of these three methods: TransferDatabase, TransferSpreadsheet, or TransferText. The syntax for the methods is similar to doing an import. Refer to the section on the import methods for the full syntax.

As with the import example, you have a lot of control over several aspects of the export process. You can manipulate the data at several points: with the specification files, during the queries to export the selected records, or during the export itself.

Done!

REVIEW

Importing and exporting is a means of extending your program's communication with other programs and the information your program can process. You have learned the general issues behind importing and exporting data. More advanced imports and exports may require further considerations. However, they all follow the same logic of the general techniques shown in this session. This session covered these topics:

- The basic logic of importing includes organizing, formatting, and mapping the data and appending the records.
- The basic logic for exporting includes collecting, formatting, and mapping the data and exporting the records.
- There is no mystery or difficulty in importing and exporting data. It tends to be a more time-consuming process than a technical one.

- After you overcome the communications barrier (determining which formats are needed, and so on) you only have to write the queries or SQL statements to pull the data you want.

- You can use the Access Import wizard to set up import and export specifications and do much of the work for you.

A key thing to note was that the code did not include any data validation routines. For the purpose of this session, that was not relevant. You should put in data validation as a standard practice when writing routines that delete or add records. An example of such a routine is one that compares the number of records to be imported with those records that actually get written to the table.

QUIZ YOURSELF

1. What is the general order you should follow when performing an import or an export? Why is the order important? (See "Importing and Exporting.")

2. Does Access allow you to export only to databases? Explain the limits, if any, that Access imposes on importing and exporting. (See "Importing and Exporting.")

3. Where in Access do you set up import/export specifications? (See "Import/export specification.")

4. What are the three VBA methods that Access provides for doing imports and exports? (See "Methods for importing and exporting.")

Techniques to Improve the Speed of an Application

Session Checklist

✔ Tuning your computer hardware for maximum performance

✔ Increasing performance dramatically by keeping your code in a compiled state

✔ Compacting your database

✔ Creating .mde databases for better performance

✔ Organizing your database into referenced libraries

✔ Improving the absolute speed of your database

✔ Improving the perceived speed of your database

30 Min. To Go

When you create an application, you want it to run as fast as possible. Sometimes, applications run slowly because they are processing hundreds of thousands of records; other applications run slowly because they are poorly written. The larger your database becomes, the slower it invariably runs. Although sloppy programming practices can be ignored in small databases, when larger databases are involved, these practices make the performance of an application unacceptable. You should employ good programming techniques with the smallest databases and make speed a priority in all your applications. This session teaches you several techniques for making Access applications run faster.

Hardware and Memory

The published minimum RAM requirement for a computer to run this version of Access on either Windows XP or Windows 2000 is 256MB RAM plus 32MB for each Office product run simultaneously — with an emphasis on minimum. If you are going to do serious development with Access, you should have at least 512MB RAM.

Memory is actually more important than the processor speed. Increasing your memory from 256MB to 512MB can easily double or triple the speed of your application. Changing the processor speed by 100 MHz and keeping the memory the same makes little difference.

Understanding the Compiled State

If your application contains even one line of Visual Basic code, it is incredibly important that you understand what compilation is and what it means for an application to be in a compiled state. There are actually two types of code in Access: the code that you write in the Visual Basic window and the code that Microsoft Access can understand and execute.

Before a procedure of Visual Basic code that you have written can be executed, the code must be run through a compiler to put it in a form that Access can understand. Access actually lacks a true compiler and instead converts the code into precompiled code and then uses an interpreter to run the code. The code in the converted form is known as *compiled code*, or as being in a compiled state.

If a procedure is run that is not in a compiled state, the procedure must first be compiled and then passed to the interpreter for execution. In reality, this does not happen at the procedure level, but at the module level. When you call a procedure, the module containing the procedure and all modules that have procedures referenced in the called procedure are loaded and compiled. You can manually compile your code, or you can let Access compile it for you on the fly. It takes time to compile the code, however, so the performance of your application suffers if you let Access compile each time you run your code.

In addition to the time it takes for Access to compile your code at runtime, decompiled programs use considerably more memory than code that is compiled. When your application is completely compiled, only the compiled code is loaded into memory when a procedure is called. If you run an application that is in a decompiled state, Access loads the decompiled code and generates the compiled code as needed. Access does not unload the decompiled code as it compiles, so you are left with two versions of the same code in memory.

Putting your application's code into a compiled state

There is only one way to put your entire application into a compiled state: Choose Debug ➪ Compile on the Modules toolbar. The Compile menu item is followed by the internal project name, as shown in Figure 18-1. To access the Debug menu, you must have a module open.

The internal project name is the filename used when you first create the Microsoft Access database file. You can change the internal project name by selecting the *project name* Properties option from the Tools menu in the Visual Basic window. The project name precedes the text Properties at the bottom of the menu. Changing the internal project name causes the database to decompile.

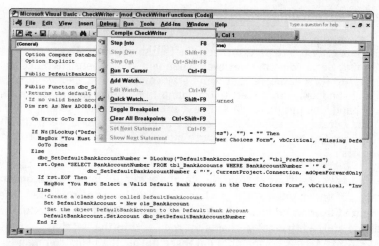

Figure 18-1 *Compiling a program.*

It can take a long time to compile complex or large applications with a lot of Visual Basic code. You should close your application after compiling. To compile all your modules, Access needs to load every single one of them into memory. All this code stays in memory until you close Access.

Previous versions of Access before 2000 included a Compile button on the Visual Basic toolbar. That is no longer the case.

Losing the compiled state

In previous versions of Access, changing any code would decompile the entire application. In this version of Microsoft Access, only portions of code affected by certain changes are put into a decompiled state — not the entire application.

The following changes cause portions of your code to be decompiled:

- Modifying a form, report, control, or module containing code. (If you don't save the modified object, your application is preserved in its previous state.)
- Adding a new form, report, control, or module. (This includes adding new code behind an existing form.)
- Deleting or renaming a form, report, control, or module.

If you modify objects such as reports or forms at runtime through Visual Basic code, portions of your application are put into a decompiled state when the objects are modified. (Wizards often do this.)

If your application creates objects such as reports or forms on the fly, portions of your application are put into a decompiled state when the objects are created. (Wizards often do this as well.)

Using the undocumented/decompile option

Sometimes, you find that no matter what you do, your database does not stay compiled. You may start your program only to see an error message telling you that Access can't find a project or library. You may get a compile error even when you know there are no code problems or syntax errors. To fix a database that won't stay compiled and then compile your database, you must run an undocumented startup command-line option called /decompile. You may have seen command-line options such as /nostartup, /cmd, and /compact. The /decompile option starts Access in a special way so that when a database is opened, all Visual Basic modules are saved as text. This works with module objects and all the code that is behind forms and reports.

Decompiling is very different from the database simply being in an uncompiled state. An uncompiled state is when any module is not compiled. The undocumented decompile command forces a decompile of every module in the database and, additionally, cleans up code within the database. Nothing else in Microsoft Access cleans up a database better than this command.

To decompile the database, choose Run from the Windows Start menu and type **msaccess /decompile**, as shown in Figure 18-2. You are asked to select the database file you want to open. As you do this, hold down the Shift key so that any Startup options in autoexec macros are not run when the database is opened. Allowing startup options to run potentially allows module code to be executed in your database. This means that Access has to compile the code before it runs. If Access begins to compile your database, the decompile option won't work. You won't know the decompile isn't working; it simply does not fix any of the problems an uncompiled database presents.

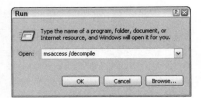

Figure 18-2   *Decompiling a program.*

Access appears to start as usual. When you open your database, you see the Access database container. This means that the decompile is finished. Immediately exit Access (close so it is not running) after it finishes decompiling and then restart Access normally.

After you exit Access and restart Access normally, you can open your database. Open any module to enter the Visual Basic Editor window. You can also open any form with Visual Basic code behind it and display the code window. Next, select the Compile *projectname* option. After the database compiles, close the module and return to the database container.

Compacting a database after compiling it

Any time you compile your database, you should also compact it. From the database container, choose Tools ⇨ Database Utilities ⇨ Compact and Repair Database. After you finish compacting, Access runs procedures much faster than usual and your database reduces to at least half the size it was before you decompiled it.

Detecting a decompiled database and automatically recompiling

Make sure that your database is always in a compiled state. Your customers may make simple or even complex changes to your application and then complain because their system is running slowly. Although some of your customers may be serious developers, many customers who make changes to Access databases do not know about compilation or compacting.

To see if your database is compiled, you can open the Visual Basic window for any module, display the Debug window, and type **? IsCompiled()**. If the database is compiled, the screen displays True. If it is in a decompiled state, the screen displays False, as shown in Figure 18-3.

Figure 18-3 *Checking to see if a database file is in a compiled state.*

To solve the problem of an uncompiled database being, you can create an interface that automatically detects if the database is not in a compiled state and then gives the user the option of compiling the application. This code is run each time the database is opened. The user still has to manually compact the database, but the hard part is compiling. Figure 18-4 shows the message that is automatically displayed if the database is not compiled.

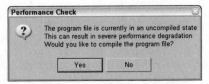

Figure 18-4 *A dialog box to help the user compile your application.*

The code in Listing 18-1 uses the Access built-in IsCompiled function to determine the compiled state of the application. If the application is not compiled, the MsgBox is displayed (refer to Figure 18-3). Users have two choices. If they are still testing, they may not want to compile yet because it takes some time and, at this stage, they may not be concerned about the speed of the application. If they want to compile, they simply have to click the Yes button.

Listing 18-1 *Visual Basic module to detect and automatically compile an application*

```
Dim MsgTxt As String
If Not IsCompiled() Then
MsgTxt = "The program file is currently in a decompiled state" & vbCrLf
MsgTxt = MsgTxt & "This can result in severe performance problems." & vbCrLf
MsgTxt = MsgTxt & "Would you like to compile the program file?"
   Response = MsgBox(MsgTxt, vbYesNo+vbQuestion, "Performance Check")
   If Response = vbYes Then
      'You could display a message box that tells the user to be patient while
      'the database is compiled
      DoCmd.Echo False     'Stop screen display to eliminate seeing the module open and
close
      DoCmd.OpenModule "anymodulename"     'Open any module you have in the database
      DoCmd.SelectObject acModule, "anymodulename" 'You must select the module 'after you
open it
      RunCommand (acCmdCompileAndSaveAllModules) 'This command does the compile and save
      DoCmd.Close acModule, "anymodulename"     'Close the module after the compile and
save is done
      DoCmd.Echo True     'Start screen display again
      MsgTxt = "          The program file has been compiled" &  vbCrLf
      MsgTxt = MsgTxt & "You should now select Tools | Database Utilities | Compact
Database"
      MsgTxt = MsgTxt & vbCrLF & "from the menu above the database container. "
      Response = MsgBox(MsgTxt, vbInformation, "Compile Completed Successfully")
   End If
End If
```

Although there is no easy way to automatically compact the open program file, the user can be instructed to choose Tools ➪ Database Utilities ➪ Compact and Repair Database. When the program database is open, this also reruns the startup or Autoexec macro file after compacting the database.

*20 Min.
To Go*

Creating and Distributing .mde Files

One way to ensure that your application's code is always compiled is to distribute your database as an .mde file. When you save your database as an .mde file, Access compiles all code modules (including form modules), removes all editable source code, and compacts the database. The new .mde file contains no source code but continues to work because it does contain a compiled copy of all your code.

Not only is this a great way to secure your source code, but it also enables you to distribute databases that are smaller (because they contain no source code) and that always keep their modules in a compiled state. Because the code is always in a compiled state, less memory is used by the application and no performance penalty is exacted for code being compiled at runtime.

In addition to not being able to view existing code because it is all compiled, you also have the following restrictions:

- You cannot view, modify, or create forms, reports, or modules in Design view.
- You cannot add, delete, or change references to object libraries or databases.

- You cannot change your database's Visual Basic project name using the Options dialog box.

- You cannot import or export forms, reports, or modules. Note, however, that tables, queries, and macros can be imported from or exported to non-.mde databases.

Because of these restrictions, it may not be possible to distribute your application as an .mde file. For example, if your application creates forms at runtime, you cannot distribute the database as an .mde file.

There is no way to convert an .mde file back into a normal database file. Always save and keep a copy of the original database! When you need to change the application, you must open the normal database and then create a new .mde before distribution. If you delete your original database, you will be unable to access any of your objects in Design view.

There are some prerequisites to meet before you can save a database as an .mde file. First, if security is turned on, you must have all applicable rights to the database when you create the .mde file. In addition, if the database is replicated, you must remove all replication system tables and properties before saving the .mde file. Finally, you must save all databases or add-ins in the chain of references as .mde files, or your database cannot use them.

You should first close the database if it is currently opened. If you do not close the current database, Access attempts to close it for you, prompting you to save changes where applicable. When working with a shared database, all users must close the database because Access needs exclusive rights to work with it.

To save the database as an .mde file, choose Tools ➪ Database Utilities and click Make MDE File, as shown in Figure 18-5.

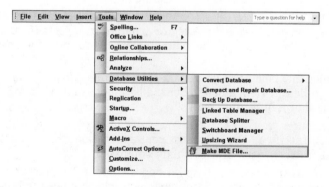

Figure 18-5 *Saving your database as an .mde file.*

If the database is closed and no database is open, specify the database you want to save as an .mde file in the Database To Save As MDE dialog box, and then click Make MDE.

If you had a database open when you selected Make MDE File, this step is skipped and Access assumes you want to use the previously opened database. If you wish to use a different database, cancel out of Make MDE File, close the database, and select Make MDE File again. At that time, you are asked to identify the database you want to save as an .mde file.

In the Database to Save as MDE dialog box, specify a name, drive, and folder for the database. Do not attempt to save the .mde file with the same filename as the original database.

Do not delete or overwrite your original database! As stated previously, there is no way to convert an .mde file to a normal database, and you cannot edit any objects in an .mde file. If you delete or otherwise lose your original database, you can never again access any of the objects in the design environment.

Organizing Commonly Used Code into a Library

After your application is finished and ready for distribution, consider putting commonly used code that is never modified by an end user into a library database.

A *library database* is an external Access program database that is referenced from your application database. You incur a little overhead by having to call code from the library rather than accessing it directly in the parent application. The benefit is that the library code will never be put into a decompiled state — even if your application creates or modifies objects on the fly or if your users add new objects or modify existing objects.

Putting code into a library database can greatly increase an application's performance and keep the performance consistent over periods of time. Most important, it separates the database file into two smaller databases; and the smaller the database, the faster it runs.

The first step in referencing procedures in an external database is to create the external database with all its modules just as you would an ordinary Access database. Any procedures that you declare as `Private` are not made available to the calling application, so plan carefully what you want and don't want to expose to other databases.

After you have created the second database and created or exported its objects (forms, reports, modules), you can create a reference from the main program file to the referenced database (the database your users run).

To create a reference, first open any module in your main application database in Design view. When you have a module in Design view, a new command becomes available from the Tools menu called References, as shown in Figure 18-6.

After you choose Tools ➪ References, you see the References dialog box (see Figure 18-7). In the References dialog box, you specify all the references your application needs for using OLE automation or for using other Access databases as library databases.

When making a reference to another Access database (as opposed to an OLE server created with another development tool such as Visual Basic .NET), you probably need to browse for the database. Use the Browse dialog box as though you were going to open the external database.

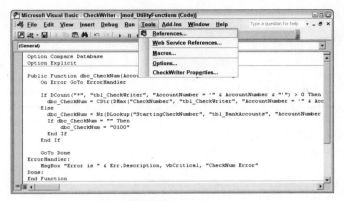

Figure 18-6   *Selecting the References option.*

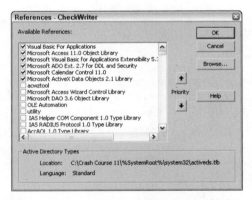

Figure 18-7   *Viewing and selecting references.*

After you have selected the external Access database, it shows up in the References dialog box with a check mark to indicate that it is referenced.

To remove a reference, access the References dialog box again and clear the referenced item by selecting its check box. After you have made all the references you need to make, click the OK button.

After a database is referenced, you can call the procedures in the referenced database as though they existed in your application database. No matter what happens in your application database to cause code to decompile, the referenced database always stays in a compiled state unless it is opened and modified directly using Access.

Improving Absolute Speed

When discussing an application's performance, the word *performance* is usually synonymous with speed. In software development, there are actually two different types of speed: absolute and perceived.

Absolute speed refers to the actual speed at which your application performs a function, such as how long it takes to run a certain query.

Perceived speed is the phenomenon of an end user actually perceiving one application to be faster than another application — even though it may indeed be slower — because of visual feedback provided to the user while the application is performing a task. Absolute speed items can be measured in units of time; perceived speed cannot.

Some of the most important items for increasing actual speed are the following:

- Keeping your application in a compiled state
- Organizing your procedures into "smart" modules
- Opening databases exclusively
- Compacting your databases regularly

You should always open a database exclusively in a single-user environment. If your application is a standalone application (nothing is shared over a network), opening the database in exclusive mode can really boost performance. If your application is run on a network and shared by multiple users, you cannot open the database exclusively. (Actually, the first user can open it exclusively, but then no other user can access the database thereafter.)

The preferred method for running an application in a network environment is to run Microsoft Access and the main program .mdb file locally on each workstation and link to a shared database containing the data on the server. If your application is used in this manner, you can open and run the code database exclusively, but everyone can share the data files.

To open a database exclusively, select the filename in the Open dialog box, click the Open command button, and then choose Open Exclusive from the drop-down list (see Figure 18-8).

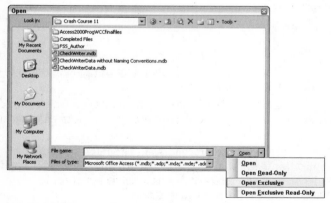

Figure 18-8 *Opening a database exclusively.*

All the preceding methods are excellent (and necessary) ways to help keep your applications running at their optimum performance level, but these are not the only ways you can increase the absolute speed of your application. Almost every area of development, from forms to modules, can be optimized to give your application maximum absolute speed. The following sections give you some tips on optimizing performance.

Minimizing form and report complexity and size

One of the key elements to achieving better performance from your forms and reports is reducing their complexity and size. Here are some ideas to help you reduce a form or report's complexity and size:

- **Minimize the number of objects on a form or report.** The fewer objects used, the fewer resources needed to display and process the form or report.
- **Reduce the use of subforms.** When a subform is loaded, two forms are in memory: the parent form and the subform. Use a list box or a combo box in place of a sub-form whenever possible.
- **Use labels instead of text boxes for hidden fields.** Text boxes use more resources than labels do. Hidden fields are often used as an alternative to creating variables to store information. You cannot write a value directly to a label as you can to a text box, but you can write to the label's caption property like this: Label1.Caption = "MyValue".
- **Move some code from a form's module into a standard module.** This enables the form to load faster because the code doesn't need to be loaded into memory. If the procedures you move to a normal module are referenced by any procedures executed upon loading a form (such as in the Form Load event), moving the procedures does not help because they are loaded anyway as part of the potential call tree of the executed procedure. A *call tree* is the potential chain of commands where one module calls another, which calls another, and so on.
- **Don't overlap controls on a form or report.**
- **Place related groups of controls on form pages.** If only one page is shown at a time, Access does not need to generate all the controls at the same time.
- **Use light forms whenever possible.** Light forms have no code module attached to them, so they load and display considerably faster than forms with code modules.
- **Use a query that returns a limited result set for the Record Source of a form or report rather than using a table.** The less data returned for the Record Source, the faster the form or report loads. In addition, return only those fields actually used by the form or report.

Using bitmaps on forms and reports

Bitmaps on forms and reports make an application look attractive and also help convey the purpose of the form or report (as in a wizard). Graphics are always resource-intensive, so use the fewest possible graphic objects on your forms and reports. This minimizes form and report load time, increases print speed, and reduces the resources used by your application.

Often you display pictures that a user never changes and that are not bound to a data-base. Examples of such pictures are your company logo on a switchboard or static images in a wizard. When you want to display an image such as this, you have two choices.

If the image never changes and you don't need to activate it in Form Design view, use an Image control. Image controls use fewer resources and display faster. If you need the image to be a linked or embedded OLE object that you can edit, use an unbound object frame. You can convert OLE images in unbound object frames.

If you have an image in an unbound object frame that you no longer need to edit, you can convert the unbound object frame into an Image control by choosing Format ⇨ Change To Image.

When you have forms that contain unbound OLE objects, you should close the forms when they are not in use to free resources. Also avoid using bitmaps with many colors — they take considerably more resources and are slower to paint than a bitmap of the same size with fewer colors.

If you want to display an unbound OLE object but don't want the user to be able to activate it, set its Enabled property to False.

Getting the most from your modules

**10 Min.
To Go**

Consider reducing the number of modules and procedures in your application by consolidating them whenever possible. There is a small memory overhead incurred for each module and procedure you use, so consolidating them may free up some memory.

Using appropriate data types

You should always explicitly declare variables using the Dim function rather than arbitrarily assigning values to variables that have not used Dim. To ensure that all variables in your application are explicitly declared before they are used in a procedure, choose Tools ⇨ Options from the Database Container window and then set the Require Variable Declarations option on the Modules tab.

Use integers and long integers rather than singles and doubles when possible. Integers and long integers use less memory and take less time to process than singles and doubles. Table 18-1 shows the relative speed of the different numeric data types available in Access.

Table 18-1 *Data Types and Their Mathematical Processing Speeds*

Data Type	Relative Processing Speed
Integer/Long	Fastest
Single/Double	Next to fastest
Currency	Next to slowest
Variant	Slowest

In addition to using integers and long integers whenever possible, you should also use integer math rather than precision math when applicable. For example, to divide one long integer by another long integer, you can use the following statement:

```
x = Long1 / Long2
```

This statement is a standard math function that uses floating-point math. The same function can be performed using integer math with the following statement:

```
x = Long1 \ Long2
```

Of course, integer math isn't always applicable. It is, however, commonly applied when returning a percentage. For example, you can return a percentage with the following precision math formula:

```
x = Total / Value
```

However, you can perform the same function using integer math by first multiplying the total by 100 and then using integer math like this:

```
x = (Total * 100) \ Value
```

You can also use string functions (**$**) where applicable. When you are manipulating variables that are of type `String`, use the string functions (for example, `Str$()` as opposed to their variant counterparts (`Str()`). If you are working with variants, use the nonstring functions. Using string functions when working with strings is faster because Access doesn't need to perform type conversions on the variables.

When you need to return a substring by using `Mid$()`, you can omit the third parameter to have the entire length of the string returned. For example, to return a substring that starts at the second character of a string and returns all remaining characters, you use a statement like this:

```
szReturn = Mid$(szMyString, 2)
```

When using arrays, use dynamic arrays with the `Erase` and `ReDim` statements to reclaim memory. By dynamically adjusting the size of the arrays, you can ensure that only the amount of memory needed for the array is allocated.

In addition to using optimized variables, consider using constants when applicable. Constants can make your code much easier to read and do not slow your application if you compile your code before executing it.

Writing faster routines

You can speed up your procedures in a number of ways by optimizing the routines they "contain. If you keep performance issues in mind as you develop, you can find and take advantage of situations like those discussed here.

Some Access functions perform similar processes but vary greatly in the time they take to execute. You probably use one or more of these regularly. Knowing the most efficient way to perform these routines can greatly affect your application's speed:

- For/Next statements are faster than `Select Case` statements.
- The `IIF()` function is much slower than a standard set of `If/Then/Else` statements.
- The `With` and `For Each` functions accelerate manipulating multiple objects and/or their properties.

- Change a variable with `Not` instead of using an `If/Then` statement. (For example, use x = Not(y) instead of If y = true then x= false.)

- Instead of comparing a variable to the value `True`, use the value of the variable. (For example, instead of saying `If X = True Then...`, say `If X Then....`)

- Use the Requery method instead of the Requery action. The method is significantly faster than the action.

- When using OLE automation, resolve references when your application is compiled rather than resolving them at runtime using the `GetObject` or `CreateObject` functions.

Using control variables

When referencing controls on a form in code, you can choose either very slow or very fast ways to use references to form objects. The slowest possible way is to reference each control explicitly. This requires Access to sequentially search for the form name, starting with the first form name in the database, until it finds the name in the forms list (`msysObjects` table). If the form name starts with a z, this takes a long time if there are many forms in the database. For example:

```
Forms![frm_CheckWriter]![BankAccountNumber] = something
Forms![frm_CheckWriter]![BankAccountName] = something
Forms![frm_CheckWriter]![Payee] = something
```

If the code is in a class module behind the frm_CheckWriter form, you can use the Me reference. The Me reference refers to the open object (forms or reports) and substitutes for `Forms![formname]`. It can go very quickly right to the form name. For example:

```
Me!BankAccountNumber] = something
Me![BankAccountName] = something
Me![frm_CheckWriter]![Payee] = something
```

If your code is not stored behind the form but is in a module procedure, you can use a control variable like the following:

```
Dim frm as Form
set frm = Forms![frm_CheckWriter]
frm![BankAccountNumber] = something
frm![BankAccountName] = something
frm!frm_CheckWriter]![Payee] = something
```

Using this code, you look up the form name only once. An even faster way is to use the `With` construct. For example:

```
With Forms![frm_CheckWriter]
   ![BankAccountNumber] = something
   ![BankAccountName] = something
   !frm_CheckWriter]![Payee] = something
End With
```

You can then reference the variable rather than reference the actual control. Of course, if you don't need to set values in the control but rather use values from a control, you should simply create a variable to contain the value rather than the reference to the control.

Improving Perceived Speed

Perceived speed is how fast your application appears to run to the end user. Many techniques can increase the perceived speed of your applications. Perceived speed usually involves supplying visual feedback to the user while the computer is busy performing some operation. This feedback might be a percent meter that updates constantly when Access is busy processing data.

Loading and keeping forms hidden

If certain forms are displayed often, consider hiding them rather than closing them. To hide a form, set its Visible property to False. When you need to display the form again, set its Visible property back to True. Forms that remain loaded consume memory, but they display more quickly than forms that must be loaded each time they are viewed. In addition, if you are *morphing* a form or report (changing the way the form or report looks by changing form and control properties), keep the form hidden until all changes are made so that the user doesn't have to watch the changes take place.

Using the hourglass

When your application needs to perform a task that may take a while, use the hourglass. The hourglass cursor shows the user that the computer is not locked up but is merely busy. To turn on the hourglass cursor, use the Hourglass method:

```
DoCmd.Hourglass True
```

To turn the hourglass back to the default cursor, use this method:

```
DoCmd.Hourglass False
```

Using the percent meter

In addition to using the hourglass, you should consider using the percent meter when performing looping routines in a procedure. The percent meter gives constant visual feedback that your application is busy, and it shows the user in no uncertain terms where it is in the current process. The following code demonstrates using the percent meter in a loop to show the meter, starting at 0 percent and expanding to 100 percent, 1 percent at a time:

```
Dim iCount As Integer, iCount2 As Long
Dim Result As Integer
Result = SysCmd(acSysCmdInitMeter, "Running through loop", 100)
For iCount = 1 To 100
    Result = SysCmd(acSysCmdUpdateMeter, iCount)
```

```
    For iCount2 = 1 To 50000: Next iCount2 ' This creates a pause so the meter is readable
Next iCount
Result = SysCmd(acSysCmdRemoveMeter)
```

The first step for using the percent meter is initializing the meter. You initialize it by calling the SysCmd function like this:

```
Result = SysCmd(acSysCmdInitMeter, "Running through loop", 100)
```

The acSysCmdInitMeter in this line is an Access constant that tells the function that you are initializing the meter. The second parameter is the text you want to appear to the left of the meter. Finally, the last value is the maximum value of the meter (in this case, 100 percent). You can set this value to anything you want. For example, if you were iterating through a loop of 504 records, you could set this value to 504. Then you could pass the record count at any given time to the SysCmd function; Access decides what percentage the meter shows to be filled.

After the meter has been initialized, you can pass a value to it to update the meter. To update the meter, you call the SysCmd function again and pass it the acSysCmdUpdateMeter constant and the new update meter value. Remember, the value that you pass the function is not necessarily the percent displayed by the meter. When the loop is completed, run SysCmd(acSysCmdRemoveMeter) to remove the meter from the status bar.

Done!

Review

In this session, you learned about ways to make your application run faster by keeping it compiled or by using a variety of techniques to increase the speed with which it runs. The following topics were covered:

- Tuning your computer hardware for maximum performance
- Increasing performance dramatically by keeping your code in a compiled state
- Compacting your database
- Creating .MDE databases for better performance
- Organizing your database into referenced libraries
- Using techniques to improve the absolute speed of your database
- Using techniques to improve perceived speed such as the hourglass and progress meter

---

Quiz Yourself

1. What is the optimum amount of memory you need to run Microsoft Access? (See "Hardware and Memory.")
2. Why would you want to compile your program? (See "Understanding the Compiled State.")
3. How do you compile your Access database file? (See "Putting your application's code into a compiled state.")

4. Should you compact your database after compiling it? (See "Compacting a database after compiling it.")

5. What are the advantages of creating an .mde file? (See "Creating and Distributing .mde Files.")

6. Why should you split your database files into libraries? (See "Organizing Commonly Used Code into a Library.")

7. What are several techniques for improving the absolute speed of an application? (See "Improving Absolute Speed.")

8. How can you display the hourglass and a progress meter when you run long processes? (See "Improving Perceived Speed.")

Creating Animated Splash Screens, About Boxes, and Startup Screens

Session Checklist

✔ Displaying startup screens

✔ Examining common startup dialog boxes

✔ Creating basic types of startup forms

✔ Getting Access to open and close the dialog boxes

✔ Adding animation

**30 Min.
To Go**

Nearly every professional application uses startup forms. These forms are important for many reasons. Your database or application might take a long time to load, and you want to keep your customers' attention while the initial processes run. You may want to make sure your customers have loaded the latest version of your software. If your customers need to link to data stored in a separate database, you may want to make sure they are aware of the data file they are attached to and also ensure that they are working with the correct database. All these items can be presented to users by way of a friendly, informational screen.

The more information your system displays, the more it can reduce the number of errors that are likely to be introduced during subsequent processes. If you can consistently present usable information to the operator of your system, you are more likely to be successful. In this session, you learn how to create three basic types of informational screens:

- Splash screens
- About boxes
- First screens

Creating a Splash Screen

A *splash screen* is a form that is displayed for a few seconds and then disappears. It is normally displayed when the user first opens the application, and it is used for two main reasons:

- To display information about the application, such as the name, version, and registration information
- To provide the user with something to look at while the application loads

Figure 19-1 shows a typical splash screen. This is the form frm_SplashScreen found in the Check Writer example database.

Figure 19-1 *The Check Writer splash screen.*

You create the splash screen form as you do any other form. Figure 19-2 shows the design of the splash screen form used in the Check Writer application. Notice the components used on this form. There is a company logo, a product logo, and several text and label controls used to display information about the program. When creating your own splash screen form, you can link to or embed your logos or other graphics in the form.

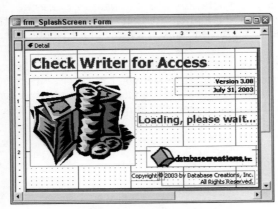

Figure 19-2 *The Design view of the Check Writer splash screen.*

You can also add to the form a background image or any other information that you want users to see when they first start the application.

When creating the form, consider its size. Pop-up forms always appear on top of other forms. Also, splash screens are not maximized to the full screen as other forms are. For this reason, you should create a form large enough to display all the information you plan to place on the form.

 Don't set the form to Modal because you want other processes to continue running while the form is displayed. When a form is set as modal, you cannot click or select anything in another window until the modal form is closed.

Figure 19-3 shows the property sheet for frm_SplashScreen. The form is set to Pop Up, whereas scroll bars, navigation buttons, and record selectors have all been disabled. You don't want the user to interact with this form; it is for display purposes only.

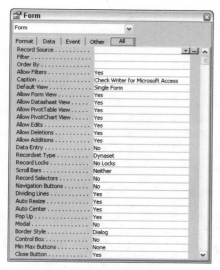

Figure 19-3   *The property sheet for frm_SplashScreen.*

Starting a form automatically when a database is opened

After you have added the objects and controls to the form, let Access know how the form should be opened. Because it is being used as a splash screen, you want Access to display this form first when the application starts. There are a few ways you can do this:

- Set the form as the startup display form.
- Call the form from the startup display form.
- Open the form from an autoexec macro.

If you use the `Startup` **property, make sure you do not have any Autoexec macros. These affect which form displays first when the application opens.**

Setting the form as the startup display form

To set the form as the startup display form, follow these steps:

1. Choose Tools ⇨ Startup. The Startup dialog box is displayed, as shown in Figure 19-4.

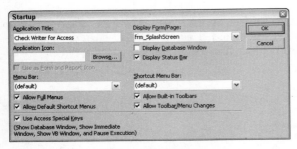

Figure 19-4 *The Startup dialog box.*

2. From the drop-down box in the Display Form/Page field, select the form you want to use as a splash screen. This box displays all forms in the current database. The dialog box also enables you to control other options displayed when the application opens, such as the database window, toolbars, and status bar.

Calling the form from the startup display form

You can also call the splash screen from another form as the startup display form. You accomplish this by opening the other form and adding code to the On Load event as shown in the following code. As this form loads, it opens the splash screen form as well.

```
Private Sub Form_Load()
    DoCmd.OpenForm "frm_SplashScreen"
End Sub
```

Using an Autoexec macro to open the splash screen

Earlier versions of Access used the Autoexec macro to carry out an *action* or series of actions when a database first opened. When you open a database, Access looks for a macro named Autoexec and, if it finds one, Access runs it automatically.

To create an Autoexec macro, create a macro containing the actions you want to run when you open the database, and then save the macro with the name Autoexec. An example of an Autoexec macro used to open a splash screen is shown in Figure 19-5.

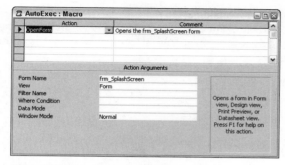

Figure 19-5   *An Autoexec macro.*

 In earlier versions of Access, Autoexec macros were commonly used to control startup options. Current versions of Access use the Startup Display form to set startup options.

20 Min.
To Go

Using Timer events

Because splash screens are displayed on screen for only a few seconds, you need to tell Access how long to display the splash screen and what to do after it closes. In some cases, you may also want to kick off other events while the splash screen is open. You can use a Timer event to do this.

By running a macro or event procedure when a Timer event occurs, you can control what Microsoft Access does at every timer interval. For example, you might want to open other forms, run macros, or control any animation used in your splash screen.

Figure 19-6 shows the property sheet for frm_SplashScreen with the Timer Interval and On Timer selections displayed. You can adjust the time period by changing the value of Timer Interval. This can also be done programmatically with the statement

```
Me.TimerInterval = x
```

where x represents the number of milliseconds. There are a thousand milliseconds in a second. To set each update of the form to 5 seconds, enter **5000** in the previous statement or in the Timer Interval property field.

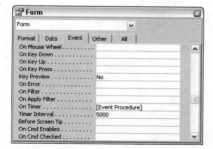

Figure 19-6   *Setting Timer events.*

The On Timer property is used to set what happens after the form is displayed for the selected timer interval. An example of a timer event is shown in the following code. Notice that when the timer interval is reached, the form named frm_AttachmentManager is opened and the frm_SplashScreen form is closed.

```
Private Sub Form_Timer()
    NumTime = NumTime + 1
    If NumTime = 1 Then
        DoCmd.OpenForm "frm_AttachmentManager", acNormal, , , , , "Startup"
    End If
    If NumTime = 3 Then
    DoCmd.Close acForm, "frm_SplashScreen"
    End
End Sub
```

Setting the timer interval to 0 prevents the timer event from executing.

You can control when events happen by using an On Load event and changing the On Timer event code to the following:

```
Private Sub Form_Load()
    intTime = 0 'Initialize variable
    Me.TimerInterval = 500 'Set timer to fire every 1/2 second
End Sub

Private Sub Form_Timer()
    intTime = intTime + 1    'increment timer count
        Select Case intTime
        Case 6  '3 seconds have passed
            'Open attachment manager form in startup mode to check for linked tables
            DoCmd.OpenForm "frm_AttachmentManager", acNormal, , , , , "Startup"
        Case 8  '4 seconds have passed
            'close this form
            DoCmd.Close acForm, Me.Name
    End Select
End Sub
```

The code in the Form_Load event sets the timer interval, named intTime, to 0. Notice the TimerInterval is set to 500, which sets the timer to one-half–second intervals. The Form_Timer event is then used to control the action that takes place when the timer reaches a certain interval. intTime=intTime + 1 tells Access to increment the timer by 1. When the interval reaches 6, the frm_AttachmentManager form is opened. When it reaches 8, the current form, frm_SplashScreen is closed.

Adding animation to a splash screen

You can create more interesting splash screens by adding animation to the form. The frm_SplashScreen form uses some simple animation techniques to enhance the form. The design of this form is shown in Figure 19-7.

Figure 19-7   *A design of an animated splash screen.*

In this form, the text Loading, please wait. . . blinks on the screen while the form loads. This is accomplished by adding one line of code to the On Timer event of the form.

Listing 19-1   *Code for Blinking Text*

```
Private Sub Form_Timer()
    intTime = intTime + 1   'increment timer count
    Me.LoadingMessage.Visible = Not Me.LoadingMessage.Visible    'Toggle loading message
    Select Case intTime
        Case 6  '3 seconds have passed
            'Open attachment manager form in startup mode to check for linked tables
            DoCmd.OpenForm "frm_AttachmentManager", acNormal, , , , , "Startup"
        Case 8  '4 seconds have passed
            'close this form
            DoCmd.Close acForm, Me.Name
    End Select
End Sub
```

The text that blinks is set as a label object named LoadingMessage. The line of code added to the Form_Timer event turns the display of the label on and off, which gives it the appearance of blinking. You can set how fast the text blinks by setting the Timer Interval property. In this example, the interval is set to 500, which means the text appears and disappears or "blinks" about every half a second. After the timer interval reaches 8, the form closes.

Creating an About Box

One of the standard interfaces found in most software is an About box. This form is often displayed by selecting an option from the Help menu or by clicking on a picture, logo, or hidden area of the screen.

The About box used for the Check Writer form is shown in Figure 19-8. This is a typical About box used in standard applications. The name of the application is displayed, the version number, copyright information, and the names of the developers.

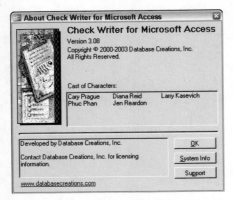

Figure 19-8   *The Check Writer About box.*

An About box is normally set up as a pop-up, modal type of form that displays basic information about the application. The user exits the form without doing anything within the application.

Adding functionality to the About box

In addition to displaying basic information about the application, you can also add more functionality to the form. This includes adding buttons to open other forms, setting hyperlinks, and adding sound to the form.

Notice that the Check Writer About box contains three buttons. The OK button is simply used to close the form, whereas the System Info button opens the frm_SystemInformation form. This form is used to display information about the user's operating system and version of Access. Likewise, the Support button displays a simple form named frm_TechSupport, which provides the user with information about obtaining technical support for the application.

The bottom of the form displays a label with the caption `www.databasecreations.com`. This is actually a hyperlink that when clicked opens the URL to the company's main Web site. Setting a hyperlink is simple. Just add the URL to the `Hyperlink Address` property of the command button, as shown in Figure 19-9.

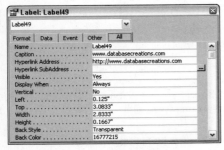

Figure 19-9   *Adding a hyperlink.*

Note If you need to use a hyperlink and connect to a remote URL, make sure that the user has a browser installed and is able to establish a connection to the URL, as well as sufficient access rights to display the hyperlinked page. If you anticipate that some users may not have a browser installed or a connection configured, you can provide them with additional functionality to establish the connection to the hyperlinked document.

Refer to the About box shown in Figure 19-8 and notice that the first character of text on each button is underlined. This means an access key has been set for each button. When you assign an access key to the button, pressing the Alt key plus the key for the underlined character moves the focus to that button. You can set the access key to any character of the button's Caption property. You do this by adding an ampersand (&) character to the left of the character you want to use as the access key.

 Note Don't use the same character as an access key for more than one button or control on the same form. When the same access key is assigned to multiple buttons, pressing the Alt + access key combination selects the first button in the tab order. However, this may not be the button you want.

Adding sound to the About box

You can add some extra pizzazz to your About box by playing a sound clip when the form opens. You do this by inserting a sound clip onto the form. The exact location and size of the clip doesn't really matter because you can set its size when the form is opened. Notice that in Figure 19-10 the sound clip in the design of the About Box form is represented by a sound icon.

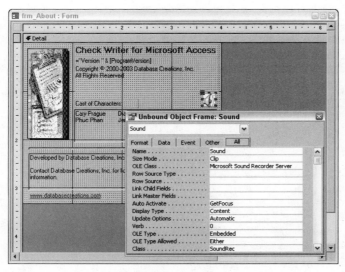

Figure 19-10   *Adding a sound clip to a form.*

In addition to adding the sound clip, you must also enable the object by setting its Enabled property to Yes and changing the Auto-Activate property to Get Focus. Finally, you set focus on the control by using the Form Load event.

The following code shows the form's On Load event. Notice the code added for the sound file named Sound. First, the focus is set to this object. This is necessary to get the sound to play. Then, the width and height of the object is set to 0. This is done so the sound icon is not displayed on the form when it opens.

```
Private Sub Form_Load()
    Me.Sound.SetFocus
    Me.Sound.Height = 0
    Me.Sound.Width = 0
End Sub
```

The sound does not play if you set its Visible **property to** No.

Creating a First Screen

A First Screen form is the form that appears the first time you run an application. It is often used to guide new users through the installation or setup of the application. It may also be used to provide a guided tour, demo, or tutorial.

As you can see in Figure 19-11, the First Screen form for the Check Writer application, named frm_FirstScreen, gives the user basic instructions on the system. It consists of several label fields, a text box, a button, a check box, and one unbound object used to display a graphic.

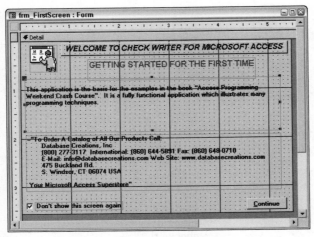

Figure 19-11 *The design of the First Screen form.*

The Continue button is used to close the frm_FirstScreen form and open the next form to be displayed. This could be the application's main menu, tutorial, or demo form.

Checking the value to display the first screen

The check box labeled Don't Show This Screen Again allows users to decide if they want to continue displaying the first screen each time the application is opened. If they choose not to have the screen displayed, the first screen is bypassed when the application starts. This is typically done by adding code to the On Open event of the First Screen form to check whether the user has selected not to view the form at startup.

In the Check Writer application, the On Close event of the frm_AttachmentManager form is used to open the First Screen form:

```
Private Sub Form_Close()
    If Me.OpenArgs = "Startup" Then
        DoCmd.OpenForm "frm_FirstScreen"
    End If
End Sub
```

Notice that this code opens the First Screen form even if the user selects not to view the form. To control whether the form should open based on the user's selections, the code behind the On Load event of the frm_FirstScreen form checks to see what the user selected:

```
Private Sub Form_Load()
    If Me.SkipFirstScreen Then
      DoCmd.Close acForm, Me.Name
    End If
End Sub
```

The frm_FirstScreen form is bound to the table named tbl_LocalSettings. This table consists of two fields. The ProgramVersion field is used to store the current version number, which is displayed on the About form. The SkipFirstScreen field is used to determine if the frm_FirstScreen form should be displayed. When the First Screen form opens, the value of the SkipFirstScreen field is checked. If the value of the field is True (the user does not want the First Screen form displayed), the form is closed. This is done by programmatically clicking the command button on the form named cmdContinue, which is the button on the form used to close the form.

Storing the value to display the screen

Because a user has control over whether the First Screen form is displayed, you need some way to store his selection so the application can determine whether the form should be opened. Because the form is bound to the table tbl_LocalSettings, you can store a value in a field in this table. The field named SkipFirstScreen is used for this purpose. The application checks the value of the field to determine whether to display the form.

This field is represented on the form by the check box labeled Don't Show This Screen Again. If the user selects this box, the value of this field is updated to True. So the next time the application is started, the First Screen form checks the value of this field. If it is True, the form closes immediately. Otherwise, the form continues to be opened each time the application is started until the user selects otherwise.

Make sure that you set the value of the `SkipFirstScreen` **field to** `False` **if you want the First Screen form to open when the user first starts the application.**

Done!

REVIEW

In this session, you learned about some of the different types of forms used in applications. These topics were covered:

- Splash Screens can be used to display information about the application while it loads.
- An About Box form is another type of form that is commonly used in most applications. This form provides detailed information about the application and can also include contact and author information.
- First Screens can be used to guide new users through an application. They provide additional assistance on getting started with the application and can even include links for starting tutorials or demos of the application. You learned how to control the display of these forms, as well as some techniques for adding advanced functionality to the form, such as animation and sound.

QUIZ YOURSELF

1. Which event can you use to control actions performed within a form? (See "Using Timer events.")
2. How can you set a hyperlink to a button on a form? (See "Adding functionality to the About box.")
3. How can you add sound to a form or a control on the form? (See "Adding functionality to the About box," and "Adding sound to the About box.")
4. How can you control whether a form is displayed based on a user's selection? (See "Creating a First Screen," "Checking the value to display the first screen," "Storing the value to display the screen.")

Creating Help Systems

Session Checklist

✔ Understanding the Help Viewer

✔ Authoring help topics

✔ Using help-authoring tools

✔ Assigning help topic IDs

✔ Calling help from forms and controls

**30 Min.
To Go**

A help system is a fundamental component of any application. Many developers omit this critical component either because they lack the skills involved in creating such a system or because they do not have the time. If you can develop and integrate a great help system, you provide a real boost to the success of your application. In this session, you learn how to integrate a help system into your application.

Understanding the Help Viewer

The Help Viewer displays the files that make up the help system. Pressing the F1 key is the quickest way to display the Help Viewer. You can also display it by choosing Help from the menu bar. Figure 20-1 shows the Help Viewer for the Check Writer sample application.

The Help Viewer displays when you press F1 anywhere on the Check Writer form. You can also choose Help ⇨ What's This? from the Help menu. The Help Viewer includes three components:

- The Topic pane
- The Navigation pane
- The toolbar

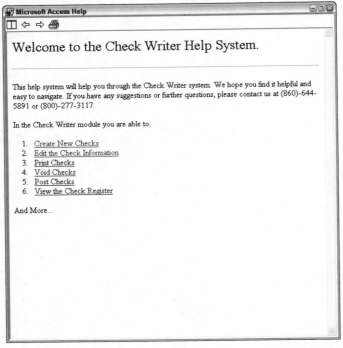

Figure 20-1 *Displaying the Help Viewer on the Check Writer form.*

The Topic pane is where the text for the help item displays. The Navigation pane displays to the left of the Topic pane and includes the Contents tab. The Contents tab lists all the topics that are included in the help system. The toolbar displays at the top of the viewer and includes buttons for the following tasks:

- Displaying or hiding the Navigation pane
- Moving forward or backward between previously viewed topics
- Printing a displayed topic
- Setting options for displaying the Help Viewer

The Contents tab displays in a tree-like format. An Open button and a book icon are displayed next to each high-level topic. To see the subtopics available for a high-level topic, you click the Open button. When you click the Open button, it changes to a Close button, the book icon changes to an open book icon, and one or more subtopics appear below the high-level item.

A question-mark icon displays next to each subtopic. When you select a subtopic, the help topic information for that subtopic displays in the Topic pane.

Creating a Help System

Building a help system requires not only a significant amount of labor, but also a tremendous amount of planning and creativity. Before you can begin writing the help contents, you need to define a list of all the important features and functions of the application and organize them into an outline format. Creating the outline is a lot like creating an outline before you write a paper or book. The order of the items should coincide with the flow of the application. After you have completed the help system, this outline should look very similar to its table of contents.

After the outline for your help system is complete, you can create the topic information that displays for each topic. You create the help content for each topic in HTML format. The content for each topic is stored in a separate HTML file.

To create the topic information for each help topic, you can use Microsoft Word or any authoring tool that can create HTML files.

HTML format provides the capability to be very creative in authoring help topics. In addition to textual content, you can also add graphics, sounds, animated images, or anything else to give users the information they need. Figure 20-2 shows the HTML file, written in Microsoft Word, for the Writing A Check topic.

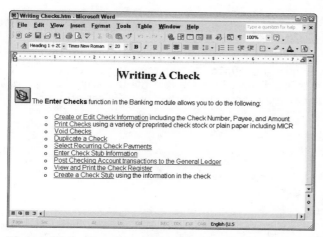

Figure 20-2 *Creating a help topic using Microsoft Word.*

The Writing A Check topic includes some informational text along with a graphic and several hotspots. The hotspots display as underlined colored text. When you move the cursor over a hotspot, the cursor changes to a hand. The hand cursor indicates that if you click on the hotspot, you can jump to the topic related to the hotspot.

To bundle all the help topic files into a format that can be accessed from the Help Viewer, you need a help-authoring tool. Help-authoring tools perform the following functions:

- Compile all the topic files into a single help file (.chm) that you can distribute with your application
- Create a table of contents, index, and full-text search utility
- Provide an interface to the Windows HtmlHelp API so that you can integrate the help system into your application

Numerous help-authoring tools are available for creating help systems. The developer version of Microsoft Access 2000 includes the HTML Help Workshop. Two other popular tools are Doc-To-Help and RoboHelp. For a list of other available tools, look for information on HTML help on Microsoft's Web site (www.microsoft.com/).

The details on how to create a help system using these help-authoring tools is outside the scope of this book. A lot is involved in using these tools effectively, and the process varies with each tool. In fact, entire books are available with a vast array of tips and techniques that these tools can provide to help you implement really professional help systems. *Building Enhanced HTML Help with DHTML and CSS,* by Jeannine Klein (published by Prentice Hall PTR), is a good one to try.

Defining Help Topic IDs

20 Min. To Go

For the purposes of this session, you need to understand how to use the help-authoring tool to set up HtmlHelp application programming interface (API) properties. The HtmlHelp API properties tell applications how to access the help system's topics. In this session, the HtmlHelp API properties are set up using the HTML Help Workshop.

Creating the header file

An application retrieves a help topic from a help system by passing the topic ID. Each topic in the help system must have a unique topic ID. To assign a topic ID to each topic, you create a header file. A *header file* is just a special type of text file that contains data in a predefined format. Figure 20-3 shows the header file for the Check Writer help system.

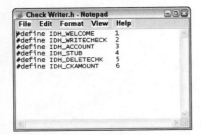

Figure 20-3   Creating the help system's header file.

The Check Writer.h file contains the header information for the Check Writer help system. You can use Notepad to create the file, or you can use any application that can create a text file.

Each line in the file assigns a unique ID to a help topic. Here is the syntax for the entries in the header file:

```
#define    <symbolic name>    <ID>
```

The entries in the header file are like a program. You use the #define command to execute the assignment statement. The symbolic name is just a descriptive name that you use to refer to a topic. It must be all alpha characters and contain no spaces. The ID is the numeric identifier that you use to refer to the topic. Each ID in the header file must be unique.

It is a good idea to create the entries in ID order to make it easier for others to work with the file later. Also, if you increment each ID by a multiplier of 10, 100, or even 1,000, it is easier to insert a topic ID later.

Adding the header file to the help project

After you have created the header file containing the topic IDs, you incorporate the file into your help project. To add the file to the help project, follow these steps:

1. Open the HTML Help Workshop.
2. Open the help project file (.hhp) for your help system.
3. Click the HtmlHelp API Information button in the HTML Help Workshop. The HtmlHelp API Information dialog box displays, as shown in Figure 20-4.

Figure 20-4   *Including a header file for the help system.*

4. Click the Header file button on the Map page of the HtmlHelp API dialog box. The Include File dialog box displays.
5. Use the Browse button to select the name of the header file you created. Then click the OK button. The header filename displays on the Map tab.

 If you prefix the symbolic ID with "IDH", the HTML Help Workshop automatically verifies that the topic exists in your help project when you compile it.

The header file is used to assign topic IDs for your help system. Now the help system needs to know which topic file, or HTML file, is associated with each topic ID. To map the topic IDs to HTML files, follow these steps:

1. Select the Alias tab of the HtmlHelp API dialog box, as shown in Figure 20-5.
2. Click the Add button on the Alias tab. The Alias dialog box displays, as shown in Figure 20-6.

Figure 20-5   Mapping the IDs to HTML files.

Figure 20-6   Adding an HtmlHelpAPI alias.

3. In the first field of the Alias tab, type the first symbolic ID you created in the header file.

4. In the drop-down list labeled "Use it to refer to this HTML file:," pick the name of the HTML topic file that you want to use for the symbolic ID. Then click the OK button. The Alias string displays on the Alias tab of the HtmlHelp API Information dialog box.

5. Enter the alias definitions for each of the symbolic IDs you created in the header file.

6. When you have finished creating the alias definitions, click the OK button on the Alias tab to save them.

 Be sure to save and compile the help project whenever you make any changes.

Testing HtmlHelp API definitions

The HTML Help Workshop provides a facility for testing your HtmlHelp API mappings. You can use this facility to make sure that your symbolic IDs are mapped to the proper help topic. To test each topic ID, follow these steps:

1. Choose Test ⇨ HtmlHelp API from the HTML Help Workshop menu. The Test HtmlHelp API dialog box displays, as shown in Figure 20-7.

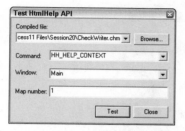

Figure 20-7 *Testing the HtmlHelp API definitions.*

2. Use the Browse button to select the name of your compiled help file if it is not automatically selected. Select HH_HELP_CONTEXT for the command. Enter the topic ID you want to test in the Map Number field.

3. Click the Test button. The Help Viewer opens and displays the help topic that corresponds to the topic ID you entered in the Test HtmlHelp API dialog box.

If the Help Viewer does not display the right topic or does not display any topic, check the following list to troubleshoot your topic error.

- Is the correct header file selected on the Map tab of the HtmlHelp API?
- Did you enter the correct symbolic ID for the HTML file you selected on the Alias tab of the HtmlHelp API?
- Does the symbolic ID on the Alias tab match the one in the mapped header file?
- Did you save and recompile your project?

After you have tested your HtmlHelp API definitions, you are ready to link the help system to your Access application.

Connecting the Help File to an Access Application

**10 Min.
To Go**

Once you have a help file in good working order, it is easy to link it up to an Access application. You can display general help for forms or specific help topics that relate to fields, command buttons, and menu items.

Specifying help for a form

Each form contains two help properties: HelpFile and HelpContextID. You use the HelpFile property to set the source for all the help topics you want to display for the form. The HelpContextID contains the topic ID to use for general form help.

To set the HelpFile property, enter the path and filename of the compiled help (.chm) file that you want to use for the form. Figure 20-8 shows the help settings for the Check Writer form.

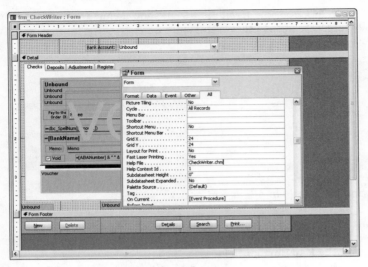

Figure 20-8 *Integrating help for a form.*

The Check Writer form is connected to the CheckWriter.chm file. If you do not specify a path name for the help file, Access looks in the application's folder for the specified filename.

Avoid hard-coding path names in an application. This process can cause run-time errors or erroneous behavior.

The Check Writer form's HelpContextID is set to 1. The HelpContextID settings that you can use come from the topic IDs you assigned in the HtmlHelp API dialog box in the help system.

For the form's HelpContextID, use a topic ID that corresponds to general help topics for the form. Topic ID 1 in the Check Writer help system corresponds to the Welcome help topic. When the user presses F1 on the form, the Help Viewer displays the Welcome help topic.

Displaying help topics for controls

You can display a help topic for an individual control on a form. When the control has focus, the user can press F1 to display the help topic that describes the active control. To link a control to a help topic, you set the control's HelpContextID. The help file used for control-level help is the one you entered for the form's HelpFile property. You can link to the IDs that you entered in the help file's header file.

When you are setting up help for the controls on a form, keep the contents of the help file's header file handy. An easy way to do this is to tile the header file and Access design windows together on the screen, as shown in Figure 20-9.

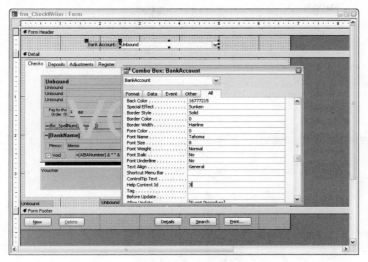

Figure 20-9 *Setting up control-level help for a form.*

When setting `HelpContextIDs` for radio buttons and option buttons, be sure to set the `HelpContextID` for the labels as well. If you do this, the appropriate help topic displays regardless of where the user clicks. (Some users may click the label instead of the control itself.)

If your help file does not include specific help for a control on the form, you can leave its `HelpContextID` set to 0 (the default). When the user requests help on the control, the form's general help topic displays.

Don't forget to set the form's `HelpContextID`. If the form's `HelpContextID` is 0, Microsoft Access help displays for form-level help and for any control with `HelpContextIDs` set to 0.

Testing custom help

After linking the help system to the controls in the form, test the form's help connections. Figure 20-10 shows the help topic that displays when you press F1 on the Bank Account field in the Check Writer form.

To test the help system links, open the form. Press F1 for each control on the form. Check to make sure the correct help topic displays for each control. Form-level help should display for controls with no specific `HelpContextID` setting.

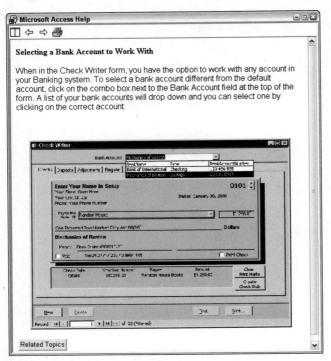

Figure 20-10 *Testing a form's custom help.*

Done!

REVIEW

A truly professional application includes a well-constructed, thorough help system. The users of your application can feel more secure as they begin to use the application if they know they can get quick and accurate help instantly. A good help system reduces the amount of time you spend performing technical support and increases the usability of the application. This session discussed these points:

- Access applications display help using the Windows Help Viewer.
- Help topics are created in HTML format.
- You need a help-authoring tool such as HTML Help Workshop to build a help system.
- The HtmlHelp API allows applications to display individual help topics from a help system.
- You can display help for an Access form by setting the help properties for the form and its controls.

QUIZ YOURSELF

1. Name the three components of the Help Viewer. (See "Understanding the Help Viewer.")

2. Identify the first step in creating a help system. (See "Creating a Help System.")

3. Name the utility that allows applications to display a help system. (See "Defining Help Topic IDs.")

4. What is the purpose of the help system header file? (See "Creating the header file.")

5. Name the two help properties you use in an Access form to display help. (See "Connecting the Help File to an Access Application.")

6. Name the source of the list of topic IDs that you can use in a form. (See "Displaying help topics for controls.")

PART

IV

Saturday Evening
Part Review

1. What are the five parameters for the MsgBox function?
2. True or false: The buttons parameter of the MsgBox function also determines the icon to be displayed.
3. Describe the difference between application modal and system modal as it pertains to the message box function.
4. Which of the following statements is/are correct?
   a. Error handling is enabled with the On Error Goto 0 statement.
   b. The Resume 0 statement disables error handling.
   c. The Resume Next statement returns execution to the line immediately following the line at which the error occurred.
   e. All of the above.
   f. None of the above.
5. List some of the file format types you are able to import or export.
6. What are the four basic steps in doing an import?
7. What is an Import/Export Specification and where would you set it up?
8. List the methods available for transferring data.
9. What is more important for improving the speed of Microsoft Access — memory or a faster processor?
10. Name three ways to lose the compiled state.
11. What is the name of the undocumented command that can greatly speed up an Access program and clean up your database file at the same time?
12. What are three things you cannot do with a .MDE database file?
13. True or false: A splash screen is a type of menu system.
14. True or false: When a form is modal, the user cannot select anything in another window until the modal form is closed.

15. True or false: An AutoRun macro is used to carry out an action or series of actions when a database first opens.

16. True or false: Setting a timer event to 0 stops the timer event from executing.

17. The _____ pane displays the text for the help item.

18. True or false: You create the content for the help topics in HTML format.

19. A help-authoring tool performs all but which one of the following features?

    a. Compiling all of the topic files into a single help file (.CHM).

    b. Creating a table of contents, index, and full-text search utility.

    c. Providing an interface to the Windows HtmlHelp API.

    d. Inserting the topic IDs into the forms and fields in your application.

20. Which property is used to connect a control to a help file?

    a. HelpContextID

    b. OnHelp

    c. OnKeyDown

    d. Caption

☑ Friday

☑ Saturday

☑ **Sunday**

Part V — Sunday Morning

Part VI — Sunday Afternoon

PART

V

Sunday Morning

Creating Search Dialog Box Forms

Session Checklist

✔ Understanding dialog boxes

✔ Creating a search dialog box

✔ Changing the searchable items

✔ Finding the selected item in the form

✔ Calling a search dialog box form

**30 Min.
To Go**

Although Microsoft Access has several built-in techniques to search for data, each technique requires that users understand, to some degree, the complexities involved. Although you may think it's easy for users to place the cursor on a field and click the binocular toolbar button, this method is simply not obvious or intuitive. It is even less likely that users who simply want to run an Access application will try the Query by Form view, especially if they have little or no experience with Microsoft Access. A search dialog box enables users to quickly select a method to view data, select a desired record, and display the record on any underlying data entry form. Because many Access applications hide some or all of the Microsoft Access interface, this programmed search dialog box is essential.

Understanding Dialog Boxes

Pop-up dialog boxes are a major part of any application because they help control the flow from one area of an application to another and provide the user with many options that, otherwise, would take hours of coding or manual intervention. By creating innovative dialog boxes that give the user many choices, you simplify an application and increase intuitiveness. Allowing the user to easily move from one selection to another decreases training costs and increases the user's productivity.

Clicking the Search button on the frm_CheckWriter form displays the Search for Check/Deposit Adjustment dialog box, which includes an option group labeled Type of Search and a list box showing the items available to search in the frm_CheckWriter form (see Figure 21-1).

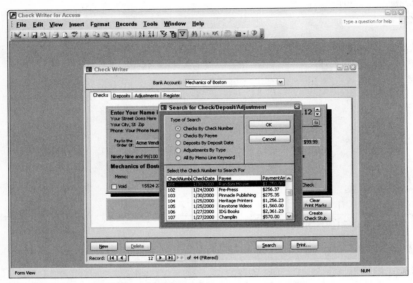

Figure 21-1   *Using a dialog box to search for a record.*

The Type of Search option group includes five different search options. When the user clicks one of the options, the content of the list box changes to reflect information corresponding to the Type of Search option. For example, the Checks By Check Number option lists all the checks in the Check Writer sorted by check number. The Deposits By Deposit Date option, on the other hand, lists all the deposits in the Check Writer sorted by deposit date. When the user selects an item in the list box and clicks the OK button, the dialog box closes and the frm_CheckWriter form displays the record that the user selects in the dialog box list box.

Although data entry forms and dialog boxes are both forms, dialog boxes have some unique characteristics. Most significantly, dialog boxes are generally not bound to any data source. Because their job is simply to guide you from one form to another or from one record to another, they do not need a data source of their own. The controls on the dialog box are all that you need to determine where to go next.

Some of the other properties unique to dialog boxes include the following:

Auto Resize	Yes (True) — Dialog box resizes to show all the form's controls.
Auto Center	Yes (True) — Dialog box is displayed in the center of the screen.
Pop Up	Yes (True) — Form pops up on top of all other windows.
Modal	Yes (True) — User cannot select another window until the dialog box is closed.
Border Style	Dialog — Displays a non-resizable thick border.

`Control Box`	Yes (True) — Displays the Control Menu box in the upper-left corner.
`Min Max Buttons`	None — Hides the Minimize and Maximize buttons.
`Close Button`	Yes (True) — Displays the Close button (Control box must be Yes).

Although these are the traditional dialog box settings, you may not always want to use them. Figure 21-2 shows the settings for the `frm_DialogCheckSearch` dialog box.

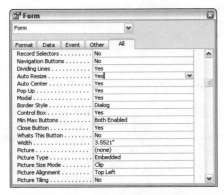

Figure 21-2   *Setting the properties for a dialog box.*

The `Pop Up` setting forces the dialog box to display in front of any other displayed window. However, if your dialog box displays another window while the dialog box is still open (a Print Preview window, for example), the dialog box remains stuck in front of the other window. If you use the `Pop Up` property, you must either close the dialog box before displaying another window, or if you need to keep the dialog box open for some reason, you can hide it.

Modal dialog boxes are being used less and less frequently. Windows and event-driven programming incorporate the concept of letting users decide what they want to do and when they want to do it. Unless you absolutely need to guide users down a specific navigation path and keep them in the dialog box until they perform some action or close the dialog box, you should avoid the modal setting.

Dialog boxes in the past have always used a thick, non-resizable border to indicate that they were modal dialog boxes. However, with today's choices of screen resolutions and a definite move to give the user more freedom of the environment, dialog boxes are showing up with a resizable thin border rather than the dialog-border style.

The `Auto Center` property works in conjunction with the `Pop Up` property to force the dialog box to appear in the center of the screen. Although the `Auto Center` dialog box can always be moved, it reopens in a centered position. The only reason to use this property is when the application's user environment employs vastly different resolutions and dialog boxes (which are often smaller than data entry forms) might be moved to a corner of a larger screen resolution. When the application is opened in a smaller resolution, a dialog box might appear partially off the screen, and in some cases, become inaccessible.

Creating Search Dialog Boxes

20 Min. To Go

The first step in building a search dialog box is to create a form — just as you would create a normal data entry form. Set the form's AutoResize, AutoCenter, PopUp properties, and so on, so that it displays as a dialog box.

Next, you can add controls to the dialog box. A typical search dialog box, like frm_DialogCheckSearch, includes the following controls:

- An option group for selecting the type of search
- A list box or combo box for displaying the searchable items
- A set of command buttons to process or cancel the dialog box

You should set one of the option buttons as the default so that when the dialog box opens, one of the options is already selected and the list box displays the corresponding set of items. Figure 21-3 shows setting the default option for the Type of Search option group. You can create as many different options as you want. You are limited only by physical space on the screen. You can always switch the option group to a combo box if you need unlimited options.

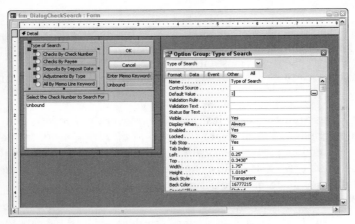

Figure 21-3   *Setting the default search option.*

If you have five search options or fewer, option buttons are the most visual and intuitive choice. If you have more than five options, it may be more practical to use a combo box.

After setting the default search option, be sure that you set the RowSource for the list box to match the default search option. This way, when the form opens, the list box automatically displays the correct items for the selected search type. Figure 21-4 shows the RowSource property setting for the list box in the frm_DialogCheckSearch dialog box.

Figure 21-4 *Setting the default list box RowSource property.*

Changing the list box items

Each time the user selects a different search option, the contents of the list box change. To change the contents of the list box, you use the `AfterUpdate` event of the option group. Figure 21-5 shows the `AfterUpdate` event for the Type of Search option group.

```
Private Sub Type_of_Search_AfterUpdate()
    Me!Keyword.Visible = False
    With Me
        ![By Search type].RowSource = ""
        Select Case ![Type of search]
            Case 1
                Forms!frm_CheckWriter.TabControl.Pages("Checks").SetFocus
                ![Search Text].caption = "Select the Check Number to Search For        "
                ![By Search type].ColumnCount = 5
                ![By Search type].ColumnWidths = ".65 in;.65 in;1.1 in;0.5 in;0 in"
                ![By Search type].BoundColumn = 5
                ![By Search type].RowSource = "SELECT [tbl_CheckWriter].[CheckNumber], [tbl_CheckWriter].[CheckDate], [tbl_Che
            Case 2
                Forms!frm_CheckWriter.TabControl.Pages("Checks").SetFocus
                ![Search Text].caption = "Select the Payee Record to Search For        "
                ![By Search type].ColumnCount = 5
                ![By Search type].ColumnWidths = "1.1 in;.65 in;.5 in;.65 in;0 in"
                ![By Search type].BoundColumn = 5
                ![By Search type].RowSource = "SELECT [tbl_CheckWriter].[Payee], [tbl_CheckWriter].[CheckDate],[tbl_CheckWrite
            Case 3
                Forms!frm_CheckWriter.TabControl.Pages("Deposits").SetFocus
                ![Search Text].caption = "Select the Deposit to Search For        "
                ![By Search type].ColumnCount = 4
                ![By Search type].ColumnWidths = ".65 in;.65 in;1.6 in;.0 in"
                ![By Search type].BoundColumn = 4
                ![By Search type].RowSource = "SELECT [tbl_CheckWriter].[CheckDate] AS [Date],[tbl_CheckWriter].[DepositAmount
            Case 4
                Forms!frm_CheckWriter.TabControl.Pages("Adjustments").SetFocus
                ![Search Text].caption = "Select the Adjustment to Search For        "
                ![By Search type].ColumnCount = 4
                ![By Search type].ColumnWidths = "1.1 in;.65 in;1.15 in;.0 in"
                ![By Search type].BoundColumn = 4
```

Figure 21-5 *Changing the contents of the list box.*

The `Type_Of_Search_AfterUpdate` event includes a `Case` statement for evaluating the option the user selected. Each branch in the `Case` statement includes the same types of statements, but the values that the statements set change depending on the type of search selected.

Using the statement before the `Case` statement `[By Search Type].RowSource = ""`, however, may be the most important technique you learn in this session. This statement sets the RowSource property of the combo box to null. This is mandatory because if the row source is set to a valid data source, the data source is requeried each time the other properties, such as `ColumnCount`, `ColumnWidths`, or `BoundColumn`, are set. If your combo box row source returns 100,000 records, you could wait a long time because the combo box must retrieve the data four times — once when the row source is set and each time one of the three properties is set.

The first statement in each branch of the `Case` statement changes the active page in the frm_CheckWriter form's tab control. The tab control page in the frm_CheckWriter form must be in sync with the type of search the user selected in the search dialog box. For example, if the user chooses to search for a deposit by deposit date, you must change the Check Writer's active tab to the Deposits tab.

The second statement sets the caption for the search dialog box's list box. The caption displays instructions appropriate to the type of search. For example, selecting the option Deposits By Deposit Date displays the caption `Select the Deposit to Search for`.

The next three lines of code set the properties for the list box columns:

ColumnCount	Number of columns in the combo box
ColumnWidths	Width of each column
BoundColumn	Column containing the key field (TransID)

Notice that the `ColumnWidth` **for the last column (**`TransID`**) in each** `Case` **statement is set to** `0`**. Setting the** `ColumnWidth` **to** `0` **hides the column in the list box. The last column in each** `Case` **statement is also the** `BoundColumn`**. Even though the column is hidden, you can still access its value through the** `BoundColumn` **property.**

The last statement in each `Case` statement sets the RowSource property for the list box. This statement uses a SQL SELECT statement to retrieve the values to display in the list box columns and also specifies the sort order for the list box rows.

See Session 9 to review the steps for creating SQL statements.

10 Min.
To Go

Finding the selected record

When the user selects a record in the search dialog list box and clicks the OK button, the selected record displays in the data entry form. The code for the OK button uses the BoundColumn property of the search dialog list box to locate the record in the data entry form's record source. There are two different methods that professional programmers use to find the record:

- Placing the cursor in the key field of the calling form and using the `FindRecord` method.
- Using the `RecordsetClone` method and the `Bookmark` property to find the record.

The `FindRecord` method can be used only if the form's `RecordSource` uses a single-field key and the form includes a control bound to the key field. You can always add a hidden field or use a concatenated key, but generally, you want to use this method only on single-field keys.

 Searching on an indexed field provides superior performance to searching on a nonindexed field. Nonindexed field searches require Access to use a slow sequential search from the first to last record in the table.

Figure 21-6 shows the `OK_Click` event procedure for the `frm_DialogCheckSearch` dialog box. The code first checks to make sure a list box item is selected. The value of the list box is null if no record is selected. Only four statements are needed to find the record. First, the calling form is selected using the `SelectObject` command. Next, the cursor is placed on the key field (TransID) using the `SetFocus` method. The `FindRecord` command is then used to position the record pointer to the correct record, and last, the search dialog box is closed.

```
CheckWriter - Form_frm_DialogCheckSearch (Code)
cmdOK                                    ▼    Click                                ▼
    Private Sub cmdOK_Click()
    Dim Response As Integer
        If IsNull(Me![By Search type]) Then
            Response = MsgBox("You Did Not Select a Record to Search For", vbCritical, "No Record Selected")
            DoCmd.SelectObject acForm, "frm_CheckWriter"
            DoCmd.Close acForm, "frm_DialogCheckSearch"
            Exit Sub
        End If
        If IsNull(Forms!frm_CheckWriter![TransID]) Then
            Response = MsgBox("You Cannot Search from a New Record", vbCritical, "New Record Search Disallowed")
            DoCmd.SelectObject acForm, "frm_CheckWriter"
            DoCmd.Close acForm, "frm_DialogCheckSearch"
            Exit Sub
        End If
        If Trim$(Me![By Search type]) = Trim$(Forms!frm_CheckWriter![TransID]) Then
            DoCmd.SelectObject acForm, "frm_CheckWriter"
            DoCmd.Close acForm, "frm_DialogCheckSearch"
            Exit Sub
        End If
        DoCmd.SelectObject acForm, "frm_CheckWriter"
        'Search by memo don't know which tab to select until they choose a search item
        If Me![Type of search] = 5 Then
            With Forms!frm_CheckWriter
                Select Case Me![By Search type].Column(0)
                    Case "Check"
                        .TabControl.Pages("Checks").SetFocus
                    Case "Deposit"
                        .TabControl.Pages("Deposits").SetFocus
                    Case Else
                        .TabControl.Pages("Adjustments").SetFocus
                End Select
            End With
        End If
        Forms!frm_CheckWriter![TransID].SetFocus
        DoCmd.FindRecord Me![By Search type]
        DoCmd.Close acForm, "frm_DialogCheckSearch"
    End Sub
```

Figure 21-6   *Using the FindRecord method to locate a record.*

Opening the Search Dialog Box from the Form

You can add a command button to the data entry form to open the dialog box you want to use for the search. Figure 21-7 shows the Search command button for the frm_CheckWriter form.

The Search command button in the frm_CheckWriter form uses an event procedure for its `OnClick` event to open the search dialog box. The code for the `Search_OnClick` event to open the `frm_DialogCheckSearch` dialog box is very simple:

```
DoCmd.OpenForm "frm_DialogCheckSearch"
```

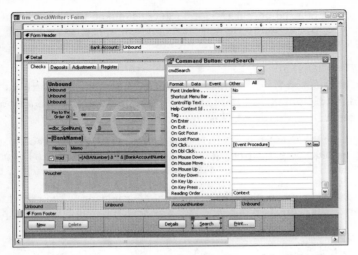

Figure 21-7 *Using a button to open the search dialog box.*

Done!

REVIEW

Search dialog boxes provide your users with a flexible tool for searching for a record. Each form in your application can have its own search dialog box, each with its own set of search criteria. This session covered the following topics:

- Dialog boxes provide an intuitive way for the user to move from one area of the application to another.
- Dialog boxes usually have no data source.
- Modal dialog boxes force the user to make a selection before moving to another form.
- Setting the RowSource property for a list box changes the items that display in the list box.
- You can use the FindRecord method to synchronize the selected record in the search dialog box with the data entry form.
- You use a command button on the data entry form to open its search dialog box.

QUIZ YOURSELF

1. Which property makes a dialog box display on top of any other form? (See "Understanding Dialog Boxes.")
2. Which property requires the user to either make a selection from the dialog box or close it before he or she can move to any other form? (See "Understanding Dialog Boxes.")
3. Name the three most common types of controls used in dialog boxes. (See "Creating Search Dialog Boxes.")

4. Which statement is mandatory when writing event procedures that change the RowSource property for a list box or combo box? (See "Changing the list box items.")

5. Which property and setting make a list box column invisible? (See "Changing the list box items.")

6. Name the two methods you can use to programmatically find a record in a form's record source. (See "Finding the selected record.")

7. Which command button event do you use to open a search dialog box? (See "Opening the Search Dialog Box from the Form.")

Programming Dialog Boxes and Reports and Working with ActiveX Controls

Session Checklist

✔ Designing a print dialog box

✔ Programming reports

✔ Working with the ActiveX Calendar control

30 Min. To Go

Although data entry and display forms are critical to handling data in any application, dialog boxes are just as important for handling selection options (menu navigation), searching, printing, and other non-data–type information. Data entry forms and dialog boxes are both forms, and they share many common features and controls. As you see in this session, dialog boxes, when properly designed, can make a system more usable and make its users more productive. This session also illustrates how programming reports with or without a print dialog box can extend the features you provide to your users. With a programmed report, you have control over the look as well as the data.

Finally, using ActiveX controls in your database is a great way to quickly enhance your product. ActiveX controls are self-contained, functional objects that you literally drop into your forms or reports. We use the Calendar control in Access to help you understand ActiveX controls implementation.

Basic Dialog Box Design

Although dialog boxes use forms as a starting point, generally, none use bound forms. This means that there is no bound data source such as a table or query behind a dialog box. A dialog box is displayed either with no predetermined selections or with some default selections from which users can choose their options so that the program can proceed. Some dialog boxes (we call them *smart dialogs*) save the last set of options chosen and maintain a table for these options. You can create this feature programmatically on the OnOpen event of the form, or you can do it through a bound selection. It simply depends on your data model.

Generally, dialog boxes have some specific properties that differ from data entry forms, and Session 21 details those differences. Refer to that session if you need a refresher on the differences.

Creating and Using Print Dialog Boxes

Print dialogs let you control what and how a user prints reports in their system. Although Microsoft Access provides a print button for data sheets, forms, and reports and a very good report writer, the average user spends too much time manipulating report record sources to print the desired data.

When you create a report using Microsoft Access, you are only creating a template for data to flow through. Although the report object produces all the great formatting and calculations that make a report look good, the data that is passed to the report is critical to accurate reporting.

Each report has a single Record Source. This record source can be a table, query, or a SQL statement. By using a query, you can work with an optimized SQL statement. More important, you enable communication between the query, your report, and an intuitive dialog box. You simply run the report and let the dialog box and query work together to pass the desired data to the report. A simple report dialog box form is illustrated in Figure 22-1, and a more complex one is shown in Figure 22-2.

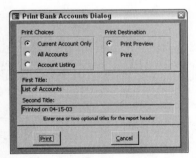

Figure 22-1 *The form frm_DialogBankPrint is a very simplified print dialog*

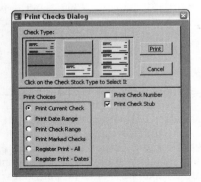

Figure 22-2 *The form frm_DialogCheckPrint is a more sophisticated print dialog form.*

As you can see in the dialog box form, there are just a few controls. Two option groups are available. One is to choose the type of check stock to print to, and the second is to control which records are printed. The two text boxes enable the user to enter optional titles to be printed in the report if entered. Finally, the From Date and To Date fields are used by the query to limit the selection to records where the Last Purchase Date field is between the From Date and To Date entered.

Displaying the print dialog box form

From the main form, you can add a button or some other method to open the dialog box you want to use in your printing. Figure 22-2, for example, includes a Print button in the Check Type section of the form. The code to open the frm_DialogBankPrint form is very simple. The following code is found in the OnClick event of the Print button on the main Check Writer form:

```
DoCmd.OpenForm "frm_DialogBankPrint"
```

Building a print dialog box

The print dialog example we use is fairly simple. The technique you want to learn here is the communication between the dialog box form and the report, and how the data is filtered for the report.

The first step is to create a form and use the desired dialog box options. As you can see if you refer back to Figure 22-1, the form includes two option groups and option buttons, several unbound text boxes, two command buttons, and associated label controls. This is the frm_DialogBankPrint form.

The option buttons are used strictly to store the selections for the records to be printed (current or all) and the print destination. The Print button contains the logic to use these values. The values in the First Title and Second Title fields are used by the report itself whereas the From Date and To Date values are used to communicate with the query, which, in turn, affects the report's record source.

Interfacing queries with print dialog forms

The frm_DialogBankPrint is a very simple example of a print dialog form. A more complex example is the frm_DialogCheckPrint in Figure 22-2. In this print dialog, depending on the choices the user makes, different records are printed in the report. The following code uses the OpenReport method and passes a SQL WHERE statement as one of the arguments to limit the data selection. For example, there is code to filter for those records whose value in the CheckDate field is between the FromDate and ToDate entered in the frm_DialogCheckPrint form. The following line of code is taken from the On Click event of the OK button:

```
DoCmd.OpenReport RptName, acNormal, , "[AccountNumber]=Forms![Check Writer] _
    ![BankAccount] And [TransType]='" & TxnSel & "' AND [CheckDate] >= _
    Forms![frm_DialogCheckPrint]![From Date] And [CheckDate] <= _
    Forms![frm_DialogCheckPrint]![To Date]"
```

When the report is run and the criteria argument used, the report looks at the values entered in the print dialog form and uses it to select records. Many applications require the user to open the query and enter the values he wants to use in the query. Other applications use parameter queries, which pop up when the query is run. Neither is acceptable in professional applications. You want to allow the user to control his application from a user interface. You do not want to control it in the programming environment. This gives the user a sense of control and flexibility.

An alternative approach to this is to open the report and then set the RecordSource of the report. You can do this by setting the RecordSource for report after you run the OpenReport. For example, if you want to run the Bank Account report and have it list just checking transactions, you can have the following line of code. This is placed after an OpenReport method. The code sets the record source with a SQL string.

```
Reports![Rpt_BankAccounts].RecordSource = "SELECT * FROM [tbl_BankAccounts]
WHERE [Type] = 'Checking'"
```

The previous line of code uses a SQL string as the record source and sets the report to print only records that are 'Checking' accounts types.

You could also substitute the name of a table or query.

```
Reports![Rpt_BankAccounts].RecordSource = tbl_BankAccounts
```

Although it is more convenient to use the Criteria argument of the OpenReport method, you have reasons to set the report's recordset programmatically. You may need to print a complex report, which does a lot of calculations or involves multiple complex queries — such as a Union Query. It is much easier to create the query and then set it to reference the controls on the print dialog than to programmatically build the SQL string to use as the criteria argument. In this case, it is easier to use a query and set it programmatically.

Printing reports from the dialog box

The report is printed after the code first hides the modal print dialog. This way if the report is printed as a Print Preview, it does not appear behind the modal dialog. The value of the Type of Output option group is checked. The ReportDest variable is set to acPreview if the Print Preview choice is selected or acNormal is the Print choice is selected.

**20 Min.
To Go**

Finally, the OpenReport method is used to print the report. For the form frm_DialogBankPrint, a variable, ReportDest, is used to select the second parameter print destination whereas a filter is also passed to the report if the current record is being printed using the value of the current Bank Account field. In the form, frm_DialogCheckPrint the OpenReport does not use a variable for the print type because all the printing is sent directly to the printer.

Remember, that the report filter created here and the criteria in the query are not mutually exclusive. If you select the current record only, and the Last Purchase Date does not fit within the date parameters from the print dialog you see no records in the report.

Interfacing reports with print dialog forms

Print dialog forms and reports can communicate with each other in many ways. By referencing controls on the dialog form, the report can display information either that the user enters or that is set programmatically.

For example, in the frm_DialogBankPrint form, two text boxes let the user enter two optional report titles. The report in Figure 22-3 uses the First Title and Second Title fields in the frm_DialogBankPrint form when printing the report. The titles are simply calculated text boxes that refer to the values in the dialog form. If you look at the control source of the two controls on the report, you see that they are set to reference the controls on the print dialog. The two controls on the report have the following lines for the controlsource.

```
=[Forms]![frm_DialogBankPrint]![First Title]
=[Forms]![frm_DialogBankPrint]![Second Title]
```

A simple but very effective technique!

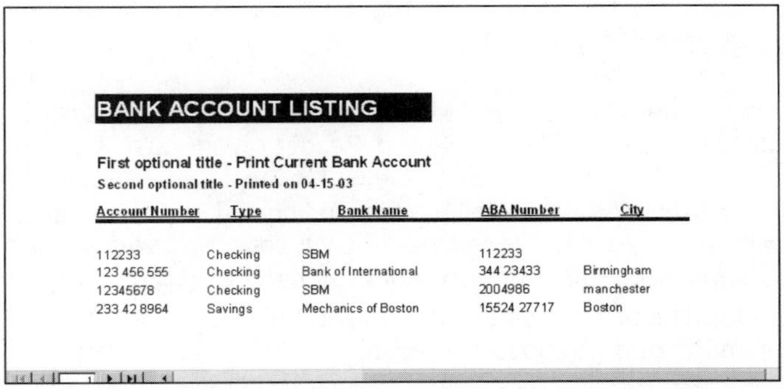

BANK ACCOUNT LISTING

First optional title - Print Current Bank Account

Second optional title - Printed on 04-15-03

Account Number	Type	Bank Name	ABA Number	City
112233	Checking	SBM	112233	
123 456 555	Checking	Bank of International	344 23433	Birmingham
12345678	Checking	SBM	2004986	manchester
233 42 8964	Savings	Mechanics of Boston	15524 27717	Boston

Figure 22-3 *The report rpt_BankAccount shows the two additional title fields. These refer to the two text box controls on the print dialog form.*

Although this example is simplistic, this technique is not limited. You can reference form values in reports, queries, and modules and even other forms. You can prompt the user for information, as well as set visible or invisible controls with information that you pull in from a setup table. Set controls on the open form and then reference them from the report. Just remember that to reference the controls, they must be on an open form. Therefore, you may at times want to set the form to `Visible = False`, which would leave the form open but hidden from the user. Then you can still reference the controls from the report. This technique is quick and easy to design. Most of all, it lets you reference information more easily.

Programming Reports

Up to this point, you have been introduced to a few techniques used to affect a report programmatically. You have seen ways to change the records that the report displays. You have also seen an example of how to place information on the report itself from the form. Access has a tremendously powerful reporting module. You have created reports up to this point. You may not as yet, however, have used the events available in reports to program the reports. Several features and properties of a report can be programmed to enhance your reporting capabilities.

Report sections

In order to understand how to program a report, you must understand the report sections and how they interact with the report and with each other. Any report has the following sections, Report Header and Footer, Page Header and Footer, and a Detail section. Access enables you to create sections in addition to these standard sections, and you set them in the Grouping and Sorting property sheet. The following list describes the standard report sections:

- **Report Header and Footer section:** Prints at the beginning and end of the report, respectively. The Report Header goes before the Page Header section. You can use this section to print a company logo or other information or as a cover page for the report. The Report Footer is the last section of the report; however, it prints before the Page Footer on the last page of the report. Use this section to display the report totals.

- **Page Header and Footer section:** Appears at the top and bottom of each page, respectively. The Page Header appears after the Report Header on the first page and is present on each page that follows. This section is ideal for displaying column headings, page numbers, or other information you want to show at the top of each page. The Page Footer section appears at the bottom of each page, and you can set up calculated fields to display page totals or page numbers in this section.

- **The Detail section:** Displays the main body of information for the report. This section is on every page and is repeated for each record.

Depending on how you set up additional sections, they go before or after the Detail section and display and group the records that you want to show.

Section events

Each section has innate events on which you can run code. The following list details the events available to you for each section of any given report:

- On Format: Enables you to set a macro or event procedure to the section. Access executes the section when it formats the particular section.

- On Print: Assigns a macro or event procedure to a section's On Print event. The macro or code is run when Access starts printing the section or displaying it in Preview.

- On Retreat: Macro or event procedure that runs after Access processes the On Format and before it processes the On Print. This event is only executed in an instance when Access must move back to the previous page when a particular section does not fit on the page. This event is important if you are using the option of Keep Together. The code is processed during the back up. After this event, the On Format is run again.

Report events

Every report created in Access has the following events that can contain code. These events can make running reports seamless:

**10 Min.
To Go**

- On Open: A macro or VBA code that Access uses when the report is run either in Print or Print Preview. This precedes all other events. Put code here to close or hide open forms or other open reports. In addition, if you want to programmatically set controls on a report you can do so here.

- On Close: Macro or code that runs when the report is closed. This is also activated when you close out of a Print Preview. Enter code here to make hidden forms or reports visible or to update records. For instance, you can have code that marks a particular record as having been printed. The code in this section can be fired off when the user closes the report.

- On Activate: An event that occurs when the report receives the focus during a Print Preview. You can write code that displays a custom menu for the user during preview.

- On Deactivate: An event that fires when the preview report loses the focus. You can turn off any custom menus or toolbars that were available during the preview.

- On No Data: An event activated when the report's record source contains no data. Put code here to display a message that indicates no data was available and closes the report.

- On Page: A macro or event procedure that is executed after the On Format event has been executed for a section but prior to the printing of that section.

- On Error: An event you can use to enter a macro or VBA code to display proper error messages in response to any errors encountered in running the report.

If you learn to program a report, you can increase its effectiveness and also expand it. To view examples of how a report can be manipulated programmatically, look at the Check Register report shown in Figure 22-4. Notice the report rpt_CheckRegister has several features that are programmatically controlled, such as the two secondary titles and the alternating colored rows of data.

CHECK REGISTER

Enter Your Name in Setup

Mechanics of Boston
Account Number: 233 42 8964

Clr'd	Check #	Date	Trans. Type	Payee	Payment	Deposit	Balance	Memo
✓		3/23/2000	VOID-Beginning Ba		$0.00	$1,600.00	$1,600.00	Initial Balance Transfer from Other Account
✓	0101	1/30/2000	Check	Random House	$1,250.00	$0.00	$350.00	Book Order #950215-23
✓		1/28/2000	Beginning Balance		$0.00	$200.00	$650.00	
☐		1/29/2000	Deposit		$0.00	$200.00	$750.00	
☐		2/8/2000	Other Income		$0.00	$60.00	$810.00	
✓	0103	1/30/2000	VOID-Check	Pinnacle Publishing	$275.35	$0.00	$534.65	For Code Print Pro Documentation
✓		1/30/2000	VOID-Deposit		$0.00	$9,500.00	$10,034.65	Monthly Check Receipts
✓	0102	1/24/2000	Check	Pre-Press	$256.37	$0.00	$9,778.28	Ad Film for Access Advisor
✓	0104	1/25/2000	Check	Heritage Printers	$1,256.23	$0.00	$8,522.05	New Yes! I Can Run My Business Brochures
✓	0105	1/25/2000	VOID-Check	Keystone Videos	$1,560.00	$0.00	$6,962.05	Access Developer Videos
☐	0106	1/27/2000	Check	IDG Books	$2,361.23	$0.00	$4,600.82	PC World Access 2 Bible Books
☐	0107	1/27/2000	Check	Champlin	$570.00	$0.00	$4,030.82	Boxes for Products
☐	0108	1/30/2000	Check	State of Connecticut	$1,256.52	$0.00	$2,774.30	January Sales Taxes
✓		1/31/2000	VOID-Deposit		$0.00	$1,000.00	$3,774.30	Deposit from Samson Corp.
✓		2/1/2000	VOID-Interest		$0.00	$10.00	$3,784.30	January 1995 Interest
✓		2/1/2000	VOID-Service Char		$18.35	$0.00	$3,765.95	January 1995 Service Charge
☐	0202	2/8/2000	Check	AA Test Supplier 1	$15.03	$0.00	$3,750.92	PO 95020111
☐	0109	2/18/2000	Check	Private Printers	$205.64	$0.00	$3,545.28	
☐	0203	3/1/2000	Check	Heritage Oil	$25.00	$0.00	$3,520.28	
☐	0110	3/17/2000	Check	Roadside Diner	$20.00	$0.00	$3,500.28	
☐		3/17/2000	VOID-Deposit		$0.00	$100.00	$3,600.28	
☐	0111	3/22/2000	Check	Acme Vending	$99.00	$0.00	$3,501.28	
☐	0112	3/22/2000	Check	Acme Vending	$99.99	$0.00	$3,401.29	
☐	0113	3/15/2000	Check	Private Printers	$52.00	$0.00	$3,349.29	
☐	0204	3/15/2000	Check	Acme Vending	$20.00	$0.00	$3,329.29	
☐	0114	3/2/2000	Check	Private Printers	$320.00	$0.00	$3,009.29	
☐	0115	3/2/2000	Check	Acme Vending	$176.00	$0.00	$2,833.29	

Figure 22-4 *The report Rpt_CheckRegister illustrates how you can program the report to include some very sophisticated visual effects.*

The Check Register uses several events in the report. When you run the report, you print the lines with alternating background colors to make it easier to see. You do this by setting the background color of the text boxes on the report. (To create the check box, a box was drawn behind the check box itself.) The first line of code to do this is in the On Format event of the Page Header. This one line of code sets a hidden field, backgroundsetting. This field is used to establish whether the background should be white (0) or gray (-1).

Rather than using a field to hold the value, a global variable for the report could have been declared. However, in this example a text box was used so that you can turn on the Visible setting and see how its value changes from −1 to 0 during the formatting and printing of the report.

The code, which turns the background from white to gray, is handled in the event in the Detail section. This code was placed in this section because it affects the detail information. The following code appears in the event:

```
Dim x As Integer   'used to count through the columns

If Me.backgroundsetting = 0 Then
    For x = 1 To 9 Step 1
        Me("column" & x).BackColor = 16777215
    Next x
Else
    For x = 1 To 9 Step 1
        Me("column" & x).BackColor = 12632256
    Next x
End If
Me.backgroundsetting = Abs(Me.backgroundsetting) + (-1)
```

The preceding code works by first declaring a variable that is used for the For Next loops. Then the code checks the current status of the backgroundsetting text box. If the value is zero, it loops through each of the nine controls and sets the back color to 16777215, which is the value of white. If the value is other than zero (-1), the back color is set to 12632256, which is the value of light gray.

The final line of code does a very neat trick. Because the values can only be true (-1) or false (0), the code takes the absolute value of the current value and adds a negative one to it. You may have to recall some elementary math, but you can see that doing this saves you from having to set the value twice, once for the negative instance and another for the positive.

The code declares a variable x that is used to count through the columns. If you look at the properties for each of the text boxes, you see that the names are set to "column1", "column2", "column3", and so on. The reason for this is to save some programming time. Rather than writing several lines of code to set the values of each control, you do a loop instead. This is an excellent technique to use when you have many controls that you want to affect programmatically.

You are not limited to making superficial types of changes to a report programmatically. You can do calculations and process data via code rather than doing it at the query or report level. For instance, to calculate the running balance as each transaction is displayed, you can set a variable via code and (in the On Format event of the Detail section) keep adding to that variable. If you review the report, rpt_CheckRegister you see how this is done. A public variable is declared, runningbalance. Then in the On Format event of the Report Header, the value for the variable, runningbalance is set to zero. The code is placed here because you want this value to run across multiple pages. If you set it in the On Format event of the Page Header, it is reset whenever a new page is started. Review the code in the On Format event of the Detail section. You see the following line of code at the end of the listing:

```
runningbalance = runningbalance + Nz([DepositAmount]) - Nz([PaymentAmount])
```

Of course, this is a simplistic example. You could also do it without any programming at all by using the Running Sum property. The emphasis, in this session, is that you are not limited to using queries to calculate and manipulate your data. In many cases, to create fast printing reports, you may want to do calculations via code if they prove to be faster.

The previous examples have focused on the On Format event of the report method. What about the On Print? When is it appropriate to use code in this event? Well, if you wanted to track if a report had ever been printed, you can write code to track such an event. Open up a recordset, move to the record that you are currently printing, and set the field Printed to True. This can be seen in the report, Check Print — Bottom. The code in the On Print event of the Detail section opens up a recordset and finds the transaction by searching for the ID. After it finds the record, it marks it as Printed.

Using the ActiveX Calendar Control

Access provides a built-in ActiveX Calendar Control that you can plug into any form. As shown in Figure 22-5, the Calendar Control displays a monthly calendar. As you click on each day of the month, the day number appears sunken. You can modify the appearance of the control using the control's properties box.

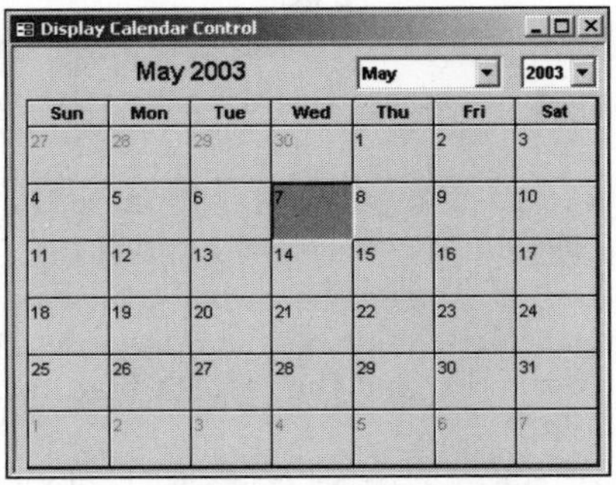

Figure 22-5   *The Access ActiveX Calendar Control displays a monthly calendar.*

Figure 22-6 shows the Calendar Properties dialog box, which enables you to change how the control displays the date components on the calendar. On the General tab, you can change the control to display the month in short format (Jan, Feb, Mar, and so on) or long format (January, February, and so on). You can also format the days of the week (Monday, Tuesday, Wednesday) to short, medium, or long. The check boxes on the right side of the Properties dialog box enable you to turn the display of the various components on and off. The Font and Color tab allow you to change the font and color of each component that displays in the control. The events provided with the control enable you to retrieve the date the user has selected in the control.

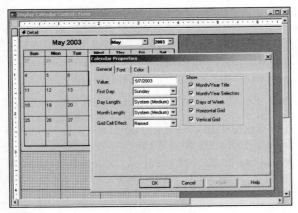

Figure 22-6 *Configuring the appearance of the ActiveX Calendar control.*

Although the Access Calendar control is easy to add to any form, it provides limited programmable features. Additionally, the Calendar control is not installed automatically when you install Access. When you distribute your application to users, you must also distribute and register the files required to run the Calendar control.

Done!

REVIEW

This session has exposed you to basic dialog box design and has shown you how to design a print dialog box. You also learned about programming reports and using the ActiveX Calendar controls. The following topics were covered:

- You can create powerful search dialog boxes that give your users searching capabilities.
- You can design and program print dialog boxes that can either limit or expand the options available to your end user.
- You can incorporate many of the techniques you learned in previous sessions with your basic understanding of the available report events to enable you to program more effective reports.
- You can do two things when you program reports: affect the display and manipulate the data. Using code to change how a report looks can expand the report's features by giving you more dynamic reports.
- You can hide and display controls according to settings or a particular field's contents.
- You can do calculations or pull in data from a source other than the report's record source. This gives you tremendous power when designing reports because it frees you from displaying only the data from the record source of the report.
- You can drop an ActiveX control into your forms and reports to enhance your end product.

QUIZ YOURSELF

1. What are the basic characteristics of a dialog box? (See "Basic Dialog Box Design.")

2. What is the significance of the properties Modal and Pop-Up? (See "Basic Dialog Box Design.")

3. What are some of the basic controls you would want to put on a print dialog? (See "Building a print dialog box.")

4. What command is the easiest to use in running the report from the print dialog via VBA code? (See "Printing reports from the dialog box.")

5. What are the main sections of a report? What events are associated with each section? (See "Programming Reports.")

6. If you wanted to put in a message displayed only when an error occurs, which event would you use? (See "Programming Reports.")

Application Architecture

Session Checklist

✔ Understanding application architecture for a complete application

✔ Structuring your VBA code and dealing with compilation

✔ Using the Program file configuration

In this session, you learn how to structure your application with functionality that is common to most applications.

30 Min. To Go

Assuming that you have created the tables, forms, reports, and so on that make up your application, you should probably include some additional items to handle the general program functionality. You normally find these items in any professionally designed software. Preceding sessions have touched on some of these, but this session helps you put the whole into perspective.

What to Include in Your Application

In addition to the custom and unique functions required for an application, you need to include items from the following categories:

- Startup forms and About boxes (Refer to Session 19.)
- Switchboard or menu systems (Refer to Session 11.)
- Security (Refer to Session 28.)
- Error handling (Refer to Session 16.)
- Help (Refer to Session 20.)
- Support

All the items listed have been discussed at some point in this book except for the support item. You should include one or more of the following categories of support functions:

- Technical support
- Preference management
- Archiving
- Backup
- Repair
- Compaction
- System information

The Technical Support screen

Providing a pop-up form, usually called from the About box or the Help pull-down menu, can give frustrated users an easy way to know how to contact the right organization to help them with their problems. List telephone numbers, fax numbers, e-mail addresses, and/or Web addresses where users can get technical support.

Preference management

The use of the word *preferences* in the context of this function includes more than just preferences. Information about the application, user, organization, and so on must be handled as well. You can hardcode this type of information, but this doesn't make the application flexible, easy to maintain, or user-configurable.

You generally create preferences when building your application. You might not give users control over system preferences such as the version or copyright, but you do let them select how an application runs. For example, each user may search for data differently or have a different default value.

Preferences can be one of three types:

1. System
2. Default
3. User

System preferences are those that exist only once and are common to all users. Preferences such as the license information, security options, startup options, and so on, fall into this category. Default preferences are those that may be different from user to user. If a set of preferences has not been established for a particular user, the Default preferences are used. User preferences are duplicates of the Default preferences but set to a specific user. You might have a file location that is user-dependent, a form color, a report heading, and so on. Just as users can have specific security options, using preferences they have specific options to control the way the application works.

Preferences are usually stored in a separate table, either locally on a client machine, on a server, or on a combination of both. There are generally two different schemes for handling preferences: the single-record method or the multiple-record method. With the single-record method, you create a field for each preference and have only one record in the table. You might actually use a record for each user if you provide for independent preferences by user.

In the multiple-record method, a record exists for each preference. This method has the advantage of not requiring a table-design change when you want to add a preference. The disadvantage is that every preference value is stored as a text value instead of as a specific field type. In most cases, a preference stored as a string value is fine, but if you need to store a preference as numeric, date/time, OLE object, or another type, the single-record method is better.

The Check Writer sample application offers the preferences table shown in Figure 23-1. This is an example of the single-record method. In Figure 23-2, the same preferences are shown in a datasheet view using the multiple-record method.

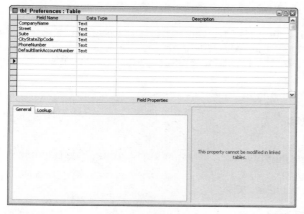

Figure 23-1   *The Design view of the single-record preferences table.*

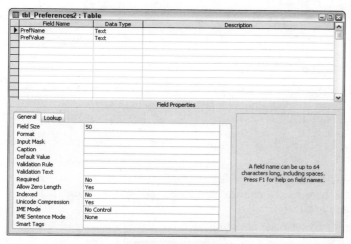

Figure 23-2   *The Datasheet view of the multiple-record preferences table.*

You can access the data in these tables directly by using your own code or functions just as you would retrieve normal table data. It is a good idea to have a function that retrieves preference values. This makes it easy to reference the values on forms, reports, and within code. In the sample application, a module called `PreferenceFunctions` contains two functions, `GetPref` and `SetPref`, that can be used to retrieve and set preferences from either type of preference table. The code listing for these functions is covered in the section "Conditional compiling" later in this session. Conditional compiler constants are used to handle the two different types of tables from the same function code base.

Using the `GetPref` function simply requires that you pass a preference name to the function. The value of the preference is then returned. The returning value type is a variant (because its type may vary). If there is an error or if the preference doesn't exist, a null value is returned. Here is an example of a call to this function:

```
StrCompanyName = dbc_GetPref("CompanyName")
```

Using the `SetPref` function is a little more involved. First, if the preference exists, its value is replaced. If the preference does not exist, the preference is added. If there are no errors, a True value will be returned by the function to indicate the successful setting of the preference.

The `SetPref` function has the following arguments:

1. The name of the preference (`String`)
2. The value of the preference (`Variant`)
3. The ADO data type, which is used only when creating a new preference (default value is `adWChar`)
4. The size of the field (default value is 255)

Arguments 3 and 4 are used only for the single-record method. Here is an example of a call to this function:

```
BlnSuccess = dbc_SetPref("Report Header","The Acme Corporation", adWChar,
100)
```

Archiving

Archiving is the process of moving data records from the active database to a separate database. Usually, the records moved are deleted from the active database. This cuts down on the number of records in the application database. Doing this has significant benefits:

- The size of data tables is reduced, improving performance in loading forms, running queries, running reports, and so on.
- The time to load forms and set values to controls is reduced.
- The number of items the user has to choose from in list and combo boxes is reduced, saving time and effort.
- The disk requirements for file storage are reduced.
- The time to do backups and the size of the media are reduced.

Archiving has far-reaching benefits that save time and money and help you maintain a better-performing application while safeguarding data that you may need later.

Backup

If you have ever had an Access database that was corrupted beyond repair, you can understand the importance of backing up your database. You can manually make a copy of your program file once, and unless you make changes to it, the copy can be stored safely. However, assuming you properly split your program and data files, the data file is changed every time you use your application. You should include some means of creating a backup.

The code in Listing 23-1 contains a function that you can use to add a backup feature to your application. You can call it from a button on a form, passing it the backend filename. It checks to see if the filename is the current database, and if it is, the function returns a message that it cannot back up the current database file. Otherwise, it makes a copy of the file. This copy has a datatime stamp and the extension .bak.

Listing 23-1 *Backup File Function*

```
Public Function dbc_BackupFile(fileBackup As String) As String
Dim FileName As String
    On Error GoTo ErrorHandler

    If fileBackup = CurrentDb.Name Then
        dbc_BackupFile = "Cannot backup the current database file"
        GoTo Done
    End If

    FileName = dbc_GetDirPart(fileBackup) & Left(dbc_GetFileNamePart(fileBackup), __
Len(dbc_GetFileNamePart(fileBackup)) - 4) & Format(Now(), "YYYYMMDDHHNNSS") & ".bak"
    FileCopy fileBackup, FileName
    dbc_BackupFile = fileBackup & " backed up to " & FileName
    GoTo Done

ErrorHandler:
    dbc_BackupFile = Err.Description
Done:
End Function
```

Repair

The Repair function allows the user to choose an MDB file and repair it. Occasionally, you may need to repair an Access database. Repairing is necessary because data files can occasionally become fragmented or corrupted. You cannot select to repair the program database you are currently using. You can repair the database as long as it is not used exclusively and no attached tables are in use by bound forms. You cannot repair a database being used by other users.

The System Information screen

You should include a System Information screen to display information that would be useful to the user or to the technical support person trying to solve a problem. The information you might display on a System Information screen includes the following: the version of Access running; the initialization file for Access; the name and location of the current program .mdb file; the location of Access; the location of any attached data files; the program version; the current user; and the system date and time.

This is a purely informational screen that requires no action from the user except to click OK to close the form. It is usually displayed from an About box or other utility form to enable the developer to help the user debug any environmental problems. A sample System Information screen is shown in Figure 23-3. This form is included in the sample Check Writer application.

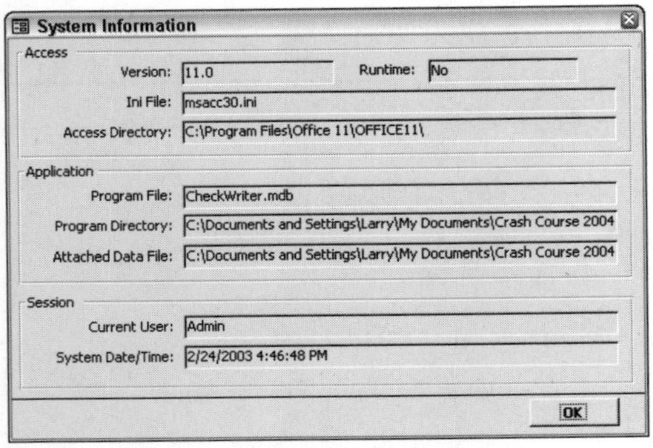

Figure 23-3   *The System Information screen.*

The code for this form is shown in Listing 23-2. Everything happens on the Form_Load event. The listing is broken down into sections: Access information, application information, and session information. The Access information is derived by using the SysCmd function. Application information comes from the object CurrentProject and from looking at the MsysObjects table. The MsysObjects table is used to determine how many attached tables there are. If there is only one, the file for the attached tables is displayed. If there is more than one, the message Use the Attachment Manager is displayed. If there are no attached tables, a message is displayed telling you that there are no attached tables. Session information is pulled from the CurrentUser function and the Now function.

Listing 23-2   *The System Information Screen Form Load Subroutine*

```
Private Sub Form_Load()

On Error GoTo ErrorHandler

With Me
    'Access information
    .AccessVer = SysCmd(acSysCmdAccessVer)
    .RunTime = IIf(SysCmd(acSysCmdRuntime), "Yes", "No")
    .IniFile = SysCmd(SYSCMD_INIFILE)
```

```
    .AccessDir = SysCmd(SYSCMD_ACCESSDIR)

    'Application information
    .ProgramFile = CurrentProject.Name
    .ProgramDirectory = CurrentProject.Path
    If DCount("Database", "MsysObjects", "Type = 6") > 0 Then
      If DCount("Database", "MsysObjects", "Database <> " & Chr(34) & _
      DLookup("Database", "MsysObjects", "Type = 6") & Chr(34)) = 0 Then
        .AttachedTo = DLookup("Database", "MsysObjects", "Type = 6")
      Else
        .AttachedTo = "Multiple files, use Attachment Manager"
      End If
    Else
      .AttachedTo = "No attached tables"
    End If

    'Session information
      .User = CurrentUser()
      .SystemDateTime = Now()

  End With
  GoTo Done

ErrorHandler:
    MsgBox err.Description
Done:

  End Sub
```

Using this type of form, you could display even more information that would be useful for technical support purposes.

 EZ Access Developer Suite from Database Creations, Inc., contains powerful and flexible interfaces that handle all the functions previously described, including a Preference Manager, Archive Manager, File Utilities, and System Information Screen. The companion Web site contains a link to a demo of this product.

VBA Code

**20 Min.
To Go**

Your VBA code can be handled in a number of different ways. This includes the methods for compiling as well as how the code is structured. The methods, in general, affect maintainability and performance.

Compiling

As discussed in previous sessions, your VBA code is stored within a Visual Basic project. For your code to execute, it must be compiled. Microsoft Access stores the code in two states: the source code version and the compiled version. Whenever the source code is changed, the compiled version is deleted. Access compiles the necessary modules when they are used if they are not in a compiled state. This is not the preferred method because it is nice to know if there are compilation errors before you attempt to execute the code. You can compile the project by choosing Debug ⇨ Compile Project in the VBA window.

Compile options

Choosing Tools ⇨ Options in the VBA window gives you some control over how Access compiles. Making this selection displays the window shown in Figure 23-4. In the lower-right corner of the General tab, you find two options for compilation:

- **Compile On Demand:** Limits what Access compiles when a form is opened. Only those functions that are used are compiled.
- **Background Compile:** Compile any uncompiled code when Access's processes are not busy.

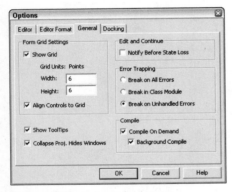

Figure 23-4   *Compiler options.*

It is always best to compile an application completely before delivering it to a user.

The IsCompiled property

You can check the status of the compiled state of a project by looking at the IsCompiled property of the Application object. This property returns a Boolean value indicating whether the project is in a compiled state. It is True (-1) if the project is in a compiled state. It is False (0) when the project has never been fully compiled, if a module has been added, edited, or deleted, or if a module hasn't been saved in a compiled state.

Conditional compiling

Sometimes certain code may not apply to a specific environment. For example, you might have an application that runs differently in different versions of Access. Or maybe some code is applicable to different versions of Windows. Other reasons include debugging statements and localizing an application for different languages. To have one code base that can run in different environments, Access and VBA provides a concept called *conditional compilation*.

You use conditional compilation to run blocks of code selectively. To do this, you need the following:

1. A conditional compiler constant identified with #Const
2. An #If... #Then... #Else directive (they can be nested)

As an example of using compiler constants can be found in the module mod_PreferenceFunctions, which is part of the sample Check Writer application. The code for this module is shown in Listing 23-3. As previously discussed, there are two methods for dealing with preferences: the single-record and the multiple-record methods. The module is coded to work with either of these methods, and the selection of the method is handled with compiler constants.

Listing 23-3   *The Preference Functions*

```
'Prior to using these functions you must set the type of preference
' system you will be using and include the appropriate table

#Const PreferenceSystem = 1 '1 = single record, 2 = multiple record
#If PreferenceSystem = 1 Then
  Const PrefTable As String = "tbl_Preferences"
#Else
  Const PrefTable As String = "PreferencesII"
#End If

Public Function dbc_GetPref(strPrefName As String) As Variant
'Function returns the preference data for the preference name
'  or null if preference cannot be determined
Dim rst As ADODB.Recordset

  On Error GoTo ErrorHandler
  Set rst = New ADODB.Recordset
  rst.ActiveConnection = CurrentProject.Connection
  rst.CursorType = adOpenKeyset

  #If PreferenceSystem = 1 Then
    rst.Open "Select * from " & PrefTable
    If rst.RecordCount = 1 Then
      dbc_GetPref = rst(strPrefName)
    Else
      dbc_GetPref = Null
    End If
  #End If

  #If PreferenceSystem = 2 Then
    rst.Open "Select * from " & PrefTable & " Where PrefName = " & Chr(34) & strPrefName
& Chr(34)
    If rst.RecordCount = 1 Then
      dbc_GetPref = rst!PrefValue
    Else
      dbc_GetPref = Null
```

Continued

Listing 23-3 *Continued*

```
    End If
  #End If

  GoTo Done
ErrorHandler:
  dbc_GetPref = Null
Done:
End Function

Public Function dbc_SetPref(strPrefName As String, varPrefValue As Variant, Optional
strPrefType = "adWChar", Optional lngPrefSize = 255) As Boolean
Dim varX As Variant
'Function sets preference data for the preference name
'  A new preference will be created if it doesn't exist
'  If it exists the previous value will be replaced
'The arguments are as follows:
' strPrefName is the name of the preference
' varPrefData is the value of the preference
' strPrefType is the ADO Data Type which is used only when creating a new preference
'   This argument is optional and will default to a string type
'Function returns a true if preference was successfully set or a false if there was a
problem
#If PreferenceSystem = 1 Then
Dim rst As ADODB.Recordset
Dim cat As New ADOX.Catalog
Dim tbl As New ADOX.Table
Dim col As New ADOX.Column

  On Error GoTo ErrorHandler
  Set rst = New ADODB.Recordset
  rst.ActiveConnection = CurrentProject.Connection
  rst.Open PrefTable, , adOpenKeyset, adLockPessimistic, adCmdTable

  'Do check to see if field exists
  On Error Resume Next
  varX = rst(strPrefName)
  rst.Close
  If Err.Number = 3265 Then
  'Field does not exist, create new field
    On Error GoTo ErrorHandler
    cat.ActiveConnection = CurrentProject.Connection
    col.Name = strPrefName
    col.Type = strPrefType
    col.DefinedSize = lngPrefSize
    cat.Tables(PrefTable).Columns.Append col
    Set cat = Nothing
  End If

  'Change value of Field
  On Error GoTo ErrorHandler
  rst.Open PrefTable, , adOpenKeyset, adLockPessimistic, adCmdTable
  rst(strPrefName) = varPrefValue
```

```
   rst.Update

#End If

#If PreferenceSystem = 2 Then
Dim rst As ADODB.Recordset

   On Error GoTo ErrorHandler
   Set rst = New ADODB.Recordset
   rst.ActiveConnection = CurrentProject.Connection
   rst.Open PrefTable, , adOpenKeyset, adLockPessimistic, adCmdTable
   rst.Find ("PrefName = '" & strPrefName & "'")
   If rst.EOF Then
     'add new preference
     rst.AddNew
     rst!PrefName = strPrefName
     rst!PrefValue = varPrefValue
     rst.Update
   Else
     'preference exists
     rst!PrefValue = varPrefValue
     rst.Update
   End If
#End If

   dbc_SetPref = True
   GoTo Done
ErrorHandler:
   dbc_SetPref = False
Done:
End Function
```

The first section of the code in Listing 23-3 contains the general declarations section. The constant `PreferenceSystem` is used to determine the Preference method. A value of 1 is used for the single-record method, and a value of 2 is used for the multiple-record method. Note that the value of the constant `PrefTable` is set to a different table name based on the compiler constant `PreferenceSystem`. This is done with the #If, #Then, #Else, #Endif directives.

Both the functions `GetPref` and `SetPref` contain the #If, #Then, #Else, #Endif directives that determine the method used to handle preferences. When the compiler processes the code, only the code appropriate to the preference method is compiled and used.

 Conditional compiler constants are always private to the module in which they appear. It is not possible to create public compiler constants using the #Const directive. To define public compiler constants, use the Project Properties window and enter the compiler constants in the Conditional Compilation Arguments field on the General tab.

VBA defines constants for use with the #If...Then...#Else directive without defining them with the #Const directive. These constants are global in scope and apply to all modules in a project (see Table 23-1).

Table 23-1   *Built-In Conditional Compiler Constants*

Constant	Description
Vba6	True if VBA version 6.0
Win16	True indicates that the development environment is 16-bit
Win32	True indicates that the development environment is 32-bit
Mac	True indicates that the development environment is Macintosh

Decompiling

Just as you can compile an application, you can also decompile an application. This is not something that is normally done, but it is sometimes necessary to correct some peculiar errors with Access. These errors occasionally occur when a new library reference is added or the operating system has changed. You can decompile the entire project in one of two ways:

1. Change the name of the project.
2. Use the /decompile command line option when starting Access.

Module structure

Access and VBA provide the capability to have multiple modules within a database or project. Each module can have one or more functions or subroutines as well as globally declared constants and variables. You might first choose to put all your code into one module. The problem with doing that, however, is that whenever you need a single function in that module, the whole module is loaded into memory. This may adversely affect the performance of your application.

On the other hand, if each function is in a separate module, every time a new function is called, Access stops the application to load the new module. The best method is to break your functions and subroutines into logical groups that make sense to load at the same time. If functions are related, put them into the same module. If a function calls another function, put them both into the same module. Another good rule is to keep public declarations and variables in a separate module.

**10 Min.
To Go**

Program File Configuration

You can control the behavior of Access and your application by configuring various options and properties. The following sections describe several of these options and properties.

Startup options

Access provides various startup options that control how an application runs. You can access these options by choosing Tools ⇨ Startup. These can be also set using VBA and ADO.

These properties are defined by Microsoft Access and aren't automatically recognized by the Jet database engine.

When the property is set for the first time, you must create the property and append it to the Properties collection of the object to which it applies. After the property is in the collection, you can set it in the same manner as you do any ADO property. When the property is set for the first time in the user interface, it is added to the Properties collection, and you can set it without appending it. When writing code to set these properties, include error-handling code to verify that the property you are setting already exists in the Properties collection.

 When you create a property, you must correctly define its Type **before you append it to the** Properties **collection.**

The following list contains some Microsoft Access defined properties that apply to the Application object: AppTitle, AppIcon, StartupShowDBWindow, StartupShowStatusBar, AllowShortcutMenus, AllowFullMenus, AllowBuiltInToolbars, AllowToolbarChanges, AllowBreakIntoCode, AllowSpecialKeys, Replicable, and ReplicationConflictFunction.

Startup procedures

You have three choices for starting your VBA code when a database is opened:

1. Use the command line argument /x *macro,* which runs the specified macro when the application starts. Have this macro call a VBA procedure.
2. Use the macro named AutoExec, which automatically runs when Access starts.
3. Set the Display Form/Page entry on the Startup dialog box available from the Tools menu. The code in the OnLoad or OnOpen event of this form is then run when the form automatically opens as Access starts.

Compacting

Compaction of a database file will significantly improve performance. You must make provisions within your application to perform this important function.

What is compacting?

You compact an Access database to remove deleted objects that are still taking up file space. When you delete data or objects in an Access database, the file can become fragmented, causing disk space to be used inefficiently. Compacting the database makes a copy of the file and rearranges how the file is stored on your disk. This optimizes the performance of the database. If you distribute your application so that data is in a separate file from your application and you have protected your application from being changed, compacting won't be necessary. Before distributing your application, be sure to compact it.

Compaction requires exclusive access by the program doing the compaction. In other words, you cannot have other users using the database file while it is being compacted. This is one of the shortcomings of Access versus a database management system like SQL Server. A DBMS allows users to use the database while the file is being compacted or backed up.

How to compact programmatically

You can compact a database using VBA and ADO/JRO by using the `CompactDatabase` method. This method copies and compacts a closed database and gives you several options. These options include changing its version, the collating order, the use of encryption, and more. The syntax is

```
JetEngine.CompactDatabase(SourceConnection, DestConnection)
```

where `SourceConnection` is a string value specifying a connection to the source database to be compacted. The SourceConnection must be closed. `DestConnection` is a string value specifying a connection to the destination database to be created by the compaction. You get an error if the `DestConnection` already exists or if another file with that name already exists. It is not possible to do a compaction of the same database, that is, one in which the source database and destination database are the same.

It is important to automate this process somehow or, at least, to give your users a way to compact their databases once in a while. You cannot compact the database you are currently using, nor can you compact a database being used by others.

The code in Listing 23-4 can be used to programmatically compact a file. The function is set up to accept one or two parameters. If the database to compact has a database password, you supply the second parameter. As part of the compaction, the function makes a copy of the database file, renames it, and compacts it back to the original filename.

Listing 23-4 *Compact Function*

```
Public Function dbc_CompactFile(fileCompact As String, Optional pwd As String = "")
Dim errloop
Dim f As Integer
Dim SizeBefore As Long
Dim SizeAfter As Long
Dim PercentCompaction As Single
Dim fileBackUp As String

    On Error GoTo ErrorHandler

    'Get file size before compaction
    f = FreeFile
    Open fileCompact For Binary Shared As #f
    SizeBefore = LOF(f)
    Close f

    'Create backup file before compaction
    fileBackUp = Mid(fileCompact, 1, Len(fileCompact) - 3) & "bak"
    If Dir(fileBackUp) <> "" Then
        'Delete if already exists
        Kill fileBackUp
```

```
        End If
        Name fileCompact As fileBackUp

        'Do compaction
        If pwd = "" Then
            DBEngine.CompactDatabase fileBackUp, fileCompact
        Else
            DBEngine.CompactDatabase fileBackUp, fileCompact, , , ";pwd=" & pwd
        End If

        'Calculate new file size
        f = FreeFile
        Open fileCompact For Binary Shared As #f
        SizeAfter = LOF(f)
        Close f

        'Calculate percent and display message
        PercentCompaction = (SizeBefore - SizeAfter) / SizeBefore
        MsgBox fileCompact & " compacted by " & Format(PercentCompaction, "Percent")
        GoTo Done

ErrorHandler:
        For Each errloop In DBEngine.Errors
            MsgBox "Compaction unsuccessful! " & errloop.Description
        Next errloop
Done:
End Function
```

Done!

REVIEW

In this session, you learned how to structure your application and provide some functionality that is common to many applications. These topics were covered:

- A complete application includes startup forms, an About box, a switchboard or menu system, security, error handling, a help system, and support.

- A support system includes technical support, preference management, archiving, backup, repair, compaction, and system information.

- There are two different schemes for handling preferences: the single-record method and the multiple-record method. There are advantages and disadvantages to each.

- The Compact function can defragment your database, save file space, and improve performance of your database.

QUIZ YOURSELF

1. What are the two different schemes for handling preferences? List the advantages and disadvantages of each. (See "Preference management.")
2. List the five benefits of archiving. (See "Archiving.")
3. What are the restrictions on repairing a database? (See "Repair.")

4. What type of information is displayed on a System Information screen? (See "The System Information screen.")

5. What method is used to compact a database programmatically? (See "Compacting.")

Packaging Your Application

Session Checklist

✔ Learning considerations for .mde files

✔ Using Runtime

✔ The Setup Program

**30 Min.
To Go**

I n this session, you learn how to prepare your application for deployment to your users. Obviously, there are many considerations, such as the media on which you create the installation, the destination computer's environment, and so on. This session presents these relevant topics from several perspectives.

.MDE files

Access provides for a special type of database file that prevents users from viewing the code and design of forms and reports. This is an .mde file. You might want to consider distributing your application in this format.

What is an .mde file?

An .mde file is a copy of an .mdb file with all source code removed and only compiled code included. It is used for distribution of applications to users who have no need to modify the code. Because it has no source code, it is smaller than the .mdb file. In addition to being a smaller file, it has the following benefits: It remains compiled, it prevents users from viewing or changing the code modules, and it prevents changes to forms and reports.

The MDE property

There is an MDE property that you can use to determine whether a database has been saved as an .mde file. When a database is saved as an .mde file, Access adds the MDE property to the database and sets it to the String value T.

The MDE property doesn't exist in a database that is not an .mde file. Trying to determine this property will cause an error in an .mde file.

How to create an .mde file

You can change a database to an .mde file by choosing Tools ⇨ Database Utilities ⇨ Make MDE File. When you create an .mde file, Access does the following:

- Removes all editable source code
- Compiles all modules
- Compacts the database

Be sure to save a copy of your original database to maintain the source code.

Runtime

With the Office Developer Edition, Microsoft has provided a means for developers to distribute Access applications without requiring the user to purchase Access. This is a great way of deploying an application to hundreds or thousands of users who may not have purchased Microsoft Office Professional (which includes Access). Although this type of distribution has a big advantage, there is a price to pay. Namely, the Runtime version of Access has limitations. These limitations basically prevent the Runtime version from being used by itself. As a developer, you need to know these limitations and provide the functionality necessary to replace these missing functions. Here is a list of the functions not included in the Runtime version:

- The database window is hidden.
- The macro and module windows are hidden.
- No design views are available.
- Menu items are limited — only menu items that you include.
- No built-it toolbars — only custom toolbars that you include.
- No Access help files — only help files you create.
- No built-in error handling — Access runtime crashes if you haven't included error handling.
- Some key combinations aren't enabled. These are generally those related to the database window, Design views, menu items, help items, and error handling.

The Setup Program

Most of the time, you distribute your application using a setup program of some sort. This is characteristic of just about all software. With the architecture of Windows-based operating systems, you need to be sure that your application will run within the operating system and that the operating environment is aware of your program. You can ensure these things with a setup program. In this session, you learn about the process of installing your software on a computer.

Why do you need a setup program?

Unless your program is a single database file without reference to any other files, you should include a setup or installation program. More than likely, your application is split into more than one database: one for data and one for the program. If this is the case, you must make sure that the links from one to the other work regardless of where a user puts your application. A setup program can help you make sure this is not a problem.

Also, you have most likely used a reference, library, ActiveX control, help file, or similar item in your application. If these add-ins are not installed on the user's computer in the correct location, your application crashes when it first starts up. The setup program properly handles the installation of add-ins on a user's computer.

Another reason for using a setup program involves creating desktop shortcuts, menu items, and including icons for the shortcuts. Without these, the user will be forced to start Access first and then search for the application using the Open dialog box. This is not only inefficient, but it's frustrating for the user.

Setup programs also contain compressed versions of your files, so distribution of the code requires less storage. This makes it more efficient for storage on a CD or for deployment over a network or the Internet.

If you are going to distribute your application with Access Runtime, a lot of files, registry entries, and so on need to be installed. Using the setup program provided with Office Professional makes including Runtime an easy process.

Finally, setup programs provide for including readme files, license agreements, other technical support information, and the ability to remove the application through an uninstall program.

Using the Package and Deployment Wizard

The Package and Deployment Wizard included with Microsoft Office Developer provides a means of creating a setup program that will work with Access, Access Runtime, and Microsoft Data Engine (MSDE)-based applications. You can create a setup program that is contained on a floppy disk or that is Web-based, and everything in between, including network-based setup programs and CDs.

The process of distributing an application with the Package and Deployment Wizard is shown in Figure 24-1.

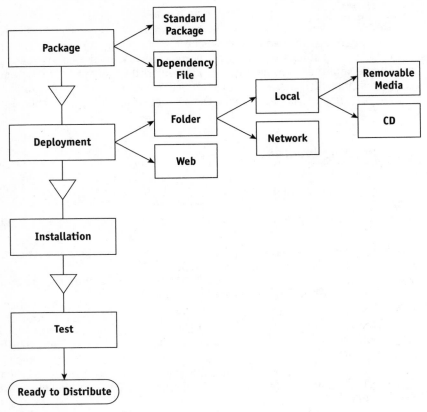

Figure 24-1 *The process of distributing an application.*

There are four major steps in distributing an application:

1. Creating a package
2. Deploying a package
3. Installing a package
4. Testing a package

Installing and testing

Before delivering the application to the user, you should run through the installation program and test the results of the installation. For the same reasons that you test your application for bugs, you should also test the setup program and verify that the setup program does its job properly. A number of problems can occur because computer environments vary significantly; many variables are associated with the computer hardware, operating systems, and other applications that may be loaded.

To run the setup program, locate the Setup.exe file as created in the deployment step. Execute the Setup.exe file and follow the prompts and screens to install the application.

The Check Writer sample application file has a setup program on the companion Web site that was created by the Package and Deployment Wizard. Download and run the Setup.exe file.

You should test the setup program and test the application in a variety of operating environments to ensure that the programs work properly for your users. Although the number of combinations of processors, speed, memory, operating system, and other variables are almost unlimited, it would be wise to choose at least a few different environments to test the application.

Considerations for using a setup program

Generally, a setup program needs to be aware of the environment on which it is installing the software. The actions taken by the setup program may vary based on the configuration of the computer and other installed software.

General considerations

Because the application you are developing is written in Access, you must consider the implications of running the application on a machine that has more than one version of Access or the wrong version of Access. Be sure to check the registry entries to see which versions are installed. You cannot perform this check within your application because that would imply that the correct version of Access exists and was loaded for the application to run. Therefore, you must perform this check within the setup program or set the menu shortcut properties to point to the correct version of Access. The problem is simplified if you include the Runtime version because the setup program should install Access Runtime and correctly create the menu shortcuts.

Considerations when using the Package and Deployment Wizard

If you are including Access Runtime, the distribution sets are quite large — at least 160MB. This prohibits the use of floppy disks.

**10 Min.
To Go**

Microsoft Internet Explorer (IE) version 5.0 or later is required when using Access data pages. IE 5.0 is installed as part of the setup program. IE will not be the default browser unless a previous version of IE existed on the target computer.

You can customize the Package and Deployment Wizard using Visual Basic 6.0 by modifying the Setup1.vbp program. Refer to Microsoft documentation for more information.

Third-party programs

There are options for creating a setup program other than using the Package and Deployment Wizard. These options are programs created by third parties. The two most popular third-party vendors are Wise Solutions, Inc. and InstallShield Software Corporation.

Wise Solutions, Inc., located in Canton, Michigan, produces several installation programs that have various features depending on which type of installation you need to perform.

Wise for Windows Installer provides more power and flexibility than the Package and Deployment Wizard.

InstallShield Software Corporation, located in Schaumburg, Illinois, also provides several installation programs. Its products include InstallShield Professional and InstallShield Developer, among others.

You also have some choices in how the setup program executes. Some programs use an engine that consists of a compiled script file and a series of CAB files that store the data files. Other programs use the Windows Installer (MSI), a configuration that consists of a series of database tables and files compiled into a single MSI file. The MSI format is an open standard created by Microsoft. For products that use Windows Installer, Microsoft's engine processes the database and files and installs the application. The Installer engine is part of the Windows 2000, ME, and XP operating systems.

SageKey, located in Penticton, BC, Canada, sells scripts for both Wise Solutions and InstallShield. These scripts include the necessary functionality not only to install your files, but also, optionally, to install all the files necessary to install Access Runtime.

Done!

REVIEW

In this session, you learned how to configure your application to install and execute in the correct and optimum environment. These topics were covered:

- An .mde file contains only compiled code and is useful for developers to distribute applications to users who have no need to modify the code.

- The Runtime version of Access has limitations that prevent the Runtime version from being used by itself. You need to know these limitations and provide the necessary functionality in your application.

- You should include a setup program to handle the multitude of files your application requires. These files include attached data files, references, libraries, ActiveX controls, help files, and so on.

- Other reasons for using a setup program include creating desktop shortcuts and menu items, providing icons for shortcuts, compressing files, installing Access Runtime, displaying readme files and license agreements, and installing other technical support information. A setup program also gives you the capability to remove the application through an uninstall program.

- You should test the setup program and test the application in a variety of operating environments to ensure that the programs work properly for your users.

- Other options in the Package and Deployment Wizard are programs created by third party vendors.

Quiz Yourself

1. What are the characteristics of the MDE property? (See ".MDE files.")

2. List the Access functions not included in the Access Runtime version. (See "Runtime.")

3. List the reasons for why you need a setup program. (See "Why do you need a setup program?")

4. What are the four steps to distributing an application with the Package and Deployment Wizard? (See "Using the Package and Deployment Wizard.")

5. What are some of the variables affecting the installation of an application on a user's computer? (See "Installing and testing.")

Programming Wizard-Type Forms for Easier Processing

Session Checklist

✔ Understanding wizards

✔ Understanding the structure of a wizard

✔ Creating a generic wizard

✔ Looking at a sample wizard

**30 Min.
To Go**

Wizards are used throughout Access and other commercial software to make the software easier to use and, in particular, to help users accomplish an activity. In this session, you learn about wizards and you look at a sample wizard created for the Check Writer application.

What Is a Wizard?

Microsoft Access has several built-in wizards to guide users through the various steps in accomplishing a task. These wizards provide a step-by-step user interface with navigational buttons to go back a step, move forward to the next step, cancel the operation, or finish the operation.

Here are some pointers to remember when designing your wizard:

- Use the wizard to step through a process.
- Each page of the wizard should be a step toward completing the process.
- The order of the steps should make sense.
- Keep buttons, fonts, and controls consistent between pages.
- Keep pages uncluttered.
- Use defaults as much as possible to simplify user input.

The Structure of a Wizard

Wizards can be created in a variety of ways with different Access objects. For example, you can use a single form with page controls to separate the pages of the wizard. Or, you can use a main form with subforms for each page. You might also see a separate form for each page of the wizard. You need to decide which is the best approach to take. In this session, we use a different approach than those just mentioned. We use a Tab control on a single form, with each page on the Tab control being a page in our wizard. This approach has the following advantages:

- The entire wizard is contained within one Access object, a form.
- The Tab control provides properties and methods that simplify coding. For example, you can set focus to a page, hide a page, and so on.
- The tabs on the Tab control can be shown or made invisible depending on your needs. They can even be buttons.
- Only one set of navigation buttons is needed.

The normal navigation buttons that a wizard requires are Next, Back, Cancel, and Finish. These won't be on the tab control but instead on the main form. It is also common, but not necessary, to have a graphic on the left side of a wizard page. With the structure we chose for our sample wizard, you have the choice of putting one graphic on the main form or different graphics on each page. This affects the size of the tab control. The tab control takes up most of the main form's area if it includes the graphics, or just part of the main form if the main form has the graphic. Our sample has only one graphic, so it requires less memory.

Creating a Tab-Controlled Wizard

The New Bank Account wizard included in the CheckWriter application enables you to explore basic architecture.

The wizard contains general controls and layout so that you can add copy and modify it for other applications. The code is also structured for easy flexibility and maintainability. Figure 25-1 shows the wizard form in Design view.

In this figure, you can see the graphic, the tab control, and the navigation buttons. The control software for the wizard controls which page is displayed as well as which navigation buttons are enabled or disabled.

The tabs are normally hidden when the form is opened, but in Design view they are visible, making them easier to work with. On the left side of the form is an unbound object frame for the graphic. You can add any picture type using one of the standard methods in Access. On the bottom of the form are the four navigational buttons: Cancel, Back, Next, and Finish. These buttons are used to move through the wizard. The check mark on the bottom left portion of the form is normally invisible. It is named StatusForward and is used to indicate the direction the wizard is going (forward/backward).

Wizard forms are generally designed with the border style set to dialog box with no scroll bars and no record selectors.

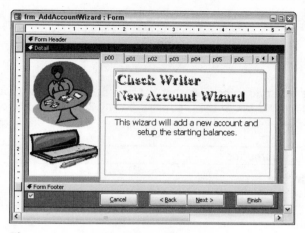

Figure 25-1   *Design view of the wizard.*

Here are a few rules for the buttons that apply to the code included with this wizard:

- The Back button is always disabled on the first page.
- The Finish button is disabled on all pages except the last page.
- The Forward button is always disabled on the last page and may be disabled on a page-by-page basis depending on whether the user has completed the information on a given page.
- The Cancel button is always enabled.

The opening page of the wizard is shown in Figure 25-2. On this page, you need to identify the wizard and its purpose.

Figure 25-2   *The title page of the wizard.*

There are nine pages built into this sample. You can add additional pages as necessary. Likewise, if you are not going to use all nine pages, you can delete pages or just ignore them.

You can add whatever controls you want to each page. There is code behind the form to control navigation between pages. The code for all the navigation buttons is described in this session, with additional comments on how to modify the code for your own needs. There is also a subroutine for the Form Open event and a general subroutine that is called to change a page.

The Form Open subroutine

The Form Open subroutine sets the tab style to none so that the user doesn't see the tabs. The buttons are initialized and the focus is set to the first page. Listing 25-1 shows the code for this subroutine.

Listing 25-1 *The Wizard Form Open Subroutine*

```
Private Sub Form_Open(Cancel As Integer)
'set tab style to none
    Me.wzdPages.Style = 2
'initialize buttons and goto first page
    Me.cmdBack.Enabled = False
    Me.cmdFinish.Enabled = False
    Me.wzdPages.Pages(0).SetFocus

End Sub
```

With a tab control, you can remove the tabs by setting the style to a value of 2. We make the change to 2 here because the default view is to show tabs so that when you're in Design view, you can navigate between pages. But when the user initiates the wizard, you generally want control over the sequence of events to prevent skipping steps. The subroutine also disables the Back and Finish buttons. To go to the first page of the wizard, you need to set focus to page 0 only. Tab control pages start with 0.

The Next button

You control the next operation of the wizard by clicking the Next button. This triggers the code shown in Listing 25-2.

Listing 25-2 *The Next Button Click Subroutine*

```
Private Sub cmdNext_Click()
Dim tbc As Control

'set status to forward
    Me.StatusForward = True

 'goto next page
    Set tbc = Me!wzdPages
    Me.wzdPages.Pages(tbc + 1).SetFocus

'enable Back button
    Me.cmdBack.Enabled = True

'if last page disable next button and enable finish button
    If tbc = Me.wzdPages.Pages.Count - 1 Then
```

```
            Me.cmdNext.Enabled = False
            Me.cmdFinish.Enabled = True
        End If

End Sub
```

This code runs when the Next button is clicked and sets focus to the next page. The StatusForward control is set to True to indicate that the direction is currently forward. The control tbc is set to the current page control and is used to move to the next page. The Back button is enabled. If the new current page is the last page, the Next button is disabled and the Finish button is enabled.

Indirectly, another subroutine runs when the Next button is clicked. This occurs when you change the focus to a different page on the tab control. The OnChange event for the tab control runs the code in Listing 25-3:

Listing 25-3   *The Wizard Page-Change Subroutine*

```
Private Sub wzdPages_Change()
'Handles navigation among pages or processing when a page changes
'You can do the following in this subroutine
'    Skip pages
'    Change the order in which the pages are displayed
'    Check for valid entries before proceeding to the next page

If Me.StatusForward Then
    'Navigation in the forward direction
    Select Case Me.wzdPages.Value
        Case 0
        Case 1
        Case 2
        Case 3
        Case 4
        Case 5
        Case 6
        Case 7
        Case 8
    End Select
Else
    'Navigation in the backward direction
    Select Case Me.wzdPages.Value
        Case 0
        Case 1
        Case 2
        Case 3
        Case 4
        Case 5
        Case 6
        Case 7
        Case 8
    End Select
End If
End Sub
```

This subroutine is called when the form is loaded — when the Next button and the Back button are clicked. The purpose of this subroutine is to handle the navigation between pages. Depending on the direction and which page is current, error checking can occur to make sure the proper inputs were made in the previous step. If not, you can add code to go back to the previous page and show a message. Listing 25-3 is a blank template for the code. The appropriate code is added for a `Case` statement depending on the direction and the page number. The value for the `Case` statement is the new current page number. If you adjust the number of pages from 9 (0–8) in the example, you can add or delete `Case` statements here. An example of this subroutine is shown later in this session.

The Back button

The code for the Back button is similar to the Next button. It sets focus to the previous page of the wizard. The control `tbc` is set to the current page control, and the Next button is enabled. If the new current page is the first page, the Back button is disabled. The Finish button is also disabled and the `StatusForward` control is set to `False` to indicate that the direction is currently backwards. The code for the `Click` event of the Back button is shown in Listing 25-4.

Listing 25-4   *The Back Button Click Subroutine*

```
Private Sub cmdBack_Click()
Dim tbc As Control

'set status to back
    Me.StatusForward = False

'goto previous page and enable next button
    Set tbc = Me!wzdPages
    Me.wzdPages.Pages(tbc - 1).SetFocus
    Me.cmdNext.Enabled = True

'if first page disable button back button
    If tbc = 0 Then Me.cmdBack.Enabled = False

'disable finish button
    Me.cmdFinish.Enabled = False

End Sub
```

The Cancel button

Because you want the user to be able to cancel the wizard at any time, the Cancel button is always enabled. The code behind the `Click` event is shown in Listing 25-5 and is simply used to close the wizard form. If you need to add any cleanup code before the wizard is closed to undo the selections that the user may have made prior to canceling the wizard, you should add it here.

Listing 25-5   *The Cancel Button Click Subroutine*

```
Private Sub cmdCancel_Click()
'Cancel wizard and close form
    DoCmd.Close acform, Me.name
End Sub
```

The Finish button

On the last page of the wizard, the Finish button is enabled. The `OnClick` event should start execution of whatever you want the wizard to do. Include a statement to close the wizard form when you are done.

 Session 26 explains how to make a wizard work with Access as an add-in.

A Sample Wizard

**10 Min.
To Go**

The Check Writer sample application contains the form frm_AddAccountWizard. This wizard is used to create a new bank account. The title page of this wizard was shown in Figure 25-2, and the first page is shown in Figure 25-3.

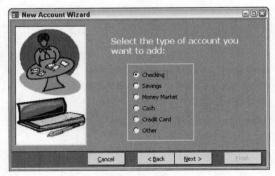

Figure 25-3   *The first page of the New Account Wizard.*

In Listing 25-6, you see only those subroutines specific to this form. The subroutines for the four navigation buttons and the Form Open subroutine remain the same no matter what the wizard is used for. Listing 25-6 contains three procedures that are unique to the New Account Wizard: Form_Load, Finish, and wzdPages_Change.

The Form_Load subroutine initializes the control xDataSource on the form so the wizard can actually use the unbound form utilities described in Session 12. The Finish function calls the Unbound Form function dbc_SaveRecord to save the new account record and then it closes the wizard form.

Listing 25-6   *The New Account Wizard Subroutines*

```
Private Sub Form_Load()
'Initialize datasource for the unbound form functions
'Assume the datasource is in the same directory as the application
    Me.xDataSource = "Data Source=" & Application.CurrentProject.Path &
"\CheckWriterData.mdb"
End Sub

Public Function Finish()
    'Call the unbound form save record function
    dbc_SaveRecord Me
    DoCmd.Close acForm, Me.Name
End Function

Private Sub wzdPages_Change()

'This Subroutine handles the navigation among pages or processing when a page changes
'You can do the following in this subroutine
'   Skip pages
'   Change the order that the pages are displayed
'   Check for valid entries before proceeding to the next page

If Me.StatusForward Then
    'Navigation in the forward direction
    Select Case Me.wzdPages.Value
        Case 0
        Case 1
        Case 2
            'Set the control for the type of account based on the caption
            for the option selected
            Me.Type = Me.Controls("TypeLabel" & Trim(str(Me.selType))).caption
        Case 3
            'Prevent the user from staying on this page if
            '  the Bank Account field is null
            If IsNull(Me.BankAccountNumber) Then Me.wzdPages.Pages(2).SetFocus
        Case 4
        Case 5
            'Prevent the user from staying on this page if
            '  the fields on the previous page are null
            If IsNull(Me.ABANumber) Or _
              IsNull(Me.StartingCheckNumber) Then
              Me.wzdPages.Pages(4).SetFocus
            End If
        Case 6
            'Skip this page if the user doesn't have the last statement
            If Me.HaveLastStatement <> 1 Then
              Me.wzdPages.Pages(7).SetFocus
            End If
        Case 7
            'Skip this page if the user has the last statement
            If Me.HaveLastStatement = 1 Then
              Me.wzdPages.Pages(8).SetFocus
            End If
        Case 8
    End Select
```

```
     Else

     'Navigation in the backward direction
     Select Case Me.wzdPages.Value
         Case 0
         Case 1
         Case 2
         Case 3
         Case 4
         Case 5
         Case 6
           'Skip this page if the user doesn't have the last statement
           If Me.HaveLastStatement <> 1 Then
             Me.wzdPages.Pages(5).SetFocus
           End If
         Case 7
           'Skip this page if the user has the last statement
           If Me.HaveLastStatement = 1 Then
             Me.wzdPages.Pages(6).SetFocus
           End If
         Case 8
     End Select
 End If

 End Sub
```

The wzdPages_Change subroutine is the significant controlling code for the wizard. In the forward direction, code runs on pages 2, 3, 5, 6, and 7. Note that the Case statement for a given page runs as soon as the given page has focus. On page 2, some processing is done based on the selection on page 1. Page 1 contains an option group, and the control Type is set to the label caption for the respective option selected. On page 3, the value of BankAccountNumber located on page 2 is checked. If it is null, then focus returns to page 2 because this is a required field. A similar check is made on page 5 based on the data on page 4, which is also required. On page 5 (see Figure 25-4), the user is asked whether he or she has the last bank statement. If the answer is Yes, page 6 is displayed (see Figure 25-5); otherwise, page 7 is displayed. This shows you how you can conditionally display pages based on user input.

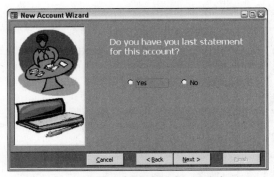

Figure 25-4 *Page 5 of the New Account Wizard.*

In the backward direction, again the only logic is to skip pages not applicable based on the user selection on page 5.

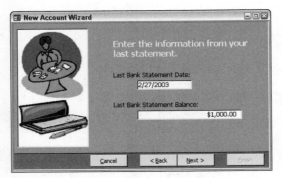

Figure 25-5   *Page 6 of the New Account Wizard.*

Done!

REVIEW

In this session, you learned about designing wizards. Wizards provide a step-by-step method to guide users through a particular process. These topics were covered:

- The standard user interface for a wizard includes the Cancel, Back, Next, and Finish buttons.
- Wizards are designed to help you step through a process, with each step taking you closer to completing the process. The order of the steps should make sense.
- The design of the user interface should be consistent between pages. Keep pages uncluttered.
- You can use a tab control on a single form with each page on the tab control also serving as a page in your wizard. If you do this, the entire wizard is contained within one Access form, and the tab control provides properties and methods that simplify coding.

QUIZ YOURSELF

1. What are some points to remember when designing your wizard? (See "What Is a Wizard?")
2. What are the different ways of designing a wizard using Access objects, and what are the advantages and disadvantages of each approach? (See "The Structure of a Wizard.")
3. What are the general rules to apply to a wizard's navigation control buttons? (See "Creating a Tabbed Controlled Wizard.")
4. What functions might be performed when changing pages on a wizard? (See "The Next button.")
5. Explain the purpose of the StatusForward control. (See "The Next button.")

Using Add-Ins with Your Application

Session Checklist

✔ Using add-ins

✔ Using the registry with Access add-ins

✔ Using the Add-In Manager

✔ Creating a library database

30 Min. To Go

This session provides you with the background to understand how to use add-ins with Access. Because there are so many possible combinations, levels, and options, this session illustrates only the first step to using a library database as an add-in.

What Are Add-Ins?

A great deal of confusion surrounds add-in terminology. You might see any of these components referred to as add-ins: wizards, builders, libraries, and menu add-ins. Simply put, an *Access add-in* is a component that is not part of the basic Microsoft Access product.

Add-ins can come from the following sources:

- Provided with Access from Microsoft
- Purchased from third-party developers
- Custom designed

Examples of add-ins provided with Access include control wizards, form wizards, chart wizards, field builders, object libraries, the Switchboard Manager, the Linked Table Manager, the documenter, the performance analyzer, and many, many more. Several add-ins are available from third parties as well.

 Database Creations, Inc., supplies add-ins as part of its EZ Access Developer Suite and, in particular, the EZ Application Builder. Other vendors include FMS and Black Moshannon Systems. Or you can design your own, as discussed later in this session.

Add-ins come from different sources, and they can be of different types. There are two basic types distinguished by the connection that is made to Access. These connections can be either references or the registry.

Add-ins connected through references are generally referred to as a *library*. Reference add-ins generally provide functionality through VBA code as a function call.

Add-ins connected through the registry fall into the categories of wizards, builders, and menu add-ins. Menu add-ins are the most obvious because they appear on the Tools menu under the Add-Ins entry. The Add-In Manager is always listed on this submenu. Ironically, the Add-In Manager is an add-in itself. Most menu add-ins are provided by third-party vendors or are a custom-designed component. This doesn't mean that you can only create an add-in that shows up on this menu. You can also create add-ins that are initiated in other ways. If an add-in does not use the Add-In menu, it falls into the category of an Access object wizard.

Wizards exist to assist the user or developer in performing some task. This task could be creating or modifying an Access object, control, or property. For each of these different tasks, the add-ins are categorized as the following:

- **Data object wizards.** For tables and queries
- **User interface wizards.** For forms, reports, and data access pages
- **Control wizards.** For creating new objects on forms, reports, or data access pages
- **Property builders.** For setting property values
- **Expression builders.** For creating expressions

Figure 26-1 can help you better understand these various categories of wizards and builders.

So where do you go from here? One of the most important elements for a programmer to understand is how to plug these add-ins into Access and make them work. The next section discusses the general considerations for add-ins.

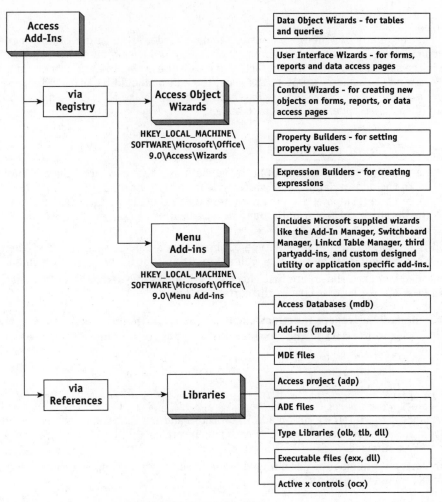

Figure 26-1 *The structure of Access add-ins.*

General Add-In Considerations

When dealing with add-ins you must consider various aspects such as the type of file, references within the different databases, form properties, and multi-user issues.

File types

Access add-ins generally use the file extensions .mda or .mde. An .mda file can be opened and the code viewed. The .mda extension is simply a way to identify an add-in, and the file structure is the same as an .mdb file. In fact, you can still use the extension .mdb for an add-in if you want. To secure or protect the code, the add-in should be an .mde file. You create this .mde file by choosing Tools ⇨ Database Utilities ⇨ Make MDE File. An .mde file contains only compiled code, not the source code.

Referring to different databases

When using an add-in, you have code in both the main database as well as the add-in database. To refer to the add-in database in which code is currently running, use the `CodeProject` or `CodeData` object to return a reference to the add-in database. If you want to refer to the database that's currently open in Access, use the `CurrentProject` or `CurrentData` object.

The add-in database can contain any type of object that a regular database can. When you refer to any object, you must be sure that you are referring to it in the correct database.

Macros called from the add-in are first checked within the add-in database. If Access doesn't find the macro there, it checks the current database.

Domain aggregate functions such as `Dcount`, `Dmin`, `Dmax`, **and** `Dlookup` **always refer to the data in the current database, not to the library database.**

General design

It is best to model the interface for an add-in on those add-ins that come with Microsoft Access. Users are probably already familiar with this interface, so ease of use is maximized and training is minimized.

You can perform a number of tasks to give your add-in the same appearance as Access add-ins. These include the following:

- Set the form's AutoCenter property to Yes.
- Turn record selectors off.
- Turn scroll bars off, unless they are required.
- Don't use navigation buttons unless you are using a form that has multiple records.
- Place controls consistently on every form.
- Use the dialog mode to prevent the user from moving to the next form until conditions in your code are met.
- Use multipage forms with navigation buttons. This keeps the add-in within a single form.

See Session 25 for more information on the technique of keeping an add-in within a single form.

Multiple-user considerations

Add-ins are always opened for shared access, giving multiple users access to the objects in your add-in. Be aware that if your add-in needs to write back to its database, you must open the add-in with read/write permissions.

Wizards

20 Min.
To Go

Wizards exist for one primary reason: to guide a user through a series of steps to accomplish a task. As is the case with the built-in wizards that come with Access, the tasks are to build databases, tables, queries, forms, reports, controls, or build values or expressions. A wizard to build a new bank account was shown in Session 25. Wizards generally use forms, graphics, and helpful text to guide the user through the operation and hide the technical details of what is going on.

Depending on the task to be accomplished, the wizards are categorized as shown in Figure 26-1.

Data object wizards and user interface wizards

Data object and user interface wizards help the user create a new table, query, form, data access page, or report. Access has a number of built-in object wizards, which are available in the New Table, New Query, New Form, New Data Access Page, and New Report dialog boxes. You can create an object wizard that will also appear in one of these dialog boxes. You accomplish this by creating registry entries, a process covered later in this session.

Control wizards

Control wizards help the user to add either an Access or an ActiveX control to a form, report, or data access page. A control wizard runs when a control in the toolbox is clicked and is dropped onto a form, report, or data access page. The wizard launches only if the control wizards' tool in the toolbox is selected.

Builders

Builders are a simpler version of a wizard. Rather than performing a task, a builder usually creates an expression or a single data element. The Expression Builder is built into Access. It is used for several different properties on a form or report. It is typically used as a control source for a control. The Query Builder can be used as the record source of a form. You can also find an Input Mask filter builder, as well as other builders.

When a builder is available for a particular property, the Build button, the small button with the ellipsis (...), appears next to that property's name in the property sheet.

Menu Add-Ins

Unlike wizards and builders, menu add-ins go beyond creating expressions or performing a single task. They generally operate on multiple objects or Access itself. Database Documenter and Performance Analyzer are examples of menu add-ins.

When a menu add-in is installed, it is available through the Add-Ins submenu of the Tools menu. Having the add-in on the menu provides a means of running the add-in outside the context of a specific object or property, as the wizards do.

Installing a wizard or menu add-in

Whether you have a wizard or menu add-in, you have two choices for how to install your add-in: directly using a setup or installer program or interactively using the Access Add-In Manager utility. In either case, registry entries are created for each add-in. A setup program can create the registry entries, or the Add-In Manager can do it. One feature of the Add-In Manager is that it can also remove add-ins. Before we explore the mechanics of the Add-In Manager, let's look at which registry entries are required.

Add-In registry entries

Figure 26-2 shows the Registry Editor with the key for the menu add-ins expanded. This entry is located under the branch HKEY_LOCAL_MACHINE\SOFTWARE\Microsoft\Office\ 11.0\Access\Menu Add-ins, which contains all entries that appear on the Add-In submenu in Access. Only the Add-In Manager is listed here, but you can add your own add-ins under this branch as well. These add-ins then appear on the menu.

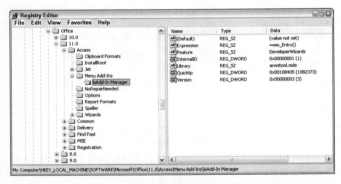

Figure 26-2   *A registry entry for the Add-In Manager.*

For wizards, the branch in the registry is HKEY_LOCAL_MACHINE\SOFTWARE\Microsoft\ Office\11.0\Access\Wizards. This branch and all the default entries are shown in Figure 26-3.

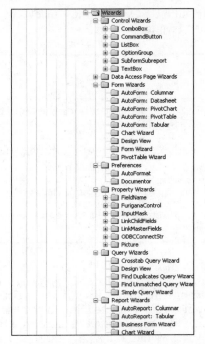

Figure 26-3 *Registry entries for the wizards.*

Placing your entry into any of these folders makes Access aware of your wizard within the context determined by the folder. For example, you can create your own query wizard and add a key in the folder Query Wizards. Then, when you run Access and create a new query, your wizard is listed along with the others in the same branch. Depending on the type of wizard, registry key values vary. Refer to Microsoft documentation for the required entries for each wizard type.

The Add-In Manager utility

To use the Add-In Manager, your add-in requires two items:

1. Database property entries for Title, Company, and Comments
2. A USysRegInfo table

The database properties Title, Company, and Comments are displayed by the Add-In Manager to let the user know what the add-in is. To set database properties before you install your add-in, do the following:

1. In the Database window, click Database Properties on the File menu.
2. Click the Summary tab.
3. Enter the values in the Title, Company, and Comments boxes to describe your add-in.
4. Click OK.

The USysRegInfo table must have specific fields and data that specify the Windows registry entries to be created when your add-in is installed (see Table 26-1).

Table 26-1 *Structure of the USysRegInfo Table*

Field	Field Type	Description
Subkey	Text	The name of the subkey that contains the registry information for the add-in
Type	Number	The type of value to create beneath the subkey: subkey (0), String (1), or DWORD (4)
ValName	Text	The name of the registry entry to be created
Value	Text	The value to be stored in the registry entry defined by the ValName field

In the Subkey field, you can use the HKEY_CURRENT_ACCESS_PROFILE*AddInType*\\ *AddInName* string to create the registry entry. This string is used by the Add-In Manager to determine the location on the user's machine of Access-specific information in the registry. This enables Access to create the entry for the add-in in the appropriate place. If the user starts Access with the /profile command-line option, this string is used to make sure the registry entry is created beneath the specified Access user profile. If not, the entry is created under the \\HKEY_LOCAL_MACHINE\\SOFTWARE\\Microsoft\\Office\\2003\\Access\\ AddInType subkey in the registry.

 There are different user profiles. The one used to start Access from the command line is not the same one as the one defined for logging on to the operating system. A user profile defined for the operating system applies to all programs on the system and is used to maintain system data for individual users. An Access user profile applies only to Access, and only when you start Access from the command line.

You can also use the HKEY_LOCAL_MACHINE\\SOFTWARE\\Microsoft\\Office\\2003\\Access\\ *AddInType* string to specify that the registry entries for the add-in should always be created under this registry subtree and that Access user profiles are to be ignored. Note that, in this case, you must include the full registry path to the add-in's subkey. Table 26-2 shows a sample USysRegInfo table.

Table 26-2 *Sample USysRegInfo Table*

Subkey	Type	ValName	Value
HKEY_CURRENT_ACCESS_PROFILE \\Menu Add-ins\\&Create Functions Table	0		
HKEY_CURRENT_ACCESS_PROFILE \\Menu Add-ins\\&Create Functions Table	1	Library	|ACCDIR\\ FunctTable.mda

Subkey	Type	ValName	Value
HKEY_CURRENT_ACCESS_PROFILE \Menu Add-ins\&Create Functions Table	1	Expression	=AddFuncToTable()

The Add-in Manager is not limited to installing menu add-ins. It can install wizards as well, as long as the registry information is located in the USysRegInfo table.

The USysRegInfo table is not automatically created for you when you create a new .mda file. You then add records to this table to match your add-in needs. This table contains the four fields shown in Figure 26-4.

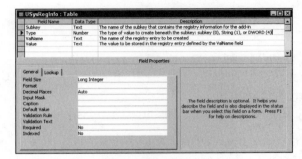

Figure 26-4   *The USysRegInfoTable structure.*

 The USysRegInfo table is a system table and is usually hidden. To view the USysRegInfo table, choose Tools ⇨ Options, click the View tab, and then click the System Objects check box.

Each record in the table is used to describe a subkey or value to be added to the registry by the Add-In Manager. Each add-in requires a minimum of three records, where each record does the following:

1. Creates the subkey for the add-in
2. Adds the library entry
3. Adds the expression entry

You can have additional records to store other values in the registry that the add-in may specifically require. Note that the different types of builders and wizards have different entries.

Library Add-Ins

**10 Min.
To Go**

Whereas Access module objects enable you to share common procedures among other Access objects, library databases allow you to share common procedures among other Access databases. This further reduces redundant code and allows for easier maintenance of the code because it is located in just one place and not in several in applications. You can also distribute a library database as an .mde file with the source code protected and distribute the main application open with source code.

A library database is like any other Access database containing tables, queries, forms, data access pages, reports, and modules. You can open it like any other database, but the difference lies in how the database is loaded.

Functions and subroutines in the library database can be addressed only from the current database if they are declared `Public`. Privately declared procedures are available only within the library database. Also, routines stored in a class module are not available from outside the library database.

Creating a library database

To create a library database, follow these steps:

1. Create the library using forms, modules, and other objects in a new database.
2. Test and debug the library functions.
3. Compile and compact the library database.
4. Rename the library database so that it has an extension of .mda or convert the database to an .mde file.

Debugging library databases

It's a good idea to test and debug the library functions before you tie a library database into an application; but sometimes this is not possible. In certain cases, you cannot test a library without it being called from an application. Sometimes the library works fine until it is called from an application. The more you can test the library by itself, the better it is.

The LoadOnStartup key

The registry entry, LoadOnStartup key, provides a way to have Access load a library database automatically when Access is started. You can add a key called LoadOnStartup to the following branch:

```
HKEY_LOCAL_MACHINE\SOFTWARE\Microsoft\Office\11.0\Access\Wizards
```

The entry for the key is the string value for the path and filename of the library to load. Also enter a data value of `rw` for the value.

 Using the LoadOnStartup key to load a library causes Access to start more slowly. The library occupies memory regardless of whether any functions are called, so use this feature judiciously.

References

References tell Access where to find a library database. To see the list of references, you open the VBA window either by opening a module or by viewing the code for a form or report. Choosing Tools ➪ References opens the References dialog box, as shown in Figure 26-5.

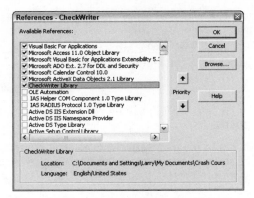

Figure 26-5 *The References dialog box.*

References become invalid if they are relocated and Access cannot find them. Because they are stored in the referencing database, references are not automatically updated when a library is moved.

When Access cannot find the reference based on the absolute path stored with the database, it tries to find it in the relative path to the database in which it is referenced. So if you store the reference in the same folder as the database that references it, and relocate both files, there is no problem with the reference. If Access cannot find it in the relative path, it then searches the directory in which Access is installed. If that still doesn't work, the Windows System directories are checked. And as a last resort, any directories included in the environmental PATH variable are checked for the reference.

You can also use the registry to store the location of a library database by using the registry key called RefLibPaths under `HKEY_LOCAL_MACHINE\Software\Microsoft\Office\11.0\Access`. For each library, create a new string value. Use the name of the library database and the value as the path to that reference.

Creating a reference

You have two choices for creating a reference: using the References dialog box (refer to Figure 26-5) or creating it programmatically.

Unlike the registry entries for wizards and menu add-ins that are established for all databases, references are done on a database-by-database basis. It works fine to use the References dialog box at the time you develop an application, as long as the references don't move or disappear. It is important in your setup or installation program that the libraries get installed in the correct location and that the versions of those libraries are correct. As an extra feature, you can add some code to programmatically add, check, or remove references.

To manually create a reference:

1. Open the VBA window.
2. Choose Tools ➪ References.

3. Select the reference you want to add from the available list or click the Browse button to search for a library to reference.

4. Set the priorities of the references. This is important if the same function name is used in more than one library. The reference with the highest priority gets referenced first.

Programmatically working with references

Access contains `Reference` objects that enable you to programmatically work with references. However, working with references is beyond the scope of this book. Check the Microsoft documentation for more information about working with references programmatically.

Calling a reference

As long as the function or subroutine in the library database is declared `Public`, you can call the procedure just as if it were in the current database. You can optionally use the `Run` method to invoke a library routine. This method gives you the capability to specify the library in which the function is located. You do this by specifying the project name used for the library:

```
[LibraryName].FunctionName.
```

Be careful when naming functions in your library database that may be the same as those in the current database. Access uses the procedure in the current database, not the function in the library database. You can get around this problem by not using the same name or by preceding the function name with the module name as shown here:

```
[ModuleName].FunctionName.
```

Creating a Library from a Module

Our sample Check Writer application contained a module that has generic use for unbound forms. This module is named mod_UnboundFormUtilities. Because it is a fairly general-purpose module and could also be used in other databases, we made it a library database. We followed these basic steps in creating the library database:

1. The development of the module was done within the application database because the code can be viewed and debugged more easily.

2. After it was tested, a new, empty database was created with an .mda extension, and the name CheckWriterLibrary.mda was used.

3. The module was moved from the application database to the new, empty library database, and it was deleted from the application database.

4. With the VBA window open in the application database, we created a reference to the new library database by choosing Tools ➪ References (refer to Figure 26-5).

5. We compiled both the application and the library databases to verify that there were no errors.

6. We tested the application with the library database.

Done!

REVIEW

In this session, you learned about expanding the functionality of Access with add-ins. You can do this at different levels and in various ways. With these capabilities, Access becomes a very customizable program. This session covered these topics:

- You can get add-ins with Microsoft Access, purchase them from third-party developers, or have them custom designed.

- There are two basic types of add-ins distinguished by the connection that is made through either references or the registry.

- The add-in may contain any type of object that a regular database can, but you must be careful when referring to an object in either the add-in or the current database.

- The Add-In Manager requires registry information located in a USysRegInfo table contained within the add-in.

- References tell Access where to find a library database. Viewing and working with the reference list is done through the VBA window and by choosing Tools ⇨ References.

QUIZ YOURSELF

1. Name the three sources of add-ins. (See "What Are Add-Ins?")

2. What distinguishes the two basic types of add-ins? (See "What Are Add-Ins?")

3. What are the characteristics of the .mda file type? (See "File types.")

4. What are the two ways of installing an add-in? (See "Installing a wizard or menu add-in.")

5. Describe the purpose and the process of creating a USysRegInfo table. (See "The Add-In Manager utility.")

6. What are the four steps to creating a library database? (See "Creating a library database.")

PART

V

Sunday Morning Part Review

1. True or false: You can use the `FindRecord` method with multi-key fields.
2. Setting the _____ property to Yes forces the user to close the dialog box before moving to another form.
3. Which one of the following properties is not typically set for a dialog box?
   a. `PopUp`
   b. `Modal`
   c. `AutoCenter`
   d. `RecordSource`
4. To change the list of items in a find dialog box, which property do you set for the dialog's list box or combo box?
5. List some of the basic features of a Search and Print Dialog.
6. Which of the lines below would be the correct syntax for printing a report via VBA code?
   a. `DoCmd.PrintReport "testreport", acNormal`
   b. `DoCmd.OpenReport acNormal, "testreport"`
   c. `Docmd.OpenReport "testreport, acNormal`
7. Where can you place events on a report?
8. What function provides a means of determining the Access version, runtime, initialization file, and Access directory?
9. True or false: The Background Compile option will compile only those functions that are used.
10. To have one code base that can run in different environments, Access and VBA provides which of the following?
    a. Global constants
    b. Conditional compilation
    c. Preference functions

    d. Decompiling

    e. None of the above

11. List the three choices for starting your VBA code when a database is opened.

12. List at least three reasons to have a setup program.

13. List at least three items to consider when designing a wizard.

14. List at least three advantages for using the Tab control in a wizard.

15. True or false: The normal navigation buttons that a wizard requires are Next, Back, and Cancel.

16. Which of the following is false?

    a. The Back button is always disabled on the last page.

    b. The Finish button is disabled on all pages except the last page.

    c. The Forward button is always disabled on the last page.

    d. The Forward button may be disabled on a page-by-page basis based depending on whether the user has completed the information on a given page.

    e. The Cancel button is always enabled.

17. True or False: An *Access Add-in* is a component that's not part of the basic Microsoft Access product.

18. List at least five examples of Add-ins provided with Access.

19. An Access Add-in uses which file extension?

    a. .MDB

    b. .MDE

    c. .MDA

    d. .ADE

    e. All of the above

20. What is the branch in the registry reserved for wizards?

PART

VI

Sunday Afternoon

Programming and Using File Attachments

Session Checklist

✔ Defining linked tables

✔ Using linked tables

✔ Using Access-provided tools

✔ Looking at ADO programming features for linked tables

✔ Creating a simple Attachment Manager form for linked tables

30 Min. To Go

I n this session, you learn about splitting a database into two parts: a front-end and a back-end. The connection between the two is made with attached or linked tables. You learn how to deal with this connection as well as with the functions available for manipulating the connection in VBA.

File Attachments

Access refers to attached tables as *linked tables*. Linking data enables you to read and, in most cases, update data in the external data source without importing. The external data source's format is not altered so that you can continue to use the file with the program that originally created it, but you can also add, delete, or edit its data using Microsoft Access as well. These sources include not only other Access .mdb files, but also Access .adp, .mdw, .mda, and .mde files. Beyond Access, you can connect to Excel, text, Outlook, Exchange, Paradox, HTML, dBASE, SQL Server, ODBC data sources and Sharepoint Team Services.

Application developers commonly keep data tables in a file separate from the program. This technique is referred to as having a *front end/back end application*. The reasons for using this method are numerous:

- Data files are better managed on a server, whereas the front-end application runs best on the workstation. This facilitates multi-user access, replication, backups, security, and so on.
- Large databases should be handled by a more powerful database management system like SQL Server rather than by Microsoft Access.
- Data files can still be maintained by a legacy system.
- Reduced network traffic improves performance.
- Separate files enable independent support and maintenance of the front-end application.

Figure 27-1 shows a typical example of how to configure linked tables in an application. This figure depicts six different connections. The number of connections could be one or many more than six. The figure shows three different data sources that can be different because they are located on different servers, relate to different department data, exist as different types of files, or can be separated based on user accessibility. In addition, the figure lists a security data source. This database may contain sensitive information about the security in your application and is, therefore, separated from the rest of the data. You might also choose to have a separate archive database where historical records are kept. These records cannot change, so frequent backups are not needed. The archived data is accessed only occasionally and is generally read-only.

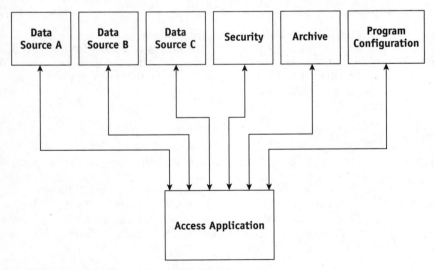

Figure 27-1 *An example of linked tables.*

Another type of linked database is program configuration data. Such items as preferences and program options are stored in this database. It gives the system administrator some control over the front-end application without actually changing the code or objects in the front-end application.

Basic Principles

You normally create a link to a table in another database by choosing File ⇨ Get External Data and then choosing Link Tables. You can also create a link by choosing Tables in the Database window and clicking New. You get a choice of how you want to create the table; one of the options is Link Table.

The File Link dialog box appears, enabling you to select a file. You can link to an Access data file or another type. The types of data sources you can link to depends on the drivers you installed with Access. If you do not see the data source you are looking for, rerun the Access setup program and install any missing drivers.

Depending on the type of file you choose from the File Link dialog box, a list of tables contained within the selected file is displayed. You can choose to link to one or several tables. Access uses different icons to represent linked tables and tables that are stored within the current database. The icon for a linked file contains an arrow pointing to the right. If you delete the icon for a linked table, you delete the link to the table, not the external table itself.

Managing these links can be somewhat tedious, especially if you have many tables and more than one data file. You are not limited to one data source, so tables can come from several different sources. You may sometimes lose the links if the data source you are linked to is not available. Some reasons that the data source may not be available include the following:

- The external data source has moved.
- The server where the external data source is located is down.
- The network is down.
- The user does not have the permissions necessary to access the external data source.
- Share names have changed.

When any of the previous actions occur, you should probably refresh your links. In addition, it is common to relink to different data files. This might happen if you have a different set of data files for multiple companies or different projects. When you want to select a different company, you have to respecify the data source to connect to.

Access Tools

In addition to the Table Link Wizard, Access comes with a Database Splitter and a Linked Table Manager. The Database Splitter provides an easy way to move tables from a single .mdb into a front end/back end set of files.

The Linked Table Manager provides a means to look at the links and refresh or change them. Figure 27-2 shows how the Linked Table Manager is started. You choose Tools ⇨ Database Utilities ⇨ Linked Table Manager.

Figure 27-2   *Starting the Linked Table Manager.*

The interface for the Linked Table Manager is shown in Figure 27-3. The linked tables are listed along with their data sources. You can choose which tables to update and whether to change the location of the linked table.

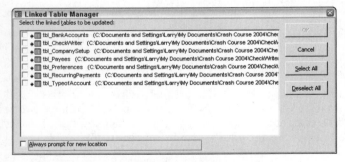

Figure 27-3   *The Linked Table Manager interface.*

The Linked Table Manager is adequate for some applications, but it has limitations. With some programming, you can create a robust attachment manager with a lot more features than the Linked Table Manager. This includes making it more suitable for use in a turnkey-type application. In this session, you continue developing a more powerful Attachment Manager.

Programming Concepts

**20 Min.
To Go**

Working with linked tables requires that VBA code use two different ADO object models:

- ActiveX Data Objects 2.7 (ADODB)
- ADO Extensions 2.7 for DDL and Security (ADOX)

There are different versions of ADODB and ADOX. As of this writing, there are versions 2.0 thru 2.7. Access can work with different versions. As a general rule, use the latest version available.

ADODB lets you work with recordsets but not Access table definitions. That is why you also need ADOX to manipulate the table structures. The models perform a variety of other functions as well, but we concentrate only on those functions needed to work with linked tables.

To use ADOX with your application, you need to establish a reference to the ADOX type library in addition to the ADODB library — which should be already established because Access defaults to this library. The description of the ADOX library is Microsoft ADO Ext. for DDL and Security. The ADOX library filename is Msadox.dll, and the program ID is ADOX.

You set up references from within the VBA Editor by choosing Tools ⇨ References. The resulting dialog box is shown in Figure 27-4.

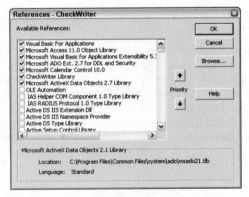

Figure 27-4   *The References dialog box.*

To begin using ADOX for table definitions, the function shown in Listing 27-1 can show you the basics. (This function is located in the module mod_UtilityFunctions in the sample Check Writer application.) When executed, this function prints a list of the tables in the Immediate window in the current .mdb, along with the table's properties.

To run a function directly in the Visual Basic code window, just move your cursor onto the code within the function and press F5. Note that this does not work in class modules.

Listing 27-1 *The ListTableProperties() Function*

```
'Function prints list of tables and their properties in Immediate window
'using ADOX ActiveX Data Objects
Dim cat As New ADOX.Catalog
Dim tbl As ADOX.Table
Dim i As Integer

    cat.ActiveConnection = CurrentProject.Connection
    For Each tbl In cat.Tables
        Debug.Print tbl.Name; Tab(20), tbl.Type
        For i = 0 To tbl.Properties.Count - 1
Debug.Print Tab(5); tbl.Properties.Item(i).Name, Tab(50); _
tbl.Properties.Item(i).Value
        Next
    Next

End Function
```

The ADOX catalog

Referring to the listing for the ListTableProperties function, you first need to define a catalog. A *catalog* contains collections of tables as well as views, users, groups, and procedures. These describe the data source structure or *schema* as it is sometimes referred to.

You create a new ADOX catalog by dimensioning a variable as a New ADOX Catalog, as shown in the statement Dim cat As New ADOX.Catalog.

The catalog has several properties, and the ActiveConnection property must be set to the current project connection. Connections are the means to interface your application to a data source. The statement cat.ActiveConnection = CurrentProject.Connection in the example sets the active connection for the newly created catalog to the connection in the current project. The CurrentProject object has several collections and properties that contain specific objects within the current Access database. In this case, the Connection property returns a reference to the current ActiveX Data Objects (ADO) Connection object and its related properties.

Accessing tables with the catalog

An ADOX catalog contains a Tables collection. Each table in the collection has the following objects: Columns, DateCreated, DateModified, Indexes, Keys, Name, ParentCatalog, Properties, and Type. We are interested in these objects:

- **Name:** The table name.
- **Type:** The type of table. For linked tables, the value for this object is LINK.
- **Properties:** A collection of properties for the table.

The Table Properties collection

For each table in the Tables collection there is a Table Properties collection. Some of these properties relate to providers. ADO accesses data and services from OLE DB providers. For Access, this is the Jet OLDDB provider, so the properties are a function of this provider.

These properties consist of the following:

- Temporary Table
- Jet OLEDB:Table Validation Text
- Jet OLEDB:Table Validation Rule
- Jet OLEDB:Cache Link Name/Password
- Jet OLEDB:Remote Table Name
- Jet OLEDB:Link Provider String
- Jet OLEDB:Link Datasource
- Jet OLEDB:Exclusive Link
- Jet OLEDB:Create Link
- Jet OLEDB:Table Hidden In Access

When you execute the function shown in Listing 27-1, you see a list of tables within the database along with the properties just listed. The basic ones, as they pertain to linked tables, are these:

- Jet OLEDB:Remote Table Name: Contains the name of the table in the remote datasource.
- Jet OLEDB:Link Provider String: A string describing the provider.
  For Access, this is a blank string.
  For Excel, it looks something like Excel 5.0;HDR=YES;IMEX=2;
  For dBASE, it looks similar to dBase 5.0;HDR=NO;IMEX=2;
  Each provider has different formats and parameters. You can include user IDs and passwords in this string as well.
- Jet OLEDB:Link Datasource: The path and filename of the external data source.

Linked tables

As you have seen, you can list the tables in a database as well as refer to the linked tables and their properties. You can also change the link's data source. This is the focus of this section because you often need to reconnect to a data source in another folder, drive, server, or even network domain.

To accomplish this, you actually delete the linked table from the catalog and define a new link. This involves learning a few ADOX methods.

To delete a table, you first create a new catalog as you did in the previous section. Then set the connection for that active catalog to the current project connection. Next, execute a

Delete Table method supplying the name of the table to be deleted, and finally, refresh the Tables collection. The following code accomplishes all this:

```
Dim cat As New ADOX.Catalog
cat.ActiveConnection = CurrentProject.Connection
cat.Tables.Delete strNameOfTableToBeDeleted
cat.Tables.Refresh
```

With the table removed from the catalog and the Access .mdb, you add a new linked table with the same name but connected to a different data source. You set up this operation by dimensioning a new catalog variable and also by dimensioning a new ADOX table variable:

1. For the newly created catalog, set its active connection to the current project connection.

2. Define the new table's parent catalog as the newly created catalog.

3. Name the table and set its properties. These properties include the data source, remote table name, and provider string. If you are reconnecting a previously deleted table, you should temporarily store the values of these properties from the old table so that they can be used for the new table.

4. Now set the property Jet OLEDB:Create Link to True. This establishes a link when the table is appended to the table's collection.

5. Append the new table to the Tables collections. All these operations are performed in the code in Listing 27-2.

Listing 27-2   *Code to Link a New Table*

```
Dim cat As New ADOX.Catalog
Dim tbl As New ADOX.Table

cat.ActiveConnection = CurrentProject.Connection
Set tbl.ParentCatalog = cat
tbl.Name = strTableName
tbl.Properties("Jet OLEDB:Link DataSource") = strDataSource
tbl.Properties("Jet OLEDB:Remote Table Name") = strRemoteTable
tbl.Properties("Jet OLEDB:Link Provider String") = strProvider
tbl.Properties("Jet OLEDB:Create Link") = True
cat.Tables.Append tbl
Set tbl = Nothing
```

 If the table that you are connecting to is a Microsoft Access table, you do not have to set the property Jet OLEDB:Link Provider String.

The Attachment Manager

In this section, you create a form that provides the general functionality needed in the Check Writer application. The form is called the Attachment Manager and provides the following functionality:

- Works with any number of attached tables connected to a single data source.
- Provides for different data sources (for example, Access, xBase, Excel, ODBC).
- Checks linked tables when the application starts up. If attachments are good, it opens the next form in the application. If there are errors with the attachments, it opens up the Attachment Manager form so the user can select a new file.
- Provides for a user interface that, when selected from an application's menu system, enables the user to change the file to which the tables are attached.
- Displays the currently linked tables and information about them.
- Displays errors on a table-by-table basis when they cannot be linked.

The form design

The frm_AttachmentManager form is a single form (it has no subforms) and relies on only one external function that is used to call the Open File dialog box, which is covered later in this session.

You can open the Attachment Manager directly from the database container window as well as from VBA code. When the Manager is opened from VBA code, if an opening argument string value of Startup is passed, the form checks the currently linked tables to see if there is an error. If not, the form immediately closes. The user doesn't even know what happened. The form then opens the next form for the application. If there is an error with the linked tables, the form becomes visible, informs the user of the problem, and provides a means to reconnect to a different file.

When the Attachment Manager is opened without the string value Startup opening argument, the form displays the current status of the tables and provides a dialog box to change the file for the linked tables.

The visual design for this form is based on a main tab control with three tabs. These tabs function as follows (see Figure 27-5):

- **Tab page 0:** The List of Currently Attached Tables tab contains a list box called ListStatus that lists the currently attached tables along with information about them.
- **Tab page 1:** The Attach Table(s) to File tab provides a message to the user as well as an interface to choose a new file.
- **Tab page 2:** The List of Attached Tables and Errors tab contains a list box called ErrorList that lists the errors associated with linking the tables.

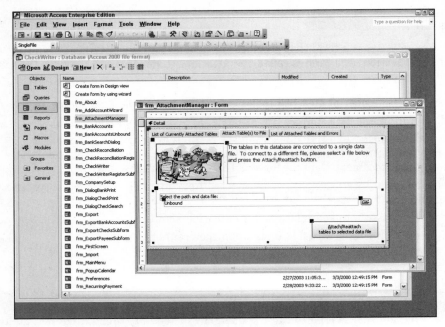

Figure 27-5   *Attachment Manager form in Design view.*

The code

The list box on the List of Currently Attached Tables tab is filled using a function named FillList. In turn, this function calls the function GetLinkedTables.

Refer to the code in the class module of the form frm_AttachmentManager in the sample application file CheckWriter.mdb.

The GetLinkedTables function gets the ADOX catalog tables collection information into an array that is used by the form. This form actually uses two arrays:

- LinkedTables: A string array of link information, one entry per table, where:
  LinkedTables(0, x) = Name of table x
  LinkedTables(1, x) = Name of remote table for table x
  LinkedTables(2, x) = Data source for table x
  LinkedTables(3, x) = Type or provider string for table x
  LinkedTables(4, x) = Error message for table x
  LinkedTables(5, x) = New data source for table x

- LinkedFiles: A string array of linked files, one entry per file, where:
  LinkedFiles(y) = Data source y

These arrays are public to the functions and subroutines of this form and are used by several of them.

Before the Form Open event even executes, the functions FillList and GetLinkedTables have been executed, the arrays have been initialized, and the list box on page 0 of the tab control has been filled. The processing associated with the Form Open event is shown in the flowchart in Figure 27-6.

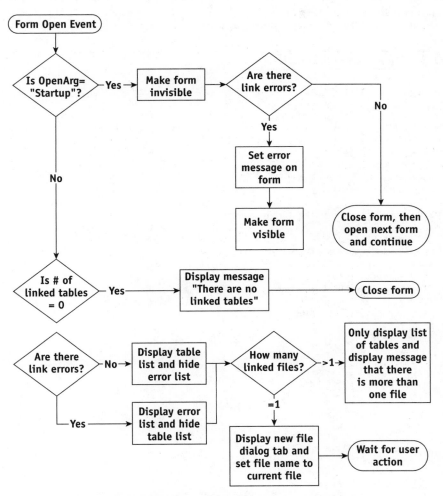

Figure 27-6   Attachment Manager Form Open event processing.

Two user buttons are on the form: one to call the File Open dialog box and select a file to attach to, and the second button to actually attach to the data source.

The subroutine cmdAttachFile1_Click runs when the user clicks the Attach/Reattach button. This function checks for a valid filename and then puts the filename in the array LinkedTables, which is used by the function dbc_AttachTable to link the tables. The dbc_AttachTable function is called for each table to be linked and returns an error message in the array LinkedTables if there is a problem with the link. After the links have been made or attempted, the Boolean variable LinkErrors is checked. If a problem exists, the Errors tab is displayed and the list box on that tab is filled with the `FillErrorList` function. If no problem exists, the List of Currently Attached Tables tab is displayed, and the list box is refreshed with the newly attached tables. The user then simply closes the form.

Because the function `dbc_AttachTable` does the majority of the work, the listing for that function is included here (see Listing 27-3). With the previous discussion and examples, you should be able to follow the logic and statements here.

Listing 27-3 *The AttachTable Function*

```
Public Function dbc_AttachTable(strTable As String, strRemoteTable As String, strProvider
As String, strDataSource As String) As String

'function attaches table "strTable" to "strRemoteTable" Table in file "strDataSource"
using "strProvider"
Dim cat As New ADOX.Catalog
Dim tbl As New ADOX.Table

    On Error GoTo ErrorHandler

    cat.ActiveConnection = CurrentProject.Connection

    Set tbl.ParentCatalog = cat
    'add new table with a suffix of 1
    tbl.Name = strTable & "1"
    tbl.Properties("Jet OLEDB:Link DataSource") = strDataSource
    tbl.Properties("Jet OLEDB:Remote Table Name") = strRemoteTable
    If strProvider <> "Access" Then
        tbl.Properties("Jet OLEDB:Link Provider String") = strProvider
    End If
    tbl.Properties("Jet OLEDB:Create Link") = True
    cat.Tables.Append tbl
    cat.Tables.Refresh

    'new table successfully attached so delete old and rename new
    cat.Tables.Delete strTable
    tbl.Name = strTable
    cat.Tables.Refresh

    Set tbl = Nothing
    dbc_AttachTable = ""

    GoTo Done
ErrorHandler:
    Select Case Err.Number
        Case 3011
            dbc_AttachTable = "Could not find the table in " & strDataSource
        Case Else
            dbc_AttachTable = Err.Description
    End Select
Done:

End Function
```

There are a few other subroutines in the Attachment Manager form. The ListStatus_DblClick subroutine executes when a user double-clicks the table list. This subroutine displays all the information about the table in a message box. A similar function occurs with the ErrorList_Click subroutine that runs when the user clicks the error list.

The button near the Filename text box runs a subroutine that displays the Open File dialog box. This is actually handled with the dbc_OpenFile function located in the module mod_FileUtilities, and the dbc_OpenFile function calls the API GetFileInfo in the Msaccess.exe library. This displays the standard Office File Open dialog box and, after the user chooses a file, it returns the name of the file along with the path.

The last bit of code in the Attachment Manager occurs in the Form Unload event. This subroutine runs when the form is closed either programmatically or by the user with the Close Window button. No processing is done unless the form was opened with the Startup argument. In that case, if link errors still exist, the user is asked if he or she really wants to exit the application. If the response is Yes, the application quits; otherwise, the form stays open until no link errors exist.

Operation

To use the Attachment Manager, you must first define your table links within Access as you normally do by choosing File ➪ Get External Data ➪ Link Tables. With the Attachment Manager, you can easily change the files that the tables point to, as well as refresh the attachments and determine which errors, if any, exist with the attachments.

When you open the Attachment Manager normally, you see the Attach Table(s) to File tab and dialog box displaying a message and prompting for a new file (see Figure 27-7).

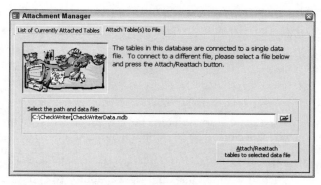

Figure 27-7 *The Attachment Manager dialog box.*

At this point, the user can choose to look at the currently attached files by clicking the List of Currently Attached Tables tab. The linked tables are displayed as shown in Figure 27-8.

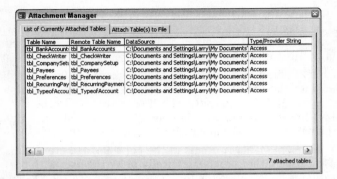

Figure 27-8   *The List of Currently Attached Tables tab.*

If more than one file is attached, the only tab that is displayed is the List of Currently Attached Tables tab, and a message box pops up that says `There is more than one attached file. Cannot process.` Double-clicking a particular table in this list opens a message box with more details about the particular table (see Figure 27-9).

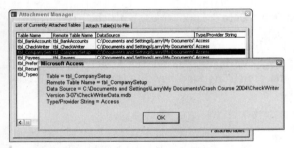

Figure 27-9   *Viewing table details.*

Additional capabilities

With the Attachment Manager, you have a good starting point for creating a more sophisticated model. Additional features include the capability to handle more than one attached file, the option to try the current directory automatically if link errors exist, the capability to provide a table-driven system with groups of tables and data sources already stored, the capability to keep a history of files attached with a name, and the capability to choose data sources based on the saved name.

Database Creations, Inc. (www.databasecreations.com) **sells as part of its EZ Developer Suite a more sophisticated Attachment Manager that can handle all the additional capabilities just mentioned.**

Done!

REVIEW

In this session, you learned about the front-end and back-end architecture and how the connection between the two is made with attached or linked tables. You also learned how to programmatically manipulate this connection using ADO objects. These topics were covered:

- A linked table is a connection to an external data source.
- Linked tables are used for better management of data separate from the front-end application. They can also improve an application's performance.
- ADO programming features for linked tables are based on the ADOX library.
- An ADOX catalog is used to store the table definitions and the link information.

QUIZ YOURSELF

1. What are some of the causes of losing a link to an attached table? (See "Basic Principles.")
2. What are the two ADO object models that allow a programmer to work with linked tables. (See "Programming Concepts.")
3. Which property of the Jet OLEDB provider contains the name of the table in the remote data source? (See "The Table Properties collection.")
4. Name three reasons why the Attachment Manager form is needed in an application. (See "The Attachment Manager.")
5. What additional functionality is provided by the Attachment Manager over the Linked Table Manager? (See "The Attachment Manager.")

Securing Access Databases

Session Checklist

✔ Options for securing an Access database

✔ Share-level security

✔ User-level security

✔ Encryption as a security option

✔ Other considerations for ensuring security

**30 Min.
To Go**

W hen you design an application, you must be concerned about its security and that of the data it supports. This session focuses on how to work programmatically with Access security. It assumes that you have some knowledge of security with Access and the Access user interface for working with security. If you need help in these areas, refer to Chapter 34 of the *Access 2003 Bible* by Cary N. Prague, Michael R. Irwin, and Jennifer Reardon (published by Wiley).

The companion Web site for this book includes an .mdb file called
`Security.MDB` **that contains sample code from this session.**

Security Options

Access gives you several options for securing a database — some simple options and some more complicated ones. Which option you implement is a function of the nature of your application, how it is designed, who the users will be, where the data is stored, and how complex you want to make the security options.

You must consider security from two aspects: the program and the data. Some methods protect the data, whereas others protect the program. Table 28-1 summarizes the various methods and the features of each. The table also includes combinations of the methods because you can use more than one method at a time.

Table 28-1   *Access Security Methods*

Method	Protects Data	Protects Program	Notes
Share level	Good	Good	Gives all users the same password
User level	Better	Better	Can control access user by user
Encryption	Better	Good	Prevents reading data using an external program
.MDE	No	Best	Protects all program code but not data
Share level and encryption	Better	Good	
User level and encryption	Best	Better	
.MDE and encryption	Better	Best	
Share level, encryption, and .mde	Better	Best	
User level, encryption, and .mde	Best	Best	Provides the best of both worlds

The next few sections take each method and describe how to implement it using VBA code.

Share-Level Security

With Access share-level security, the database is secured with a password. To open the database, the user must specify the correct database password. To open a database connection with a password, you specify the password in the Open method of the ADO connection, as shown here:

```
Dim cnn As New ADODB.Connection

    cnn.Open "Provider=Microsoft.Jet.OLEDB.4.0;" & _
        "Data Source=C:\nwind.mdb;Jet OLEDB:Database Password=password;"
```

To change a database password, you use the JRO object model not ADOX, which is typically used for the Jet database. The Jet and Replication Objects (JRO) object model contains the objects, properties, and methods for creating, modifying, and synchronizing replicas as well as for dealing with such things as a database password.

The reference for JRO to be set in the VBA window is Microsoft Jet and Replication Objects 2.6 Library.

Unlike ADO and ADOX, JRO cannot be used with data sources other than Microsoft Jet databases. Changing the password is possible only when compacting a database. The following listing shows the code needed to change a database password:

```
Dim je As New JRO.JetEngine

    je.CompactDatabase "Data Source=C:\nwind.mdb;", _
        "Data Source=C:\nwind2.mdb;" & _
        "Jet OLEDB:Database Password=newpassword"
```

In the sample file Security.mdb on the companion Web site, the module mod_SecurityFunctions illustrates the technique for changing a database password based on this listing.

Because you cannot compact a database onto itself, you must compact to a copy of the database. Therefore, you will want to add some code to check whether the file that you want to compact to already exists. If it is there, delete it. Then, after compacting the database, you can delete the original database and rename the compacted database with the original name.

User-Level Security

The Access security model consists of workgroups, groups, users, and permissions. The groups and user information is contained within a workgroup file. This file has an .mdw extension. The default filename is System.mdw, but it can be different. Therefore, you can have more than one workgroup file, but only one file can be associated with an application in a given session. Multiple applications can share a single workgroup file as well.

The permission information is stored within the Access database file. This includes assignments of permissions for each object by group or user. Permissions can include up to eight different types depending on the object being secured. Figure 28-1 shows the User and Group Permissions window, which lists the permissions available.

When designing an application, you can provide the security system with a different user interface that has features not found in the standard Access security interface. This is particularly true if you distribute your application in the runtime environment because the standard Access security interface is not available. Probably the most common functionality you can offer is the capability for a user to change his or her password. In addition, the following list covers the functions most frequently needed by an administrator who handles the security system:

- Changing a user password
- Adding a new user
- Assigning a user to a group
- Removing a user from a group
- Removing a user

Figure 28-1   *The User and Group Permissions window.*

You can programmatically create groups and assign permissions as well. Because these are not the most commonly needed interfaces and the depth of this session is limited, these functions are not covered here. But be aware that you can provide many other capabilities by using techniques similar to those explained in this session.

20 Min.
To Go

The ADOX security objects

Before starting on the code to perform the common security interfaces, you must understand the security objects with which you are working. The security objects are contained within the ADOX object model, not the ADO object model. ADOX contains extensions to the ADO model specifically designed to handle the security information. Figure 28-2 graphically illustrates the model.

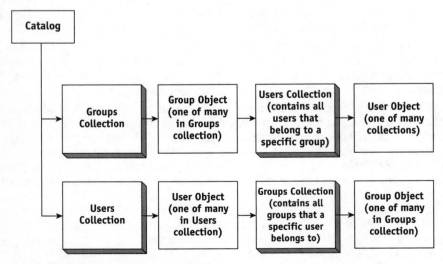

Figure 28-2   *The ADOX security object model.*

Two collections are part of the `Catalog` object: `Groups` and `Users`. These collections, in turn, have an additional collection. The `Groups` collection includes a `Users` collection, and the `Users` collection has a `Groups` collection. This cross-referencing provides the capability to look for users that are part of a group and for groups of which the user is a member.

Changing a user password

Two common functions are required for changing a user password:

- A function that enables the user to change his or her password
- A function that enables the administrator to change a user's password

Listing 28-1 shows a function that prompts the current user for a new password. If successful, the function returns a `True` value. Otherwise, if there is a problem, the function returns a `False` value.

Listing 28-1   *The Change Current User Password Function*

```
Public Function ChangeCurrentPassword() As Boolean
Dim cat As ADOX.Catalog
Dim strOldPassword As String
Dim strNewPassword As String

  Set cat = New ADOX.Catalog
  cat.ActiveConnection = CurrentProject.Connection
  strOldPassword = InputBox("Enter your old password", _
"Password Change for " & CurrentUser())
  strNewPassword = InputBox("Enter your new password", _
"Password Change for " & CurrentUser())
  If strNewPassword <> InputBox("Reenter your new password", _
"Password Change for " & CurrentUser()) Then
    MsgBox "Error entering password"
    GoTo Done
  End If
  cat.Users(CurrentUser()).ChangePassword strOldPassword, strNewPassword
  ChangeCurrentPassword = True
  MsgBox "Password successfully changed"
  GoTo Done
ErrorHandler:
  MsgBox Err.Description
  ChangeCurrentPassword = False
Done:
End Function
```

Note that the `CurrentUser()` function is used here, which returns the currently active user name. A new ADOX catalog is set first with the current project connection established. The function then prompts the user for the old password, and then twice for the new password. The `ChangePassword` method is then used with the `Users` collection of the catalog to change the password. If everything completes successfully, the function displays a message saying that the password was successfully changed and then returns a value of `True` to the calling code. In Listing 28-2, the function is not interactive (no `InputBox` functions), and the passed parameters allow any user password to be changed. This function would typi-cally be called in the administrator mode.

Listing 28-2   *The Change User Password Function*

```
Public Function ChangePassword(strUserName As String, strOldPassword As String,
strNewPassword as string) As Boolean
Dim cat As ADOX.Catalog

   Set cat = New ADOX.Catalog
   cat.ActiveConnection = CurrentProject.Connection
   cat.Users(strUserName).ChangePassword strOldPassword, strNewPassword
   ChangePassword = True
   GoTo Done
ErrorHandler:
   MsgBox Err.Description
   ChangePassword = False
Done:
End Function
```

Adding a new user

The function in Listing 28-3 adds a new user to the workgroup. The required parameters are the username and the password. The function works by creating a new catalog object and appending the new username with a password to the Users collection in the catalog. If the function executes without any errors, a value of True is returned; otherwise, a value of False is returned to the calling procedure.

Listing 28-3   *The Add User Function*

```
Public Function AddUser(strUserName As String, strPassword As String) As Boolean
'Adds a new user
Dim cat As ADOX.Catalog

   On Error GoTo ErrorHandler
   Set cat = New ADOX.Catalog
   cat.ActiveConnection = CurrentProject.Connection
   cat.Users.Append strUserName, strPassword
   AddUser = True
   GoTo Done
ErrorHandler:
   MsgBox Err.Description
   AddUser = False
Done:

End Function
```

Assigning a user to a group

To assign a user to an existing group, you append the group name to the group's collection of the specific user. Listing 28-4 illustrates how this is done. The function requires two parameters: the username and the group to which to add the user. If the function executes without any errors, it returns a True value. Otherwise, a False value is returned to the calling procedure.

Listing 28-4   *The Assign User to Group Function*

```
Public Function AssignUserToGroup(strUserName As String, _
        strGroupName As String) As Boolean
'Adds a user to an existing group
Dim cat As ADOX.Catalog

  On Error GoTo ErrorHandler
  Set cat = New ADOX.Catalog
  cat.ActiveConnection = CurrentProject.Connection
  cat.Users(strUserName).Groups.Append strGroupName
  AssignUserToGroup = True
  GoTo Done
ErrorHandler:
  MsgBox Err.Description
  AssignUserToGroup = False
Done:

End Function
```

Removing a user from a group

Removing a user from a group is similar to adding one: The group name is deleted from the user's group collection. In Listing 28-5, the Delete method is used against the Groups collection for the specified user. If the function executes without any errors, it returns a True value. Otherwise, a False value is returned to the calling procedure.

Listing 28-5   *The Remove User from Group Function*

```
Public Function RemoveUserFromGroup(strUserName As String, strGroupName As String) As
Boolean
'Removes a user from an existing group
Dim cat As ADOX.Catalog

  On Error GoTo ErrorHandler
  Set cat = New ADOX.Catalog
  cat.ActiveConnection = CurrentProject.Connection
  cat.Users(strUserName).Groups.Delete strGroupName
  RemoveUserFromGroup = True
  GoTo Done
ErrorHandler:
  MsgBox Err.Description
  RemoveUserFromGroup = False
Done:

End Function
```

Listing 28-6 shows how you remove a user from the workgroup. This function receives as a parameter the username to be removed. As with the previous functions, a new catalog object is created with a connection to the current project. By using the `Delete` method for the `Users` collection, a user can be removed. If the function executes without any errors, it returns a `True` value. Otherwise, a `False` value is returned to the calling procedure.

Listing 28-6   *The Remove User Function*

```
Public Function RemoveUser(strUserName As String) As Boolean
Dim cat As ADOX.Catalog

   On Error GoTo ErrorHandler
   Set cat = New ADOX.Catalog
   cat.ActiveConnection = CurrentProject.Connection
   cat.Users.Delete strUserName
   RemoveUser = True
   GoTo Done
ErrorHandler:
   MsgBox Err.Description
   RemoveUser = False
Done:

End Function
```

Opening a secured database

With security enabled on a database, opening the database using an ADODB connection method requires an ID and password parameter to be passed:

```
Dim cnn As New ADODB.Connection

    cnn.Provider = "Microsoft.Jet.OLEDB.4.0"
    cnn.Properties("Jet OLEDB:System database") = "c:\system.mdw"
    cnn.Open "Data Source=c:\northwind.mdb;User Id=Admin;Password=password;"
```

A Microsoft Jet provider-specific connection property, `Jet OLEDB:System database`, specifies the workgroup file. Before you can reference provider-specific properties from the `Properties` collection, you must define which provider you are using. Therefore, the provider is specified first, and then the property for the workgroup file can be specified. Finally, the connection can be opened with the data source, the user ID, and the password.

**10 Min.
To Go**

Encryption

Despite everything that is accomplished with share-level or user-level security, someone could still open an .mdb file with a text editor and read the contents of a file as a series of ASCII characters. This may not be a problem when the code is routine, but it could compromise sensitive data. To overcome this security breech, Access provides for encryption. Encrypting a database compacts the file and makes it indecipherable by any program like a utility program or word processor.

You perform encryption using the JRO compact database method:

```
Dim je As New JRO.JetEngine

    je.CompactDatabase "Provider=Microsoft.Jet.OLEDB.4.0;" & _
        "Data Source=C:\nwind.mdb", _
        "Provider=Microsoft.Jet.OLEDB.4.0;" & _
        "Data Source=C:\nwind2.mdb;" & _
        "Jet OLEDB:Encrypt Database=True"
```

Always back up your files before you do any major file conversion such as encrypting or converting to an .mde.

The encryption method creates a compacted copy of the original database. You must add code to check for the existence of a file of the same name. You also need to add code to rename the file to the original name after it has been encrypted.

.MDE

An option for protecting your application code is to distribute the program as an .mde file. As discussed in Session 24, an .mde file is a copy of an .mdb file with all source code removed and only compiled code included. This obviously protects the code because source code is not available. This prevents anyone from going into an object's Design view. It doesn't protect any data, the opening of an object, or the execution of any code. Therefore, it is a limited, but important, security option.

Refer to Session 24 for more information about the .mde file.

Other Considerations

Besides the specific security features built into Microsoft Access, other items must be considered to be certain that an application and its data are secure. These include such things as file security, hiding the database objects from the user, and disabling various keys that provide access to areas where the user should not go.

File security

With all the security features discussed so far, unless you have operating-system protection for your files, someone with access to a database file can simply use Windows to copy, move, replace, or delete files. It is imperative that you consider a method to protect the database application and data using operating system security. Windows 95/98/ME don't offer much security. Consider using Windows NT/2000/XP to handle the security that you really need. It is outside the scope of this book to discuss the details of a security approach using

Windows, but there are many references on the market that can steer you in the right direction. One such reference is *Windows 2000 Server Security For Dummies* by Paul Sanna (published by Wiley).

Hiding the database window

A good method for maintaining control of the application and data from within Access is to hide the database window. You can do this by choosing Tools ⇨ Startup Options. Figure 28-3 shows the dialog box used to set this option. The option is Display Database Window. When this option is unchecked, the database window is hidden and users cannot access the objects. Of course, there are ways to redisplay the database window. The methods to redisplay the database window and the ways to prevent redisplay are discussed in the following two sections.

Figure 28-3 *The Start-Up Options dialog box.*

`Startup Show DBWindow` is a property of the database object. To set this property in code, you execute the code in Listing 28-7. The code in this listing uses an error condition to detect whether the property exists. On the line following the `On Error resume next` statement, the property is set to `False`; but if the property does not exist, an error 3270 occurs. If this error is detected, the property is added with the appropriate value of `False`.

Listing 28-7 *Setting the StartupShowDBWindow Property*

```
Dim db As Object
Dim prp As Property

   Set db = CurrentDb
   On Error resume next
   db.Properties("StartupShowDBWindow") = False
   If err.Number = 3270 then 'Property not found
     Set prp = db.CreateProperty("StartupShowDBWindow",1, False)
     db.Properties.Append prp
   Endif
```

The sample form frm_DatabaseSecurityStartupProperties in the Security.mdb file on the companion Web site illustrates the technique for changing the database properties based on Listings 28-7, 28-8, and 28-9.

Disabling the Bypass key

When a database application is first loaded, execution immediately starts with the command-line argument /x *macro*, the AutoExec macro, and/or the Startup Form set with the database properties. If the user holds down the Shift key when starting an application he bypasses these actions. Doing this could violate security and provide your users with access to objects in your application that you do not want them to access. Therefore, setting the AllowBypassKey property to False can prevent the Shift key from stopping the execution of these items. To disable the Bypass Key, set the corresponding database property AllowBypassKey to False. Listing 28-8 shows you how to do this. The error handling in this listing is similar to that described in the Listing 28-7.

Listing 28-8   *Setting the AllowBypassKey Property*

```
Dim db As Object
Dim prp As Property

  Set db = CurrentDb
  On Error resume next
  db.Properties("AllowBypassKey") = False
  If err.Number = 3270 then 'Property not found
    Set prp = db.CreateProperty("AllowBypassKey",1, False)
    db.Properties.Append prp
  Endif
```

Disabling special keys

You can use the AllowSpecialKeys property to prevent the user from gaining access to areas of the application that could violate security. Special keys are listed in Table 28-2. The code to disable the Special Keys is shown in Listing 28-9. In this code, the property AllowSpecialKeys is set or added if it is not there, as done in the previous two listings.

Table 28-2   *Special Keys*

Special Key Combination	Action
Alt+F1 (F11)	Displays the database window
Ctrl+F11	Toggles between the custom menu bar and the built-in menu bar
Ctrl+Break	Breaks code execution
Ctrl+G	Displays the immediate window

Listing 28-9 *Setting the AllowSpecialKeys Property*

```
Dim db As Object
Dim prp As Property

  Set db = CurrentDb
  On Error resume next
  db.Properties("AllowSpecialKeys") = False
  If err.Number = 3270 then 'Property not found
    Set prp = db.CreateProperty("AllowSpecialKeys",1, False)
    db.Properties.Append prp
  Endif
```

All options are sensitive to order, later ones overriding earlier ones.

Done!

REVIEW

In this session, you learned about the importance of security. The various options for protecting the application and data were discussed. In addition, material and examples were presented that showed you how to programmatically work with Access security. The following topics were covered:

- Several security options are available, each with its advantages based on the type of application you have, how it is designed, who the users are, and how the data is stored.

- Security options exist to protect the program and the data.

- With Access share-level security, the database is secured with a password that all users use.

- The ADOX object provides the extensions to handle user-level security, whereas the JRO object provides the methods to handle share-level security.

- Encrypting a database protects the data from being read by a program outside of Access.

- .mde files primarily protect the program code.

- A developer should also address other security considerations These include file security from an operating system perspective, hiding the database window, disabling the bypass key, and disabling other keys that could violate security.

Quiz Yourself

1. What is the best security method to protect data? (See "Security Options.")

2. What is the best security method to protect both the data and the program? (See "Security Options.")

3. In which file are the security permissions stored? (See "User-Level Security.")

4. The Groups and Users collections are part of which object? (See "The ADOX security objects.")

5. What additional precautions should you take beyond using Access security to secure an application? (See "Other Considerations.")

6. What is accomplished by encrypting a database? (See "Encryption.")

7. What property is used to disable the bypass key? (See "Disabling the Bypass Key.")

Access and Client Server Data

Session Checklist

✔ Understanding client/server architecture

✔ Understanding Microsoft Data Engine 2000 (MSDE 2000)

✔ Choosing the right database engine

✔ Working with Access and SQL Server databases

✔ Upsizing an Access database to SQL Server

*30 Min.
To Go*

When you design a database application, you must understand the needs of the users in current and future environments. An application needs to be flexible enough to easily accommodate users' expanding needs. Access databases can accommodate most small-workgroup environments. However, environments with large numbers of users or those that process large volumes of data require a true client/server database engine.

Understanding Client/Server Architecture

In a client/server computing environment, two or more network workstations can share a centrally located data source. An application is split into two components: the front end (client component) and the back end (server component). The client component is usually installed on the user's workstation and includes the user-interface functions like switchboards, forms, and reports. The server component is usually located on a network server and stores only the database data. The server database performs functions that are invisible to the user — delivering data to the client to display on a form or report, receiving updated data from the client, and restricting access to its data through database security.

You have already taken steps toward a client/server architecture by using linked Access tables for your application. However, the Access database environment is not a true client/server architecture. Jet, the database engine for Access databases, is called a file server database engine. File server database engines merely move data back and forth between the client and the server. Running an Access query requires Jet to send all the data for the tables used in the query to the client workstation. The client workstation must then process the query to produce the result.

True client/server database engines do more than simply move data. When you run a query or stored procedure against a client/server database, the server processes the query or stored procedure. The server then sends the result to the client. In addition to minimizing traffic on the network, this strategy also makes more efficient use of the client's and the server's processors.

Microsoft Data Engine 2000 (MSDE 2000) is a client/server database engine that is included with Access 2003. It is a scaled-down version of Microsoft SQL Server 2000, optimized to run on the desktop or in a small network environment.

Understanding Microsoft Data Engine 2000

MSDE 2000 is a good solution if you are creating an application for a workgroup that consists of a few users today, but it is likely to grow to hundreds or even thousands of users. MSDE 2000 is designed using the same database engine as SQL Server 2000. Databases you build in it are directly portable to SQL Server 2000. Although MSDE 2000 is 100 percent compatible with SQL Server 2000, it does not include all the SQL Server features.

MSDE 2000 runs under Windows NT 4.0, Windows 98, Windows 2000, Windows ME, and Windows XP. Therefore, you can install MSDE 2000 either on a network server, or even on your local workstation. MSDE 2000 gives you the power of SQL Server 2000 by providing functions such as transaction logging, database recovery, database security, and true client/server-distributed processing right on the desktop.

If the target workgroup for your application includes many users or heavy transaction volumes, you should use SQL Server2000 as your database engine instead of MSDE 2000. Although MSDE 2000 has no limit on the number of simultaneous users, it is optimized for five users. Other limitations include a 2GB-database size limit, the capability to use (at most) only two processors, and the inability to support all database replication features.

One of the primary reasons to use MSDE 2000 is that the developer does not have to be connected to SQL Server 2000 to develop the application. Both the front end and the database can be developed using Access and MSDE 2000. The back-end database can easily be transferred to SQL Server for user testing and, ultimately, for implementation.

Deciding between Jet and MSDE

Because MSDE 2000 provides so much power and scalability, it might be tempting to use it with all your applications. But, as is often the case, with maximum flexibility comes higher complexity. With Jet databases, after Access is installed you simply install the application's database — Jet is automatically included in Access.

Creating and maintaining MSDE 2000 databases are more complicated processes than creating a Jet database. Whereas MSDE 2000 has automatic features for dynamically reconfiguring and recovering from errors, larger databases usually require configuration by a database administrator. On the other hand, damaged Jet databases often cannot be repaired.

You need to analyze the business environment of the intended workgroup before you choose the database for your application. Does the business environment include skilled staff who are capable of maintaining a server database like MSDE 2000? How much memory and disk space do the workstations and server have? Does the application require a solid security system to protect sensitive data? Will there be a large number of users or high volumes of data?

Although security is optional with Jet databases, MSDE 2000 requires database security similar to Windows NT security. Your application requires someone skilled enough to set up user accounts and passwords.

MSDE 2000 requires a computer with a Pentium 166-MHz or higher processor with 32MB of RAM, although 64MB or more is recommended. MSDE 2000 requires approximately 45MB of hard drive space for a typical installation — 25MB for program files and 20MB for data files. Most workstations in the business world today easily meet these requirements. Optionally, you can store the program files and data files on separate drives. Remember that you need additional space for your database files. If you find that the organization's equipment is closer to the minimum requirements, however, keep in mind that a Jet database generally requires less memory and hard disk space than the same database developed in MSDE 2000.

In reality, you should have a minimum of 128MB on any computer system running Microsoft business software purchased in 2001 or later.

Determining the number of potential users and the volume of transactions for an application can be unpredictable in some situations. If there are only a few users and relatively low volumes of data for, at least, the near future, Jet may be the best solution for the sake of simplicity.

Access includes the Upsizing Wizard to automatically import a Jet database into MSDE 2000.

Using MSDE

20 Min.
To Go

Before you can work with an MSDE 2000 database, start the SQL Server Service Manager. It manages the connections between applications and MSDE databases.

Starting SQL Server Service Manager

To start SQL Server Service Manager, choose Service Manager from the MSDE folder in your Start menu. SQL Server Service Manager displays, as shown in Figure 29-1.

MSDE 2000 is not installed automatically when you install Office 2003. You can install it manually from the Office 2003 CD-ROM. See the Office 2003 documentation for information on how to perform the installation.

Figure 29-1   *Starting the SQL Server Service Manager.*

To connect to an MSDE 2000 database, select SQL Server for Services. Then click the Start/Continue button to start it. When the SQL Server service has started, a green arrow displays next to the server in SQL Server Service Manager, and the Pause and Stop buttons become enabled. Figure 29-2 shows the SQL Server Service Manager with SQL Server running.

SQL Server starts each time you boot up the computer if you select the option Auto-Start Service when OS starts.

Figure 29-2   *Running the SQL Server service.*

With SQL Server Service Manager running, you can create and connect to MSDE 2000 databases. To create an MSDE 2000 database from Access, you must first create an Access project.

Understanding projects

You can use an Access project to create and maintain an MSDE database. You can also use an Access project to create the user-interface objects — forms, reports, data access pages, macros, and modules — that get their data from MSDE 2000. The database window for a project looks very similar to the Access database window you are already accustomed to. In fact, creating the user-interface objects is virtually the same as creating them in Access. Figure 29-3 shows the database window for a new project.

Even though you can create the data objects — tables, views, and stored procedures — in a project, the data objects are actually being stored in a separate MSDE 2000 database (.MDF) file. The MSDE 2000 file is created automatically when you create a new project.

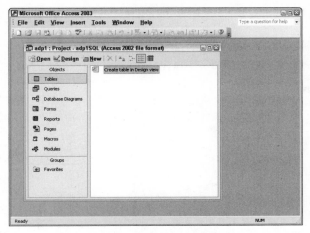

Figure 29-3   *Viewing the database window for a project.*

 Views and stored procedures are comparable to Access queries. Views are select queries. Stored procedures are action or parameter queries. Database diagrams are just like relationships in an Access database.

Creating a project

To create an Access project, follow these steps:

1. Start Microsoft Access, choose File ➪ New from the Access menu. The New File task pane displays, as shown in Figure 29-4.

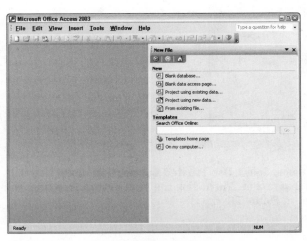

Figure 29-4   *The New File task pane.*

2. Choose New ⇨ Project Using New Data. The File New Database dialog box displays, as shown in Figure 29-5.

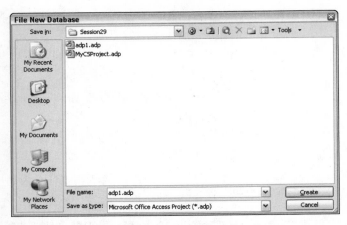

Figure 29-5   *The File New Database dialog box.*

3. Choose a folder for the new project and enter **MyCSProject** for the filename. Then click the Create button. The Microsoft SQL Server Database Wizard displays, as shown in Figure 29-6.

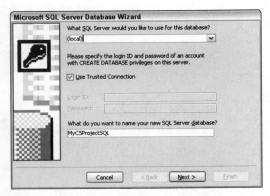

Figure 29-6   *The Microsoft SQL Server Database Wizard.*

4. Enter **(local)** for the server name. Select **Use Trusted Connection**. Enter **MyCSProjectSQL** for the database name. Then click the Next button. The final wizard screen displays, as shown in Figure 29-7.

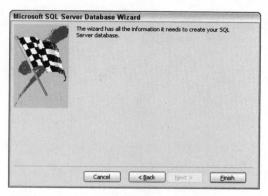

Figure 29-7 *The final Microsoft SQL Server Database Wizard screen.*

You use (local) when creating an MSDE 2000 database on a desktop computer. If you want to create the database on a server on your network, select the server name from the list.

5. Click the Finish button. The Microsoft SQL Server Database Wizard creates the new MSDE 2000 database and the new Access project. The Database window for the new project displays.

Creating the new MSDE 2000 database and new Access project can take several minutes.

Working with data objects in a project is a little different from working with tables and queries in an Access database. But using the project data design tools is really just as easy as creating tables and queries in Access once you get the hang of it.

Creating a table

Creating a table in an Access project is just like creating a table in an Access database. To create a new table, follow these steps.

1. Select the Tables object in the Database container. Then select the Create Table in Design View item in the Tables object window. The Choose Name dialog box displays.

2. Enter **MyTable** for the new table name. Next, click the OK button. The Design view for the new table displays. Figure 29-8 shows the Design view for the BankAccounts table.

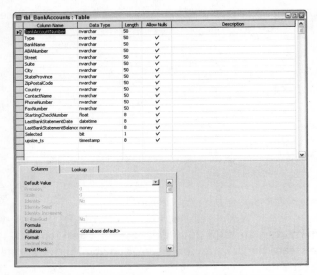

Figure 29-8 *The Design view of an MSDE 2000 table.*

The Design view of an MSDE 2000 table displays in a spreadsheet-style format. The first two columns are just like the Access database table design window. The Column Name column is where you enter the names of the fields for the table. The second column contains the datatype for each field. The AllowNulls column displays a check box to indicate whether the field can contain Null values. Just as in an Access database, you can use the Description column to enter information describing the purpose of the field. The remaining properties that you can define for each field or column name, display in the Properties window in the bottom pane of the Table Designer.

Creating the tables and queries for a new SQL Server database can be a time-consuming job. If you are moving an existing Access database to MSDE 2000 or SQL Server, you do not have to start from scratch. The Microsoft Access Upsizing Wizard does most of the work for you.

10 Min.
To Go

Upsizing to MSDE

You can convert an existing Microsoft Access database (.MDB) to a SQL Server database automatically using the Microsoft Access Upsizing Wizard. The Upsizing Wizard creates a new SQL Server database and imports all the Access database tables. It imports the table structures, indexes, validation rules, defaults, autonumbers, relationships, and — of course — the data. At the same time, it fine-tunes the new database structures to take advantage of SQL Server functionality wherever possible. You can also convert the Access application's forms, reports, macros, and modules into a new Microsoft Access project.

Before upsizing, make a backup copy of your Access database.

The following example upsizes the Check Writer database. To upsize an Access database, follow these steps.

1. Open the Access database that you want to convert. Start SQL Server Service Manager.
2. Choose Tools ➪ Database Utilities ➪ Upsizing Wizard. The first screen of the Upsizing Wizard displays, as shown in Figure 29-9.

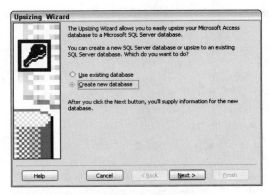

Figure 29-9   *The Upsizing Wizard.*

3. Choose the Create new database option. Then click the Next button. The second Upsizing Wizard screen displays, as shown in Figure 29-10.

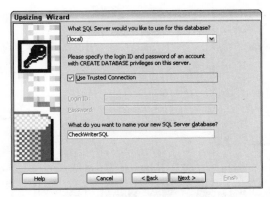

Figure 29-10   *Setting up the new SQL Server database.*

4. You use this screen to define the connection information for the new SQL Server database. Type **(local)** as the location for the new SQL Server database. Check Use Trusted Connection. Type **CheckWriterSQL** for the name of the new database. Finally, click the Next button.

5. Use the next screen, as shown in Figure 29-11, to select the tables to include in the new database. Click the >> button to select all the tables in the Available Tables list. Click the Next button.

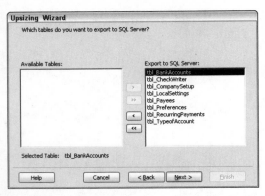

Figure 29-11   *Selecting the tables for the new SQL Server database.*

6. On the screen shown in Figure 29-12, you can take advantage of many SQL Server features such as indexes, validation rules, defaults, relationships, and timestamp fields. Make the appropriate selections. Click Next to continue.

Figure 29-12   *Taking advantage of SQL Server features.*

7. Figure 29-13 shows the screen for creating the new Access project to use with the SQL Server database. Type the path and filename for the new project. Click the Next button.

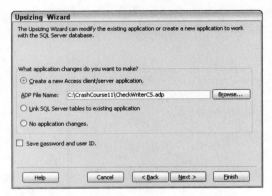

Figure 29-13   *Creating the Access project.*

8. Click the Finish button on the final Upsizing Wizard screen, shown in Figure 29-14.

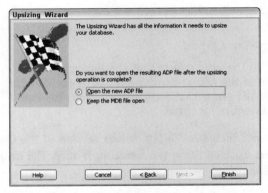

Figure 29-14   *The final Upsizing Wizard screen.*

It takes several minutes to create the new SQL Server database and Access project. A message box with a progress meter tracks the conversion process while you wait.

When the conversion process is complete, the Upsizing Wizard displays the Upsizing Wizard Report. An example of the report is shown in Figure 29-15. It includes information about how the Access database and application were converted and information about any errors that were encountered.

You can close the Upsizing Wizard Report window when you have finished reviewing it. The Upsizing Wizard automatically loads the new Access project.

You can view the Upsizing Wizard Report later. The filename is your Access application filename with the extension .snp (for example, CheckWriter.snp).

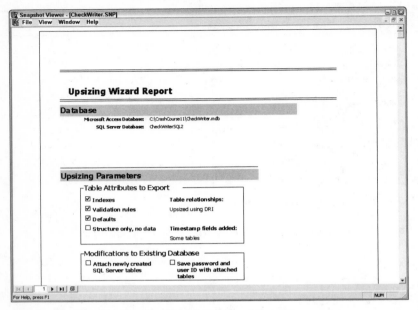

Figure 29-15 *Viewing the Upsizing Wizard Report.*

When the new project displays, review all the new objects that the Upsizing Wizard created. You may find, however, that some of the Access queries did not upsize. See the Upsizing Wizard Report for information on the errors that were encountered. You can manually create either a view or stored procedure for these.

This book's companion Web site includes the SQL Server version of the Check Writer application, which was upsized using the Upsizing Wizard. The project filename is CheckWriterCS.adp.

Done!

REVIEW

Using Access and MSDE 2000, you can implement true client/server database applications. MSDE 2000 provides virtually all the functionality and power of SQL Server, yet you can run it on a desktop workstation. These topics were covered:

- Client/server databases process queries on the server and send only the result to the application.

- MSDE 2000 and SQL Server are examples of true client/server database engines.

- MSDE 2000 is a scaled-down version of SQL Server 2000 that can run on a desktop computer or on a network server.

- Jet is a file/server database engine that is sufficient for use in smaller, low-volume databases.

- Access projects are used to work with MSDE 2000 databases.

- The Upsizing Wizard automatically converts an Access database to a client/server application.

QUIZ YOURSELF

1. How do file/server databases differ from client/server databases? (See "Understanding Client/Server Architecture.")
2. Which operating systems can run MSDE 2000? (See "Understanding Microsoft Data Engine 2000.")
3. For which environments is Jet the most practical database solution? (See "Deciding between Jet and MSDE 2000.")
4. What is the purpose of SQL Server Service Manager? (See "Using MSDE 2000.")
5. A project's tables, views, and stored procedures are stored in what type of file? (See "Understanding projects.")

Creating SQL Server Queries

Session Checklist

✔ Checking a project's SQL Server connection

✔ Working with SQL Server queries

✔ Manipulating data with stored procedures

✔ Using a user-defined function to perform a calculation

**30 Min.
To Go**

I n Session 29 you learned how to upsize an Access database to SQL Server and how to use an Access project to work with SQL Server tables. In this session, you continue on this path by learning how to use an Access project to create queries that retrieve and manipulate SQL Server data.

Even though you can create SQL Server data objects (tables and queries) in a project, the data objects are actually being stored in a separate MSDE 2000 database (.MDF) file. The MSDE 2000 file is created automatically when you upsize data from an Access .mdb file or when you create a new project. Access provides a tool to display the name of the project's database file.

Checking a Project's Database Connection

You can determine the name of the MSDE 2000 database that is connected to the current project by choosing File ⇨ Connection. This option displays the Data Link Properties dialog box shown in Figure 30-1. This box shows the properties for the database connection for the current project.

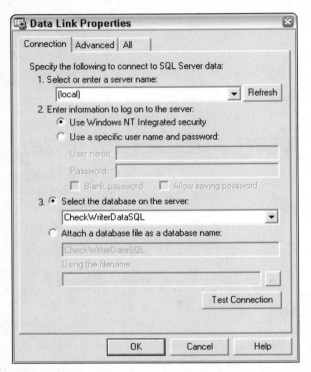

Figure 30-1   *Determining a project's database connection.*

The data link properties shown in Figure 30-1 are the properties for the connection to the CheckWriterDataSQL database.

The properties for creating an MSDE 2000 database connection are covered in Session 29.

Understanding Project Queries

You use queries in an Access project the same way you use them in an Access database — to view, change, add, or delete data.

Projects provide three types of queries for working with data:

- Views
- Stored procedures
- User-defined functions

Creating a view

Views are like queries in an Access database. You work with views in the Query Designer, which works very much like the Access Query Design window. Views are used for retrieving rows of data from one or more tables. You can use a view as the record source for a form or as the row source for a combo box. To create a view, follow these steps.

1. Select the Queries object in the database window. Then choose Create View in Designer in the Queries object window. The Query Designer opens.

2. To add a table to the Query Designer, right-click the Query Designer window. Then choose Add Table from the shortcut menu. The Add Table window appears. Select one or more tables and then click Add to add the tables to the Query Designer window.

3. You can select columns and enter criteria the same way you design queries in an Access database.

Figure 30-2 shows the vwBankAccountList view in the Query Designer. You use the grid pane (lower section) of the Query Designer just like the grid pane of an Access query. However, the rows and columns of the view are pivoted — that is, the column names included in the query are listed as rows in the grid pane. The table name and criteria for each column are displayed as columns across from each of the column names.

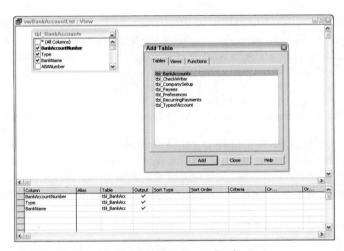

Figure 30-2 *Working in the Query Designer.*

You cannot use a view to perform Access query actions such as UPDATE, INSERT, or APPEND. Views also cannot receive parameters. You must create a stored procedure for these types of queries.

20 Min. To Go

Creating a stored procedure

A stored procedure is a special type of query that enables you to use commands that update data in the database. Creating a stored procedure is more like writing a Visual Basic procedure than like creating a view or a query. To create a stored procedure, first select the

Queries tab in the database container. Then select Create Procedure in Designer. The Query Designer displays. You use the Query Designer for a stored procedure the same way you use the Query Designer to build a view. The Design window for the spBankAccountsAlphabetized stored procedure is shown in Figure 30-3.

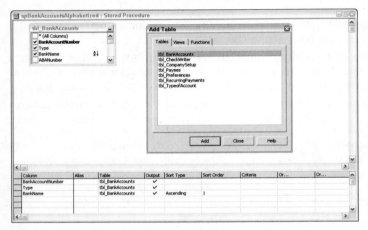

Figure 30-3   *Working with stored procedures.*

The spBankAccountsAlphabetized stored procedure includes the same table, columns, and criteria as the vwBankAccountListing view. The difference is that spBankAccountsAlphabetized specifies a Sort Order for the BankName column.

You can specify a Sort Order for a column in a view. However, to sort a view requires the use of the TOP 100 PERCENT clause with the Select statement. When you add a Sort Order to a view, Access automatically adds the TOP 100 PERCENT clause to the Select statement.

The TOP clause degrades performance because it causes the sorting to be done on the client machine instead of on the server. The TOP clause is not required for sorting Select queries in a stored procedure. The server performs sorting of stored procedure data.

You can add a view to a stored procedure.

When you use the graphical tools of the Query Designer to create a stored procedure, Access converts what you create into the Transact-SQL programming language. The Transact-SQL commands are what SQL Server actually executes when the query runs. You can view the Transact-SQL program for the stored procedure by choosing View ⇨ SQL View from the Query Designer menu. Figure 30-4 shows the SQL view for the spBankAccountsAlphabetized stored procedure.

Figure 30-4 *Viewing the SQL view of a stored procedure.*

You can make changes to the stored procedure using either the Design view or the SQL view. As you are working with the stored procedure, you can switch between view modes. If you are viewing in the SQL view window, you can return to the Design view by choosing View ➪ Design View. Any changes that you made to the query in SQL view are reflected in the Design view. When you make changes to the query in the Design view window, the changes are immediately updated in the SQL view window.

 If you are proficient in creating stored procedures on your own, you can even create a new stored procedure directly in the SQL window.

If you want to run a stored procedure with different criteria values every time you run it, you can add a parameter to the stored procedure's criteria. A *parameter* is a placeholder for the column's criteria. For example, you may want to retrieve all checks issued during a specific date range. But, you may want to retrieve all checks issued during January, 2000, one time, or all checks issued during December, 2000, another time. The spChecksIssuedReport stored procedure uses the @begindate and @enddate parameters, as shown in Figure 30-5.

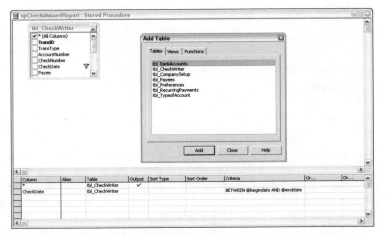

Figure 30-5 *Creating a stored procedure with a parameter.*

The spChecksIssuedReport stored procedure receives two datetime parameters: begindate and enddate. This stored procedure is a simple SELECT statement that selects all of the fields from the tbl_CheckWriter table for the date range specified by the parameters.

You can't specify a parameter in a view.

**10 Min.
To Go**

Creating User-Defined Functions

User-defined functions combine the best features of views and stored procedures into a single query. You can pass parameters to user-defined functions. They can also include views, stored procedures, or other functions. User-defined functions can't be used to update, insert, or delete data in a database.

To create a function, select the Queries object, and then select the Create function in designer. The Query Designer opens. You can add a table, a view, or another function to the new function by selecting from the list of tables, views, and functions shown in the Add Table window.

Figure 30-6 shows the SQL view for the fnCheckIssuedDateRange function. The fnCheckIssuedDateRange function returns the check writer information for checks issued during a specific date range. The datetime variables @begindate and @enddate contain the beginning and ending dates for the date range passed by the calling program. The RETURNS TABLE statement shows that the function returns a table of data containing one or more records. The RETURN statement contains a single SQL statement. When the function executes, it performs the query specified in the SELECT statement. The SELECT statement retrieves the row or rows of data from the database. The table that results from the SELECT statement becomes the RETURN value for the function.

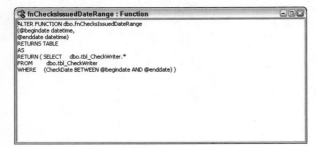

Figure 30-6 Creating a user-defined function.

Basically, the user-defined function is a simpler version of the stored procedure. If your query needs to accept one or more parameters and return a single value or a single table, you should use a user-defined function for the query rather than a stored procedure. Stored procedures are geared for performing more complex query operations, such as multiple Select statements, table updates, and returning multiple result sets.

Done!

REVIEW

Using Access and MSDE 2000, you can implement true client/server database applications. MSDE 2000 provides virtually all the functionality and power of SQL Server, yet you can run it on a desktop workstation. This session covered the following topics:

- Access projects are used to work with MSDE 2000 databases.
- The Data Link Properties dialog box displays the name of the project's database.
- SQL Server views and stored procedures are similar to Access queries.
- Views and user-defined functions can retrieve but not update data.
- Stored procedures and user-defined functions can accept parameters.

QUIZ YOURSELF

1. A project's tables, queries, and database diagrams are stored in what type of file? (See "Understanding projects.")
2. Which type of object is used to update a database: a view, a user-defined function, or a stored procedure? (See "Creating a view.")
3. How can you determine which database your project is connected to? (See "Checking a project's database connection.")
4. True or False: If you need to sort the results of a query, you should use a view. (See "Creating a Stored Procedure.")

PART

VI

Sunday Afternoon
Part Review

1. List at least two reasons you may lose the table links in a database.
2. True or false: You use ADODB to work with Access table definitions.
3. Which of the following is used to create a new catalog object?
   a. Dim cat as ADO.catalog
   b. Dim cat as New ADO.catalog
   c. Dim cat as New ADOX.catalog
   d. Dim cat as ADOX.catalog
   e. Dim cat as New ADODB.catalog
4. What line of code would you use to set a newly created catalog object to the current database connection?
5. True or false: Excel can be used as a source for a linked table.
6. List four security methods that protect the program code.
7. True or false: The security objects are contained within the ADOX object model.
8. Which of the following is (or are) true of encryption in Access?
   a. Encryption is done using the JRO compact database method.
   b. Decryption requires a password.
   c. Encryption does not protect the database from being read by a utility program.
   d. Encryption uses the ADOX object model.
   e. None of the above.
9. List methods other than Access security for protecting an application from unauthorized users.
10. True or false: The AllowBypassKey is a property of the Access Application object.

11. Two or more network workstations can share a centrally located data source in which architecture?

12. True or false: Access is a good example of a true client/server environment.

13. A ____ _____ database engine simply moves data back and forth between the server and the workstation.

14. The maximum database size of an MSDE 2000 database is _____.

15. True or false: The data objects of an MSDE 2000 database are stored in an .mdb file.

16. Which one of the following is not an MSDE 2000 object?

    a. Table

    b. Stored Procedure

    c. View

    d. Query

17. Which of the following environments is best suited for developing an application using MSDE 2000?

    a. Ten or more simultaneous users with high volumes of updates.

    b. The business environment has a SQL Server 2000 database and you are an off-site application developer.

    c. Five or fewer simultaneous users with modest volumes of updates.

    d. The business environment consists of outdated workstations with lower memory and minimal hard disk space.

18. Which of the following operations can be performed using a view?

    a. INSERT

    b. UPDATE

    c. SELECT

    d. None of the above

19. To sort the result set of a SQL Server query efficiently, you should use what type of query?

20. True of false: A SQL Server user-defined function can be used to update data.

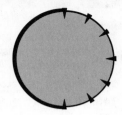

APPENDIX

Answers to Part Reviews

This appendix provides the answers to the review questions found at the end of each part of the book.

Friday Evening Review Answers

1. Database management systems include the ability to build tables and relationships and the ability to store data.

2. The Visual Basic editor window is a separate window in Access 2003.

3. The two types of procedures are *subprocedures* and *functions*. The difference is that a function returns a value to the calling procedure and a subprocedure does not.

4. Visual Basic for Applications (VBA) is the language used within Microsoft Access modules. Jet is the standard database engine used to hold the data tables in Microsoft Access and Visual Basic. The Microsoft Database Engine (MSDE) is a scaled-down version of SQL Server and used as an alternate engine.

5. False.

6. d.

7. Auto List Members.

8. b.

9. General design, detail design, programming and documentation, testing, and debugging.

10. Compiling checks your program for syntax errors and resolves some of your references. It converts your program to a form your computer can understand. It allows your programs to run much faster. You should also compact your database after you compile your program.

11. The Immediate, Locals, and Watches windows.

12. A breakpoint stops a program when a specific line of code is reached. A watchpoint is set by the user and stops a program when a specific variable of control reaches a preset value.

13. Property sheet.

14. False.

15. a.

16. c.

17. Dim.

18. Access will run a VBA program much faster if `Option Explicit` is used once at the top of each module and all your variables are declared.

19. Public or Global define a variable to your entire program and Private limits the scoping to one procedure.

20. a, d. Text is nonsensical and is named String. Number is not a Visual Basic numeric data type. Integer, Currency, Long, Single, and Double are valid.

Saturday Morning Review Answers

1. *Logical constructs* are a certain class of VBA statements that control the way a program runs. Generally, programs run one statement after another in the order in which they appear. Logical constructs are used to make the program run in the order that makes sense for the business purpose.

2. Logical constructs include conditional processing (`If-Then-Else`, `Select Case`), and Looping (`Do While`, `For Next`).

3. *Nesting* occurs when you put an `If-Then-Else` statement within another `If-Then-Else` statement. This allows you to write complex Boolean expressions.

4. The `Do Until` clause code always runs at least once and runs until the condition is met to terminate the loop. The `Do While` clause runs as long as the condition is true.

5. True.

6. Function.

7. d.

8. c.

9. d.

10. True.

11. b.

12. Select a file to open.

13. c.

14. False.

15. Recordset.

16. False.

17. False.

18. Pessimistic locking.

19. a.

20. c.

Saturday Afternoon Review Answers

1. True.

2. False.

3. False.

4. False.

5. e.

6. False. You need to handle functions that are automatic with Access bound forms including record locking and the functions that connect the form to the data source.

7. The functions you need to include on an unbound form include: connecting to the record source, selecting/finding a record or records from a record source, loading up the controls on the form with data, retrieving the record(s), editing a record, saving a record, adding a new record, deleting a record, moving among multiple records like going to the first record, last record, next record, and previous record, and undoing changes made to the record before it is saved.

8. You would not want to use unbound forms because a lot of code is required to duplicate the functionality of a bound form. It is also difficult to provide continuous forms or a datasheet view, which a bound form can easily do.

9. A single check box can only have one of three states: True, False, or Null. In a situation where you need more values for the user to select, it is best to use an option group. With an option group you can have more than just three values.

10. False. Only one value can be selected in a combo box. A list box would allow you to select multiple items from the listing. This is because of the nature of the two controls. A combo box only displays one item whereas a list box can be set up to display multiple rows of records or items.

11. b, e, f, and g. Review the "Basic Elements of Combo and List Boxes" section of Session 13.

12. d. Remember that to properly use the Not In List event, you need to set the Limit to List property to No. When you set this up, any entries you enter that are not in the list will initiate the code in the Not In List event. The reason for setting the Limit to List to No is that if you select Yes, any entries that are not a part of the list will trigger an error message, forcing you to select an item in the list.

13. Forms, Datasheet and Continuous.

14. False. A subform can be unlinked from the main form.

15. A continuous form allows you to format all rows and columns and use any control for each column, whereas a datasheet gives you little control over the display grid.

16. Link Child Fields and Link Master Fields.

17. You would use a tabbed control for any number of reasons. Aesthetically, you may want to standardize the Windows "look and feel." Logically, you want to segregate your data or controls by group or functionality. In addition, the physical constraints of the limited desktop area may require that you use a tabbed control in order to save space.

18. c. The On Change event is fired each time the tab selection is changed. This event can be very useful because it lets you process code in a single event for any changes in the tabs. You can add code that runs with each tab's On Change event to check for the current tab page and then to display controls or run code accordingly.

19. False. You can set the Visible property of each tab individually in addition to the entire tabbed control itself. This lets you control which pages are visible and when.

20. None, Tabbed, and Buttons. Please review "Tabbed Control Styles" in Session 15.

Saturday Evening Review Answers

1. The five parameters of the MsgBox function are the prompt text, buttons, title, helpfile, and context.

2. True. The buttons parameter also determines the icon to be displayed as well as the default button and the modality of the message box.

3. The application modal state requires the user to respond to the message box before continuing within the current application, which is suspended until the message box is cleared. The system modal state suspends *all* applications until the user responds to the message box.

4. c.

5. Access provides a few different means for importing and exporting data. In addition, you can import and export to several standard formats. The formats are listed in Session 17 in detail. The following is an abbreviated list.

   a. Excel (all versions)

   b. dBase (III, III+, IV, 5, and 7)

   c. Lotus (versions upto version 4)

   d. Text files (delimited and fixed width)

6. The four basic steps in doing an import are:

   a. Organizing the data.

   b. Formatting the data.

   c. Mapping the data.

   d. Appending the records.

   You will first need to gather and organize the data to be imported. You then must format the data in a manner that Access can recognize and that works with your data structure. Next you will perform the most important step, mapping the data.

This is the process of matching up the data being imported with the data structure you are working with. You will need to consider such issues as which tables, fields, data type, size, and so on will be matched to which corresponding parts of your data structure. These are all important aspects of the mapping process. Incorrectly matching up the field size could result in the loss of data. Likewise, matching the wrong key field from one table to another could result in corrupting the data so that it is no longer valid.

7. An import/export specification is a file that gives Access a set of rules for importing or exporting data from/to a text file. Once you've created an import/export specification, you can use it over and over, on both delimited and fixed-width text files. The specification is stored in the database and is an Access system object. You can access this feature when you initiate an import. To create a specification file you can use either of the Import or Export Text Wizards. The wizard creates a listing of information that would be critical to the import or export process such as the format of the file, field mappings, field properties, and so on. Refer to "Import/Export Processes" in Session 17.

8. There are three main methods available for transferring data. Which method you choose depends on where the data is and whether you are exporting or importing.

   a. TransferDatabase Method

   b. TransferSpreadSheet Method

   c. TransferText Method

   Refer to the section "Methods for importing and exporting" in Session 17.

9. Memory is actually more important than the processor speed. Increasing your memory from 64MB to 128MB can easily double or triple the speed of your application, while changing the processor speed and keeping the memory the same will make little difference.

10. Modifying a form, report, control, or module containing code. (If you don't save the modified object, your application is preserved in its previous state.)

    Adding a new form, report, control, or module. (This includes adding new code behind an existing form.)

    Deleting or renaming a form, report, control, or module.

11. Decompile.

12. You cannot view, modify, or create forms, reports, or modules in Design view.

    You cannot add, delete, or change references to object libraries or databases.

    You cannot change your database's VBA project name using the Options dialog box.

    You cannot import or export forms, reports, or modules. Note, however, that tables, queries, and macros can be imported from or exported to non-MDE databases.

13. False.

14. True.

15. True.

16. True.

17. Topic.

18. True.
19. d.
20. a.

Sunday Morning Review Answers

1. False.
2. Modal
3. d.
4. RowSource.
5. A Search Dialog would have several basic elements. The easiest way to derive the answer is to look at what information is required in order to do a search. In order to do a search, you must obtain the "what" — that is, the value to be searched for — from the user. You also need to determine the "where" — that is, the location(s) in which to search for the value. Therefore, you need a control to obtain the value to search for and one to select where to search. There are other elements which may be useful — for instance, adding criteria or Boolean operators — but at a minimum, the "what" and "where" are required..

   A Print Dialog would have the following basic features: a control for the user to select the report to print; the number of copies; and the type of output (Preview or Print). In addition, you may want to add additional controls that give greater control of the printing options to your user — for instance, additional titles and filter options. Review the form yBank Print Dialog for an example of a basic print dialog; the form "yCheck Print Dialog" is more advanced.

6. b. The syntax and arguments for the OpenReport command are as follows:

   Report Name: The actual name of the report object.

   View: The type of view, either Print to the printer or Print Preview.

   Filter Name: The name of a query that can be used to filter the records in the report.

   Where Condition: The WHERE clause of a SQL statement that can be used to restrict the records in the report.

7. You can place code in the following events for the report:
   - On Open
   - On Close
   - On Activate
   - On Deactivate
   - On No Data
   - On Page
   - On Error

In addition, you can also place code that is associated with a particular section or group. These events include:

- On Format
- On Print
- On Retreat

8. The SysCmd function.

9. False. The Background Compile option will compile any uncompiled code when Access's processes are not busy.

10. b.

11. Use the command line argument /x *macro*, use the macro named AutoExec, and set the Display Form/Page entry on the Startup dialog box.

12. To make sure the data links between a front-end and back-end database are correct, to install the required references, library, ActiveX control, or help file, and to create desktop shortcuts and menu items.

13. You should make each page of the wizard step toward completing the process; order the steps to make sense; keep buttons, fonts, and controls consistent between pages; keep pages uncluttered; and use defaults as much as possible to simplify user input.

14. The entire wizard is contained within one Access object, a form; it provides properties and methods that will simplify coding; the tabs on the Tab control can be visible or invisible depending on your needs; there needs to be only one set of navigation buttons.

15. False. You also need a Finish button.

16. a. The Back button is always disabled on the *first* page.

17. True.

18. Examples of Add-ins provided with Access include control wizards, form wizards, chart wizards, field builders, object libraries, the switchboard manager, the link table manager, the documenter, the performance analyzer, and many, many more.

19. e. all of the above.

20. HKEY_LOCAL_MACHINE\SOFTWARE\Microsoft\Office\11.0\Access\Wizards.

Sunday Afternoon Review Answers

1. You may lose the table links if the data source you are linked to is not available because: the external data source has moved; the server where the external data source is located is down; the network is down; the user does not have the permissions necessary to access the external data source; or share names have changed.

2. False. You use ADOX to work with Access table definitions.

3. c.

4. cat.ActiveConnection = CurrentProject.Connection

5. True.

6. Security methods that protect the code are share level, user level, encryption, and MDE.

7. True.

8. a.

9. Other methods of protecting an application from unauthorized users include operating system security, hiding the database window, disabling the bypass key, and disabling special keys.

10. False.

11. Client/server.

12. False.

13. File Server.

14. 2GB.

15. False.

16. d.

17. c.

18. c.

19. Stored procedure.

20. True.

Index

Symbols and Numerics

Continued

Continued

Continued